A Composer's Insight

Thoughts, Analysis, and Commentary on Contemporary Masterpieces for Wind Band

VOLUME 1

Edited by
Timothy Salzman

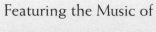

Featuring the Music of

Timothy Broege
Michael Colgrass
Michael Daugherty
David Gilligham
John Harbison
Karel Husa
Yasuhide Ito
Cindy McTee
Alfred Reed
Joseph Schwantner
David Stanhope
James Syler

Published by
MEREDITH MUSIC PUBLICATIONS
a division of G.W. Music, Inc.
4899 Lerch Creek Ct., Galesville, MD 20765
http://www.meredithmusic.com

MEREDITH MUSIC PUBLICATIONS and its stylized double M logo are trademarks of
MEREDITH MUSIC PUBLICATIONS, a division of G.W. Music, Inc.

Library of Congress Control Number: 2002117814

International Standard Book Number: 0-634-05827-4
Printed and bound in U.S.A

DEDICATION

To my family; Jodi, Leigh and Jonathan.

And with love and gratitude to the One who gave you to me.

CONTENTS

FOREWORD

When the New England Conservatory offered me a commission in 1984 to write a work for wind ensemble, I tried to get out of it. Memories of playing mediocre music in high school and college bands, with multiple clarinets doubling the melody and an army of tubas booming out the bass line, still rang in my ears. My love was the symphony orchestra, which I felt offered a better balance of instruments, especially with the beauty of the strings. But I was curious: why had wind ensemble conductor Frank Battisti asked for me?

When I talked to Battisti he told me that I did not have to stick to any standard band orchestration, but could pick and choose my instruments from a smorgasbord of winds, brass and percussion. This appealed to me because one of the weaknesses of the standard band orchestration in my opinion has always been the overly thick middle—horns, plus saxophones, plus bassoons, plus euphoniums—especially when doubling each other, creates for me a kind of sonic stomachache. Battisti's complete flexibility on that and every other creative aspect of the project began to excite me. I could create my own ensemble and set it up my own way, and my imagination began to fly. This freedom allowed me to write *"Winds of Nagual."*

After the piece was premiered, I began to find more advantages to writing for wind ensemble. The band director has time to study and learn the score and time to rehearse it, and time to talk to the composer about details as rehearsals progress. My experience with symphony orchestras is that the orchestra sees the music maybe as far as 48 hours in advance of the premiere, and I may never have the chance to talk details with the conductor.

Another old impression I had was that band directors were kind of military-minded or singularly education-minded and were not really sensitive musicians, certainly not to new trends in music. But I found in Frank Battisti, and subsequently in many of the other conductors who performed my works for wind ensemble, that this new generation of conductors contained musicians of the highest caliber. Moreover, they communicate with each other about new pieces, and are just as interested in doing a second or third performance as they are in a premiere. And bands rent music just the way orchestras do, so a composer can actually develop an income from the performances that follow a premiere. And I learned that the university or conservatory wind ensemble is no longer the dumping place for musicians who didn't make it into the school orchestra. The playing level in student wind ensembles today is astounding, and the performances I receive from them are often better than those from professional symphony orchestras.

As this compilation of composers' insights will show, today's wind ensembles are commissioning top composers and offering them the chance to express themselves freely. In this way the symphonic wind band is constantly reinventing itself, which will give it a fresh appeal for listeners. Much of this music is being recorded as well and is beginning to reach into the music world at large.

In my view, the future success and development of the wind ensemble depends on the quality of the music. The modern symphony orchestra exists because great composers wrote great music for it. And the symphonic band, still in its artistic infancy, is beginning to gain new audiences as it performs and records exciting new music. The energy is there. The new generation of wind ensemble directors is bubbling with resourceful and imaginative minds, and they are commissioning new works hand over fist. This publication, *"A Composer's Insight: Thoughts, Analysis and Commentary on Contemporary Masterpieces for Wind Band,"* attests to the ever-developing communication between band directors and the living composer.

Something just has to come of all this—and it will.

—Michael Colgrass

PREFACE

The initiative for this project was borne of the specific need for reference material that would serve to introduce teacher/conductors to the wind works of contemporary composers in an overview format.

In my career, composer/conductor interaction has been a particular catalyst for musical inspiration, change and, subsequently, growth. Composers have had much to say regarding the construction process of their works, the way in which they would like to hear them, the sources for the inspiration of their music and other intriguing information that has illuminated my own attempts at performance. As I've had opportunity to watch students engage with composers in rehearsal situations it has always been fascinating to note the substance of the interaction that ultimately seems to spark effective performance. Our attempt here is to capture a bit of that.

Without question the past three decades of composition for the wind band have been marked by a significant increase in the quality and quantity of new repertoire. This body of thoughtful new work has been a remarkable development on the part of 'serious' composers in that they have, to some degree, chosen to forsake earlier career tradition in devoting their time to create music for what their predecessors would have certainly termed an 'educational' idiom. Our gratitude for their efforts is felt every day in rehearsal rooms and concert halls throughout this country and in many others.

This publication is not intended to serve as an exhaustive analysis of a composer's style or to be any sort of final word as to the importance of their contributions to the field of wind band repertoire; the latter seems a hopelessly arbitrary pursuit. It is more an attempt to bring into clearer focus the substance of each composer's approach to music; it's inspiration, creation and performance.
　—Timothy Salzman
　　March, 2002

ACKNOWLEDGMENTS

Thank you to the composers who have not only crafted the beautiful music that has benefited so many but have also been so gracious in the gift of their time. Obviously without their creativity and willingness to be involved in our idiom this project would not exist.

Thank you to the co-authors...your dogged determination and team work ethic has been truly inspirational. Thanks for your contributions.

Thanks to my colleague (and co-author for one chapter) Dr. J. Bradley McDavid for helping one of our friends and former students during a time of real need during this process.

Thanks to Jacob Winkler, David Reeves, Eric Wiltshire and other students who have helped with computer-related questions.

And, most of all, to the students of the University of Washington Bands, thank you. Without you this wonderful world of band music has no 'live' voice in my own day-to-day experience. I have always felt privileged to have the very best of front row seats quite near to your contagious sense of adventure during our travels through so many new musical landscapes. Thanks for risking.

AUTHOR BIOS

Timothy Salzman, (co-author and compiling editor), is Professor of Music at the University of Washington where he serves as conductor of the University Wind Ensemble and teaches students enrolled in the graduate instrumental conducting program. Prior to his appointment at the UW he served as Director of Bands at Montana State University where he founded the MSU Wind Ensemble. From 1978 to 1983 he was band director in the Herscher, Illinois, public school system where the band program received several regional and national awards in solo/ensemble, concert and marching band competition. Professor Salzman holds degrees from Wheaton (IL.) College (Bachelor of Music Education), and Northern Illinois University (Master of Music in low brass performance), and studied privately with Arnold Jacobs, former tubist of the Chicago Symphony Orchestra. He has numerous publications for bands with the C. L. Barnhouse, Arranger's Publications, Columbia Pictures and Hal Leonard Publishing companies, has served on the staff of new music reviews for the Instrumentalist magazine and is currently the President of the Northwestern Division of the College Band Directors National Association. Mr. Salzman is a national artist/clinician for the Yamaha Corporation of America and has been a conductor, adjudicator or arranger for bands in over forty states, Canada, England, Japan, South Korea, Indonesia and Russia. In the fall of 1997 he was Visiting Professor at the Senzoku Gakuen Uozu School of Music in Uozu, Japan.

Raydell Cecil Bradley is currently Director of Concert Bands and Associate Professor of Music at Pacific Lutheran University in Tacoma, Washington. He has served on the faculties of Fort Hays State University in Hays, Kansas; Truman State University in Kirksville, Missouri and Omaha North High School in Omaha, Nebraska. Dr. Bradley received the Bachelor of Music Education and Master of Arts degrees from Truman State University in 1981 and 1986. He completed the Doctor of Musical Arts degree in Instrumental Conducting from the University of Washington in June 2000, where he was the recipient of the Dorothy Danforth-Compton Foundation fellowship. He has served as guest conductor, clinician, and adjudicator in over 25 states and Canada.

Stephen DeLancey Clickard, Jr. received his Bachelor of Arts degree from San Jose State University in California and his Master of Music degree from the University of Northern Colorado. In August 1999, he received his Doctor of Musical Arts degree in Instrumental Conducting from the University of Washington, where he studied conducting with Peter Eros and served as a graduate assistant to Dr. J. Bradley McDavid and the Husky Marching Band. He is currently Associate Professor of Music at Bloomsburg University of Pennsylvania. He has served as president of the California Music Educator's Association Central Coast Section and as Administrator of the Monterey Jazz Festival's Summer Music Camp.

David Fullmer earned his BM and MM degrees from Brigham Young University. He is a candidate for the DMA in instrumental conducting from the University of Washington where he served as the teaching assistant to Professor Tim Salzman during the 1997–1998 school year. He is currently Director of Bands at Timpview High School in Provo, Utah where he has established a regional and national reputation for excellence in Symphonic Band, Jazz Ensemble, Marching Band and Percussion Ensemble. He has served as the Utah State Chair for the National Band Association and is President-Elect of the Utah Music Educators Association. He has received the UMEA Superior Accomplishment Award, the Mid-West Medal of Honor, Provo Educator of the Year and twice received the NBA Citation of Excellence.

Scott G. Higbee received a Bachelor of Music Education degree from Saint Olaf College in Northfield, Minnesota, where he studied conducting with Miles H. Johnson and Steven Amundson, and trombone with Paul Niemisto. He received a Master of Music degree from the

University of Washington where he studied conducting with Timothy Salzman and Peter Eros, and trombone with Stuart Dempster. He has been on the staff of the University of Washington Husky Marching Band and is currently a high school band director and freelance trombonist in the Seattle area.

Miriam Krueger holds an undergraduate degree in flute performance from the University of Denver and graduated from the University of Washington in 1999 with a M.M. in flute performance. She is a freelance performer in the Seattle area.

J. Bradley McDavid is currently Director of Athletic Bands and Assistant Professor of Music at the University of Washington in Seattle, Washington. He has taught instrumental music at the elementary, middle school and high school levels in the public schools of Ohio and Arizona. He received his Bachelor of Music Education degree from The Ohio State University in 1985, Master of Music degree from Arizona State University in 1990 and Ph.D. in Music Education from The Ohio State University in 1999. He has served as guest conductor, clinician, and adjudicator throughout the United States and China.

Judson J. Scott is a candidate for the DMA in instrumental conducting from the University of Washington where he served as the teaching assistant to Professor Tim Salzman during the 1999–2000 school year. Formerly trumpet instructor and wind ensemble conductor at Brandeis University, he is now on the faculties of the University of Puget Sound and Pacific Lutheran University. Mr. Scott holds degrees from Baldwin-Wallace College and New England Conservatory. A former member of the Mexico City Philharmonic, he has performed with the Seattle and Tacoma symphony orchestras, the Seattle Opera Company, the 5th Avenue Theatre, and the Northwest Sinfonietta among others. A keen advocate of new music, Mr. Scott is a founding member of the Warebrook Contemporary Music Festival in Vermont and has performed locally with the Seattle Creative Orchestra and the Contemporary Chamber Composers and Performers. He has given local or world premieres of works by John Harbison, Gunther Schuller, William O. Smith, and Michael Colgrass among many others.

Miho Takekawa is currently studying for the Doctor of Musical Arts degree in percussion performance at the University of Washington. She also teaches undergraduate percussion students at the UW as a graduate fellow. She has received the Boeing Scholarship for excellence in percussion performance for the last two years. Originally from Tokyo, she received her B.A. in percussion performance and music education at Kunitachi School of Music in Tokyo and her M.M. in percussion performance from the University of Washington. Ms. Takekawa started playing piano at age three and percussion at age thirteen as a student of Professor Tomoyuki Okada. A fine marimbist, Ms. Takekawa is also a very active multi-percussionist in the Pacific Northwest and is involved in the performance of all styles of music including West African, jazz and classical.

In 1990, **David Waltman** was the youngest conductor ever selected for the United States Army Band Officer conductor program after auditioning with the United States Army Band (Pershing's Own) in Washington, D.C. As a bassoonist, Mr. Waltman has performed with the Denver Symphony Orchestra, the Greeley Chamber Orchestra, the Jefferson Symphony and many United States and European military bands. In association with Western Washington University, Mr. Waltman and his wife, Marisa Hartman, are producing the Masters of Wind Music video series showcasing the world's finest wind conductors and composers including Frederick Fennell, H. Robert Reynolds and Dr. Alfred Reed. Mr. Waltman is Music Director and Artistic Advisor for the Port Gardner Bay Chamber Music Society and Conductor of the Boeing Employees Concert Band. He holds the Bachelor of Music Degree from Northern Colorado University.

Timothy Broege

by
David Fullmer

The music of Timothy Broege (b. 1947) has been performed throughout the United States, as well as in Canada, Europe, Australia, Japan and China. He has received grants and commissions from Meet the Composer, Inc., the Tidewater Music Festival, the Evanston Symphony Orchestra, the Monmouth Symphony Orchestra, Gruppa Nova-Germany, Emory University, the Indianapolis Children's Choir, and many others. His compositions are published by, among others, Bourne Company, Hal Leonard, Manhattan Beach Music, Allaire Music and Daehn Publications. Recordings released on compact disc include *Sinfonias III, V, IX, and XVI; Concerto for Piano & Wind Orchestra, Concerto for Marimba & Wind Orchestra; The Waukesha Rondo; No Sun No Shadow;* and *Runes.* Northwestern University Recordings has released a compact disc featuring his harpsichord music.[1]

The compositions of Timothy Broege include the series of *Sinfonias* for large ensembles, and the series of *"Songs Without Words"* for chamber ensembles. Several of his keyboard compositions have been recorded and broadcast by Deutschlandfunk and WDR in Cologne, Germany. His music has been showcased at conventions and festivals, including those of the Music Educators National Conference, the National Band Association, the National Wind Ensemble Conference, and the College Band Directors National Association. He is a Past-President of the Composers Guild of New Jersey, Inc and is an affiliate of Broadcast Music, Inc. (BMI). As a guest composer/conductor, Timothy Broege has appeared at the Wisconsin and Ohio Music Educators State Conventions, the Mid-West Band & Orchestra Clinic, the 1990 Annual Spring Conference on Wind & Percussion Music at Western Michigan University, and the 1994 & 1999 Wind Band Symposiums at the University of Minnesota. His *Songs Without Words* for clarinet, cello & piano was awarded First Prize in the New Jersey Chamber Music Society's 20th Anniversary Composition Competition and received its premiere in the spring of 1994. For his compositional efforts on behalf of school musicians Timothy Broege was given the 1994 Edwin Franko Goldman Award of the American School Band Directors Association.

He currently holds the position of Organist and Director of Music at First Presbyterian Church, Belmar, New Jersey, where he has served since 1972. In addition to his compositional activities, Timothy Broege is an active recitalist on harpsichord, organ, and recorder and has appeared in numerous duo recitals with the lutenist and guitarist Francis Perry. He resides in Bradley Beach, New Jersey.[2]

BIOGRAPHICAL INFORMATION

Timothy Broege was born November 6, 1947 in Belmar, New Jersey, and studied piano and theory with Helen Antonides during his childhood years. As an undergraduate student at Northwestern University in Evanston, Illinois he studied composition with M. William Karlins, Alan Stout, and Anthony Donato; piano with Frances Larimer; and harpsichord with Dorothy Lane. He received the degree Bachelor of Music with Highest Honors in June 1969.[3]

From 1969 to 1971 Broege taught 6th grade in the Chicago Public School System. He then served as an instrumental and general music teacher at Manasquan Elementary School in New Jersey from 1971 until 1980. After teaching for eleven years, Broege, in need of a new challenge, contemplated performing full time but was concerned about attempting to "eke out a living" as a freelance musician. He knew that this work would not provide regular income especially since he was not willing to travel. His brother, an attorney, suggested that he consider paralegal work—a profession with regular salary, benefits and flexible hours. Since that time, and until his recent retirement, Broege worked 20 hours per week as a claims manager for a Chapter 13 Bankruptcy Trustee in New Jersey becoming something of a bankruptcy expert in that area of the country. Broege typically spent Monday through Wednesday at the office dividing the remainder of the week between composing and performing. The financial security that he enjoyed freed his creative process as he did not feel pressure from publishers to write something that had to be commercially viable.[4]

COMPOSITIONAL PHILOSOPHY

Timothy Broege thinks of himself first as a composer, rather than an 'educational' or 'band' composer as others have tried to label him.[5] He feels that his calling to this work comes from composers of the past, especially those from the 17th and 18th centuries. His understanding of, and connection to that time period are rooted in his harpsichord study and performance.

His compositional approach, simply stated, is to write the best work possible within the given technical capabilities of the commissioning ensemble. He believes that if a composer cannot write well with limited resources that he or she is not ultimately professional; he points to the great composers of the past who, when faced with a highly structured set of practical parameters, repeatedly proved that music "stripped down to essentials" is capable of being high art. Young bands have their own unique limitations that must be taken into consideration by any composer, a challenge that Broege meets with a particularly beautiful and developed sense of craftsmanship.

Broege acknowledges the highly practical dimension found in his work and harbors a clear vision of his music speaking to the masses now.[6] It is his strong feeling that composers need to adopt a "mandate to be useful" by making music a part of every day life; only then are they making a contribution to society. He has little patience for composers that delight in their own obscurity by waiting for the day when they are finally 'understood.' Broege's own ideal includes a high standard of craftsmanship that utilizes an eclectic compositional language; he believes that school bands are a logical place to further this vision.[7]

Broege has experienced a certain prejudice that has been occasionally levied against band composers and has been criticized for exercising poor professional judgment by choosing to write music for children. His prolific compositional output stands as a testament to his commitment to create a body of music that is intended for performers of all experience levels and abilities. He believes that there exists in America the rather lofty notion that the arts are not for everyone and, as a consequence, a high percentage of the general population is largely unfamiliar with prominent poets and/or composers. This seems to be somewhat of a cultural phenomenon, as both Europe and Japan appear to embrace a more inclusive approach to the arts in general and bands in specific. However, in major American cities, bands or even wind ensembles are rarely mentioned and Broege believes that the bands will not be truly accepted as equal to orchestras in the professional musical world until foreign wind bands begin touring in America's finest concert halls. There is hope for the future of wind music in that respect as a growing number of orchestral conductors, (Leonard Slatkin, and Pierre Boulez for example), are beginning to program more wind music and are also aware of the quality of the wind repertoire.

While many composers seek positions at universities, Broege has felt the need to be more directly connected to the world of music making. He has always felt that certain aspects of composition are difficult, if not impossible to teach and that, at times, composition professors are a bit suspect in this regard. He asserts that certain 'nuts and bolts' aspects of the craft can be learned through books and firmly believes that the best way to learn how to compose is by composing.

Broege warns of a 'cheap' aesthetic in the public schools where deliberate decisions by educators as to what students read and play seems to reinforce the notion that "the only thing of value is commercial." He has frequently confronted his music educator friends who purchase compositions of questionable value and asked them to use their financial resources to commission new works from composers of quality repertoire. His own rich experiences with school bands have contributed to his zeal for writing for those groups.[8]

COMPOSITIONAL STYLE

Many composers of the 20th century chose to work in experimental idioms because of the belief that the possibilities of the traditional approaches had been exhausted. Broege believes that the same challenges may now face contemporary composers. However, he has chosen to embrace many tested musical expressions especially in terms of the formal organization of his music.

Broege's music is formally organized via the highly structured, fixed forms of the baroque period including rondo, theme and variations, passacaglia and simple song form.[9] He believes that these older organizational approaches are still quite valid and that their strong architecture communicates musical contrast most effectively. He is not comfortable composing 'organic' music that grows freely out of germinal ideas feeling that such music can be expressive but typically lacks narrative. He points to Shostakovich, Stravinsky, Sibelius and other great 20th century composers who may have had similar feelings regarding the formal organization of their music. Sibelius is one of Broege's favorite composers because of his inherent structural approach, an approach that is not easily formally identifiable. Haydn is equal to, or even greater than Mozart in Broege's mind, because of the originality of the older composer's structural procedures.[10]

The compositional language employed is not of primary importance to Broege as he typically writes in a practical manner, often tailoring the work to the technical abilities of the commissioning ensemble. In doing so all available creative resources are utilized which leads one to identify his compositional approach as truly 'polystylistic.'[11] Efficiency marks his work as Broege agrees with Milton Babbitt's notion that every note in the piece must be justifiable in terms of the overall linear and vertical structure.

Within almost every Broege composition a section of increased pulsation and rhythmic 'groove' appears. These ostinato-like segments can be quite extended or may only occur for a few measures. While some have been critical of these sections, Broege contends that they develop quite naturally, almost unconsciously. There are times when he finds that he must fight the urge to include them, a particular problem when that sort of compositional expression does not stylistically complement the given work. This appearance of strong pulsation is typically a variation of orchestration and thematic material and in a practical sense serves as a dependable way of creating narrative flow. While not intended as comic relief, these groove sections have the same effect in that they create a significant change in tension. Broege also considers these sections to be a connection to the vernacular, a reminder to the listener to pay particular attention; that what is being performed is not that far removed from everyday life.

There is a great deal of jazz influence throughout Broege's compositions which can be attributed to his early experience of listening to jazz and his practical experience of playing in small dance bands as a teenager. *No Sun, No Shadow: An Elegy for Charles Mingus* was composed without any reference to written scores; Broege simply recalled the Mingus tunes from his aural memory, a memory built up from many years of listening. *No Sun, No Shadow,* which in essence is a tenor saxophone concerto, and the concertos for piano and marimba all share sonic and structural aspects. Considered a trilogy by Broege, they represent his effort to work with larger time frames. In these works his earlier subscription to the formal brevity of a 'Webern model' has given way to a new appreciation for the more extended forms of Bruckner and other large-scale composers.[12]

OVERVIEW OF SELECTED WORKS FOR BAND

The following six Broege compositions for band represent a wide range of complexity reflecting the experience levels of the commissioning ensembles of each work.[13] Each analysis includes formal structure, unique rehearsal and performance challenges and composers' comments.

The Headless Horseman Grade 2. 2:00 Manhattan Beach

The Headless Horseman was composed in 1973 and first performed by the Manasquan, New Jersey Summer School Concert Band. This programmatic work is based on the well-known character in Washington Irving's short story, The Legend of Sleepy Hollow. The music depicts the Horseman, his whinnying stallion, and their frightening ride through the countryside as they snatch unsuspecting souls.[14] It is Broege's first published work for band and it continues to enjoy widespread popularity.[15]

In a technical sense, players must have the ability to shift dynamics, articulations, and tone qualities quickly. The introduction should be allowed to develop in an even slower manner than the indicated tempo of quarter = 60. Blending is critical in the tonal clusters. There are some challenging chromatic passages in the brass and glissandi work for trombones. The snare drum player must be able to perform the eighth-two sixteenth rhythms consistently at a variety of dynamic levels.[16]

The work displays the composer's eclectic style by utilizing contemporary compositional techniques inside of conventional rondo form.

Peace Song Grade 2. 5:00 Bourne

Peace Song is derived from material drawn from the third movement of Broege's *Three Pieces for Clavichord.* The band version is re-worked from an earlier arrangement for orchestra and is broader in scope than either of the earlier versions.[17]

The work is intended to have the effect of a magical incantation—a prayer for an end to suffering, violence and injustice. With an atmosphere of solemnity, *Peace Song* requires sustained legato playing throughout, similar to the sound produced by a cathedral organ. Fully supported tone is needed to sustain the lyrical melodic lines and the perfect fifths that dominate the harmonic structure. The first trumpet and horns are written in extended ranges. Given the fact that the work is written for a younger band a somewhat extended percussion section is utilized including vibraphone (with motor), chimes, xylophone, marimba, bass drum, suspended cymbals, crash cymbals, triangle, and gong.[18]

Sinfonia XVII: The Four Winds Grade 3. 7:00 Manhattan Beach
I. A Prelude for the East Wind
II. A Dance for the West Wind
III. A Musette for the South Wind
IV A Fantasia for the North Wind

The Charles D. Evans Junior High School Band and Orchestra Boosters of Ottumwa, Iowa commissioned *Sinfonia XVII: The Four Winds* for the Evans Junior High School Wind Symphony, Philip C. Wise and Jena S. Hawk, directors. The piece was composed during June and July of 1989 and is derived from the musical materials in movements one, four, five and seven of the composer's *Suite on the First Tone* for organ solo.[19] Broege wrote the following explanation regarding the title of the work:

The four winds blow variously from north, south, east, and west, causing clouds to race across the sky, fires to blaze high in the great forests, melancholy to permeate the souls of dreamers, and promises of adventure to permeate the air with excitement.

In the great organs of baroque cathedrals, the four winds bring to musical life the pipes of the main wind chests: grand organ, positive organ, solo organ and pedal.

The instruments of the wind ensemble are characterized by their sounds—flutes, single reeds, double reeds, brasses—and it is the four-fold richness of timbre in the band to which the composer pays tribute. From the world of natural wonders, the great pipe organs, and the timbral diversity of wind instruments, *Sinfonia XVII* draws its inspiration.[20]

Sinfonia XVII: The Four Winds is carefully scored for concert band. The oboe part is doubled in the second flute and the score requires only two horn and two trombone parts.

Students are expected to change styles drastically from one movement to the next. Other than a bassoon solo (cued tuba) in the second movement (m. 3–7) and a sixteenth note flourish by solo alto saxophone in the third movement (m. 14–18), the technical demands are moderate. The percussion scoring requires seven players on the following instruments: chimes, tam-tam, tambourine, cymbals, xylophone, marimba, snare drum, bass drum, timpani, bells, and vibraphone.

Sinfonia XVI: Transcendental Vienna Grade 4 7:00
Manhattan Beach
I.   Star Gazing: Aldebaran
II. Incantation—Allegro misterioso
III. Waltz—Temp di Valse
IV. Star Gazing: Sirius

Sinfonia XVI: Transcendental Vienna was composed during January and February of 1989 on commission from Richard H. Sanger and the Henry David Thoreau Intermediate School Symphonic Band of Vienna, Virginia. Mr. Sanger and his students premiered the work on May 22, 1989 in Vienna, Virginia. Broege gives the following explanation about the work:

It was a happy coincidence that the commission for *Sinfonia XVI: Transcendental Vienna* came from the Henry David Thoreau School located in Vienna, Virginia. Thoreau is one of the 'magic' names in American culture: Henry David Thoreau, one of the leading figures of the Transcendentalist movement, centered in 19th-century New England, left us a body of unique philosophical and poetical writings. To utter the words, Walden Pond, is to invoke an America long past in physical actuality, but still present in the minds and hearts of many American citizens.

The name, Vienna, of course, summons thought of the Old World: culture, fine food, wine, civilized cities. While contemplating the form that *Sinfonia XVI* should take, I found myself thinking of two of the pillars found in Viennese culture; expressionism, and the waltz.

Musically speaking, expressionism reached a zenith in the works of Arnold Schoenberg and Alban Berg. It was Berg, in particular, that I wanted to invoke in the outer movements of my composition. I knew I would also have to include a waltz, and an invocation of the mysterious forces that are contained in both expressionism and transcendentalism. Thus was the structure of the work generated.

The outer movements with their vision of the night sky and the stars Aldebaran and Sirius, frame the central movements, which are essentially two versions of the same material, and are quieter and less dramatic. The outer movements are symmetrical, and share both pitch and rhythmic materials. Accordingly, I see the work as a ternary form, with the central movements forming a unit within the outer 'frame.'[21]

Sinfonia V: Symphonia Sacra et Profana Grade 5 7:00
Manhattan Beach

Prelude
Rag
Alla Turca
Chorale
Rag
Ragtime Alla Turca
Chant and Pavanne

Sinfonia V: Symphonia Sacra et Profana is one of Broege's first great compositional successes. Both *Sinfonia V* and *Sinfonia III* have contributed greatly to his wind composing reputation and are still frequently performed.[22]

Sinfonia V could be thought of as a divertimento in that the composition is made up of short sections of varying character. Broege alters this form slightly by using seven sections performed without interruption. The composition may appear to be through-composed; however, traditional formal structures are present and later sections of the composition are actually developments of earlier sections. Composed in 1973 on commission from the University City, Missouri High School Wind Ensemble, the work presents unique musical challenges including improvisation, use of piano and electric piano, extended brass and bassoon ranges, ragtime style, singing by the instrumentalists, highly technical percussion writing, rhythm and meter.[23]

This work is a clear example of Broege's polystylistic approach to composition as it demonstrates his ability to develop two or three different styles simultaneously. They are frequently presented as sound layers separated into woodwind, brass, and percussion choirs. The chorale and chant (sacred) seem to be responsorial to the jazz elements (profane).[24]

No Sun, No Shadow: Elegy for Charles Mingus Grade 6 35:00 Allaire

No Sun, No Shadow: Elegy for Charles Mingus was composed through a commission from the Emory University Wind Ensemble of Atlanta, Georgia, Dr. Jack Delaney, conductor, and was premiered on April 22, 1988 with Mr. Stutz Wimmer as tenor saxophone soloist. The piece was composed during the months of June to October in 1987 at Oceanport, New Jersey.[25]

The music of Charles Mingus has had a tremendous influence in Broege's musical life. In fact, *No Sun, No Shadow: Elegy for Charles Mingus* was written without Broege referring to any single written note. He credits Mingus with demonstrating the advantages of extreme musical contrast (tempo, style, instrumentation, and dynamics, especially) and shares Mingus' preference for well developed compositional structures and narratives. Broege writes the following about his elegy for "a towering figure of 20th century music":[26]

The late Charles Mingus—composer, bassist, and band leader—was a leading figure in the Afro-American improvisational music tradition. Like his revered predecessor, Duke Ellington, Mingus was a composer for whom the performing jazz ensemble was the true 'instrument,' and the many groups led by Mingus in the 1950's, 1960's, and 1970's played and recorded some of the most passionate and innovative music America has produced. Fortunately, many recordings of the music of Charles Mingus remain available on such record labels as Columbia, Candid (reissued on Mosaic), Impulse, Prestige, and Atlantic, among others. The composer of *No Sun, No Shadow* urges those who are unfamiliar with this great musical legacy to investigate these recordings.

A number of brief references to Mingus compositions are contained in *No Sun, No Shadow*. Pieces referred to include "Half Mast Inhibition", "Goodbye Pork Pie Hat", "Better Get Hit in Your Soul", "The Black Saint and the Sinner Lady", and "Fables of Faubus." Careful listeners may hear other references.[27]

No Sun, No Shadow: Elegy for Charles Mingus is a polystylistic work with a strong jazz influence and could be considered to be a concerto for tenor saxophone due to the prevalence of that instrument in many sections of the composition.

Concerto for Marimba and Wind Orchestra Grade 6/5
25:00 Allaire

The Concerto for Marimba and Wind Orchestra was begun in September 1990 and completed in June 1991 on a commission from the University of Washington Wind Ensemble, Timothy Salzman, conductor. The work, while quite eclectic in nature, draws its' central programmatic inspiration from the John Boorman film *The Emerald Forest*. The plot of the movie is based upon the true story of an American engineer whose responsibility it was to supervise the construction of a huge hydroelectric plant on the Amazon river. One day, while on the construction site, the engineer's five-year-old son was abducted by a native tribe. The engineer spent the next ten years of his life desperately searching for the boy. Their ultimate meeting and the ensuing cultural clash give Boorman the opportunity to make a powerful statement regarding the destruction of the Amazon rainforest.[28]

The work is cast in three movements. The first movement opens with fanfare-like energy and culminates by using text in the musical dialogue. The text is derived from the following poem:

Song of the Termite People
　　Who are the Termite People?
　　What do they do?
　　They cut down the grandfather trees
　　In the rainforest.
　　They are the bringers of war,
　　They are destroyers of peace
　　In the rainforest.
　　—after John Boorman's film, *The Emerald Forest*

The second movement is very slow and lyrical and allows the soloist and ensemble much room for musical expression. The third movement, spirited and energetic, in rondo form, requires the soloist to use unusual sticking techniques, such as playing the marimba with the wooden handles of the mallets, rather than the mallet head.[29]

CONDUCTING APPROACH

Broege offers the following in his advice to conductors who are contemplating the rehearsal and performance of his music:

> . . . primarily, the form/structure of the music must be presented clearly, and the gestural (expressive) vocabulary of the music must be allowed to speak with maximum effectiveness. Since my music seeks to reach across centuries and to reconcile the expressive worlds of the 17th and 18th centuries with those of the present day (including the entire 20th century), it is important for conductors and performers to have a musical background at least as varied as my own, i.e., fully conversant with all "serious" music traditions, as well as vernacular, improvisatory, and experimental traditions from all over the world. My music needs conductors and players especially well versed in early music, and equally well-versed in 20th century jazz traditions. Generally speaking, performers should approach my music with an open mind, seeking always to determine the "affect" of the music, as if performing C.P.E. Bach. It is important to understand that the broad stylistic vocabularies ("polystylism") in my music are always servants of expressive gesture and emotional rhetoric.[30]

When asked about 'reference' music for a conductors who are interested in a more illuminated performance of his music Broege offers the following:

> For conductors of my larger ensemble pieces, it is helpful to listen to my solo piano music, which serves as a microcosm of much of my stylistic vocabulary, and to my series of *Songs Without Words* for chamber ensembles, which are the purest expressions of my gestural vocabulary. Composers which have had a pronounced influence on my work, with which conductors and performers of my music should be on intimate terms, include: Girolamo Frescobaldi, Louis Couperin, Francois Couperin, Rameau, J.S. Bach, C.P.E. Bach, Haydn, Schubert, Bruckner, Stravinsky, Schoenberg, Webern, Britten, Shostakovich, Copland, and Morton Feldman.[31]

For reference recordings of his music Broege recommends:

> . . . the recently issued (September 2000) CD set from Indiana University of Pennsylvania, containing performances of my *Waukesha Rondo, Concerto for Marimba and Wind Orchestra* and *Sinfonia No. 9*, is recommended without reservation. The conductor on *Waukesha Rondo* is Jason Worzbyt, and the conductor for the other two pieces is Jack Stamp, one of the very best interpreters of my ensemble music. An earlier CD from Indiana University of Pennsylvania contains an excellent performance of *Sinfonia No. 3*, conducted by Jack Stamp. Another equally fine conduc-

tor of my wind ensemble music is Jack Delaney, presently at Southern Methodist University. Privately issued recordings from SMU featuring the estimable Meadows Wind Ensemble, all superbly played, include my *Songs Without Words for Clarinet and 15 players*, *Concerto for Marimba and Wind Orchestra* and *Sinfonia No. 14*. Commercial promotional recordings issued by Daehn Publications, and conducted by Jack Stamp, include my band pieces *The Child & the Kings*, *Concert Piece for Trumpet and Band*, *Procession & Torch Dance*, *Three Bruckner Preludes*, and *Sonata for Wind Band after C.P.E. Bach*, and all are enthusiastically recommended. A generous sampling of my harpsichord music is available on a CD from Northwestern University Recordings, beautifully played by Paul Rey Klecka.[32]

DISCOGRAPHY

AVAILABLE ON COMPACT DISC

Concerto for Marimba & Wind Orchestra
 Indiana University of Pennsylvania Wind Ensemble, Jack Stamp, conductor
 "Whiplash", Klavier Recordings

No Sun, No Shadow: Elegy for Charles Mingus
 University of Miami Wind Ensemble, Gary Greene, conductor
 "Christina's World" Albany Records

Runes and *Mets Rule* for flute & harpsichord
 Richard Soule, flute; John Metz, harpsichord
 RUNES, Trope Note/Cambria

Sinfonia V
 California State University/Fullerton Wind Ensemble;
 Mitch Fennel, conductor
 Cal State/Fullerton Recordings GVCD-9006

Concerto for Piano & Wind Orchestra
 Mary Mark Zeyen, piano
 California State University/Fullerton Wind Ensemble
 Mitch Fennel, conductor
 Cal State/Fullerton Recordings GVCD-9112

Sinfonia V
 Rutgers University Wind Ensemble
 William Berz, conductor
 Mark Recordings MCD-2940

Sinfonia XVI: 'Transcendental Vienna'
 Rutgers University Wind Ensemble
 William Berz, conductor
 Mark Recordings MCD-2002

Sinfonia III
 Indiana University of Pennsylvania Wind Ensemble
 Jack Stamp, conductor
 IUP CD (issued 1996)

The Waukesha Rondo
Concerto for Marimba & Wind Orchestra
 Sinfonia IX
 on "IUP Bands 2000"
 IUP CD (issued 2000)

The Headless Horseman
Peace Song
 North Texas Wind Symphony
 Eugene Corporon, conductor
 GIA Publications CD-418

Three Pieces for American Band, Set No. 2
Dreams & Fancies
 North Texas Wind Symphony
 Eugene Corporon, conductor
 GIA Publications CD-446

No Sun, No Shadow: Elegy for Charles Mingus
 on "Christina's World"
 University of Miami Wind Ensemble
 Gary Green, conductor
 Whit Sidener, saxophone
 Albany Records CD-Troy403

Runes
Mets Rule
 on "Runes: American Music for Flute & Harpsichord"
 Richard Soule, flute
 John Metz, harpsichord
 Troppe Note/Cambria CD-1432

Partita No. 2
Prelude "on the return of his beloved harpsichord from the workshop of Willard Martin"
Sonata for Harpsichord
Two Sonatas/Two Rondos
Suite in F Major
 on "Music from Northwestern, Volume 7"
 Paul Rey Klecka, harpsichord
 Northwestern University Recordings CD (released 1999)

Surfboard Blues
 "Band Music of Distinction, Volume 7"
 Daehn Publications/West Coast Music Service DP-1813

Rhythm Machine
 "Distinguished Music for the Developing Band, Volume 3"
 Rutgers University Wind Ensemble
 William Berz, conductor
 Daehn Publications/West Coast Music Service RUWE-1783

Available on Cassette

Five Minimal Songs
    Steven Combs, Baritone
    The Monmouth Symphony Orchestra
    Roy Gussman, conductor
    Monmouth Symphony Recordings (issued 1996)

'*Live in Concert: Francis Perry & Timothy Broege*'
(contains *Franciscan Variations* for guitar & harpsichord)
Allaire Music Recordings TCS-1993
    Recordings are available through the respective university music departments, or by calling Jim Cochran at Shattinger Music Co. in St. Louis, MO (phone 314/621-2408 or fax 314/621-2561).

Appendix

Chronological List of Works (includes year composed, title, scoring)

Year	Title	Scoring
1965	Prayer of Saint Francis	satb chorus, acapella
1965	Two Sacred Songs	med-low voice with organ or piano
1966	Three Lamentations	tenor, horn, piano
1967	(revised 1993) Rosa Mystica	ttbb, organ
1967	Quintet	flute,clar,violin,bassoon, harpsichord
1967	Mourning	clarinet, strings
1968	Spiritual Bell	tuba, harpsichord (or piano)
1968	Sweet Romance at Ninny's Tomb	flute, piano
1968	Studies and Songs	baritone voice, piano
1969	Runes	clarinet, harpsichord (or piano)
1970	Quintet	flute, tenor sax, piano, bass, drums
1971	Chicago Songs	piano, keyboard
1971	Serenata	trumpet, piano
1971	Sinfonia I	orchestra
1971	Benedictus	mezzo soprano, tuba (or bass), piano
1972	Brass Quintet No. 1	2 trumpets, horn, trombone, tuba
1972	Three Piano Rags	piano or keyboard
1972	Southern Suite	band
1972	Suite for Winds & Percussion	band
1972	Vom Himmel Hoch	satb chorus, bass, piano
1972	Sinfonia II	band
1972	Partita for Harpsichord	harpsichord or keyboard
1972	Sinfonia IV	band
1972	Sinfonia III	wind ensemble
1973	The Headless Horseman	band
1973	Songs without Words Set 1	chamber orchestra
1973	Songs from the Gold Key	soprano, flute, clarinet, percussion
1973	Sinfonia V	wind ensemble or band
1973	(revised 1995) The Child and the Kings	band
1974	Rhythm Machine	band
1974	Old Hundredth	handbells
1974	Adagio Religioso and Allegro	handbells
1974	Sinfonia VI	band
1974	Three Pieces for American Band Set 1	band
1974	Songs without Words Set 2	clarinet, mixed ensemble
1975	Quintet for Saxophones	saxophones (sop, alto, 2 tenors, bari)
1975	Blue Goose Rag	band
1975	Serenade for Percussion and Band	band
1975	Sinfonia VII	mixed ensemble
1975	Concert Piece for Trumpet & Band	band
1976	Songs without Words Set 3	marimba, chamber ensemble
1976	Streets and Inroads	band or wind ensemble
1976	Songs of Walt Whitman (Sinfonia VIII)	ssa chorus, piano (or band)
1976	Sinfonia VIII	treble chorus, band
1977	Bolzano	organ, keyboard
1977	Songs, Dances and a Chorale	trumpet, marimba
1977	Sinfonia IX	band
1978	Suite in F	harpsichord, keyboard
1978	Three Pieces for American Band Set 2	band
1978	Four Motets of the Revelation	satb chorus, acapella
1978	Six Early Songs	trumpet, percussion
1978	Nine Arias	alto saxophone, piano
1979	One Week	piano, band
1980	Seven Studies for Piano	piano, keyboard
1980	Solo for Flute	flute, wind ensemble
1980	Sinfonia X	band
1981	Serenata for Trumpet and Band	trumpet, band
1981	Seven German Dances	piano, keyboard

Year	Title	Instrumentation
1982	Sinfonia XI	chamber orchestra, orchestra
1982	Five Sonatas	harpsichord, clavichord, piano, organ
1983	Three Chinese Lyrics	satb chorus, acapella
1983	Sonatas and Fantasias	wind octet
1984	Mets Rule	flute, piano
1984	Sinfonia XII	wind ensemble
1985	Sinfonia XIII	wind ensemble, band
1985	The Kingfisher	harpsichord, keyboard
1985	A Garden in Winter	clavichord, harpsichord, keyboard
1985	Sonatas & Fantasias	wind octet
1985	Characteristic Suite	tenor saxophone, piano
1985	Fantasia for Guitar	guitar
1986	Seven Songs	high voice, piano
1986	Meadows	saatb recorders
1986	A Prayer of Moses	satb chorus, organ (or piano)
1986	Sinfonia XIV	wind ensemble
1987	The Diamond Rule	band, wind ensemble
1987	Fantasia for Flute & Harpsichord	flute, harpsichord (or piano)
1987	Musette/Chaconne/ Forlorn/Time's Telling	alto saxophone, organ
1987	Sonata for Harpsichord	harpsichord, keyboard
1987	Prelude, Dance and Forced March	orchestra
1987	Sinfonia XV	wind ensemble, band
1987	Elegy in Memory of Morton Feldman	piano, keyboard
1987	No Sun, No Shadow; Elegy for Charles Mingus	tenor sax, piano, bass, drums, orchestra, (wind ensemble)
1987	Three Pieces for Clavichord	clavichord, keyboard
1987	Quartet 1987 for strings	string quartet
1988	O Lord, Thou Art My God	chorus
1988	Suite on the First Tone	organ, keyboard
1988	Dreams and Fancies	band
1988	Alien Grounds	guitar ensemble, guitar
1988	Brass Quintet No. 2	2 trumpets, horn, trombone, tuba
1988	Three Pieces	orchestra
1988	Three Psalms	treble chorus, wind ensemble
1989	Peace Song	band
1989	Sun Heart: Three Poems of Octavio Paz	satb chorus, piano
1989	The Four Winds	band
1989	Sinfonia XVI	band
1989	Sinfonia XVII	band
1989	Two Sonatas, Two Rondos	harpsichord, keyboard
1989	Sinfonia XVI: Transcendental Vienna	band
1989	Songs without Words Set 4	clarinet, cello, piano
1989	Five Minimal Songs	baritone voice, piano
1989	Fantasia for Harpsichord	harpsichord, keyboard
1989	Jody	band
1989	Fantasia for Organ	organ
1989	Two Sonatas, Two Rondos	harpsichord
1989	Fantasia for Organ	organ, keyboard
1990	Concerto for Piano & Wind Orchestra	piano, wind ensemble
1990	Visions of Li T'ai-Po	baritone, piano
1990	Three Gremlin Pieces	harpsichord, piano, keyboard
1990	Schuyler Songs	med voice, harpsichord (or piano)
1991	Concerto for Marimba & Wind Orchestra	wind ensemble
1991	Songs without Words Set 5	fl, guitar, cello, harpsichord
1991	Wedding Song with Two Variations	keyboard
1992	Bill Karlins' Ground	piano
1992	An Anniversary Air	organ
1992	Two Rivers: A Ceremony for the Earth	treble chorus, recorders, Orff instruments, percussion, guitar, keyboards, dancers
1993	Franciscan Variations	guitar, harpsichord
1993	Serenade	violin, harpsichord
1993	For Solo Recorder	alto recorder
1993	Grizzly Bear Rag	band
1993	Theme & Variations	band
1993	Sonata for Wind Band	band
1993	A Sabbath Mood	sab chorus
1993	Fanfare & Lullaby	piano
1994	Schumann as Metaphor	piano
1994	Micah's Words	satb chorus, piano
1994	Seven New Carols	satb, fl, piano, bass
1995	Freedom's Necessary Tones	band
1995	Three Preludes	piano
1995	Prelude	harpsichord
1995	Franciscan Variations	(guitar & orch) orchestra
1995	Arioso Sopra Ciacona	(violin & orch) orchestra
1995	Three Preludes (Anton Bruckner)	band
1995–97	The Nostalgia Series (six songs)	orchestra
1996	Five Minimal Songs (voice & orch)	orchestra
1996	The Endless Way	tenor solo, satb, keyboard
1996	Partita Marietta Suite	ssaattb recorders
1996	Stone Garden	flute, bassoon
1996	Seventeen Verses	fl, bssn, harpsichord

1997	Train Heading West & Other Outdoor Scenes	band	
1997	America Verses	band	
1997	Three Sonatas	keyboard	
1997	Procession & Torch Dance	band	
1998	Songs Without Words, Set 6	cello, four percussion	
1998	Chant & Invocation to the Archangel Michael	satb, organ	
1998	The Waukesha Rondo	band	
1999	Sinfonia XIX	band	
1999	Narrative, Ground & Variations	band	
1999	Ricercar	organ	
1999	Talisman	piano (publ. Allaire)	
1999	Talisman II	vibraphone (publ. Allaire)	
2000	Muir Woods	orchestra	
2000	Mysterian Landscapes	band	
2000	The Garden of Hope	voice, flute, clarinet, piano, str. qt.	
2000	*El Jardin de Esperanza*	band	
2000	Two-Part Elegy for LaNoue Davenport	solo recorder	
2000	Sinfonia XXI	wind orchestra	
2000	Slow March with Celebration	band	
2001	Three Pieces for American Band, Set No. 3	wind ensemble	
2001	Mysterian Landscapes	band	
2001	Song with Variations	band	
2002	Grand Festival Music	band	
2002	Charlotte Doyle's Voyage	band	
2002	Sinfonia XX	orchestra (Allaire)	
2002	Old Church Music	organ (Allaire)	
2002	Surfboard Blues	band (Daehn) Gr. 2.5 4'	
2002	Yuletide Dances	band (Grand Mesa Music) Gr.3 5'	
2002	Bartok Variations	band (Grand Mesa) Gr. 2 3'	

CATEGORICAL LIST OF WORKS (INCLUDES TITLE, GRADE, TIME, PUBLISHER)

BAND

TITLE	GRADE	TIME	PUBLISHER
America Verses	2.5	6'	Manhattan Beach
Blue Goose Rag (by Raymond Birch, arr. Broege)	3	3'	Manhattan Beach
Charlotte Doyle's Voyage	3	9'	manuscript
Concert Piece for Trumpet & Band	4/2	5'	Daehn
Dreams & Fancies	2.5	7'	Hal Leonard
Freedom's Necessary Tones	2.5	5'	Manhattan Beach
Grand Festival Music	4	13'	manuscript
Grizzly Bear Rag	2.5	4'	Daehn
Jody 'Variations on a Texas Work Song'	2.5	5'	Manhattan Beach
Mysterian Landscapes	4	8'	Boosey & Hawkes
One Week for solo piano & band	4/2.5	6'	Manhattan Beach
Peace Song	2	5'	Bourne
Procession & Torch Dance	2	3'	Daehn
Rhythm Machine	2	4'	Bourne
Serenata for Percussion & Band (section feature)	2.5	4'	Bourne
Serenata for Trumpet & Band	2.5/2	5'	Bourne
Sinfonia II	3	6'	Manhattan Beach
Sinfonia VI	3	6'	Manhattan Beach
Sinfonia IX 'A Concert in the Park'	4	10'	Manhattan Beach
Sinfonia X	3.5	7'	Allaire
Sinfonia XIII 'Storm Variations'	4	18'	Bourne
Sinfonia XVI 'Transcendental Vienna'	4	8'	Manhattan Beach
Sinfonia XVII 'The Four Winds'	3	9'	Manhattan Beach
Sinfonia XVIII 'Aurora'	2	10'	manuscript
Sinfonia XIX	3	9'	Boosey & Hawkes
Sinfonia XXI	6	20'	manuscript
Slow March with Celebration		5'	Boosey & Hawkes
Sonata for Wind Band (after C.P.E. Bach)	3	6'	Daehn
Song with Variations		3'	Daehn
Southern Suite	2	5'	Hal Leonard
Streets and Inroads	2	4'	Manhattan Beach
Suite for Winds & Percussion (Sinfonia IV)	3	5'	Hal Leonard
The Child and the Kings	2.5	4'	Daehn
The Diamond Rule: Concert Rag	4	5'	Allaire

TIMOTHY BROEGE

The Headless Horseman	2	2'	Manhattan Beach
The Waukesha Rondo	3.5	8'	Manhattan Beach
Theme & Variations	1	3'	Manhattan Beach
Three Pieces for American Band, Set No.1	5	6'	Bourne
Three Pieces for American Band, Set No. 2	2.5	7'	Bourne
Three Pieces for American Band, Set No. 3		10'	manuscript
Three Preludes (Anton Bruckner)	3	6'	Daehn
Train Heading West & Other Outdoor Scenes	1.5	4'	Manhattan Beach

WIND ORCHESTRA/ENSEMBLE

Concerto for Marimba & Wind Orchestra	6/5	25'	Allaire
Concerto for Piano & Wind Orchestra	6/5	29'	Allaire
No Sun, No Shadow: Elegy for Charles Mingus	5/4	30'	Allaire
Sinfonia III "Hymns & Dances"	5	10'	Manhattan Beach
Sinfonia V "Symphonia Sacra et Profana"	5	7'	Manhattan Beach
Sinfonia VII "The Continental Saxophone"	5	12'	Manhattan Beach
Sinfonia XII "Southern Heart/ Sacred Harp"	5	14'	Manhattan Beach
Sinfonia XIV "Three Canzonas"	5	9'	Manhattan Beach
Sinfonia XV "Ursa Major"	5	12'	Manhattan Beach
Solo for Flute (flute, mixed ensemble 22 players)	6/5	8'	Allaire
Three Psalms (tr.chorus & wind ens., instr.mvnts)	4/4	14'	Allaire

CHAMBER ENSEMBLE

Mourning (clarinet & strings)	9'	Allaire
Sonatas & Fantasias (wind octet)	18'	Manhattan Beach
Songs without Words Set No.1 (winds,perc,harp,piano,strings)	13'	Allaire
Songs without Words Set No.2 (clarinet, 15 players)	12'	Allaire
Songs without Words Set No.3 (marimba, 10 players)	9'	Allaire
Songs without Words Set No.6 (cello, 4 perc.)	15'	Allaire

CHAMBER MUSIC

Brass Quintet No. 2	12'	Allaire
Brass Quintet No.1 'O For a Thousand Tongues to Sing'	7'	Allaire
Quartet 1987 for strings	16'	Allaire
Quintet (fl,cl,violin,bssn, harpsichord)	10'	Allaire
Quintet (fl/alfl,tenor sax, electric bass, piano, drums)	12'	Allaire
Quintet for saxophones	8'	Dorn
Seventeen Verses (fl, bsn.,harpsichord)	10'	Allaire
Songs without Words Set No. 4	22'	Allaire
Songs without Words Set No. 5	10'	Allaire

CHORUS

A Prayer of Moses	4'	Allaire
A Sabbath Mood (text by Wendell Berry)	3'	Allaire
Chant & Invocation to the Archangel Michael	5'	Allaire
Four Motets of the Revelation	5'	Bourne
Micahãs Words	4'	Bourne
Prayer of Saint Francis	3'	Bourne
Rosa Mystica	4'	Allaire
Seven New Carols	15'	Allaire
Songs of Walt Whitman (Sinfonia VIII)	7'	Allaire
Sun Heart: Three Poems of Octavio Paz	7'	Allaire
The Endless Way	4'	Allaire
Three Chinese Lyrics	7'	Allaire

Two Rivers: A Ceremony for the Earth	45'	manuscript
Vom Himmel Hoch	3'	Allaire

GUITAR

Alien Grounds (for two or more guitars)	9'	Allaire
Fantasia for Guitar	8'	Allaire
Franciscan Variations	8'	Allaire

HANDBELLS

Adagio Religioso & Allegro	4'	Bourne
Old Hundredth	3'	Bourne

INSTRUMENTAL DUO

Characteristic Suite (tenor saxophone, piano)	15'	Dorn
Franciscan Variations (guitar, harpsichord)	8'	Allaire
Mets Rule (flute, piano)	4'	Allaire
Musette/Chaconne/Forlorn/ Time's Telling True (alto sax,organ)11' Dorn		
Nine Arias (alto saxophone, piano)	22'	Dorn
Runes (clarinet or flute, harpsichord)	5'	Dorn
Serenade (violin, harpsichord)	8'	Allaire
Serenata (trumpet, piano)	5'	Bourne
Six Early Songs (trumpet, percussion)	7'	Allaire
Songs, Dances and a Chorale (recorder, guitar)	10'	Allaire
Spiritual Bell (tuba, harpsichord)	5'	Allaire
Stone Garden (flute, bassoon)	12'	Allaire
Sweet Romance at Ninny's Tomb (flute,piano)	8'	Allaire

KEYBOARD

A Garden in Winter (for clavichord)	12'	Carl Fischer
An Anniversary Air (for organ)	3'	Allaire
Bill Karlins' Ground (for piano)	4'	Allaire
Bolzano (for organ)	5'	Allaire
Chicago Songs (for piano)	13'	Carl Fischer
Elegy 'In Memory of Morton Feldman'	15'	Allaire
Fanfare & Lullaby (for piano)	4'	Allaire
Fantasia for Harpsichord	10'	Allaire
Fantasia for Organ	9'	Allaire
Five Sonatas (for any keyboard instrument)	12'	Allaire
Partita for Harpsichord	9'	Allaire
Prelude (for harpsichord)	3'	Allaire
Ricercar (for organ)	4'	Allaire
Schumann as Metaphor (for piano)	12'	Allaire
Seven German Dances (for piano)	7'	Carl Fischer
Seven Studies (for piano)	15'	Allaire
Sonata for Harpsichord	10'	Allaire
Suite in F Major (for harpsichord)	12'	Allaire
Suite on the First Tone (for organ)	14'	Allaire
The Kingfisher (Suite for harpsichord)	16'	Allaire
Three Gremlin Pieces (for harpsichord or piano)	5'	Allaire
Three Piano Rags	9'	Allaire
Three Pieces for Clavichord	11'	Allaire
Three Preludes (for piano)	5'	Allaire
Three Sonatas (for keyboard)	6'	Allaire
Two Sonatas, Two Rondos (for harpsichord)	14'	Allaire
Wedding Song with Two Variations (for keyboard)	3'	Allaire

ORCHESTRA

Arioso Sopra Ciacona (violin, orchestra)	5'	Allaire
Five Minimal Songs (voice, orchestra)	15'	Allaire
Franciscan Variations (guitar, chamber orchestra)	8'	Allaire
Muir Woods	11'	Allaire
Prelude, Dance and Forced March	9'	Allaire
Sinfonia I 'Eland' (vocalist, jazz/rock ensemble, orchestra)	15'	Allaire
Sinfonia XI (chamber orchestra)	15'	Bourne
The Nostalgia Series		
Ah! Sweet Mystery of Life (Victor Herbert)	4'	Kalmus
The Bells of St. Mary's (A. Emmett Adams)	4'	Kalmus

When Irish Eyes are Smiling (Ernest R. Ball)	4'	Kalmus
If You Were the Only Girl in the World (Nat Ayer)	4'	Kalmus
April Showers (Louis Silvers)	4'	Kalmus
If You Wore A Tulip	4'	Kalmus
Three Pieces for Orchestra	11'	Allaire

RECORDER

For Solo Recorder (suite for alto recorder)	7'	Allaire
Meadows (saatb recorders)	6'	Polyphonic Publ.
Partita Marietta (saat recorders)	12'	Polyphonic Publ.
Two-Part Elegy for LaNoue Davenport	4'	Allaire

VOICE

Benedictus (mezzo soprano, tuba & piano)	6'	Allaire
Deliverer (tenor or baritone, piano)	4'	Allaire
Five Minimal Songs (baritone, piano)	15'	Allaire
Schuyler Songs (medium voice, harpsichord or piano)	7'	Allaire
Seven Songs on text from madrigals of John Wilbye	15'	Allaire
Songs from the Gold Key (soprano, flute, clarinet, perc)	10'	Allaire
Studies & Songs (baritone & piano)	10'	Allaire
Two Sacred Songs (medium voice & keyboard)	6'	Allaire
Visions of Li T'Ai-Po (baritone, piano)	18'	Allaire

COMMISSIONS

1971   Sinfonia I 'Eland'
       Evanston Symphony Orchestra, Evanston, Illinois

1972   Brass Quintet No. 1 'O For a Thousand Tongues to Speak'
       Chicago Brass Quintet

1973   Songs from the Gold Key
       Gruppe Nova, Germany

1973   Sinfonia V 'Symphonia Sacra et Profana'
       University City High School Wind Ensemble. University City, Missouri

1975   Sinfonia VII 'The Continental Saxophone'
       Southern Illinois University Wind Ensemble (for the U.S. Bicentennial)

1976   Songs Without Words, for marimba & ten players
       Tidewater Music Festival. Gordon Stout, marimba

1976   Sinfonia VIII 'Songs of Walt Whitman'
       Sherman Middle School, Madison, Wisconsin

1977   Sinfonia IX 'A Concert in the Park'
       Friends of the conductor John Rafoth, Madison, Wisconsin

1978   Three Pieces for American Band, Set No. 2
       Gilbert S. Lance Junior High School, Kenosha, Wisconsin

1978   Nine Arias for saxophone & piano
       Philip De Libero

1978   Pentatonic Variations (formerly One Week), for piano & band.
       Cherokee Heights Middle School, Madison, Wisconsin. Karen Becker, piano

1980   Sinfonia X
       Galien Township High School Band. Galien, Michigan

1980   Solo for Flute
       Northern Michigan University Wind Ensemble

1984   Sinfonia XII 'Southern Heart/Sacred Harp'
       Campbell University Wind Ensemble (submitted for Big Ten Band Commission)

1985   Sinfonia XIII 'Storm Variations'
       Oconomowoc Senior High School Symphonic Band, Oconomowoc, Wisconsin. In memory of Kevin Jackson

1986   Sinfonia XIV 'Three Canzonas'
       Hanover College Wind Ensemble

1986   The Diamond Rule, Concert Rag
       Georgia Southern College Wind Ensemble

1987   Musette-Chaconne-Forlorn-Time's Telling True
       Frederick Hemke, saxophone

1987   Sonata for Harpsichord
       Paul Rey Klecka and Deutschlandfunk, Germany

1987   No Sun, No Shadow, Elegy for Charles Mingus
       Emory University Wind Ensemble

1987   The Manawquan Rag
       Manasquan Centennial Committee, Manasquan, New Jersey

1987   Prelude, Dance and Forced March
       Monmouth Symphony Orchestra, Red Band, New Jersey 1988

1987   Sinfonia XV 'Ursa Major'

Gamma Phil Chapter, Kappa Kappa Psi National Honorary Band Fraternity Stephen F. Austin State University, Nacogdoches, Texas

1988   Three Psalms

Indianapolis Children's Choir and Butler University Concert Band

1989   Sun-Heart, Three Poems of Octavio Paz

Ocean County College Community Chorus, Toms River, New Jersey. Charles Read, conductor

1989   Sinfonia XVI 'Transcendental Vienna'

Thoreau Intermediate School Symphonic Band, Vienna, Virginia. Richard H. Sanger, conductor (submitted for Big Ten Band Commission)

1989   Sinfonia XVII 'The Four Winds'

Charles D. Evans Junior High School Band and Orchestra Boosters, Ottumwa, Iowa

1989   Jody, Variations on a Texas Work Song

Lincoln Middle School Band, Abilene, Texas

1990   Concerto for Piano & Wind Orchestra

California State University–Fullerton Wind Ensemble, Mary Mark Zeyen, piano soloist. Mitchel Fennell, conductor

1991   Concerto for Marimba & Wind Ensemble

University of Washington Wind Ensemble, Timothy Salzman, conductor

1992   Two Rivers: A Ceremony for the Earth

Meet the Composer & Rumson Country Day School, Rumson, New Jersey

1994   Seven New Carols

The Ocean County College Community Chorus; Charles Read, director

1995   Sinfonia XVIII 'Aurora'

The Waubonsie Valley High School Wind Ensemble. Charles Staley, Jr., conductor

1996   Stone Garden: Preludes & Inventions for flute & bassoon.

Duo Arpeggio, Phoenix, Arizona

1996   Marietta Suite

McCleskey Middle School Recorder Ensemble, Jody Miller, director

1998   Sinfonia XIX

Berwick, PA Middle School Band

1998   The Waukesha Rondo

Central Middle School Band, Waukesha, WI, Laura Katz Sindberg, director

1999   Narrative, Ground & Variations

Thoreau Middle School, Vienna, VA, Richard Sanger, director

2000   Sinfonia XXI

The Keystone Wind Ensemble, Jack Stamp, conductor

2000   The Garden of Hope

Northern Valley Regional High School, Old Tappan, NJ, Kurt Ebersole, director

2000   Mysterian Landscapes

Bald Eagle, PA High School Band, Scott Sheehan, director

2001   Three Pieces for American Band, Set No. 3

The U.S. Military Academy Band, LTC David Deitrick, conductor

2002   Sinfonia XX

The Monmouth Symphony Orchestra, Red Bank, NJ

2002   Sinfonia XXI

Keystone Winds, Jack Stamp, conductor

2002   Grand Festival Music

Kenosha Unified School District #1, Kenosha, Wisconsin

2002   Charlotte Doyle's Voyage

East Stroudsburg, Pennsylvania, 7th & 8th Grade Band

NEW WORKS

Songs Without Words Set No. 7, commission for Southern Methodist University Meadows Wind Ensemble, Jack Delaney, conductor. Chamber orchestra work for mezzo soprano (mostly wordless), harpsichord, and an ensemble of five woodwinds, three brass, percussion (1) and five strings.

Commissioning project for the New Jersey Education Association for a new work for the New Jersey All-State Chorus & Orchestra's November, 2003 All-State concert.

ENDNOTES

1. T. Broege, letter to author (October 27, 1997).
2. T. Broege, letter.
3. Ibid.
4. T. Broege, phone conversation with author (November 10, 1997).
5. A. Cohen, "Modern Composer goes for Baroque", in Asbury Park Press (Asbury Park, New Jersey, March 1, 1997).
6. T. Broege, phone.
7. Ibid .
8. Ibid.
9. A. Cohen.
10. T. Broege, phone.
11. Ibid.
12. Ibid.
13. Ibid.
14. R. Miles, Teaching Music through Performance in Band (Chicago: GIA Publications, Inc., 1997), 96.

15. T. Broege, phone.

16. R. Miles, p.97.

17. T. Broege, phone.

18. R. Miles, p.129.

19. T. Broege, Sinfonia XVII: The Four Winds (Brooklyn, New York: Manhattan Beach Music, 1996)

20. Ibid.

21. T. Broege, Sinfonia XVI: Transcendental Vienna (Brooklyn, New York: Manhattan Beach Music, 1995)

22. T. Broege, phone.

23. R. Miles, p.300.

24. Ibid., p.301.

25. T. Broege, No Sun, No Shadow: Elegy for Charles Mingus (Bradley Beach, New Jersey: Allaire Music Publishing, 1987)

26. T. Broege, No Sun, No Shadow: Elegy for Charles Mingus.

27. Ibid.

28. T. Broege, letter.

29. Ibid.

30. Ibid.

31. Ibid.

32. Ibid.

Michael Colgrass

by
Stephen Clickard

I'm not trying to pull any tricks or dazzle anybody. I'm trying to make a music which convinces me, and which is interesting to me. It's as simple as that.[1]

Pulitzer Prize-winning composer Michael Colgrass has composed five brilliantly crafted works for wind ensemble that represent a significant contribution to the repertoire by one of America's most important contemporary composers.

The programmatic originality and unusual orchestrations found in Colgrass' wind ensemble music are a decisive departure from traditional band repertoire, and as such, he is regarded as a true sound innovator. His works, while involving the standard acoustic wind and percussion instruments, are characterized by highly unusual orchestrations and performance techniques that shape the overall sound into a truly unique sonic experience. By viewing the band as a large chamber ensemble as opposed to a symphonic one, his music can, at times, sound like a consortium of soloists as opposed to a large wind ensemble. Of Colgrass' music New York Times critic Harold Schonberg said:

> Mr. Colgrass is something of a maverick. He will use serial textures, but will mix them with jazz, or outright romanticism, or dissonance á la Ives. He has also evolved a distinct kind of miniature style that is extremely personal and poetic. [2]

In describing Colgrass' inclination toward highly descriptive programmatic music, music annotator Leonard Burkat said:

> In his work, the differences that distinguish program music, which is related in some way to extra-musical subject matter, from absolute music, in which the music itself is the subject, blend and disappear. [3]

As an internationally recognized, prize-winning composer for the symphony orchestra and a variety of other media, Colgrass' contributions to the wind repertoire have given a significant measure of credibility to the wind band genre.

BIOGRAPHICAL INFORMATION

Michael Colgrass was born in Chicago on April 22, 1932. After graduating from the University of Illinois in 1956 in music performance and composition, Colgrass relocated to New York City where he free-lanced as a percussionist with such diverse groups as the New York Philharmonic, Dizzy Gillespie, the original West Side Story orchestra on Broadway and numerous ballet, opera and jazz ensembles.

His compositions have been commissioned and performed by The New York Philharmonic, The Boston Symphony, The Minnesota Orchestra, The Detroit Symphony, The Toronto Symphony, The Lincoln Center Chamber Music Society, The Corporation for Public Broadcasting, the Manhattan and Muir String Quartets, The Brighton Festival in England, The Fromm Foundation and Ford Foundation, and numerous other orchestras, chamber groups, choral groups and soloists.

Colgrass' works have been played by major symphony orchestras in the United States, Canada, and throughout Europe, Great Britain and Japan, and have been recorded by the St. Louis Symphony, the Boston Symphony, the American Symphony Orchestra, the Toronto Symphony Orchestra and numerous chamber groups and soloists.

Colgrass has received many prizes and awards: the 1978 Pulitzer Prize in Music for "Deja Vu," commissioned and premiered by the New York Philharmonic; First Prize in the Barlow and Sudler International Wind Ensemble Competitions; Guggenheim fellowship awards in 1964 and 1968; a Rockefeller Grant; and the 1988 Jules Léger Chamber Music Prize for Strangers: Irreconcilable Variations for Clarinet, Viola and Piano.

Although he makes his living as a composer, for the past 25 years Colgrass has also been giving workshops in performing excellence, combining Grotowski physical training, Neuro-Linguistic Programming (NLP) and hypnosis. Most recently he has given these workshops in Indonesia, South Africa, Argentina, Uruguay, Moscow, and Taiwan. These techniques were featured on the PBS documentary about Michael Colgrass called "Soundings: the Music of Michael Colgrass" which won an Emmy Award in 1982. His strategies for creativity are explained in Robert Dilts' book Tools For Dreamers. He is the founder of Deep Listening, a technique for using hypnosis for audiences, which is featured in the book Leaves Before The Wind. His ideas on new approaches to performing are outlined in his new book, My Lessons With Kumi, published by Real People Press.

Michael Colgrass currently resides with his wife in Toronto, writing music and giving workshops on an international scale. For more information see www.michaelcolgrass.com.

COMPOSITIONAL APPROACH

Michael Colgrass began his musical life at the age of eleven when he began taking private lessons on drums—within a year he played in his first band. His performance experience was largely in the area of jazz until he was nineteen when he began studying percussion at the University of Illinois where his interest in classical music was initially kindled. His early attempts at composing also took place at Illinois. Colgrass describes his first compositional experiences:

> I was a percussion major playing in a percussion ensemble and we needed literature. Our teacher, Paul Price, was asking everyone to write music because there wasn't too much. So, I tried my hand at it and wrote Three Brothers. That was my first piece and it was a successful premiere. So he asked me to write another one and that was it. I just kept writing from that time on. People were always asking me to write music so I was always responding to a need. It was not an academic process for me; in fact it was a functional process. It was not until I graduated from university [that] it occurred to me to write for something other than percussion. . . . I always thought I was a percussionist who was fulfilling a need for my instrument; I did not think of myself as a composer. [4]

Colgrass' compositional style shows influence from a wide variety of sources but his early influences were all jazz musicians—Max Roach, Charlie Parker, Dizzy Gillespie, from the bop era, as well as Stan Kenton, and Woody Herman from the big bands. He feels that his early love of big band jazz has provided a certain inspiration for his compositions for wind ensemble.

> . . . one reason why I like to write for bands, is because the first musical aggregations that impressed me were bands, jazz bands, big bands, although that is not the instrumentation of wind ensemble or concert band. Nevertheless a band's a band . . . ensembles without strings were my first influence. [5]

Colgrass makes extensive use of one of the key organizing elements of jazz, theme and variation, to structure his own compositions. In jazz performance, the melody is played and the soloists follow with their own variations on the melody, although sometimes played quite freely, over the same chord progression. To accomplish this sort of thematic evolution in his wind compositions Colgrass has created a type of theme and variations form that he refers to as "developmental variations." In this format he begins with a theme that is slowly transformed via numerous stylistic and textural manipulations within the orchestration. The central difference between this form and a standard theme and variations is that the listener does not necessarily hear a distinct theme followed by a clear series of variations. Rather, episodes form

as the piece develops and, due to the skill of the composer, no apparent aural 'seam' is necessarily evident between each variation or episode. This technique is used most effectively in his tone poems for wind ensemble, particularly Winds of Nagual, Arctic Dreams and Urban Requiem.

Of course Colgrass has also been influenced by 'main stream' classical music composers whose works were initially introduced to him during his student days at the University of Illinois. He names Stravinsky, Bartok and Hindemith among those whose music first impacted him.

In 1958 Colgrass was exposed to the music of Anton Webern, Alban Berg, and Arnold Schoenberg, composers whose music influenced him to focus his writing in a more atonal style. However, after a period of intense study and practice of atonality he found that it was not altogether artistically satisfying for him.

> I gradually started to write pieces that mixed atonality with a more lyrical style, giving it some kind of emotional base, which was difficult to [achieve] with atonality except [for] high intensity, terror, or mysteriousness, like in quiet atonality. Those are the moods that you can get with that type of material, and if you are very clever and work it out just right, humor. But to a broad range of emotion is extremely difficult. Subtle moods of tenderness etc. seem to be effected by some kind of an aspect that atonality just does not lend itself to. I have never heard anyone do it. The closest . . . is Alban Berg but it still has that feeling of being a semi-nightmare—and although beautiful . . . is just limited. [6]

Although Colgrass found atonality somewhat limiting, he credits the time he spent writing in an atonal manner with shaping his current compositional style and feels strongly that an important dimension in his musical understanding would be missing without that experience. For example, he credits atonality for shaping his highly unique orchestrations for band:

> My way of orchestrating comes very much from an atonal way of thinking. In atonality, for example, you don't lean on the octave. I became very cautious of the octave and it began to sound clangy and out of tune. As a result I rarely use octaves in my orchestration . . . sometimes I will have to reinforce, but in a lot of my writing even in loud sections you won't find much in the way of octaves if any. [This compositional style] forces you to find a really strong harmonic way of doing things instead of just stretching your left hand or your right hand into octaves on a piano and going "clang". It sounds loud because you are doubling c, c, c, and c. It gives you more weight, but to me it often sounds cheap. So I thought "Well, what if I do want to have a note that sounds loud but I won't let myself have the octave...what will I do?" It really becomes a tremendous challenge. You start thinking texturally and in colors much more. As a result, my orchestration took on a sense of color it would not have had, had I not studied atonality. [7]

Colgrass studied composition with Darius Milhaud in the summer of 1953 in Aspen and with Wallingford Riegger in New York during the summer of 1958, but those experiences had little impact on his composition. However, his lessons with Lukas Foss in the summer of 1954 were more useful due to a concentrated study of the sonata form, the result of which was valuable to Colgrass for formal application to his modern pieces. It is in the sonata form that Colgrass learned the principle conflict of two themes, the primary and the secondary, a "kind of a suggestion of masculine and feminine". [8]

Colgrass' two most influential composition teachers, creatively speaking, were Eugene Weigel and Ben Weber. In Colgrass' view Weigel, from the University of Illinois, was a composer who had the rare ability to teach one how to access the raw materials within one's mind. After viewing Colgrass' work Weigel would make suggestions that encouraged his imagination and helped him to look at his compositions with a renewed perspective.

In 1958 when Colgrass decided he wanted to begin composing atonally, he began studies in New York with Ben Weber, one of the first American atonal composers who had been already composing atonal music for about twenty-five years. Colgrass says he chose Ben Weber as a teacher because he wanted to study atonality from someone "with a heart". Weber insisted that Colgrass create music that was more than mere mathematical accomplishment by requiring that his compositions have shape; he further assisted Colgrass in breaking free of some of the restrictions that atonality imposed. [9]

> I remember one time when going through something of mine with him, we were kind of picking it out together on the piano and I said, "Oops this sounds like a dominant 7th" . . . he looked at me and smiled and said "You aren't free yet". I never forgot that because to me, I was always trying to write every bar, every beat, with no tonality, no major or minor key relationship at all. It is virtually impossible. But by trying to do it, you certainly tune your mind and sharpen your ear. You become extremely aware of all intervals and their meanings. So, at one point I heard a "C" and "B flat" occurring together and I thought dominant 7th and he said, "it's not a dominant 7th, [it's] just a coincidence of 2 notes moving in their own directions. You're the one who's hearing it as a dominant 7th." That really sent me home thinking. It could not, of course, have a dominant 7th function at all. And just because I was hearing 2 notes that define a dominant 7th characteristically, I was thinking that I was falling into tonality. So, when he said I was "not free" I began to allow myself to hear. When I heard a major 3rd, I didn't think, well that's B flat major, and that an augmented 4th had to have some kind of a modulation function. So I would say [that] Ben is responsible for me as a composer. [10]

Colgrass approaches a new composition in a very personal way in that he begins the compositional process by personally familiarizing himself with the commissioning artist or ensemble. When he wrote a quintet for the Canadian Brass, he interviewed the members and found that while one of the trumpet players liked the loud characteristics of his instrument, the other liked the softer qualities found in baroque style trumpet playing; so, in his writing of the work he attempted to give

them parts that best fit their nature. Obviously this cannot be done with each member of an orchestra, but when Colgrass wrote Déjà Vu, his 1978 Pulitzer Prize winning work, for the New York Philharmonic (a group in which he had been a regular extra player), he asked to sit with the orchestra during rehearsal to re-familiarize himself with the group as well as to experience the ambient environment of the new concert hall. He found that the brightness of the hall coupled with the energy and brightness of the orchestra gave clear inspiration to the approach he utilized in the piece.

Colgrass credits the programmatic nature of his music to his study of acting, dance, and mime at the Commedia dell'Arte of the Piccolo Teatro di Milano and the Polish Theater Laboratory. In addition to his theatrical training Colgrass' programmatic approach also comes from his early days as a jazz musician as he believes strongly that composers need to strive to communicate with audiences of non-specialists;

> . . . what impressed me all along, and I got it from the Charlie Parkers and Dizzy Gillespies, was that the great musicians of any given time communicate with an audience. If you're really a good composer, then you should be able to contact people who are non-specialists in your art. And it happened that the world I was living in was contradictory to that. The only people who were coming to the concerts were specialists, mainly the composers themselves. [11]

WORKS FOR WIND ENSEMBLE

Colgrass has given the wind band world five large 'tone poems' each of which is a distinctive and exceptional musical odyssey. His unique use of acoustic instruments to accomplish the programmatic intentions of each work is particularly fascinating and, for the conductor and performers, quite challenging.

Winds of Nagual A Musical Fable on the Writings of Carlos Castaneda (1985) 25'
6flt(2dbl.pic,2dbl.alt),6Bb,1Eb,bscl.,1Ebcontalt,1Bbcontbs,cbsn,sop.sax,alt.sax/6tpts(2dblcor),flhn,6hns,6trbs,2euph,2tba/2cb/pf-cel/timp.5perc
Archive score for sale (Carl Fischer)

Although Colgrass' early works were for percussion, he gradually began to include other instruments in his works. In 1962, he wrote his first piece without percussion, Rhapsody for Clarinet, Violin and Piano. He did not write a piece for wind ensemble until 1984 when Frank Battisti commissioned him to write a composition for the New England Conservatory Wind Ensemble. The result of this commission was Winds of Nagual, originally a piano piece entitled Tales of Power written in 1980 and based on the writings of Carlos Castaneda. Originally, Colgrass' publisher thought that Tales of Power would make a good orchestra piece. However, when the commission came from Frank Battisti, (at that time the wind ensemble conductor at the New England Conservatory of Music), Colgrass said that he "thought of band and all the instruments you have and all the extended winds . . . it seemed like band was a good medium for that piece."[12] At the time Colgrass did not particularly want to write for band as he was considering offers for six other commissions that were to be written for different media, and having never written for band before, he was unsure as to why a band commission had been offered to him. But, Colgrass felt that because Frank Battisti was so specific in his choice of composer, he would consider the commission seriously. The New England Conservatory Wind Ensemble premiered Winds of Nagual in February of 1985 in Jordan Hall in Boston. Colgrass recommends the recording of this premiere as well as Mallory Thompson's Northwestern Wind Ensemble recording on Summit Records as the definitive performances.

Colgrass provides clear program notes in the score of Winds of Nagual;

> Winds of Nagual is based on the writings of Carlos Casteneda about his 14-year apprenticeship with Don Juan Matis, a Yaqui Indian sorcerer from Northwestern Mexico. Casteneda met Don Juan while researching hallucinogenic plants for his master's thesis in Anthropology at UCLA. Juan became Casteneda's mentor and trained him in pre-Columbian techniques of sorcery, the overall purpose of which is to find the creative self—what Juan calls the nagual.[13]

Colgrass directs the listeners towards the identifying character motives found throughout the work:

> Each of the characters in the piece has a musical theme: Juan's is dark and ominous, yet gentle and kind. Carlos' is open, direct and naive. We hear Carlos' theme throughout the piece from constantly changing perspectives, as Juan submits him to long desert marches, encounters with terrifying powers and altered states of reality. A comic aspect is added to the piece by don Genaro a sorcerer friend of Juan's who frightens Carlos with fantastic tricks like disappearing and re-appearing at will.[14]

Additional programmatic annotations are found throughout the score and are meant to assist the conductor and performers in the interpretation of the various moods and feelings in the work rather than to more directly provide a dramatic script for the audience.

> My object is to capture the mood and atmosphere created by the books and to convey a feeling of the relationship that develops as a man of ancient wisdom tries to cultivate heart in an analytical young man of the technological age.[15]

Of critical importance to the understanding of the structure of the piece are the character themes, which reoccur throughout the work and whose manipulations are essential elements in character development. After a brief introduction, he introduces don Juan's theme beginning in measure 29. (see figure 1)

FIGURE 1: Juan's Theme (condensed from score), mm 29–39
Winds of Nagual
Copyright © 1977 Carl Fischer
International Copyright Secured. All Rights Reserved. Reprinted by Permission.

FIGURE 2: Carlos' Theme, mm 59-61
Winds of Nagual
Copyright © 1977 Carl Fischer
International Copyright Secured. All Rights Reserved. Reprinted by Permission.

Carlos' theme is first heard "in fragmented form and in sparse textures in measures 59, 61, and 65–69."16 (see figure 2) The score indication is "Carlos approaches don Juan."

The second half of the theme occurs under the marking "Carlos unsure of himself". To communicate a rather unsteady Carlos, Colgrass manipulates the tempo via a "rush/drag" technique, which, when coupled with dynamic contrasts, achieves a clear programmatic intent. The harmonic support is sustained throughout allowing the solo clarinetist to take full advantage of the written directions given by Colgrass. (see figure 3)

Another character is introduced with the appearance of don Genaro who provides a sense of comic relief in the work. He is introduced in measure 79 and "clowns for Carlos" in measure 84 via fragmented allusions to Carlos' theme. Colgrass scores the accompaniment in a comical way; trombones play crude glissandi, cowbells play a loping beat figure, and piccolos mimic chirping birds. (see figure 4) This light feel is intermittently interrupted by ominous sustained tone clusters in the bass instruments.

After don Genaro "clowns with Carlos", the score indicates that "Genaro satirizes Carlos". Here, Colgrass creates a dance-like version of Carlos' theme utilizing the Eb clarinet, Bb clarinet, soprano sax, and piano right hand. The piano left hand plays the only accompaniment. Colgrass calls for a tinny sound, perhaps in imitation of an old saloon upright. (see figure 5)

These examples briefly demonstrate a few of the many programmatic techniques employed in Winds of Nagual to relate the story of Carlos. Because there are not always breaks between the main titled sections or extensive program notes for the audience, the listener gains a general impression of the storyline but may not be aware of all the programmatic details as they occur. The many score indications are for the conductor and performer to assist in an accurate portrayal of the storyline.

Déjà Vu (1977) 18'
4 solo perc;6flt(pic,alt),0,6Bb,Ebcl,bscl,Bbcontbs,2bsn.+cbn,
sop.sax(alto)/4tpts,6hns,6trbs,1euph,1tuba/pf cel/2hp/2cb
Archive score for sale (Carl Fischer)

Déjà Vu was the next piece scored for wind ensemble and is a re-scoring of a work originally written for percussion quartet and orchestra. Commissioned and premiered by

FIGURE 3: Carlos Unsure, mm 65-69
Winds of Nagual
Copyright © 1977 Carl Fischer
International Copyright Secured. All Rights Reserved. Reprinted by Permission.

FIGURE 4: Genaro clowns, mm 84-87
Winds of Nagual
Copyright © 1977 Carl Fischer
International Copyright Secured. All Rights Reserved. Reprinted by Permission.

FIGURE 5: Carlos' Theme Satirized, mm 110-116
Winds of Nagual
Copyright © 1977 Carl Fischer
International Copyright Secured. All Rights Reserved. Reprinted by Permission.

the New York Philharmonic, Erich Leinsdorf, conductor on October 20, 1977 Déjà Vu earned Colgrass the 1978 Pulitzer Prize for Music. The wind ensemble version of the work was premiered at the 24th National Convention of the College Band Directors National Association held at Northwestern University on February 26, 1987 by the Central Michigan University Symphonic Wind Ensemble, Dr. John E. Williamson, conductor. The wind ensemble premiere was the result of a commission from the Mid-American Conference Band Directors Association.

K. Robert Schwarz, in a review for "High Fidelity" magazine described Déjà Vu in the following manner:

"'Deja vu' evokes both personal and universal pasts. On the one hand, it recalls the composer's early career as a percussionist; on the other, it uses vague historical allusions, apparent when the unifying theme is transformed into styles ranging from classic to romantic to jazz to serial. Colgrass, as can be expected, handles his huge percussion section with aplomb, and he is a fine orchestrator. The melodic parameter is cultivated from the lush lyricism of the strings to the passionate outbursts of the brass. Most important, his wild eclecticism—which might spell destruction in the hands of a lesser composer—never threatens the work's unity and integrity. An almost Ivesian joy in juxtaposing disparate material is obvious in one section, where Colgrass adroitly combines hushed, sustained strings with intrusions of jazz and Webernian pointillism."[17]

Although a wonderful addition to the repertoire, this piece will not be discussed extensively as it was not originally scored for wind ensemble.

Arctic Dreams (1991) 24'
6flt(4,5,6 dbl. alt, all dbl.pic),3ob,8Bb,bscl,Bbcontbs,3bsn,
1cbsn,3sax(sopr,alt,bar)/6tpts,6hns,6trbs,2euph,2tuba,pf
cel/hp/2cb/timp.5perc
Archive score for sale (Carl Fischer)

Colgrass' third work for wind ensemble is Arctic Dreams, a work commissioned by the University of Illinois for the 100th anniversary of the University of Illinois symphonic and concert bands and to honor Jack McKenzie who was retiring as Dean of the College of Fine and Applied Arts. It was premiered on January 16, 1991 by James Keene, conducting the University of Illinois Symphonic Band, in the Foellinger Great Hall of the Krannert Center for the Performing Arts. Colgrass investigated his subject matter thoroughly by living and interacting with the Inuit people near the Arctic Circle;

I did a lot of reading and lived there [Pangnirtung, Baffan Island] for about one month with [an Inuit] family. Barry Lopez' book, Arctic Dreams, was a particularly beautiful book. This is a book to read whether you are interested in the arctic or not. He is a wonderful writer. He had a lot of interesting stuff about the Arctic, but it is also a philosophical book. He uses the arctic as a metaphor for life. It is quite a compelling book…some aspects were informative to me about the piece and I liked the title so I used that. But, I was perhaps most influenced by a book called People of the Deer by Farley Mowat. It is a really interesting book about his adventure up in the arctic and it is partly fiction partly non-fiction. He was asked by the government to investigate what happened to a certain tribe of Inuit people called the Ihalmiut from north of Winnipeg. He went up there with a couple of Eskimo guys and they trekked through and finally found a lot of skeletons of people who died of small pox. He writes the book almost like a novel and it is so mysterious and interesting—it is evocative and magical and it gave a kind of aura to the Arctic that I had not [gotten] from a lot of the other books that were more factual. So, all that stuff came together when I lived up there for a while. I got a feeling just being there, stuff you can't get without being there . . . for example, the wind is always blowing, even when its not blowing it is blowing, even when its not a windy day it is always going on and that turns up in the piece. There are several movements where the winds come in and out and you hear ice cracking. It sounds kind of like distant explosions, a quiet or subtle explosion, and those sounds made their way into the piece—gently hitting the inside of the piano with a bass drum beater sounds like ice shifting. The other aspect is the playfulness of the Inuit people. You don't quite pick that up unless you're there. They are always kidding around. They are like children in that way; they like to kid and play tricks on you. They like to laugh; maybe it is because they are so close to death all the time. The Arctic is a very dangerous place. I mean to say, death is a way of life there. They don't live in igloos anymore. They live in little framed Quonset type huts. You can, in winter, go walking out from your house and get caught in a white-out where the wind is blowing, its snowing and everything is white. I have never experienced anything quite like it. It is like an overexposed film. You can't see the ground, the sky or the horizon and you can't see a foot in front of you. You lose your balance it is so disorienting physically. You don't realize how much you use things around you to orient your equilibrium. So when all that is taken away from you, you teeter . . . you certainly lose your sense of direction. So you can walk out 25 feet from your house and get caught in a white-out . . . you may walk in the wrong direction and they will find your body in the morning, or they may find your body 10 feet from the front door; it is possible, it happens all the time. But, the Arctic is like this and so they have a high respect for nature. Unlike us, thinking we can control the world with our technology, they know they don't control nature. This is my analysis as to why they have a good sense of humor. Because they just more

or less say, well God, you take over and you are more or less in control and we are just lucky to be here so let's have a good time. They are healthy people. Except they have a morbid side to them if they drink, [so] it is illegal to drink there.[18]

Arctic Dreams is the most highly programmatic of the three works to be discussed and each section of the piece is programmatically titled. In the score Colgrass describes it as ". . . a tone poem inspired by the Arctic and by the lives and legends of the Inuit who live there. . . . I was fascinated by their way of life, their humor, and their sense of mystery and wonder at the awesome nature around them."[19]

The opening section entitled Inuit Landscape depicts the stormy wind-swept vast open space of the Arctic. A solo trombonist, standing on the edge of the stage, is the performer instructed to play as if calling out like a "lone human being" over the polar expanse; the solo is to be performed lyrically but without vibrato in a recitative style. (See figure 6)

In measure two the ambient sounds of the Arctic are introduced by adding the low brass and woodwinds in sustained pitches under the trombone solo. Colgrass then adds the upper woodwinds to create the sound of a brittle icy wind achieved by moving glissandi in parallel motion clusters, an effect intensified by the use of swelling crescendi. (see Figure 7)

FIGURE 6: Trombone Solo, mm 1-2
Arctic Dreams
Copyright © 1991 Carl Fischer
International Copyright Secured. All Rights Reserved. Reprinted by Permission.

FIGURE 7: Icy Woodwinds, mm 3
Arctic Dreams
Copyright © 1991 Carl Fischer
International Copyright Secured. All Rights Reserved. Reprinted by Permission.

Movement two, entitled Throat Singing with Laughter, depicts the jovial, playful, childlike quality of the Inuit. As this movement opens, the plaintive sustained notes are retained in the horns, trombones, contrabassoon, and contrabassi. Colgrass again uses tone clusters moving in parallel glissandi to achieve the effect of wind. This effect is enhanced by the addition of a whistling sound in the piccolos and flutes that are instructed to blow partially across the embouchure hole while playing their respective glissandos.

The dramatic effect that is the most unique in this movement is Colgrass' use of "Throat Singing". Throat singing is a unique form of Inuit music created by rapid in-and out-takes of breath on fast rhythms, which incites almost continual laughter in the singers and onlookers alike.[20] The effect of producing sound on both the inhalation and exhalation produces a very primitive animalistic grunting sound. Colgrass specifies the syllables to be sung and uses arrows to depict whether each syllable should be sung while inhaling or exhaling. (see figure 8)

To achieve acceptable ensemble balance Colgrass specifies that the throat singers be amplified.

Colgrass is very innovative in his attempts to conjure up visual images in the mind of the listener, a wonderful example being his orchestrational realization of the aurora borealis.[21] The overall effect being that of "gossamer curtains undulating in the sky."[22] This effect is mainly achieved via the percussion section, with the addition of the celeste, harp, and contrabassi, utilizing a wide variety of very specific and sometimes unusual instructions. For example, the percussionist who is playing the piano, must, with the sustain pedal depressed, "caress strings inside the piano . . . w/ the visor of a baseball cap in figure-8 motions." The instrumentalists are given different shapes and instructions for implementing a variety of glissandi. The varied nature, by means of intensity and timing of the glissandi, are responsible for the undulating effect. The wide range of metallic sounds gives the collective timbre an ethereal feel which is grounded by the depth of sound produced by the piano and harp glissandi. A unique effect is created by the use of the water cymbal, an instrument played with a yarn stick while the cymbal is

raised and lowered in and out of water. The resultant wash of sound adds to the ambiance of a haunting wind. This effect is further enhanced by the glissandi on harmonics in the contrabassi.[23] (see figure 9)

These are but a few examples of the unique orchestrations employed by Colgrass in Arctic Dreams to communicate his programmatic intentions. His effective use of alternate tone production techniques combined with his unusual instrumental combinations, work together to create a true "Arctic" sound image in the listeners mind.

Urban Requiem (1995) 28'
Saxophone quartet; 1pic,1fl,1altfl,1ob+Enghn,1E♭cl,1B♭ cl,1bscl,2bsn+cbn /4tpts,3hns,3trbs,1tuba/ synth/ hp/ 2cb/ timp.4perc
Archive score for sale (Carl Fischer)

Colgrass' most recent work for wind ensemble is Urban Requiem, a work for saxophone quartet and wind ensemble commissioned by Gary Green and the University of Miami Wind Ensemble through its Abraham Frost Commission Series. It was first performed in Biloxi, Mississippi on January 27, 1996 and was officially premiered at the Southern Division CBDNA Conference on March 5, 1996 by the University of Miami Wind Ensemble, Gary Green, conductor. When Colgrass received the commission the only criteria stipulated were that the work should reflect the city of Miami

> . . . the city and the ethnic groups there, the problems of crime and the conflict of cities and tension was one aspect of writing the piece. Also, the University of Miami has one of the best Jazz Departments . . . and a great Sax Department. From time to time people have asked me to write a sax quartet and I had never done it. So when I thought about writing for a city, and what instrument represents a city. I thought saxes seemed to be a really urban instrument representing urban life. So those were the connections that all went into the melting pot in my mind.[24]

In the forward to the score Colgrass supplies the following program notes:

> A requiem is a dedication to the souls of the dead. Urban Requiem might be described as an urban tale, inspired by a

* Exhale (▲) and inhale (▼) catching sound in the throat so we can hear the syllables.

The effect is somewhat like loud panting with the pitches unspecific.
Note: Pitches will vary on inhale& exhale.

FIGURE 8: Throat Singing, mm 46
Arctic Dreams
Copyright © 1991 Carl Fischer
International Copyright Secured. All Rights Reserved. Reprinted by Permission.

diversity of random impressions. I thought of our urban areas, where the saxophone was spawned, and of the tragedies and struggles that occur in this environment daily. But I was also inspired by the energy and power of our cities, and the humor inherent in their conflicts. I feel that the saxophone is particularly well suited to express the variety of emotions required for this idea, because it can be not only highly personal and poignant in character but also powerful and commanding. It can howl like a banshee or purr like a kitten. In short, the saxophone is perhaps more like the human voice than any other instrument. In my mind I heard four saxophones singing like a vocal quartet, a music that was liturgical in nature but with a bluesy overtone, a kind of "after hours" requiem.[25]

Urban Requiem is a more chamber-like work than Colgrass' other works for wind ensemble and the physical set-up of the instrumentalists plays an important part in establishing the performance geography of the musical 'city'.

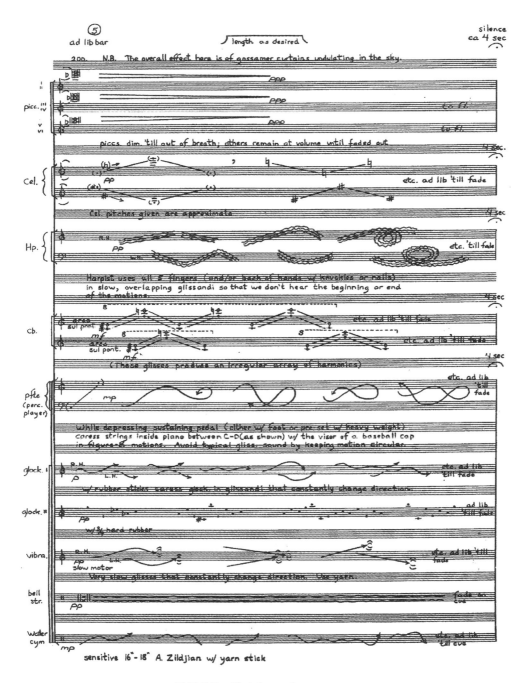

FIGURE 9: Undulating Curtain, mm 200
Arctic Dreams
Copyright © 1991 Carl Fischer
International Copyright Secured. All Rights Reserved. Reprinted by Permission.

The size of the wind ensemble for Urban Requiem matches the non-string instrumentation of a symphony orchestra (triple winds and brasses, tuba, four horns, harp, synthesizer, timpani, and four percussion). The players are divided into four groups surrounded by the larger wind ensemble, with each sax having its own little "neighborhood." The soloists interact in virtuoso display and play duets and trios with principal players in their bands. The sax players are called upon to improvise occasionally over basic material in sometimes jazz, sometimes ethnic musical traditions.[xx]

Urban Requiem is the least programmatic of his works for wind ensemble and Colgrass does not include programmatic indications in the score. The principal theme of the work is reminiscent of the Musical Offering by J. S. Bach. The unifying characteristic of the piece is the transformation of the opening theme as it travels through the various neighborhoods of this brilliantly portrayed 'urban soundscape.'

Colgrass also makes a clear distinction between the 'external' programs of Arctic Dreams and Winds of Nagual and the 'character portrayals' found in Urban Requiem.

I found that I was dramatizing, not necessarily programmatically as I did in Winds of Nagual or Arctic Dreams. . . . The instruments have a personality and a character; the protagonist, the antagonist, an aggressive person, and a romantic quiet personality. And then a shift where one personality makes a change into a violent personality from a quiet personality. So it is like theater. I always have a feeling of conflict urging the music to go on and change so that the instruments go through transformations. . .[26]

In the opening of the work the Bach-like theme is introduced by the saxophone quartet in a reverent chorale-like setting, with the theme appearing in the soprano saxophone. (see figure 10)

FIGURE 10: Theme Excerpt, mm 42-49
Urban Requiem
Copyright © 1996 Carl Fischer
International Copyright Secured. All Rights Reserved. Reprinted by Permission.

A synthesizer set to a "Fender-Rhodes" patch[27] accompanies the sax quartet in an organ-like style. During the course of the composition Colgrass introduces a vast array of musical styles and textures easily allowing the listener to conjure up a number of urban atmospheres and images. Among the many musical atmospheres utilized in the work; Afro-Cuban, up-tempo jazz, salsa, an urban, "asphalt jungle" type of feeling, and a remarkable section of 'hotel band jazz'.

This first example is written in an "afro-Cuban" style, reflecting the Cuban barrio of the city. The section begins with the glockenspiel and vibraphone providing a mild, quasi salsa montuno. Montuno is the term often used to describe the piano ostinato pattern played over the vamp section in Cuban music.[28] (see figure 11)

The salsa feel is echoed by the soprano sax. (see figure 12)

Throughout this section, Colgrass sporadically hints at salsa by using characteristic rhythms and instruments including timbales, cow bells, pans, and marimba. This continues until measure 291 where all the elements come together to create a dynamic Afro-Cuban effect. (see figure 13)

FIGURE 11: Mallet Montuno, mm 211-214
Urban Requiem
Copyright © 1996 Carl Fischer
International Copyright Secured. All Rights Reserved. Reprinted by Permission.

FIGURE 12: Soprano Character #1, mm 213-216
Urban Requiem
Copyright © 1996 Carl Fischer
International Copyright Secured. All Rights Reserved. Reprinted by Permission.

FIGURE 13: Full Salsa Feel, mm 291-294
Urban Requiem
Copyright © 1996 Carl Fischer
International Copyright Secured. All Rights Reserved. Reprinted by Permission.

Throughout this section the theme is still undergoing transformation in the soprano saxophone. (see figure 14a & b)

In measure 297 a clever transformation of character begins via a series of one bar solo breaks[29] in the timbales, soprano sax and tenor sax. The tenor sax occupies the musical spotlight, trading measures with the soprano and timbales until the focus ultimately shifts to the drum set in measure 304.

With that change, an instant stylistic change of character from latin to jazz is heard suggesting a shift to an "uptown" jazz club. (see figure 15)

The tenor sax/drum set duet continues through measure 234, where an optional open improvisation section can be inserted. Colgrass writes an optional figure for the tenor to be inserted in measure 324, which acts as a cue for the con-

FIGURE 14A: Soprano Thematic Variations, mm 246-249
Urban Requiem
Copyright © 1996 Carl Fischer
International Copyright Secured. All Rights Reserved. Reprinted by Permission.

FIGURE 14B: Soprano Theme Variations, mm 258-266
Urban Requiem
Copyright © 1996 Carl Fischer
International Copyright Secured. All Rights Reserved. Reprinted by Permission.

FIGURE 15: Transition to Jazz Feel, mm 299-306
Urban Requiem
Copyright © 1996 Carl Fischer
International Copyright Secured. All Rights Reserved. Reprinted by Permission.

ductor and ensemble that the duo is returning to the written page. (see figure 16)

The jazz atmosphere continues and becomes more frenzied. The tenor/drum set duo interacts with the other three members of the saxophone quartet beginning a four way conversation punctuated by members of the wind ensemble playing accented chordal interjections. Timpani and tam-tams provide alternating fills. This section culminates in a "sax soli",[30] with the main theme, in variation, providing the basis for the soli. (see figure 17)

The soli evolves into a mass free improvisation for the sax quartet and drum set in measure 372, which is an open bar. In addition to the improvisers, there are aleatoric figures written for flute 1, Eb clarinet, trumpets 1–3, horn 1–3, trombones 1–2, and tuba, adding to the cacophony of sound in the measure. Colgrass includes the following directions:

Free improvisation. Basic chord C#7 and C#9, but gradually stray from there harmonically as in free-style jazz ala Coltrane. All soloists are totally free and separate from each other. Exploit altissimo register, as well as honks, shrieks and growls, especially as you approach climax at bar 386.[31]

Colgrass then employs a jazz technique called "trading"[32] by having the soloists alternate in four second intervals (beginning in measure 373) with the alto saxophone who plays four seconds of solo improvisation. This is followed by four seconds of ensemble aleatory combined with drum set solo. He continues this pattern, a soloist from the quartet followed by an ensemble aleatory, building excitement by gradually shortening the time frame, first to two seconds, then to one. To create even more fervor the four saxophones solo simultaneously over the ensemble aleatory and drum set, a common technique frequently found in the jazz idiom.

These examples clearly illustrate Colgrass' masterful

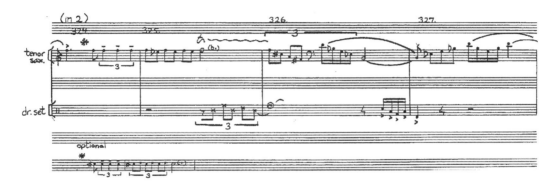

FIGURE 16: Tenor Sax Optional Cue Figure, mm 324-327
Urban Requiem
Copyright © 1996 Carl Fischer
International Copyright Secured. All Rights Reserved. Reprinted by Permission.

FIGURE 17: "Sax Soli" Theme Variation, mm 365-367
Urban Requiem
Copyright © 1996 Carl Fischer
International Copyright Secured. All Rights Reserved. Reprinted by Permission.

technique of a clever thematic metamorphosis used to clearly delineate his urban landscape.

Dream Dancer Fantasy of a Soul Moving Between Cultures (2001) 21'
Soloist: alto saxophone
Wind Orchestra: 3 fl,(2 db picc, 3 db alt),2B♭cl(2nd db E♭),bscl,2oboes,(2nd dbl Eng hn), 2bsn,cbn,4hns,3tpts,3tbn s(3d is bass),tuba,piano,celeste,harp,2cb(w/ C ext.),timp and 4 perc: glockenspiel, crotales, vibraphone, chimes, marimba, timbales & sn dr, 2 darabukas, bs dr, tam-tam, 1 large sizzle cymbal (with real sizzles), 3 large suspended cymbals (20", 22", 24").

Dream Dancer is a new composition which was commissioned by World-Wide Concurrent Commissions and Premieres, Inc., for 25 wind ensembles. European premiere given by Kenneth Radnofsky with the Royal Northern College of Music Wind Orchestra in Manchester, England, April 6, 2001. U.S. premiere by Kenneth Radnofsky with the New England Conservatory of Music Wind Ensemble at Jordan Hall in Boston, April 26, 2001.

The composer has provided the following program notes:

The musical cultures of the world are opening up to us as never before. Dream Dancer is a fantasy about a musical instrument that feels attracted to various styles of music, trying to decide which one to play. One theme is presented at the beginning, which the saxophone uses throughout to exploit the musical styles of three cultures—Mideastern, Asian and American, the latter represented by jazz. These cultures each have their own scale—the Arabic harmonic minor, the Asian pentatonic and the Western diatonic. I imagined the saxophone attracted to all these musical styles and struggling to reconcile them into one kind of music. This almost impossible goal is the central idea of Dream Dancer.

In the early stages of the piece, the saxophone seems satisfied to respond alternately to these musics and enjoy what each has to offer. But soon a sequence occurs where the soloist feels called upon to make a decision between styles, even moving to different locations onstage to interact with groups that represent each of these musics. As the conflict increases, the soloist no longer knows which style to respond to and howls in frustration. The piece ends with the saxophone trying to merge these divergent styles into one.

I think of Dream Dancer as a kind of musical play with the soloist and the other instruments being actors who respond to each other dramatically. I have been developing this idea for some years and have often found that novels, theatre and world events add to my inspiration in shaping musical ideas. The concept of mixing cultures in music is natural to me living in Toronto, perhaps the world's most cosmopolitan city, which offers a rich palette of authentic folk music from around the world. Dream Dancer was commissioned by 25 wind ensembles under the aegis of the World-Wide Concurrent Premieres and Commissioning Fund, Inc., an organization that in many ways reflects the musical scope of this work.—Michael Colgrass

Mr. Colgrass has provided the author with some special notes for soloists and conductors of Dream Dancer:

Dream Dancer presents the solo saxophone in multiple musical styles—primarily Mideastern, Asian and American (jazz). A natural way for the soloist to achieve the sometimes subtle, sometimes sudden, shifts of musical style would be to think like an actor shifting personalities, playing a person in search of an identity. Ideally, the solo part would at times sound almost like it's being played by three different saxophones, as we hear continual shifts in tone, timbre, intensity and vibrato. The conductor helps by seeing that the accompanying "orchestras" also change styles accordingly.

For example, in bars 8–31, the sax thinks of itself as a French horn. The idea here is to make the sax sound as much like the horn as possible, so that the listener can hardly tell which instrument is playing. Large, round, warm sound, with only the sublest wave of vibrato (if any), would be appropriate here. In bars 52–67, the sax decides to be like a clarinet, and we hear a different tone quality, with the sax tone perhaps thinning out, yet still remaining warm. In bars 69–101, the saxophone's jazz nature comes through, but rejects that style and enters another state of mind (118) suggesting a mideastern musical style (25–26). In bars 130–33, the sax hears the echo of Asian music, but doesn't respond to it. A subtle stylistic back-and-forth begins with the suggestion of mideastern style again in bars 139–40, shifting to a bluesy feeling in 141–43, and then back to a mideastern in 144–45. And so on.

Now the three basic elements of the musical conflict are evident— jazz, Asian and Mideastern. Confused by the stylistic contradiction, the sax rejects all of them, responding in a modern style in bar 185. But, that doesn't satisfy either and the sax finds itself gradually drawn again back to the other three styles, perhaps attracted by certain similarities in tonal gesture, like the bent notes of Mideastern music and the blues notes of jazz.

Then "Dream I" occurs (234), where the sax hears its theme played in an openly Mideastern style, and it responds for the first time by playing directly in that style (238–40). (Note that quarter tone inflections and slides are written in here to achieve the style, but in succeeding bars of mideastern music, I leave it to the soloist to make the appropriate stylistic inflections.).

"Dream II," a heavy, intense jazz style, occurs in bar 251, and the sax responds to that in a hard driving manner, reminiscent of John Coltrane. "Dream III" is Asian (271), and the sax responds with a light, innocent tone. The primary challenge for the soloist is to make vivid these stylistic shifts between light innocence, to dark mysteriousness, to a proclamatory blues— sometimes within only a few bars of each other.

In "Return Dream I," the sax is now so strongly attracted to the Mideastern style that it moves from the Home Stand at midstage to Music Stand I, where it interrelates with this music. Then it hears a strong call from the blues in "Return Dream II," and moves to Music Stand II to join that music, and finally to Stand III in "Return Dream III." Now the sax is hooked on all three musics and needs to make a decision, as all three start coming at the sax alternately and then all at once. The sax tries unsuccessfully to respond to all three and finally howls in frustration in bar 398. The howling effect should be very high and sound almost other-worldly, like a person grieving heartrendingly. In bar 401 the sax slowly gets on its feet again and plays its basic theme, while echos of the other styles recur one by one, with the sax suggesting it has satisfactorily absorbed elements of these disparate musics into one.

Note that my tempo markings are approximations only. Also, I have not always written in tempo changes where they might be appropriate, as for example where the musical styles shift back and forth within a few bars of each other. I leave it to the conductor and soloists to use judgement here and move with the nature of the music, using very subtle tempo shifts to help mark changes in style.

CONDUCTING APPROACH

Colgrass music is remarkable on many levels but especially so for its communicative power, an attribute achieved through carefully orchestrated programmatic effects. However the program in his music is more atmospheric than clearly intentional or specifically discernable. The preservation and presentation of the various atmospheres found in his works via a texturally sensitive layering of the orchestration is critical to a successful performance. Further, each player is required to have a sensitive and wide-ranging repertoire of dynamics at their disposal with a particularly highly developed sense of a true pianissimo. The conductor's gestures need to be reflective of the extreme range of dynamic contrast that is required in each work. As is expected of a composer who, based upon his scores, is obviously a meticulous craftsman, Colgrass has definite ideas of what it is that would constitute a successful performance of his work.

Well, in the first place, I want the first performance to be the way I want it. Not to say that I won't let a conductor make a suggestion. He might think the tempo is too fast or slow, and he is right, and I hear that, so I made a misjudgment. Generally a conductor will defer to me because he does not know the piece at all, it is brand new . . . there is no precedent for it. Also, I want my conception as much as possible to be rendered. So the degree to which a conductor will understand and render what I have put down on paper is what I would call a successful performance. [The conductors] sensitivity to tempo changes, mood changes [is important]. I have a lot of tempo changes in my music, not always ritardando or accelerando but suddenly a quarter will equal 68 or 66, then 72, so there are subtle jumps in moods. . . . I like a really sensitive feeling of tempo. Any sensitive feeling for tempo will rarely be in the same tempo from bar to bar. I mean from beat to beat if you have say 60 to a quarter, you can't lock into a metronome to conduct it, it just won't work. There has to be give and take with the musicians, so in this bar you are 60 to a quarter and you might find that by the time you get to the third quarter note, you might be at 62. By the time you get to the down-beat of the next note, you might be at 58. This is the feeling of music, the subtle feeling of emotion. Some conductors just lock in and beat time, really quite strictly, and with the idea that "you follow me, I am the conductor, you are the performer." I am not like that as a composer or conductor. When a performer is playing I am listening to everything that the performer is doing. I might find a performer in one performance who is inclined one way and then a month later, another performer is inclined another way and I will go with each according to that performer's nature. They are contributing something. So in other words, to me, a piece of music is not finished when you finish composing it —the composer is not the only creator. The performance is an extremely important, indigenous basic part [of] the recreation

and the continuing creation of the work. So the work will go through alteration over the years and I think probably over the centuries. Now we can play Mozart in ways Mozart did not even conceive, because of the technical skills we have and also because of the knowledge we have of so many other styles. We can say "what if I played Mozart through a filter of Debussy". So, a kind of certain mysterious impressionist quality is added to the music—we can do that now and that is a wonderful thing. I think that way in performance. I think, "what do these performers give me?" I encourage performers to be creative. So, these are all things that make a performance for me. What I ultimately want is emotion…a powerful feeling of emotion in the musicians and I want that to come across to the audience. That is what the audience comes out to hear. That is why I love jazz. It is so emotional, soulful and emotional, and I don't care about a perfect performance. I don't care if you play a wrong note sometimes. I am just looking for your reaching for feeling, and if you are doing that you are just not going to be playing on a click track. Emotion in music is produced by subtle changes in tempo that we are totally unaware of consciously. Anybody who conducts something strictly has got to be insensitive. [Music] is just not made that way. Emotion does not express itself that way. Even if the character of this music is supposed to be in a locked tempo all the way, it will not be locked when the musicians are playing it.... also, sometimes my written tempos are wrong, made in haste or after long hours of work when I'm no longer objective. So a conductor needs to have a 'sense of the musician' in order to 'find' the really best tempo for any given section. [33]

The careful balancing and coloration of Colgrass' music are also vital components in a successful performance, because those elements have a great bearing on the texture . . . and texture is what distinguishes this music from most of the other repertoire. Colgrass notes

[A conductor should pay] careful attention to the textures, which are a very important element in my music. [34]

When asked about 'reference recordings' or other music that a conductor should be familiar with when conducting Colgrass' music he responded;

I think the conductor would do best to just study my scores in a very detailed and careful way…and to understand that jazz is an underlying element in my music. I want the conductor to know the music well enough so that he/she can feel ownership of it and therefore feel free to perform it in a unique way, not just an imitation of another performance or recording. [35]

Colgrass does not listen to recorded versions of the works of many composers of band literature, but of those he has heard, he likes the music of Michael Daugherty, David Maslanka, Karel Husa, and Joseph Schwantner. He says that he admires their way of writing "colors and textures that get away from that 'band sound'." He strongly dislikes the more traditional band sound which he describes as "too thick". He feels that even Paul Hindemith "fell into it" when writing the Symphony in B♭. As previously discussed, he finds most writers rely too heavily upon unisons, octaves, and doublings throughout their scoring for the band, especially in the middle register.

Colgrass recommends the following recordings of his works;

> Both the University of Miami Wind Ensemble and the University of Minnesota Wind Ensemble recordings of "Urban Requiem" are excellent. Also the New England Conservatory Wind Ensemble recording of "Arctic Dreams" is very fine.[36]

Michael Colgrass is still actively composing, but does not like to talk about current projects. In addition to his composing he is involved with his own workshop presentations in the psychology and technique of performance and has just finished a book, *Lessons with Kumi, How to Perform with Confidence in Life and Work*.

SELECTED LISTING OF WORKS [37]

SOLO

Tales of Power (1980) 24'
  Piano solo
  For sale (CF)
Te Tuma Te Papa (1994) 12'
  Solo percussionist
  For sale (CF)
Wild Riot of the Shaman's Dreams (1992) 8'
  Solo flute
  For sale (CF)
Wolf (1976) 17'
  Solo cello
  Score for sale (CF)
Chameleon (1999) 4'
  Solo alto sax

SONGS

Mystery Flowers of Spring (1985) 4'
  Soprano w/ piano
  Score for sale (CF)
New People (1969) 18'
  Mezzo soprano, viola and piano
  Score for sale (CF)
Night of the Raccoon (1979) 14'
  Soprano, harp, alto flute, 1 perc, piano (dbl. cel + elec pf)
  Score for sale (CF)

CHAMBER MUSIC

Flashbacks A Musical Play for Five Brass (1979) 35'
  2 tpt, tbn, hn, tba
  Rental (CF)
A Flute in the Kingdom of Drums and Bells (1994) 35'
  Flute (dbl.pic and afl) and percussion quartet
  Parts on rental, score for sale (CF)

Folklines: A Counterpoint of Musics for String Quartet (1988) 22'
  Parts on rental, score for sale (CF)
Hammer & Bow (1997) 10'
  Violin and marimba
  Score for sale (CF)
Light Spirit (1963) 8'
  Flute, viola, guitar, 2 perc
  Theodore Presser Inc.
  Parts on rental, score for sale (TP)
Memento (1982) 16'
  2 pianos
  Score for sale (CF)
Rhapsody (1962) 8'
  Clarinet, violin, piano
  (CF)
Strangers: Irreconcilable Variations for Clarinet, Viola and Piano (1986) 24'
  Parts on rental, score for sale (CF)
Wind Quintet (1962) 8'
  Duration 8'
  Parts on rental, score for sale (TP)

ORCHESTRA

As Quiet As (1966) 14'
  3(pic,alt)3(Enghn)3(bs)3/4331/2hp/pf,cel,hpschd/
  Timp,3perc/str
  Score for sale (TP)
Letter From Mozart (1976) 16'
  2(pic,alt)22(bs)2+cbn/2221/pf,cel/hp/acc/timp,3perc/str
  Score for sale (CF)
The Schubert Birds (1989) 18'
  2(pic)2(Enghn)2(Ebcl,bscl)1+cbn/2200/1perc/65432
  Score for sale (CF)
Ghosts of Pangea (2000) 22'
  3(pic), 2(Eng hn), 2(Eb), bs cl., 3(cbn), 4331, pno, cel, hp,
  stgs, 5 perc.
  Score for sale (CF)

SOLOIST AND ORCHESTRA

Arias (1992) 26'
  Solo clarinet: 2(pic,alt)1(ob)1(Enghn)1(bs)1(bsn)1(cbn)/
  4331/pf.cel/hp/tim p,3perc/65432
  Archive score for sale (CF)
Auras (1972) 15'
  Solo harp: 2(pic,alt)2(Enghn)2(bs)2/222(bs)/cel/3perc/str
  Archive score for sale (CF)
Chaconne (1984) 26'
  Solo viola; 3(pic)0,3(bs)2+cbn/4331/pf,cel/hp/
  timp,4perc/str
  Archive score for sale (CF)
Concertmasters (1974) 22'

3 solo violins; 2(pic)22(bs)2(cbn)/4331/cel-hpsch/2hp/
timp,4perc/str
3 vln/pno reduction for sale (CF)

Déjà vu (1977) 18'
4 solo perc; 3(pic,alt)0,3(E♭cl,bscl)2+cbn/4331/cel/2hp/str
Score for sale (CF)

Delta (1979) 20'
Solo vln,cl,perc; 1+alt.1+Enghn.bscl.1+cbn/22/54332
Archive score for sale (CF)

Memento (1982) 16'
Two solo pianos; 2(pic)+altfl.Enghn.3(E♭cl,bscl)2+cbn43
30/cel/hp/ timp,4perc/str
Archive score for sale (CF)

Rhapsodic Fantasy (1964) 8'
Solo perc; 1(pic)111/1110/timp.3perc/cel/hp/str
Score for sale (TP)

Snow Walker (1990) 20'
Solo organ, 2(pic), 22(E♭cl,bscl), 1+cbn/2221/pf-cel/hp/
timp,3perc
Archive score for sale (CF)

Crossworlds (Boston Symphony Orchestra premiere, March
8th, 2002)
Solo flute/piano. Orchestra. (CF)

CHORUS AND ORCHESTRA

Best Wishes USA (1976) 34'
Sopr/mez/ten/bs/black and white chor: 2(pic,alt)2(Enghn)2
(E♭,bs)1+cbn/4331/hp/pf-cel-syth/guit-banj /harm/uk/acc/
jazzqt/timp.4perc, str
(CF)

Theater of the Universe (1972) 18'
Sopr/mez/ten/bar/bass/SATB: 3(pic)3(Enghn)3(E♭,bs)2+
cbn/4331/cel(pno)2hp/timp.3perc/str
(CF)

Image of Man (1974) 20'
SATB: 2(pic)22(bscl)1+cbn/4331/cel/elec.pno/
timp.3perc,str
Score for sale (CF)

The Earth's A Baked Apple (1969) 10'
Teen chor: 2222/4331/cel/timp/perc/str
Choral score for sale (TP)

WIND ENSEMBLE

Arctic Dreams (1991) 24'
6flt(4,5,6 dbl. alt, all dbl.pic),3ob,8B♭,bscl,B♭contbs),3bsn
,1cbsn,3sax(sopr,alt,bar)/6tpts,6hns,6trbs,2euph,2tuba,pf
cel/hp/2cb/timp.5perc
Archive score for sale (CF)

Deja vu (1977) 18'
4 solo perc;6flt(pic,alt),0,6B♭,E♭cl,bscl,B♭contbs,2bsn.+c
bn,sop.sax(alto)/4tpts,6hns,6trbs,1euph,1tuba/pf cel/2hp/
2cb

Archive score for sale (CF)

Urban Requiem (1995) 28'
Saxophone quartet; 1pic,1fl,1altfl,1ob+Enghn,1E♭cl,1B♭
cl,1bscl,2bsn+cbn /4tpts,3hns,3trbs,1tuba/ synth/ hp/
2cb/timp.4perc
Archive score for sale (CF)

Winds of Nagual A Musical Fable on the Writings of Carlos
Castaneda (1985) 25'
6flt(2dbl.pic,2dbl.alt),6B♭,1E♭,bscl.,1E♭contalt,1B♭contbs,
cbsn,sop.sax,alt.sax/6tpts(2dblcor),flhn,6hns,6trbs,2euph
,2tba/2cb/pf-cel/timp.5perc
Archive score for sale (CF)

Dream Dancer (2001) 21' Soloist: alto saxophone
Wind Orchestra: 3 fl,(2 db picc, 3 db alt),2B♭cl(2nd db
E♭),bscl,2oboes,(2nd dbl Eng hn), 2bsn,cbn,4hns,3tp
ts,3tbns(3d is bass),tuba,piano,celeste,harp,2cb(w/ C
ext.),timp and 4 perc: glockenspiel, crotales, vibraphone,
chimes, marimba, timbales & sn dr, 2 darabukas, bs dr,
tam-tam, 1 large sizzle cymbal (with real sizzles), 3 large
suspended cymbals (20", 22", 24").
Score for sale (CF)

MUSICAL THEATER

Something's Gonna Happen (1978) 45'
A musical play for approx. 20 children (4 leads) between
age 10–13, based on an updated version of Jack and the
Beanstalk. Text by the composer.
Flute and piano.
Score for sale CF)

Virgil's Dream, A Satiric Fantasy for Music Chamber Theater
(1967) 35'
Text by the composer.
Confused mezzo, naive tenor, hysterical tenor, conserva-
tive bass baritone, clar/elec.pno/cb/1 perc.
Score on sale (CF)

PERCUSSION MUSIC

Chamber Music for Percussion Quintet (1954) 5'
Score and parts on sale from MFP
Concertino for timpani (1953) 10'
3tpt, 3tbn, tuba, timp/2 perc.
Score and parts on sale from MFP
Fantasy Variations (1961) 12'
Perc.solo/6 perc
Score and parts on sale from MFP
Inventions on a Motive (1955) 8'
Percussion quintet
Score and parts on sale from MFP
Percussion Music (1953) 5'
Percussion quartet
Score and parts on sale from MFP
Three Brothers (1951) 4'

Percussion nonette
Score and parts on sale from MFP
Variations for Four Drums and Viola (1957) 17'
Vla/1perc
Score and parts on sale from MFP

DISCOGRAPHY[38]

ARCTIC DREAMS for large wind ensemble.
Frank Battisti conducts the New England Conservatory Wind Ensemble with members of the New England Conservatory choruses under Tamara Brooks.
Centaur Records, CRC 2288.

CHACONNE for viola and orchestra
Soloist, Rivka Golani
The Toronto Symphony Orchestra, Andrew Davis, conductor.
CBC Records 2-5087. Music also by Bloch, Hindemith and Britten.

CONCERTMASTERS for Three Violins and Orchestra
Soloists: Robert Rudie, red violin, Masako Yanagita, yellow violin, Ronald Oakland, blue violin.
The American Symphony Orchestra, Kazuyoshi Akiyama, conductor.
Vox 5158.

DÉJÀ VU for percussion quartet and orchestra.
Soloists: Richard Holmes, Richard O'Donnell, John Kasica, Thomas Stubbs.
The Saint Louis Symphony Orchestra, Leonard Slatkin, conductor.
New World Records, NW 318.

DREAM DANCER for alto saxophone and wind ensemble.
Soloist: Lynn Klock, alto saxophone.
The University of Miami Wind Ensemble, Gary Green, conductor. UMIA-1806

LIGHT SPIRIT for flute, viola, guitar and two percussion players.
The Saint Louis Symphony Players, Catherine Comet, conductor.
New World Records, NW 318.

URBAN REQUIEM for four saxophones and wind orchestra.
Soloists: George Weremchuck, soprano sax, David Ferndandez, alto sax, Tom McCormick, tenor sax, Stephen Welsh, baritone sax, The University of Miami Wind Ensemble, Gary Green, conductor.
Albany Records, Troy 212.

URBAN REQUIEM: Second Recording
Soloists: Brian Handley, soprano sax, Chris Thompson, alto sax, Robert Schrepel, tenor sax, Jeffrey Fulton, baritone sax.
The University of Minnesota Wind Ensemble, Craig Kirchhoff, conductor.
Innova Records CD 517. (Release date, July 1998)

VARIATIONS FOR FOUR DRUMS AND VIOLA
Violist Rivka Golani and percussionist Ryan Scott.
Centrediscs CMC CD 5798. (June 1998, not yet reviewed)

WINDS OF NAGUAL A Musical Fable for Wind Ensemble
The University of Cincinnati College-Conservatory of Music Wind Ensemble, Eugene Corporon, conductor.
Music also of Diamond, Hartley, Murray and Nelson.
Mark Records, MCD 780.

WINDS OF NAGUAL A Musical Fable for Wind Ensemble.
Northwestern University Wind Ensemble, Mallory Thompson, conductor. Summit Records DCD-313.

HAMMER & BOW for violin and marimba
Jacques and Michael Isrealievitch, violin and marimba
Fleur de Son Classics FDS 57941

DÉJÀ VU for four percussionists and wind ensemble
Eugene Corporan conducting the North Texas State Wind Symphony
Soloists: Troy Breaux, Shawn Hart, Jeff Prosperie, Edward Stephan
Klavier Gold Edition KCD-11091

END NOTES

1. Michael Colgrass, "Compositions—From interview with Joseph Horowitz"; available from http://www.michaelcolgrass.com/4.html; Internet; accessed 15 August 2001
2. Canadian Music Centre, "Directory of Associate Composers: Bio Michael Colgrass"; available from http://www.ffa.ucalgary.ca/cmc/dac_rca/eng/a_/Colgrass_Michael.html; Internet; accessed 2 December 1997.
3. Ibid.
4. Michael Colgrass, interview by author, 02 May 1997, telephone interview, Toronto, Canada.
5. Ibid.
6. Ibid.
7. Ibid.
8. Ibid.
9. Ibid.
10. Ibid.
11. Joseph Horowitz, "Musician of the Month: Michael Colgrass", Musical America, Nov. 1978, p.8.
12. Colgrass, Interview with author.
13. Colgrass, Winds of Nagual, Program Notes.
14. Ibid.
15. Ibid.
16. James Mathes, "Analysis: Winds of Nagual by Michael Colgrass," Journal of Band Research 20 no. 1 (1987), 10.
17. Michael Colgrass, Comment and Concert Reviews; available from http://www.michaelcolgrass.com/4.html#dv; Internet;

accessed 14 August 2001.

18. Colgrass, Interview with author.

19. Michael Colgrass, "Arctic Dreams", score. 1991.

20. Ibid.

21. Luminous bands or streamers of light sometimes appearing in the night sky of the Northern Hemisphere; northern lights, Webster's New Universal Unabridged Dictionary, 2nd ed. (New York: Simon and Schuster, 1972), 125.

21. Michael Colgrass, "Arctic Dreams", 61.

22. Ibid.

24. Colgrass, Interview with author.

25. Colgrass, Urban Requiem, Program Notes.

26. Colgrass, Interview with author.

27. An early electric piano whose sound was produced by hammers striking amplified, tuned tines. This instrument produced a unique sound that is now a standard patch on most synthesized or sampled keyboards.

28. Rebecca Mauleón-Santana, 101 Montunos, (Petaluma, CA: Sher Music Co., 1999), iv–v.

29. Solo Break is a term used in jazz for a device in which the rhythm section is tacit during a short, unaccompanied, improvised solo.

30. A sax soli is a compositional device frequently used in the jazz big band idiom consisting of a harmonized virtuoso melodic line, written for the saxophone section, which moves in parallel rhythm.

31. Colgrass, Urban Requiem, Score, 28.

32. In jazz, two or more players trade a certain number of measures, alternating improvisations. So if a jazz trio was "trading fours" on one chorus of a twelve-bar blues, each member would play four bars of improvisation.

33. Colgrass, Interview with author.

34. Ibid.

35. Ibid.

36. Ibid.

37. Michael Colgrass, "Compositions"; available from http://www.michaelcolgrass.com/2.html#SOLO; Internet; accessed 15 August 2001

38. Ibid.

Michael Daugherty

by
Judson Scott

To say that a composer's style is unique merely states what should be true of every composer, and yet when confronted with Michael Daugherty's music one feels compelled to make this claim. Enzo Restagno, Artistic Director of *Settembre Musica* in Torino, Italy describes an encounter with Daugherty in 1999 this way:

> To observe the American landscape in Michael Daugherty's company is an unforgettable experience which I had during a long nocturnal walk through the streets of New York. Naturally we talked about music, but our talk was interrupted every minute because he kept stopping ecstatically outside a show window or some public building. He wanted to call my attention to some gadget or individual abounding in symbolic value. Clothing, menus, items for everyday use, gestures, posters, billboards, photographs, and architecture, all inspired lengthy observations endowed with great insight, but, at the same time, an affectionate irony. Like the energy that radiates from the icons housed in our European museums and art galleries, Michael Daugherty's music successfully releases the poetic power of American icons.

It is in part this fascination with the vernacular that sets Daugherty's music apart. By using sophisticated compositional techniques to develop his melodic motives combined with complex polyrhythmic layers, he has created a style bursting with energy that is truly unique. *Niagara Falls* for symphonic band will be the principal work considered here, though general background and performance considerations would apply to *Desi* and *Bizarro* for symphonic winds, *Motown Metal* for brass ensemble and percussion, *Timbuktuba* for euphoniums, tubas, and percussion, and *UFO*, *Rosa Parks Boulevard* and *Red Cape Tango* for symphonic band.

Daugherty's connection to the pop world infuses his work at every level. The inspiration for much of his music comes from icons of the American pop culture. He acknowledges his debt to pop culture, saying:

> For me icons serve as way to have an emotional reason to compose a new work. I get ideas for my compositions by browsing through second hand bookstores, antique shops, and small towns that I find driving on the back roads of America. The "icon" can be an old postcard, magazine, photograph, knick-knack, matchbook, piece of furniture or roadmap. Like Ives and Mahler, I use icons in my music to provide the listener and performer with a layer of reference. However, one does need the reference of the icon to appreciate my music; it is merely one level among many in the musical, contrapuntal fabric of my compositions.

Red Cape Tango and *Bizarro* are based on the comic book Superman legend; the television character Ricky Ricardo inspired the composition of *Desi*. One hears urban Detroit in the industrial sounding *Motown Metal* and the courage of an Afro-American civil rights icon in the emotionally charged *Rosa Parks Boulevard*. *UFO* is inspired by the unidentified flying objects that have been an obsession in American popular culture since 1947.

Not surprisingly, *Niagara Falls* draws its inspiration not only from the falls themselves, but also, most importantly, from the pop culture that surrounds this natural wonder.

> My parents went on their honeymoon and I've visited there many times as I have in-laws in Syracuse so we stop at Niagara Falls on the way. Niagara Falls is a destination for honeymooners and its also one of the biggest "tourist traps" in North America. I think that to even write a piece inspired by this sort of concept is still uncommon in concert music. Yet when I am writing the music I am extremely serious about the notes, the dynamics and the articulations, the timbre, the structure and the counterpoint. When I compose, I think in a very structural logical way as Webern and Bach did.

Daugherty's melodic material—usually short motives that are repeated in sequences or canons—frequently comes straight from jazz or Latin musical idioms with strong syncopation. Often the accompanying figures are rooted in big band jazz, whether the closely harmonized scale fragments typical of a saxophone section or the explosive interjections by the brass. All of this occurs over rhythmic ostinati or grooves in the bass and percussion sections—the classic rhythm section of pop and jazz.

BIOGRAPHICAL INFORMATION

Michael Daugherty was born in 1954 in Cedar Rapids, Iowa. His fascination with pop music is rooted in his youth—his father was a dance-band drummer and Daugherty himself played keyboards in a rock band. That experience has impacted his compositional life dramatically:

> Growing up in Cedar Rapids, Iowa, in the late fifties and early sixties, I was involved in a lot of different kinds of musical groups. I played in the Grenadiers and Emerald Knights Drum and Bugle Corps. I also started a rock band called the Soul

Company when I was a teenager; it was a band that had two black singers, sax, trumpet, trombone, organ, guitar, bass, and drums. I played the M3 Hammond organ. We played tunes by Sly and the Family Stone; Blood, Sweat and Tears; and James Brown. There was a big division between black and white music at that time. There still is.

That was my first experience with kind of crossing over, breaking down boundaries. Everything that I've been doing since then, in any genre that I am working in, and what I'm trying to do in classical music is that—breaking down boundaries. What I try to do is to bring an American feel to concert music. I have done that through the music I write and by using provocative titles and concepts as a way to draw the listener in.

He attended North Texas State University (now the University of North Texas) studying jazz piano, and during his freshman year heard a concert that changed his life:

North Texas State was one of the few places where you could study jazz in 1972, but up to that point, I really hadn't heard much live twentieth century orchestral music. When I was a freshman—I was eighteen years old at the time—I went to a concert of the Dallas Symphony. They played the Samuel Barber *Piano Concerto* and the Hindemith *Mathis der Maler;* those pieces really blew me away. I really loved the sound of the orchestra, so ever since then I have wanted to take my interest in rock and jazz music and combine it with the instruments of the orchestra. To this day I am still doing that.

After graduating from North Texas State University in 1976 with his first orchestral work completed, he moved to New York City where he continued composition studies at the Manhattan School of Music and worked as an accompanist for modern dance classes. From 1979–1980 a Fullbright scholarship took him to Paris, France, where he composed computer music at IRCAM.

After living a few years in New York, I decided I wanted to check out the European new music scene. I was invited by Pierre Boulez to study at IRCAM which was at the cutting edge of new music at the time. I had a chance to hang out with composers at IRCAM like Boulez, Berio and Stockhausen—to be around those people was important to me. I had to go through the European *avant-garde* music experience, and I learned a lot about "intellectual" ways to think about and construct new music that I still use today when I compose. I have always been someone who asks questions and listens to what is happening in the new music scene. I couldn't just get what it meant to be a contemporary music composer out of a textbook—I had to live it. And being around those historically important European composers—most of whom didn't give American music a thought—gave me the courage and the strength to come back to America and write what I was hearing. I think if I hadn't gone to Europe I would be looking over my shoulder every time I composed.

From 1980–1982 he studied composition at Yale University with Earle Brown, Jacob Druckman, Bernard Rands and Roger Reynolds, and was an assistant to the jazz arranger and pianist Gil Evans in New York. Moving to Europe again from 1982–1984, he studied with György Ligeti. Of contemporary musicians, he considers Ligeti and Gil Evans his two biggest influences:

I think that the composer from Europe that has had the most influence on me is György Ligeti. I like the way he deals with complex counterpoint, and his music always seems to mean something. Ligeti also encouraged me to look seriously at American rock and jazz music and to think about composing new music using this as a musical backdrop along with, of course, classical and *avant-garde* music as well.

Also, Gil Evans, the jazz arranger/pianist for Miles Davis in the fifties and sixties, was a big influence on me. I worked with him for a couple of years—1980 through '82—in New York as his assistant. That was really great hanging out with Gil in his loft and at the jazz clubs in the Village; seeing the way that he listened to all styles of music and how he would hear chords and instrumental colors. But I think that the most important thing was seeing how Gil trusted his ears to compose. I've played by ear ever since I was a kid, and I learned to compose that way. There is always a rigorous structure and planning going on in my music—like Ligeti—but at the same time my music is very ear-influenced music. Some composers say, 'I never know what my music is going to sound like until I hear it.' That never happens to me. I know exactly what my piece will sound like at the first rehearsal. I have an extensive computer/MIDI home studio where I can sequence my music using synthesizers and samplers. I also have a large collection of real percussion instruments that I use to compose with. But hearing your music played live is always a shocking experience! While I do make orchestrational changes at rehearsals of a new composition, I rarely make changes of pitches, rhythms or structure in a new work.

Returning to America, he received his doctorate in composition at Yale University in 1986 and held a position on the faculty of the Oberlin Conservatory from 1986–91. It was at Oberlin that Daugherty's compositional voice began to emerge:

Most of the American concert music composers of my generation in New York were writing music like Elliott Carter or Steve Reich in the 1980's, and I thought, you know I just don't want to do this . . . it is not me! So I didn't write any music for about five years [1982–87]. I went to Europe and played jazz in piano bars, started an avant-gardé improvisaton band with the German trumpet "wunderkind", Markus Stockhausen, son of Karlheinz, and studied with Ligeti. I came back to the states in 1984 and I played piano bar and gigged with avant-gardé jazz groups, but I didn't really compose anything. I ended up teaching composition at the Oberlin Conservatory of Music in this tiny, little, Ohio town. . . in isolation. At Oberlin I wrote *Snap, Blue Like an Orange* for large chamber ensemble. That was my first important composition after thinking for a long time about what kind of music I wanted to write. Then I composed the *Metropolis Symphony, Bizarro* and *Desi.* I felt at Oberlin I found my "voice" as a composer. I think that being in an isolated environment forced me to look inward; to find inspiration as to what I wanted to write and say as a composer.

In 1991, he joined the faculty of the University of Michigan (Ann Arbor), where he is Professor of Composition. Daugherty was also composer-in-residence with the Detroit Symphony Orchestra from 1999–2003 and the Colorado Symphony Orchestra from 2002–2003. His music is published by Peermusic, New York, and is represented in Europe by Faber Music, London. Daugherty's music has been performed by, among others, the New York Philharmonic, the Tonhalle Orchester Zurich, the Netherlands Wind Ensemble, the BBC Symphony Orchestra (London), the symphony orchestras of Baltimore, Los Angeles, Cleveland, Philadelphia, San Francisco, and Detroit, the Kronos Quartet and bands and wind ensembles throughout the world.

Daugherty's music is a gateway for new listeners. By giving the audience, conductor, and the performers a recognizable starting point he is able to create music that they can connect to without lessening the rigor of the music. His zeal for attracting new listeners to the concert hall is evident:

> I'm trying to find a way to make a future for concert music. And the way that's going to happen, I think, is to somehow write music that will pull the listener in, since most listeners today don't know anything about classical music or especially contemporary music. So how can I do that without compromising the kind of music I want to compose? I'm not a Hollywood film composer, because I don't want anyone telling me what to write. I'm writing what I hear, I'm composing what I want to do. . . I'm writing what I feel, but I'm not writing to necessarily please everybody. I'm composing what's important to me and I want the music to somehow be an important experience to someone who is listening or performing it. And the way that I have done that up to now is through taking American icons, like Route 66, Rosa Parks, Niagara Falls, Jackie O., Elvis, Desi Arnaz or whatever. I start with these icons as an emotional basis even though what I am writing is fairly abstract music.

Daugherty sees himself as an American iconoclast composer like Charles Ives, a composer who created unique sound worlds not part of the musical vocabulary of his time. Daugherty composes music that he hears, and what he hears is heavily influenced by the pop culture influences of his youth and his experiences with the European *avant-garde* music. Interestingly, his approachable music made him an *avant-garde* composer.

> Current thought about musical aesthetics is complicated. I've spent a lot of time in Europe and every country that you go to has different arguments and different aesthetics about what new music should be. The credo I go by is, 'I write music that, first of all, I hear in my head.' If you are a painter you're not painting with a blindfold. When I'm composing, I'm not composing with ear plugs. The idea for some *avant-garde* composers is that you write music that you can't hear—but I do consider myself an *avant-garde* composer, actually. I feel like I am always pushing the envelope, taking risks and trying to compose music I think is unusual and off-beat. Since I can historically reference any music I hear, the way I compose "new" music is by "framing" and layering musical gestures that are recognizable in unexpected ways with musical gestures that are unrecognizable in expected ways.

ANALYSIS OF *NIAGARA FALLS*

Lurking under the exuberant energy of *Niagara Falls* for symphonic band is a taut construction built on a few fundamental motives. By layering and repeating these motives over pop style grooves in the bass and percussion, Daugherty is able to generate immense drive that leads to shattering climaxes.

The piece does not conform to any traditional formal pattern such as sonata or rondo, but is through-composed, proceeding from the working out of its material. The work can be divided into an exposition, a development, ending with a substantive return of the principal theme, and a coda. Within each of these larger sections, Daugherty divides his music into smaller sections as he develops his motivic material.

The principal theme, based on the syllables "Ni-a-gra Falls" (see figure 1) is first presented in measure two and has a decidedly "film noir" or gothic edge. Daugherty built this theme in two parts: motive 1—the treble clef melody, is used throughout the work either alone or with its consequent, the bass clef fragment; the consequent serves to connect presentations of motive 1 and never appears alone.

The secondary theme (see figure 2) appears in measure 32. At first glance it seems more like a harmonic underpinning or an accompaniment figure than a theme and yet it consistently appears at key moments in the work as an important structural element. This theme is constructed with an interior rising chromatic line and pulse obfuscating-rhythm.

Driving percussion and bass ostinati (grooves) support the secondary theme which are important in establishing the character of this theme.

FIGURE 1. Daugherty: Niagara Falls, measures 2–3
Niagara Falls
© Copyright 1997 by Peermusic III, Ltd.
Reprinted by Permission

FIGURE 2. Daugherty: Niagara Falls, measures 32–35
Niagara Falls
© Copyright 1997 by Peermusic III, Ltd.
Reprinted by Permission

FIGURE 3. Daugherty: Niagara Falls, measure 12
Niagara Falls
© Copyright 1997 by Peermusic III, Ltd.
Reprinted by Permission

In addition to these two themes there is a motive {see figure 3} which Daugherty uses extensively.

First appearing in measure 12 in the alto saxophone, this motive serves as a unifying element and as a structural punctuation mark. Daugherty uses this motive to generate the exuberant rhythmic drive in the final coda of the work. These three motivic elements, shown in figures one, two and three, are audibly responsible for almost every note in *Niagara Falls*. One could, perhaps, delve more deeply to draw connections that are not obvious to the ear, but Daugherty insists on the primacy of hearing, and it is not unreasonable to limit the motivic analysis to clearly audible structure.

The clearest large section of *Niagara Falls* is the exposition of the principal and secondary themes. Measures 1–20 present the principal theme. Measures 21–27 are transitory. In measure 28 the accompaniment to the secondary theme is presented with the second theme appearing in measure 32. With some interesting interruptions and transitions this section continues through measure 81. The principal theme makes a brief return in measures 82–87, signaling the end of the first large section of the work.

The presentation of the second theme is heralded by the establishment of a strong rhythmic groove in the bass and percussion based upon the tympani solo of measure 1. The secondary theme is presented by the horns and then by the horns in canon with the euphoniums. There is a four measure interruption, followed by the theme's presentation by the horns in canon with the trumpets and trombones. After another interruption, shortened to two measures, Daugherty re-establishes the groove, inverts the bass line and leaving out the theme, gives the clarinets and saxophones an "improvised" solo. In this solo line resonates the work of the jazz group SuperSax, which took improvised solos by famous jazz musicians and played them as quartets in parallel harmonies. This solo line never reappears.

The middle of the work is less easy to define though it functions similarly to a classical development section. This large section is divided into numerous smaller subsections.

After leaving the exposition the music immediately loses its aural footing, sliding around on a whole-tone scale. Similar to a classical development section, Daugherty manipulates his material, injecting his basic motivic material with new character.

The material from measure 89 through measure 106 is new and is built on a whole tone scale. The melody presented in the alto sax in measure 92 falls in major thirds; one could draw a connection to the principal theme, which also falls in major thirds, but this is not a connection that is aurally evident. The whole-tone harmonies create a floating, dreamlike quality that are reminiscent of the atmosphere created around the first presentation of the principal theme. The frenetic texture of the mallet percussion will return at key points throughout the remainder of the work and could be considered a textural motive.

At measure 107 Daugherty leaves behind the whole-tone scale in most, though not all, of the instrumental choirs, while maintaining elements of the frenetic percussion writing. Here he introduces three layers of motive 1 stripped of their original rhythm, presented in each voice in half notes. The flutes and mallets enter on the down beat of measure 107, the oboes, bassoons and horns begin on beat two and the clarinets begin on beat three. These overlapping presentations of motive 1 work to dissolve a clear sense of meter; added to this are the trumpets working to obscure the quarter note pulse. This developmental subsection is brought to a close by *tutti* reiterations of motive 3 with a brief interjection of the secondary theme by the horns in measures 126–128.

In measure 130 Daugherty makes a more concerted assault on the sense of pulse and meter and returns to the dream-like texture for further manipulation of motive 1: four soloists each with their own concurrent version of this material. The oboe presents the motive in its original, pristine state; the bass clarinet in steady dotted eighths sounds the intervals; the glockenspiel starts on the 'and' of beat two with an ornamented presentation of these same intervals; and the English horn inverts the motive, sounding the intervals in triplet quarter note figurations. Later arrivals, using similar methods, are the E♭ clarinet, the piccolo, and the first B♭clarinet. The tutti ensemble brings this developmental subsection to a close sounding motive 1 with accelerating chromatic lines in the tenor voices and mallet percussion.

These accelerating chromatic lines propel the work into the next developmental subsection and rush toward measure 156, where motive 3 becomes a motto perpetual and the backdrop for a mocking presentation of the secondary theme in the saxophones. In measure 193 the principal theme—motive 1 with its consequent—returns, presented similarly to the beginning. This return functions as a recapitulation, even occurring at the pitch level of the opening presentation, though the structures for a classical recapitulation are not present, and Daugherty has not finished developing his materials.

This recapitulation of the principal theme is left in a haze of shifting chromatic harmony where most of the twelve half-steps are constantly present. The saxes take up the pulse-obfuscating rhythm used by the trumpets in measure 107, and are later joined by the trumpets who present a different idea of where the pulse should be. Finally, with the saxes joined by the upper winds, motive 3 is mocked by the trombones. A percussion break, just as one might find in a jazz band chart, leads to the final climax of this section: the entire wind section creates a *motto perpetual* from motive 3, juxtaposed against the trumpets and horns offering motive 2. The trombones continue to mock motive 3—double time from their previous statement—creating a huge climax to end the development section.

From measure 252 to the end of the work motive 3 is glorified. It is presented simultaneously at three different tempi via thematic augmentation and diminution. Winds and percussion are at the fastest tempo, the saxes and horns at half that tempo and the trumpets at half the tempo of the saxes and horns. A short percussion break at measure 266 interrupts this texture briefly. When the *motto perpetual* is rejoined the trumpets have given up their slow tempo, joining the saxes and horns. Two brief reiterations of the secondary theme interrupts in measure 278, and a chromatic sweep rushes to the final chord, an open fifth between 'C' and 'G'.

Although motivic development is the principle structural element of *Niagara Falls*, there are a few interesting points to be made concerning tonality and harmony. The question of tonic is surprisingly ambiguous in *Niagara Falls*. Though the work deals largely with tonal melodic fragments, there is not a strong sense of a tonic. The timpani solo in measure one suggests a tonic of 'A' minor, though the presentation of the main theme in measure 2 immediately refutes that assertion, appearing instead in 'E♭' minor. The secondary theme is presented over a bass line derived from the opening measure, again suggesting 'A' minor, though, when first presented by the horns, the theme itself clearly pivots on 'B'. During the first repetition while the horns remain fixated on

'B', the euphoniums are clearly centered on 'E'. The trumpets and trombones further confuse the issue by harmonizing the theme in parallel major thirds. The third motive seems content to appear in the prevailing tonic of the moment. The work ends with the open fifth 'C–G' suggesting a home key of 'C'. By the end of the work 'C' seems a reasonable tonic—relative major of the opening A minor tonality?—and is prepared by some convincing pedal points on 'C'. One can't help but assume that had Daugherty decided the work needed an extra forty measures he could easily have come round to the key of 'F#'!

Daugherty's use of harmony is colorative rather than progressive. It is true that the principal motive is harmonized with a short progression (i–VI); this is, however, as far as the progression goes before modulating to a new pitch level, prepared melodically, though not prepared by this harmonic sequence. Motive 1 is harmonized with traditional, functional harmony, though much of the work employs nontraditional harmonies. Frequently he creates a non-traditional harmonic structure and exactly transposes the harmony to fit the melody. In so doing, large areas of harmonic plateaus are established. Important harmonic movements, therefore, tend to coincide with structural moments.

PERFORMANCE CONSIDERATIONS FOR *NIAGARA FALLS*

When preparing Michael Daugherty's *Niagara Falls* for performance, one must address three primary issues in rehearsal: balance, rhythmic integrity and style. Of course these issues are important in any music; in Daugherty's music, however, cohesive ensemble playing is the foundation needed to achieve the strong kinetic energy at the heart of the work.

Though much of *Niagara Falls* is dynamically notated at forte and above, in a properly balanced wind ensemble there should be enough 'aural room' for the melodic material to come to the fore. However, players can easily be swept into the energy of their individual parts and lose sight of the piece as a whole, reducing a fine wind ensemble to little more than a pep band. Keeping the brass and percussion sections within the parameters of their indicated volumes and encouraging them to listen for the more intricate woodwind lines is most important as a great deal of the melodic charm of the work resides in the woodwind scoring. Volume is not a viable substitute for the high energy generated in this work.

The player of the ship's bell starting at rehearsal F must realize that the bell's contribution is part of a whole and should never be mistaken as a line of principal interest—the part is marked *piano* as compared to the *fortissimo* indicated in the winds. The strong rhythmic groove can seduce even the well-intentioned, experienced player into overplaying the part. The strident sound produced by the instrument can easily obscure other layers of interest. Of course, sustained brass choir harmonic structures in any work can obliterate detailed woodwind passages and *Niagara Falls* is no exception. In the measure after rehearsal letter P, it is necessary to insist that the trumpets play a sincere *piano* in an effort to expose the horn writing. Daugherty carefully notates the subsequent crescendo as beginning on beat three and his notation must be followed scrupulously. Depending on the comparative strengths of these sections in a given ensemble, one may consider saving the bulk of the crescendo for the end of the measure. Similarly at rehearsal V, where the main theme is presented simultaneously in three different tempi—the quarter note equaling 80 in the trumpets, 160 in the saxophones and horns and 320 in the upper winds and percussion—the conductor may need to again ask the trumpets to be 'supportive' of the tenor voicing—saxophones and horns—to allow them to be heard in the texture.

Rhythmic integrity, though important in any performance, is fundamental to a successful performance of *Niagara Falls*. An important structural device in this work is the presentation of the same melodic materials at different tempi; rehearsal letter V, mentioned above, is the most striking example. There are many other instances throughout the work, however, where the relationship between layers is even more complex. For example, from virtually the first measure the marimba line makes a strong case for the dotted eighth note to be the basic unit of pulse, though the bass clarinet and bassoons seem to be unwilling to relinquish their quarter note pulse. Similarly, at rehearsal L, the bells, bass clarinet, English horn and oboe are presenting different pulses—while the oboe presents the principal theme in a quarter note pulse, the English horn plays in triplet quarters, and the bells and bass clarinet in dotted eighths—in canon separated by an eighth note. This layering of tempi will be lost if the players do not maintain absolute rhythmic integrity. As Daugherty observes:

> The complexity lies in combining the different rhythmic layers, in the polyphony. So the only difficulty with my piece is putting it together, the individual parts are not difficult. It helps to rehearse my works by breaking up the various rhythmic groups which play together and rehearse them separately, then combine the layers one by one.

Achieving proper style in *Niagara Falls* may be the most formidable challenge facing the conductor. Part pop, part classical in style, the work must project a knowledge of the pop world, though never fully inhabit it. Rhythms should not be swung, though sixteen note runs (see, for example, measure 12, alto saxophone and vibraphone) should be driven in a way foreign to classical style, rather more in the progressive jazz styles of Miles Davis or John Coltrane. The trombone interjections beginning in measure 12, the horn line beginning in measure 70 and the trumpet line beginning in measure 78 should be approached with a big band jazz style of articulation: "hot, with clean attacks and releases." Daugherty, when asked what music a conductor should be familiar with when approaching his wind music, mentioned

composers as stylistically diverse as James Brown, György Ligeti, Miles Davis, J. S. Bach and Webern.

Niagara Falls has been written with a thorough knowledge of the idiomatic potential of each instrument, a tribute to the composer's dogged determination to be familiar with any potential idiosyncrasies that may effect his orchestrational choices:

> The idea in post World War II, "Darmstadt," *avant-garde* music—a lot of if anyway—was that if you wrote idiomatically for instruments, you were accepting a limitation. I always work with instrumentalists when I compose, because I want to compose music that is "experimental" yet "idiomatic". That is why I have players come to my studio and play certain passages for me accompanied by my MIDI-computerized orchestra. I want to make sure that the notes are in the right "energy zone" and to make sure that the instrument can play what I have composed as I "hear" it. I feel that is one of the reasons that players enjoy performing my works. They say, "Wow, this sounds right to me." When I compose, I think of the "energy zones" of the instrument because I like music that is intense. The beginning notes of the *Rite of Spring* sound intense because Stravinsky selected a bassoon, not a clarinet, to play them.

However, a successful performance will require solid performers throughout the ensemble, particularly in the percussion section. Daugherty asks for truly delicate playing from the glockenspiel beginning at rehearsal letter L, a knowledge of Latin style from the conga and claves at rehearsal letter C, and simply impeccable rhythmic ensemble from the four mallet players executing difficult, unison passage work beginning at rehearsal letter V. About the percussionists Daugherty states:

> You have to have good players, but they don't have to be virtuosos. College level instrumentalists can usually play my music with no problem, because I write music that is idiomatic and my musical intentions are clear. The polyrhythmic complexity in my music occurs when the various layers of counterpoint are combined.

Because *Niagara Falls* is built on pop style grooves, the tuba and string bass players must be able to not only maintain indicated tempi but must drive the ensemble forward with a pulsation dedicated to the 'front side' of the beat.

ADDITIONAL WORKS FOR WINDS

Daugherty is particularly pleased with the reception that *Niagara Falls* has received in wind-band circles, as numerous college and university ensembles have performed it. About writing for the wind-band Daugherty says:

> I love composing for the wind-band world because the conductors and the student performers are so enthusiastic and really excited about new music. I feel that I have written some of my most interesting works because there are no restrictions on style or content in the wind-band world: I feel artistically free to let my imagination run wild and indeed it has. When I write for wind-band, I write with the same complexity that I would for

an orchestral work for the Philadelphia Orchestra. The playing level at the university level is quite high and I am always amazed at the incredible artistic and emotional level of playing that I hear at wind-band concerts.

Niagara Falls does not stand in isolation in Daugherty's output as a lone work for winds but rather has proven to be the starting point of a long list of works. Though *Bizarro, Desi* and *Motown Metal* predate *Niagara Falls*, it was *Niagara Falls* that ignited a widespread interest among wind musicians in Daugherty's music that has led to new commissions and a reexamination of Daugherty's previous works.

Desi (1991) for symphonic winds is inspired by Desi Arnaz (1917–1986) who, as a singing bongo player in various RKO film musicals of the forties, popularized Latin American music. Along with this wife, Lucille Ball, Desi Arnaz also appeared as Ricky Ricardo, a Cuban bandleader in *I Love Lucy* (1950–1961) which is widely regarded as one of the most innovative comedy shows in television history. The opening rhythmic motive in *Desi*, played by the piano and horns, is derived from the Conga dance rhythm closely associated with Desi Arnaz. *Desi* was commissioned and premiered by the Stephen F. Austin State University Symphonic Band, John Whitwell, conductor, at the 1991 CBDNA conference in Kansas City, Missouri..

Completed in 1993, *Bizarro* for symphonic winds was composed concurrently with the *Metropolis Symphony*. This work, like the *Metropolis Symphony* for symphony orchestra, was inspired by the comic book Superman. In *Bizarro* Daugherty features three rock or funk drummers making it one of his most energetic works. The character Bizarro was created by Lex Luther's duplicating ray and is an imperfect copy of Superman. The University of Texas Wind Ensemble, Jerry Junkin, Music Director, commissioned and premiered *Bizarro* at Austin, Texas in 1993.

Motown Metal (1994) for brass and percussion employs only metallic instruments. The work combines two aspects of Detroit's history: the city's place as the center of automobile manufacturing and the "Motown sound" important in popular music of the fifties and sixties. The work was commissioned by the Detroit Chamber Winds and the Summit Brass and funded by the Arts Foundation of Michigan, in conjunction with the Michigan Council for the Arts and Cultural Affairs. The Detroit Chamber Winds under the direction of H. Robert Reynolds premiered the work in Detroit, Michigan in February, 1994.

Timbuktuba (1996) for euphoniums, tubas and percussion was commissioned by Fritz Kaenzig, Professor of Euphonium and Tuba at the University of Michigan, and first performed at the 1996 Euphonium/Tuba Convention at Northwestern University, Evanston, Illinois.

Composed in 1993, *Red Cape Tango* was commissioned by the Albany Symphony Orchestra through a generous gift of the Audrey M. Kaufman Music Fund and supported by the National Endowment for the Arts. Originally for sym-

phony orchestra, the work was conceived as the fifth and final movement of his *Metropolis Symphony* and is based on the comic book character Superman. The fight to the death between Superman and Doomsday inspired this movement. The Latin chant of the dead, *Dies Irae*, is the primary musical motive in the work. The wind version of *Red Cape Tango* was commissioned in 1999 by the University of Texas Wind Ensemble, Jerry Junkin, music director. Arranged by Mark Sped, under supervision of the composer, the first performance was by that ensemble at the 1999 CBDNA convention in Austin, Texas.

The University of Michigan Symphony Band, in honor of its one hundredth anniversary, commissioned *Niagara Falls*. It was first performed October 4th, 1997 in Hill Auditorium, Ann Arbor with H. Robert Reynolds conducting the University of Michigan Symphony Band.

UFO (2001) for solo percussion and symphonic band was commissioned by Michigan State University, University of Michigan, Baylor University, the Arizona State Symphony, and the University of North Texas and was written for Evelyn Glennie. An orchestral version of UFO for solo percussion and orchestra (1999) also exists and was commissioned and premiered by the National Symphony Orchestra, Leonard Slatkin, music director and soloist Evelyn Glennie. The first performance of the final wind version of UFO—adapted by Michael Daugherty—was given by the Michigan State University Symphony Band, John Whitwell, conductor, Allison Shaw, soloist, on October 7, 2000, at Michigan State University, East Lansing Michigan. Regarding UFO the composer writes:

> *UFO* is inspired by the unidentified flying objects that have been an obsession in American popular culture since 1947. The percussion soloist is an alien, arriving unexpectedly and playing mysterious percussion instruments. During the three major sections of the composition—Unidentified, Flying, Objects—the soloist travels to different percussion stations on the stage. There are also brief interludes during which the percussion soloist performs sleight-of-hand improvisations that may leave the listener wondering: Is this another UFO sighting?

Rosa Parks Boulevard (2001) for symphonic band was commissioned by the University of Michigan and pays tribute to the woman who, in 1955, helped set in motion the modern civil rights movement by her refusal to move to the back of the bus in Montgomery, Alabama. Since her association with the Reverend Martin Luther King Jr. in the fifties, Parks has viewed the words spoken by African-American preachers as a source of strength. In *Rosa Parks Boulevard*, three solo trombones along with the trombone section are featured echoing the voices of many generations of African-American preachers across the country. These lyrical sections alternate with a turbulent bus ride, evoked by atonal polyrhythms in the trumpets, horns and non-pitched percussion. An orchestral version of *Rosa Parks Boulevard* (2000) also exists and was commissioned and premiered by the

Detroit Symphony Orchestra, Neeme Jarvi, music director. The University of Michigan Symphony Band, H. Robert Reynolds, conductor, at the University of Michigan, Ann Arbor, Michigan in April 2001, gave the first performance of the wind version of the work.

Bells for Stokowski (2002) for symphonic band is a reorchestration of the third movement of his 2001 orchestral work "Philadelphia Stories." Daugherty provides the following program note regarding the work:

> *Bells for Stokowski* is a tribute to one of the most influential and controversial conductors of the 20th century. Born in London, Leopold Stokowski (1882–1977) began his career as an organist. Moving to America, Stokowski was fired from his organ post at St. Bartholomew's Church in New York in 1908, after he concluded a service with "Stars and Stripes Forever." As maestro of the Philadelphia Orchestra (1912–36) he became known for his brilliant interpretations of classical music, his enthusiasm for new concert music, and for taking risks by constantly pushing the envelope of what was acceptable in the concert hall.
>
> In Philadelphia he created a sensation by conducting world premieres of orchestral works by composers such as Stravinsky and Varese. He also enraged classical purists by conducting his lavish Romantic orchestral transcriptions of Bach. It was in Philadelphia that he created the famous "Stokowski sound," making the orchestra sound like a pipe organ. Stokowski was so intrigued by timbral and visual complexity that he often experimented with the seating of players by moving sections of the orchestra to different parts of the stage. He also started one of America's first wind ensembles in Philadelphia. Stokowski appeared as a conductor in various Hollywood films such as "Fantasia", the 1940 collaboration with Walt Disney, which resulted in the orchestral soundtrack being recorded in stereophonic sound for the first time.
>
> In *Bells for Stokowski* I imagine Stokowski in Philadelphia visiting the Liberty Bell at sunrise, and listening to all the bells of the city resonate. To create various bell effects, I frame the ensemble with two percussionists positioned stereophonically on the stage performing on identical ringing percussion instruments such as tubular bells, crotales, bell trees, and various non-pitched metals. I also echo Stokowski's musical vision and legacy in order to look to the past and the future of American concert music.
>
> In the first section I introduce an original theme that I have composed in the style of Bach. This baroque fantasy is modulated in my musical language through a series of tonal and atonal variations. In the second part of the first section, we also hear the ensemble play a long hymn-like tune in unison which is developed as the composition unfolds. Later I also introduce my own "transcription" of Bach's C Major Prelude from *The Well-Tempered Klavier*. I employ multiple musical canons, polyrhythms, and counterpoints to achieve a complex timbral layering. Through unusual orchestrations and an alternation between chamber and tutti configurations in the ensemble, I recreate the musical effect of Stokowski's experimental seating rearrangements. In the coda I evoke the famous "Stokowski sound," by making the ensemble resound like an enormous, rumbling gothic organ. In the last chords of the composition we hear the final echoes of a long legacy of great performances by Stokowski.

WORKS LIST

SYMPHONIC BAND

Niagara Falls (1997), 10:00

Commissioned by the University of Michigan Symphony Band in honor of its hundredth anniversary and dedicated to H. Robert Reynolds. Premiered by the University of Michigan Symphony Band, H. Robert Reynolds, conductor, on October 4, 1997 in Hill Auditorium, University of Michigan, Ann Arbor, Michigan.
piccolo, 4 flutes, 3 oboes, English horn, E♭ clarinet, 3 B♭ clarinets, bass clarinet, 3 bassoons, contra bassoon; 2 alto saxophones, tenor saxophone, baritone saxophone; 4 F horns, 4 C trumpets, 2 trombones, bass trombone, 2 euphoniums, 2 tubas; timpani, 6 percussion, harp, pipe organ or synthesizer; contrabass. Parts may be doubled at the discretion of the conductor. Percussion parts may be divided among multiple players.

Red Cape Tango (1993) (arr. Mark Spede, 1999), 13:00

Originally for symphony orchestra and subsequently arranged by Mark Spede, under the supervision of the composer. The arrangement was commissioned by Jerry Junkin on behalf of the University of Texas Wind Ensemble. Premiered by the University of Texas Wind Ensemble, Jerry Junkin, conductor, at the 1999 CBDNA convention in Austin, Texas.
piccolo, 2 flutes, 2 oboes, English horn, E♭ clarinet, 4 B♭ clarinets, bass clarinet, contrabass clarinet, 2 bassoons, contrabassoon; 2 soprano saxophones (II doubles alto saxophone), tenor saxophone, baritone saxophone; 4 F horns, 4 C trumpets, 2 trombones, bass trombone, euphonium, tuba; piano, timpani, 5 percussion; contrabass. Parts may be doubled at the discretion of the conductor. Percussion parts may be divided among multiple players.

Rosa Parks Boulevard (2001), 12:00

Commissioned by the University of Michigan. Premiered by the University of Michigan Symphony Band, H. Robert Reynolds, conductor, on April 6, 2001 in the Hill Auditorium, University of Michigan, Ann Arbor, Michigan.
piccolo, 4 flutes, 2 oboes, English horn, 4 B♭ clarinets, bass clarinet, 2 bassoons, contrabassoon; soprano saxophone, alto saxophone, tenor saxophone, baritone saxophone; 4 F horns, 4 C trumpets, trombone 1 (solo), trombone 2 (solo), bass trombone (solo), 2 trombones (tutti), bass trombone, (tutti), 4 euphoniums, 2 tubas; timpani, 4 percussion, harp; 2 contrabass. Parts may be doubled at discretion of the conductor. Percussion parts may be divided among multiple players.

UFO (2000) with Solo Percussion, 40:00

Commissioned by Michigan State University, University of Michigan, Baylor University, University of North Texas and

the Arizona State Symphony. Premiered by theMichigan State University Symphony Band, John Whitwell, conductor, Allison Shaw, soloist, on October 7, 2000, at Michigan State University, East Lansing Michigan.
I.   Traveling Music
II. Unidentified
III. Flying
IV. "???"
V.   Objects
Solo Percussion
The entire solo percussion part may be played by one professional soloist. In university/educational settings, the solo percussion part could be divided between more than one student soloist. For example, the first soloist could play movements I and IV which requires extensive improvisational skills, the ability to be theatrical, and the know how to create new percussion sounds/instruments. A second soloist could play movement II which requires expertise on xylophone. A third soloist (or again the second soloist) could play movement III which requires expertise on vibraphone. Finally, a fourth soloist could be play movement V which requires expertise on drums and ability to both read and improvise on non-pitched percussion instruments.
piccolo, 4 flutes, 2 oboes, English horn, E♭ clarinet, 4 B♭ clarinets, bass clarinet, 2 bassoons, contrabassoon; soprano saxophone, alto saxophone, tenor saxophone, baritone saxophone; 4 F horns; 4 C trumpets; 3 trombones, 3 euphoniums, 2 tubas; solo percussion; 2 contrabasses. Parts may be doubled at discretion of the conductor.

Bells for Stokowski (2002) 14:00

Bells for Stokowski for Symphonic Band was commissioned by a consortium of universities including the University of Michigan (Michael Haithcock), Arizona State University (Gary Hill), Baylor University (Kevin Sedatole), University of Colorado (Allan McMurray), Ithaca College (Steve Peterson), Louisiana State University (Frank Wickes), Michigan State University (John Whitwell), Riverside, CA Community College (Kevin Mayse), University of Tennessee (Gary Sousa), University of Texas (Jerry Junkin), Texas Tech University (John Cody Birdwell), and the University of Washington (Tim Salzman).
piccolo (doubling on flute), three flutes, two oboes, English horn, two B♭ clarinets, bass clarinet, two bassoons, contrabassoon, 2 alto saxes, tenor sax, baritone sax, four horns, four C trumpets, three trombones, 2 euphoniums, tuba, timpani (five drums), four percussion, harp, pipe organ (or synthesizer), double bass. Players can be doubled at the discretion of the conductor.

SYMPHONIC WIND ENSEMBLE

Bizarro (1993) 10:00

Commissioned by Jerry Junkin on behalf of the University of Texas Wind Ensemble. Premiered by the University of Texas Wind Ensemble, Jerry Junkin, conductor, in 1993 at the University of Texas, in Autin, Texas.
piccolo, 2 flutes, 3 oboes, 3 clarinets; E♭ clarinet, B♭ clarinet, bass clarinet, 2 bassoons, contrabassoon; alto saxophone; 4 F horns, 4 trumpets, 2 trombones, bass trombone, euphonium, tuba; 4 percussion, piano, electric bass/amplified contrabass. Parts may be doubled at the discretion of the conductor.

Desi (1991) 6:00

Commissioned and premiered by John Whitwell and the Stephen F. Austin State University Symphonic Band in 1991 at the CBDNA convention in Kansas City, Missouri.
Piccolo, 2 flutes, 2 clarinets, 2 oboes, 2 bassoons; 4 F horns, 4 B♭ trumpets; 2 trombones, bass trombone, tuba; 4 percussion, piano; electric bass/amplified contrabass. Parts may be doubled at the discretion of the conductor.

LARGE BRASS ENSEMBLE

Motown Metal (1994) 7:00

Commissioned by the Detroit Chamber Winds and the Summit Brass. Premiered by the Detroit Chamber Winds, H. Robert Reynolds, conductor, in February 1994, in Detroit, Michigan.
4 F horns, 4 trumpets, 2 trombones, bass trombone, tuba; 2 percussion

Timbuktuba (1996) 7:00

Commissioned by Fritz Kaenzig, Professor of Tuba and Euphonium at the University of Michigan. Premiered in 1996 at the Euphonium/Tuba Convention at Northwestern University, Evanston, Illinois.
4 euphoniums, 2 tubas; percussion (one player)
Brass parts may be doubled at discretion of the conductor.

ORCHESTRA

Flamingo (1991), 9:00
pic, 1–1–1–1; 1 (2)–1–1–0; 2 perc, pn, strings.

Hell's Angels (1998–99), 16:00
Solo bassoon quartet; pic, 2–0–0–0; 4–4–3–1; timp, 4 perc, harp, cel; strings.

Leap Day (1996), 5:00
pic, 2–2–2, bcl–2; 4–3–3–1; timp, 4 perc; strings.
Composed for high school level orchestra.

Metropolis Symphony (1988–93), 42:00
[movements may be performed separately]

1. *Lex* (1991), 9:00
pic, 2–2, Eh, 2, bcl, 2, cbn; 4–4–3–1; timp, 4 perc, synth; strings.

2. *Krypton* (1993), 7:00
pic, 2–3, Eb,1, bcl, 2, cbn; 4–4–3–1; 4 perc, pn; strings.

3. *Mxyzptlk* (1988), 7:00
2 fl solo (II. doubles pic); 0–2–2–2; 2–1–1–0; synth, 1 or 2 perc; strings.

4. *Oh, Lois!* (1989), 5:00
2–2–2–2; 4–3–3–0; timp, 2 perc, synth; strings.

5. *Red Cape Tango* (1993), 13:00.
pic, 2–2, Eh, 2, bcl, 2, cbn; 4–4–3–1; timp, 4 perc, pno; strings.

Motor City Triptych (2000), 31:00
[movements may be performed separately]

1. *Motown Mondays* (2000), 9:30
(pic) 2–2, Eh, Eb cl, 1, bcl, 2, cbn; 4–4–3–1; timp, 4 perc, harp; strings.

2. *Pedal-to-the-Metal* (2000), 9:30
(pic) 2–2, Eh, Eb cl, 1, bcl, 2, cbn; 4–4–3–1; timp, 4 perc, harp; strings.

3. *Rosa Parks Boulevard* (2000), 12:00
(pic), 2–2, Eh, Eb cl, 1, bcl, 2, cbn; 4–4–3–1; timp, 4 perc, harp; strings.

Philadelphia Stories (2001), 29:00
[Movements may be performed separately]

1. *Sundown of South Street*, 7:00
(pic) 3–2, Eh, 2, bcl, 2, cbn; 4–4–3–1; timp, 4 perc, 2 harp, gtr, strings.

2. *Tell-Tale Harp*, 8:00
(pic) 3–2, Eh, 2, bcl, 2, cbn; 4–4–3–1; timp, 4 perc, 2 harp, gtr, strings.

3. *Bells for Stokowski*, 14:00
pic, 2–2, Eh, Eb cl, 1, bcl, 2, cbn; 4–4–3–1; timp, 4 perc, 2 harp, gtr, strings.

Route 66 (1998), 7:30
pic, 2–2, Eh–1, Eb cl, b cl–2, cbn; 4–4–3–1; timp, 4 perc, pno, hp; strings.

Spaghetti Western (1998), 20:00
Solo Eh; pic, 2–0–0–0; 4–4–3–1; timp., 4 perc., pno/cel, hp; strings.

Sunset Strip (1999), 15:00
Pic., 1–2–1, bcl., 2; 2(4)–2–0–0; perc, pno; strings.

Le Tombeau de Liberace (1996),16:00
Solo pno.; (pic), 1–1–1–1; 2–1–1–1 ; 2 perc.; strings.

UFO (1999), 40:00
Solo perc.; pic, 2–2, Eh., Eb cl.,1, bcl., 2, cbn; 4–4–3–1; strings.

Fire and Blood (2003)
Violin concerto. (Premiere May, 2003, Pamela Frank, violin, Detroit Symphony, Neeme Järvi conducting.)

STRING ORCHESTRA

Strut (1989/94), 6:00

LARGE CHAMBER ENSEMBLE OR CHAMBER ORCHESTRA

Flamingo (1991), 9:00
pic, 1–1–1–1; 1(2)–1–1–0; 2 perc, pn; strings (1 ea. or small complements)

Le Tombeau de Liberace (1996), 15:00
Solo piano; (pic), 1–1–1–1; 2–1–1–1; 2 perc; strings (1 ea. or small complements)

Snap! (1987), 7:00
fl(pic), ob, cl(Eb,Bb), b cl; hn, tpt, b tbn; 3 perc, synth; strings (1 ea. or small complements)

Blue Like an Orange (1987), 10:00
fl(pic), ob, cl(Eb,Bb), b cl; hn, tpt, b tbn; 3 perc, synth; str (1 ea. or small complements)

What's That Spell? (1995), 13:00
2 amplified sopranos; fl(pic), ob, cl, bn, A sax, T sax; hn, tpt, tbn; 1 perc, pno; str (1 each, amplified or small complements, unamplified)

OPERA

Jackie O (1997), 90:00
Chamber Opera in Two Acts
Libretto by Wayne Koestenbaum
2 Sop, 2 Mez Sop, Tenor, High Bar, Bass; fl(pic), ob(Eh), cl(b cl), sop sax(al, tn sax), bn; hn, tr, tbn(euph), tb; 2 perc,hp,gui,pno; str (1 each or small complements)

SMALL CHAMBER ENSEMBLE

Bounce (1998), 8:30
2 bassoons

Dead Elvis (1993), 10:00
Solo bn, Eb cl, tr, tbn, perc (one player), vn, cb

Firecracker (1991), 15:00
Solo ob; fl(pic), b cl, vn, vc, perc (one player), kybd

The High and the Mighty (2000), 7:00
Piccolo and piano

Jackie's Song (1996), 15:00
solo vc, vn, fl(pic), b cl, pno, perc

Lex (1991–93), 12:00
elec. vn, 2 synth, timp, 4 perc

Lounge Lizards (1994), 15:00
2 pno, 2 perc

Shaken Not Stirred (1994), 10:00
3 perc, elec bass or acoustic bass with amplification

Sinatra Shag (1997), 5:00
solo vn, fl, b cl, vc, 1 perc, pno

Timbuktuba (1996) 7:00
4 euph, 2 tba, 1 perc

Used Car Salesman (2000), 10:00
percussion quartet

Viola Zombie (1991), 10:00
2 viola

Yo amaba a Lucy (I Loved Lucy) (1996), 8:30
flute, guitar

STRING QUARTET AND PRE-RECORDED performance CD

Beat Boxer (1991), 10:00

Elvis Everywhere (1993), 8:30

Paul Robeson Told Me (1994), 8:30

Sing Sing: J. Edgar Hoover (1992), 11:00

SOLO INSTRUMENT

Jackie's Song (1996), 7:00
cello

Piano Plus (1985), 12:00
piano

Venetian Blinds (2002) 10:00
piano

DISCOGRAPHY

UFO /Motown Metal/Red Cape Tango/Desi/Niagara Falls
"UFO: The Music of Michael Daugherty"
North Texas Wind Symphony, Eugene Migliaro Corporon, Conductor. Evelyn Glennie, percussion soloist (UFO)
Klavier CD 1112

Metropolis Symphony; Bizarro
"Metropolis Symphony"
Baltimore Symphony/David Zinman
Argo 452-103-2
"Michael Daugherty: American Icons"

Dead Elvis/Snap!/What's That Spell?/Jackie's Song/Le Tombeau de Liberace/Motown Metal/Flamingo
London Sinfonietta/David Zinman; London Sinfonietta/Markus Stenz, w/ Paul Crossley, piano; Dogs of Desire/David Alan Miller; London Sinfonietta/Michael Daugherty, w/Christopher van Kampen, cello
Argo 458-145-2

Desi
"Who's Afraid of 20th Century Music, Vol. 2"
Hamburg PO/Ingo Metzmacher
EMI Classics CDC5571292

Desi
"Dance Mix"
Baltimore Symphony/David Zinman
Argo 444-454-2 ("Dance Mix")

Elvis Everywhere
"Released"
Kronos Quartet
Elektra Nonesuch 7559-79394-2

Sing Sing: J. Edgar Hoover
"Howl,"
Kronos Quartet
Nonesuch 7559-79372-2

Jackie O
"Jackie O"
Houston Grand Opera/Christopher Larkin
Argo 455 591-2

Motown Metal
"Urban Requiem"
University of Miami Wind Ensemble/Gary Green
Albany (Troy 212) ("Urban Requiem")

Paul Robeson Told Me
"Smith Quartet"
Smith Quartet
Smith Quartet Records 4001CD

Shaken Not Stirred
"Launch"
Ensemble Bash
Sony Classical SK 69246

Niagara Falls
"The University of Texas Wind Ensemble at Carnegie Hall"
University of Texas Wind Ensemble, Jerry Junkin, conductor
Mark Custom Recording Service, Inc., Clarence, NY. 2697-MCD markcustom@aol.com

Niagara Falls
"Sojourns"
North Texas Wind Symphony, Eugene Migliaro Corporon,
Conductor
Klavier CD 11099

Red Cape Tango
"Rendezvous"
North Texas Wind Symphony, Eugene Migliaro Corporon,
Conductor
Klavier CD 11109

Timbuktuba
"La Morte dell 'Oom
Symphonia two
Mark Custom Service, Inc., Clarence, NY 2808-MCD;
markcustom@aol.com

Rosa Parks Boulevard
"H. Robert Reynolds—The Retirement Concert"
University of Michigan Symphony Band, H. Robert Reynolds,
Conductor
Equilibrium EQ45

Michael Daugherty's publisher is:
Peermusic Classical
810 Seventh Avenue
New York, NY 10019
tel. 212-265-3910
fax. 212-489-2465
http://www.peermusic.com/classical

For sales and rentals of Michael Daugherty's music in North
and South America and Japan contact:
Theodore Presser Co.
588 North Gulph Road
King of Prussia, PA 19406
tel. 610-525-3636
fax. 610-527-7841
http://www.presser.com/

For sales and rentals of Michael Daugherty's music in Europe,
Australia and New Zealand, contact:
Faber Music Ltd.
3 Queen Square
London WC1N 3AU
ENGLAND
tel. +44 (0) 20 7278 7436
fax. +44 (0) 20 7833 7939
http://www.fabermusic.co.uk/

ADDITIONAL RESOURCES

BOOK

"The Muse That Sings"
Ann McCutchan
Oxford University Press, 2000
(Chapter on "Michael Daugherty")

WEB-SITES

http://www.michaeldaugherty.net//
http://www.music.umich.edu/faculty/daugherty.michael.html

David Gillingham

by
Raydell Bradley and J. Bradley McDavid

...when I heard my first band at the age of three I knew I would be involved with bands. My dad had always wanted to be a high school band director but was needed on the farm. I realized his dream when I became a middle school band director for four years. I paid my dues...and I understand the band world...D.R.G.

David R. Gillingham (b.1947) is currently Professor of Theory and Composition and also serves as Theory and Literature Area Coordinator at Central Michigan University in Mt. Pleasant, Michigan a position he has held since 1984. He earned the Bachelor and Master degrees in Music Education from the University of Wisconsin-Oshkosh in 1969 and 1977, and the Ph.D. in Music Theory and Composition from Michigan State University in 1980. His principal composition teachers were Roger Dennis, Jere Hutcheson, James Niblock and H. Owen Reed. Dr. Gillingham's national reputation as a composer of quality wind and percussion music has precipitated numerous future commissions for a wide range of commissioning institutions. He is the recipient of several awards and honors including first Prize in the International Barlow Composition Contest in 1990 for *"Heroes, Lost and Fallen—A Vietnam Memorial,"* a Summer Fellowship, a Research Professorship (at Central Michigan University) and composer-in-residence at several universities and colleges including the University of Michigan and the University of Illinois. The Prague Radio Orchestra conducted by Vladmimir Valek with soloists Daniel Koppelman and Ruth Neville recorded one of his most recent works, "Interplay for Piano Four-Hands and Orchestra" in 1996. His compositions have been performed throughout the United States, Europe, and Japan. C. Alan, Carl Fischer, Moon of Hope, Dorn, TUBA Press, ITA Press, Hal Leonard, MMB, and Southern Music companies publish Dr. Gillingham's works.

COMPOSITIONAL APPROACH

Gillingham's background in American hymnology provides the foundation for the majority of his works, compositions most aptly described as tone poems marked by the combination of liturgical themes with distinctively programmatic atmospheres. For Gillingham, the commitment to program music is a highly personal one:

...writing music with a specific program is a great point of orientation and inspiration. I firmly believe that any piece of music that a composer writes is an extension of the soul...there must be something of the mood of a composer in any composition. (You can tell the mood of Beethoven in many of his works.) You cannot say that there is nothing programmatic in a certain symphony just because a certain key names the work. You hear turmoil, you hear calm, etc. in the music of Beethoven.

Gillingham attributes the liturgical inspiration frequently found in his music to his parents, as consummate spiritual role models, and to early childhood relationships with his aunt Jeanne and his first piano teacher, Mrs. Chamberlain, who also served as organist for the local Methodist Church.

I grew up as a member of a very large family in a farming community in Wisconsin. My uncle and his family lived upstairs in a large Midwestern style home...our families would frequently get together and my aunt would play many hymns on an old pump organ. That's how I got my keyboard start...from her. I was raised in the Methodist tradition and later became a church organist for many years....I could actually quote the hymn tunes better than I could the actual text of the pieces.

He is drawn to the tone poem as a form due to what he views as his obligation to attempt to connect directly with the listener:

The tone poem gives the listener an inside edge to the music. I feel that the audience has frequently been left out and that [certain] composers have been writing for shock value. I think many composers say, "look at the marvelous craft that I have achieved...look at how I can shock people...." While it might be artistic and it might be somewhat of a feat in itself, I question if [they] have reached anyone with their music?

Richard Strauss is the composer whose tone poems he most admires:

My biggest influences must be the large symphonic poems of the late 19th century and early 20th century....I'm particularly fascinated with the 19th century heritage that we have of program music. I'm a big fan of Richard Strauss, the Romantic period composer of the tone poem (not all-contemporary band composers are) but I enjoy his scoring...it is incredible. There are, however, certain 20th century composers that have influenced me...Bernstein and Copland among them. I think I have, however, found my own voice.

In 1992 Gillingham received a Central Michigan University Summer Fellowship that he utilized to study composition with H. Owen Reed, a composer Gillingham describes as being a "major influence" on his writing:

> I learned several important things from Owen; 1) how to be rhythmically inventive; 2) how to express mood through a variety of instrumental colors; 3) how important the title of the work is in expressing the overall mood of the piece and as an important point of inspiration; 4) why writing for band is important as opposed to choosing the orchestra as a large ensemble medium of compositional expression.

He also notes that David Maslanka (another former student of H. Owen Reed) is "also a major influence in my style...he is a deep thinker and I like that".

In describing his work "A Crescent Still Abides", Gillingham offers insight into the musical materials that he is attracted to in composing his wind band music:

> I use the Lydian mode quite a bit. I like the raised fourth scale degree...it makes it sound a bit brighter than a normal scale. I like the chromatic mediant relationship. I like the use of polychords, and the use of the diminished seventh chord. I like overlapping two diminished seventh chords....I like low brass featured with some sort of chorale. I love the brass sections, especially the horns. I work very hard at making my rhythms original, but since I use ostinato quite a bit, the percussion writing is often similar.

Gillingham's wind band orchestrations are powerfully scored and demonstrate an intimate understanding of the instruments and their potential for unique coloristic contributions:

> ...I have a very strong feeling about band scoring [as] the band is a very powerful instrument. The band should be remembered as being quite different from the orchestra, and the scoring should be considerably different. Some of the band scoring by [certain] composers sounds like a big accordion. I like to work with a lot of colors and feature a number of soloists. I think the "bandstrations" should be considered from the beginning. I tell my students that you can have great material, but if it is not scored properly, it just won't make it....

The emotional component that is so pervasive throughout many of Gillingham's works can be partly attributed to his experiences during the Vietnam conflict.

> Having served as a member of a military band in Vietnam, I was able to meet the Vietnamese people and I have a special place in my heart for them. Obviously being so closely adjacent to it, the fighting itself had a profound effect on me. I could have been killed...you lived with that every day that you were there....I was there for fourteen months. There are some that say that I should not have glorified such an unpopular war through music, but I say that we can never dismiss the fact that thousands of our young men committed themselves to fight the war. They were there. Many survived, many died and many were simply lost.

Gillingham finds the wind band idiom to be a more 'performance friendly' environment for composers and is highly aware of the unfortunate perception by certain composers that the orchestral medium is more worthy of their compositional efforts:

Many perceive contemporary orchestral composers (Michael Torke, for example) to be on a higher artistic level than band composers. If the orchestral composers are not careful they will find that the band compositions are being performed more often than the orchestral compositions. The band is performing the 'cutting edge' music.

He is hopeful that some of his works will be remembered as significant contributions to the wind band repertoire:

> I would want "Heroes Lost and Fallen" to be remembered, although I don't think it is some of my best writing. I would like "Waking" and "Apocalyptic" to be remembered in that way also. I think that the "Concertino" should be remembered. I received the nicest email from composer David Holsinger about "Heroes..."; He had been asked to do a Vietnam remembrance piece...and refused. He said that "Heroes" was the definitive Vietnam piece...if I've made that type of mark then I think that it is just great. The piece can be so very powerful...and a bad performance is just grueling. I consider "Heroes" to be my "signature" work, in other words, the one by which most people seem to identify me with. I consider "Cantus Laetus" (Joyful Noise) to be my most definitive work for band. It is a concerto for wind ensemble and uses most of the scoring, harmonic, rhythmic, and melodic devices that are identified with my work.

OVERVIEW OF SELECTED WORKS FOR BAND

Concertino for Four Percussion and Wind Ensemble
Performance Time = 9:30; C. Alan Publications, 1997. Premiere—April 17, 1997 by Oklahoma State University Wind Ensemble, Joseph Missal, conductor. 8th World Association for Symphonic Bands and Ensembles (WASBE) Conference in Schladming, Austria.

Concertino for Four Percussion and Wind Ensemble is a more abstract Gillingham work in the sense that it does not have specific programmatic intent. In speaking to the issue of the abstract nature of the composition he notes:

> This piece does not have a program. Many students and conductors have put me on the spot and asked, "Is there a program with this work?" I must say that I was originally striving for a programmatic title, and the idea was something that comes from the abyss, something that is very dark...from the ocean. I like Debussy's "The Sunken Cathedral" and I always tell my students that this [Concertino] is like something rising out of the water. The opening tune is so dark and mysterious that I envision looking down a black hole of sorts. That theme then becomes transformed into a wonderful closing theme. Unlike many of my works, it does not suggest a program, but in my thinking in writing the piece was a vision of hope rising out of the darkness of an abyss in the ocean and into the daylight above the water. One can certainly understand this when following the motive first heard in the bells and vibraphone in the opening section of the piece.
> *Concertino for Four Percussion and Wind Ensemble* is not particularly challenging relative to wind instrument ranges and rhyth-

mic content but conductor and ensemble must maintain a keen sense of pulse as melodic motives are rapidly passed between winds and percussion amidst a variety of compound meters. The piece provides a technical challenge to the percussion section, particularly the keyboard instruments. With the exception of an essential harp part, this piece adheres to traditional instrumentation.

Lamb of God

Performance Time = 12:20; C. Alan Publications, 2001.
Premiere—March 31, 2001 by University of Nevada Wind Ensemble, A. G. McGrannahan III, conductor. Western States Collegiate Wind Band Festival, California State University, Fresno.

Lamb of God is a highly dramatic tone poem for wind band based on the Christian Passion. The work is cast in five connected sections chronologically coinciding with the events of the Easter story. Uniting the work is motivic material taken from the Easter sequence, *Victimae paschali laudes* (Praise to the Paschal Lamb). In the Catholic Church, the "Paschal Lamb" is representative of Christ who was sacrificed on the cross to redeem the people, or 'sheep', of the world.

The first section, *O crux, portare talentum mundi* (O cross, to bear the treasure of the world) seeks to depict Christ's tortuous walk in bearing the weight of his own cross. The three opening sonorities are meant to flash a picture of pain, as would an opening scene of a motion picture. The tortuous walk immediately continues over which the horns render a version of the first phrase of the chant. Intermittent cracks of the whip can be heard amidst the texture of the section. Density and dissonance accrue, and the motion and intensity finally halt signifying the arrival at Calvary, the site of the crucifixion. The quiet, mysterious nature of this moment reflects the ultimate realization of what lies ahead. The intensity resumes as the walk continues to the point of crucifixion, the xylophone signaling in nervous anticipation.

In the next section, *Dux vitae mortuus* ("The leader of life is slain"), timpani and snare drum rolls precede the sound of hammered nails into the cross—each nail followed immediately by a flash of a dissonant sonority. As the ever-increasing impression of suffering intensifies familiar melodic material, based on the chorale tune *O Sacred Head Now Wounded* by Hans Hassler, is initially sounded by solo alto saxophone. The pain strengthens and culminates with the seven last words of Christ represented by seven brief motives voiced in unison by the piccolo, bass clarinet, bells and piano. The vibraphone, bells and chimes strike a final chord ending the section with an inverted B♭ major chord representing Christ's last breath.

The third section, *Sepulcrum Christi viventis* ("I saw the sepulchre of the living Christ"), represents an outpouring of grief; thunder and blackening sky signify the death of Christ harmonically framed by a C♯ minor chord. The fourth section, *Surrexit Christus spes mea* ("Christ my hope has risen"), depicts the miracle of resurrection with bells, crotales and

cascading passages in the flutes and clarinets leading to a joyous musical resolution. Phrases of *Victimae paschali laudes* permeate the section and segue into the final 'benediction' in G major, *Agnus redimit oves* ("The lamb has redeemed the sheep"), beginning with a chant-like solo in the alto saxophone that ultimately expands throughout the winds. The work closes by chromatically modulating to E major, a chromatic mediant change, which Gillingham suggests depicts eternity or Christ's ascension into Heaven.

Lamb of God utilizes extensive percussion writing, challenging piano and upper woodwind ostinati, and dynamic extremes in an effort to accentuate the programmatic foundation of the work. Although the piece contains a moderate level of compound meter changes, tempi rarely rise above an andante equivalent in an attempt to reverently portray the events of the Passion. The piece does not contain any substantial range concerns for the winds, however the percussion and piano writing does present several formidable technical challenges. Enthusiasts of *Heroes Lost and Fallen* will undoubtedly be attracted to the beautifully sonorous scoring of the low brass and horns in several prominent passages.

Cantus Laetus

Performance Time = 15:00; C. Alan Publications, 2001.
Premiere—Feb 22, 2001 by University of Georgia Wind Symphony, H. Dwight Satterwhite, conductor. College Band Directors National Association (CBDNA) National Convention, University of North Texas, Denton, Texas.

Cantus Laetus (Joyful Noise) is a work cast in three major sections framed by an introduction, *Initium*, and a coda, *Finis*. Virtually all of the melodic material for this concerto is based on the Gregorian Hymn, *"Veni Creator Spiritus"* and there is also obvious and intended reference to Psalm 100 ("Make a joyful noise to the Lord, all the lands!"). The three middle sections feature the three families of the ensemble, *Calamus* (reeds/woodwinds), *Aes* (brass), and *Ictus* (percussion) with the percussion, piano and harp being scored prominently throughout.

Initium begins the work with a hammered three-note motive constructed on a minor third over the prevailing tonality of B♭ minor. Phrases of the chant make brief appearances throughout the section. A sense of building tension continues driven by repetition of the three-note motive navigating through a variety of compound meters. The frequency of the hammering, and the level of the dynamics intensify until resolution is provided via a B♭ major chord that signals the introduction of the *Calamus* section.

Calamus follows in stark contrast to the introduction and is marked by a whimsical playfulness in the upper woodwinds. Over harp arpeggios, clarinets allude briefly to primary hymn tune, *Veni Creator Spiritus*, and are quickly followed by an oboe duet which sets the pace for series of vignettes by various instruments in the clarinet solo passage; a spirited saxophone quartet, swirling flutes, and bassoon/piano and piccolo/bass clarinet duos. *Calamus* culminates with a three-part fugue in grand canonic style that is ultimately interrupted by the entire brass section announcing, via a solemn B minor chord the beginning of the *Aes* section. The solemnity continues with a chain of suspensions in the low brass followed by a mysterious ostinato in muted trumpets under which the horns darkly state the chant motive. Darkness is broken by the first phrase of the hymn dramatically intoned by the brass choir followed by the lyricism of the euphonium performing the last phrase of the chant. The brasses then break into fanfare presentation utilizing motivic material from the third phrase of the chant and ultimately culminating in first phrase fragments. Low brasses follow in march style above which the horns and trumpets make a unison declaration of the first two phrases of the chant. Again, the euphonium makes an appearance in a quotation of the third phrase of the chant in simple and beautiful elegance. The tempo changes quickly and the brass pass motives in scherzo-like style. They segue into compound meter enhanced by timpani articulations with a declamatory statement of the first phrase of the chant in minor tonality by unison horns and trumpets. This leads ultimately to a concluding burst of a C major chord.

As *Aes* interrupted *Calamus*, *Ictus* interrupts *Aes* with a thunder of drums. The timpani are featured in a soloistic passage marked by two against three rhythms ornamented by piano and xylophone. The mood calms via the use of harp and bass marimba arpeggios adorned by bowed marimba and vibraphone. The entire keyboard ensemble then collaborates to accompany singing by the wind players on motives from the chant. The keyboards quietly end this section using material from the final phrase of the chant.

An exposed percussion transition into the *Finis* ensues beginning with the timpani and joined by the xylophone, bass drum and marimba. Brass and woodwinds begin to infiltrate the texture until the *Finis* recaps the hammered motive from the *Initium*. Though the darkness of Bb minor has returned, it is soon interrupted by a joyous brass choir statement of *Veni Creator Spiritus* in Bb major, modulating to D major, and ultimately driving to a rousing conclusion in A major.

Cantus Laetus requires rapid articulation skills on the part of the wind players while the ensemble must maneuver deftly through a flurry of compound meter changes. Gillingham's extensive scoring of percussion, especially keyboard percussion, is utilized throughout. Instruments employed include brake drums, crotales, bowed marimba and vibraphone as well as bass marimba. Although significant prolonged episodes of exposed wind playing do not exist, the skillful performance of exposed arpeggiated ostinati for piano, harp and percussion is essential to a mature performance of this work. Instrumentation includes contra bassoon and soprano saxophone although parts are rarely exposed and generally doubled within the ensemble. Additional ensemble demands include singing through a brief passage and a section in which trumpets and horns are asked to sustain concert F's and G's at the lowest end of their range.

CONDUCTING APPROACH

The preservation of melodic and harmonic balance in Gillingham's 'signature' treatment of the brass choir should be of primary concern to any conductor intent on communicating the essence of Gillingham's programmatic works. Generating sonorous warmth from the entire ensemble with an ever-present awareness of each liturgical or dramatic theme will greatly assist in the clear presentation of each programmatic atmosphere that the composer has so carefully constructed.

Also, the importance of the timbre and effect of Gillingham's percussion writing on the effective communication of the dramatic intentions in his music cannot be overstated. Conductors should carefully examine the size and skill level of their ensemble's percussion section before committing themselves to a performance of many of Gillingham's compositions such as the three pieces examined in this chapter. From an issue of notation and technical demands, percussionists should be prepared to execute a wide variety of effects; it is helpful that Gillingham is precise in his notation and in his instructions relative to the issues of mallet selection and preferred damping technique. Sudden changes in dynamics and rapid crescendi/diminuendi are only part of the enormous pallet of color and effect from which Gillingham draws when scoring for percussion. Steadfast commitment to an unshakeable pulse is definitely essential, particularly in light of the abundance of compound meters and tempo changes typically incorporated by the composer.

Lastly, one of the exciting challenges for many conductors preparing to perform a Gillingham composition is the research effort required to ultimately communicate a mature understanding of the programmatic and emotional intentions on which many of his pieces are founded. As a result of concentrated score study on the aforementioned compositional components, coupled with the conductor's own interpretation and sense of creativity, the result can be a performance that leads to a high degree of not only artistic satisfaction but one that is uniquely personal for conductor as well as ensemble.

It is apparent that Gillingham has heard several live performances of his works and offers this advice to conductors:

1) Pay special attention to the percussion writing: mallet choices, types of instruments and intended effect. Percussion color is a big issue in my music.

2) Adhere as closely as possible to the marked tempos. Many conductors try to second guess my intention and tell me that "it doesn't work" at the marked tempo....I know better, as I have heard other groups play the particular work very successfully.

3) Analyze the music carefully, so that it is clear what parts need to project...the melodic line, the accompaniment, etc. It is apparent, at times, that conductors haven't done their homework.

4) Since much of my music if programmatic (i.e. tells a story or is based on some sort of extra-musical idea), it is imperative that the "effect" reach the listener. Adhere closely to marked dynamics/tempos/style markings/articulations and exaggerate if needed.

Gillingham feels that conductors contemplating a performance of his music should be familiar with four of his major works, utilizing them as reference points for the interpretation of the remaining body of his wind compositions:

…"Heroes, Lost and Fallen"; "Serenade for Winds and Percussion"; "A Crescent Still Abides"; "Waking Angels". These pieces exhibit the scoring color that identifies my style and three of them are in the sort of somber "adagio style" that I have a predilection for.

He recommends, with enthusiasm, the following recorded versions of his music:

The Klavier recordings under Corporon are very good as is the recent recording on Summit records of my trumpet concerto. I am also very fond of Jim Keene's recording of "Heroes" with U of Illinois and the recordings of my works by Steve Steele at Illinois State and by Oklahoma State University with Joe Missal.

DISCOGRAPHY

Corporon, Eugene, conductor. (1999) **Sojourns**. The North Texas University Wind Ensemble. *"Concertino for Four Percussion and Wind Ensemble"* Klavier KCD 11099

Corporon, Eugene, conductor. (1998) **Dream Catchers**. North Texas University Wind Ensemble. *"Waking Angels"* Klavier: KCD 11089

Corporon, Eugene, conductor. (1995) **Songs and Dances**. Cincinnati College-Conservatory Wind Symphony. *"Songs of the Night"* Klavier KCD 11066

Corporon, Eugene, conductor. (1992) **Memorials**. Cincinnati College-Conservatory Wind Symphony. *"Heroes Lost and Fallen—A Vietnam Memorial"* Klavier KCD 11042

Green, Gary, conductor. **Christina's World – New Music for Wind Ensemble**. The University of Miami Wind Ensemble. *"Concertino for Four Percussion and Wind Ensemble"* UMIA-1518

Keene, James F., conductor. (1999) University of Illinois Symphonic Band. *"Heroes Lost and Fallen—A Vietnam Memorial"* UI Bands 127

Locke, John R., conductor. (2001) **internal combustion!** University of North Carolina Greensboro Wind Ensemble. *"Internal Combustion"* CD-107 UNCG School of Music

McGrannahan, A. G. III, conductor. (2001) **Western States Collegiate Band Festival**. University of Nevada-Reno

Wind Ensemble. *"Be Thou My Vision"* / *"Lamb of God"* Vestige Recordings: GR 01-0501

Missal, Joseph P., conductor. (1999) **WASBE Convention performance**. Oklahoma State University Wind Ensemble. *"New Century Dawn"*

Mizushina, Katsuo, conductor. Hokazono, Shoichiro, euphonium. (1998) **Vintage:Fantastic Euphonium**. The Central Band of the Japan Air Self Defense Forces. *"Vintage"* CRCI 35012. Nippon Crown.

Nakayawa, Tetsuya, conductor. (1998) **A Crescent Still Abides**. *"A Crescent Still Abides"* Goodlife, Inc.

Satterwhite, H. Dwight and Culvahouse, John C., conductors. (2001) **Triumphs**. The University of Georgia Wind Symphony. *"Cantus Laetus"* Summit Records, DCD 306 Compact Disc.

Satterwhite, H. Dwight and Culvahouse, John C., conductors. (2000) **Milestones**. The University of Georgia Wind Symphony. *"New Century Dawn"* Summit Records, DCD 281 Compact Disc.

Satterwhite, H. Dwight and Culvahouse, John C., conductors. Mills, W. Fred, featured soloist. (1999) **When the Trumpets Call**. The University of Georgia Wind Symphony. *"When Speaks the Signal-Tone Trumpet"* Summit Records DCD247 Compact Disc.

Satterwhite, H. Dwight and Culvahouse, John C., conductors. (1998) **The Riddle of the Sphinx**. The University of Georgia Wind Symphony. *"Concertino for Four Percussion and Wind Ensemble"* Mark Custom Recording Service, 2871-MCD Compact Disc.

Satterwhite, H. Dwight and Culvahouse, John C., conductors. (1997) **New Lights**. The University of Georgia Wind Symphony. *"Waking Angels"* Mark Custom Recording Service, 2550-MCD Compact Disc.

Satterwhite, H. Dwight and Culvahouse, John C., conductors. (1996) **Apocalyptic Dreams**. The University of Georgia Wind Symphony. *"Apocalyptic Dreams"* Mark Custom Recording Service, 2677-MCD.

Steele, Steven, conductor. (1996–1997) The Illinois State University Wind Symphony and Symphonic Winds. *"Prophecy of The Earth"* / *"Heroes Lost and Fallen—A Vietnam Memorial"* / *"Quintessence"*

Stamp, Jack, conductor. (2001) **Internal Combustion**. Indiana University of Pennsylvania Wind Ensemble. *"Internal Combustion!"* Klavier CD 11119

MUSIC FOR LARGE ENSEMBLE

And Can It Be?
Ensemble: Band
Publisher: C. Alan Publications, 2000
Premiere: Feb. 20, 2000. California All State Honor
Band, H. Robert Reynolds, conductor.

Apocalyptic Dreams Symphony
Ensemble: Band
Publisher: Southern Music Co., 1996
Premiere: Mar. 2, 1995. University of Georgia Symphony Band, Dwight Satterwhite, conductor.

Au Sable River Festival
Ensemble: Band
Publisher: C. Alan Publications, 2002
Premiere: May 20, 2002. Grayling (MI) H.S. Band,
David Gillingham, conductor.

Bells of Freedom
Ensemble: Beginning band
Publisher: C. Alan Publications, 2002

Be Thou My Vision
Ensemble: Symphonic Band
Publisher: C. Alan Publications, 2000
Premiere: October 26, 1999. Indiana University Wind
Ensemble, Ray Cramer, conductor.

Cantus Laetus
Ensemble: Wind Ensemble
Publisher: C. Alan Publications, 2001
Premiere: Feb. 22, 2001 at the CBDNA National Convention. University of Georgia Wind Symphony, Dwight Satterwhite, conductor.

Council Oak
Ensemble: Band
Publisher: C. Alan Publications, 2002
Premiere: Jan. 12, 2002 at the Florida Bandmasters
Association convention. Florida All State
Honor Band, John Whitwell, conductor.

Chronicle
Ensemble: Band
Publisher: Carl Fischer, 1986 (Rental)
Premiere: Apr. 18, 1984. Eastern Michigan University
Concert Winds, Max Plank, conductor.

A Crescent Still Abides
Ensemble: Winds and Percussion
Publisher: C. Alan Publications, 1998
Premiere: May 7, 1998. Hofstra University Wind
Ensemble, Peter Boonshaft, conductor.

Concertino for Four Percussion and Wind Ensemble
Ensemble: Wind Ensemble
Publisher: C. Alan Publications, 1997
Premiere: April 17, 1997. Oklahoma State University
Wind Symphony, Joseph Missal, conductor.

Forward Motion
Ensemble: Orchestra
Publisher: C. Alan Publications, 2002
Premiere: Feb. 5, 2000. Midland (MI) Symphony Orchestra, Midland, Carlton Woods, conductor.

Foster's America (Stephen Foster Suite)
Ensemble: Band
Publisher: C. Alan Publications, 2003
Premiere: March 5, 2003. Grand Ledge (MI) High
School Symphonic Band, Michael Kaufman,
conductor.

From This Time Forth
Ensemble: Orchestra, Choir, and organ
Publisher: C. Alan Publications, 2002
Premiere: Mar. 6, 200. Hope College Choir and
Orchestra, Brad Richmond, conductor.

Galactic Empires
Ensemble: Band
Publisher: C. Alan Publications, 1998
Premiere: Mar. 14, 1998. Bands of America (Indianapolis, IN) Honor Band of America, Gary Green,
conductor.

Heritage of Faith
Ensemble: Band and choir
Publisher: C. Alan Publications, 2003
Premiere: Feb. 23, 2003. Grand Rapids (MI) Christian
High School Wind Ensemble and Choir,
John Blakemore, conductor.

Heroes, Lost and Fallen
Ensemble: Band
Publisher: Hal Leonard, Inc., 1991
Premiere: May 7, 1989. Ann Arbor (MI) Concert Band,
Victor Bordo, conductor.

Internal Combustion
Ensemble: Symphonic Band
Publisher: C. Alan Publications, 2000
Premiere: Dec. 1, 1999. New York State Schools of
Music Association All-State Symphonic
Band, Jerry Junkin, conductor.

Intrada Jubilante
Ensemble: Band
Publisher: C. Alan Publications, 1999
Premiere: May 4, 1979. Webster Stanley Middle
School Band, Oshkosh, WI, Roger Lalk, conductor.

Lamb of God
Ensemble: Band
Publisher: C. Alan Publications, 2001
Premiere: Jan. 26, 2001. Illinois Music Educator Association All-State Conference. Southern Illinois University-Edwardsville Wind Symphony, John Bell, conductor.

A Light Unto the Darkness
Ensemble: Band
Publisher: C. Alan Publications, 1998
Premiere: April 16, 1998. University of Oklahoma; Mt. Pleasant (MI) High School Wind Ensemble, Roger Sampson, conductor.

New Century Dawn
Ensemble: Symphonic Band
Publisher: C. Alan Publications, 1999
Premiere: July 6, 1999. 6th International WASBE conference; Oklahoma State University Wind Ensemble, Joseph Missal, conductor.

A Parting Blessing
Ensemble: Band with optional choir
Publisher: C. Alan Publications, 2002
Premiere: May 19, 2002. Apple Valley (MN) High School Wind Ensemble, Craig Kirchoff, conductor.

Prophecy of the Earth
Ensemble: Band and Pipe Organ
Publisher: C. Alan Publications, 2000
Premiere: May 20, 1993. Dallas, TX. J. J. Pearce High School Band, Matthew McInturf, conductor. Paul Riedo, organ.

Proud and Immortal
Ensemble: Band
Publisher: C. Alan Publications, 2001
Premiere: Nov. 15, 2001. Oklahoma State University Wind Ensemble, Joseph Missal, conductor.

Return to Innocence
Ensemble: Choir and Percussion
Publisher: Moon of Hope Publications, 1995
Premiere: Apr. 11, 1993. Carnegie Hall, NY. Central Michigan University Choir and Percussion, Nina Nash-Robertson, conductor.

Revelation
Ensemble: Band
Publisher: Hal Leonard, Inc., 1989
Premiere: May 22, 1983. Grand Ledge (MI) High School Symphonic Wind Ensemble, Michael Kaufman, conductor.

Sub-Saharan Rhythm
Ensemble: Band-grade 3
Publisher: C. Alan Publications, 1998
Premiere: March 19, 1998. Traverse City (MI) East J.H. Symphonic Band, Peter Deneen, conductor.

Symphonic Proclamation
Ensemble: Band
Publisher: Jenson Publications, Inc., 1979 <OUT OF PRINT>
Premiere: Nov. 16, 1977. Michigan State University Symphonic Band, Kenneth Bloomquist, conductor.

With Heart and Voice
Ensemble: Band
Publisher: C. Alan Publications, 2001
Premiere: May 20, 2001. Apple Valley (MN) High School Wind Ensemble, Scott A. Jones, conductor.

To be released

Aerodynamics
Ensemble: Band
Publisher: C. Alan Publications, 2003
Premiere: Spring, 2003. Sinclair Community College, Dayton, OH

LifeSongs
Ensemble: Wind Ensemble, Choir, Soprano and Baritone
Publisher: C. Alan Publications, 2003
Premiere: Spring, 2003. Illinois State University Wind Ensemble and Choir; Stephen Steele, conductor. Michelle Vought, soprano. John Koch, baritone.

Music for Large Ensembles with Soloists/Concerti

Concerto for Alto Saxophone and Wind Ensemble
Ensemble: Alto Saxophone and Wind Ensemble
Publisher: MMB Music, 1990 (Rental)
Premiere: Mar. 17, 1990. Central Michigan University Wind Ensemble, John Williamson, conductor. John Nichol, alto saxophone soloist.

Concerto for Bass Trombone and Wind Ensemble
Ensemble: Bass Trombone and Wind Ensemble
Publisher: Carl Fischer, Inc., 1986 (Rental)
Premiere: June 4, 1981. Michigan State University, Stanley DeRusha, conductor. Curtis Olson, bass trombone soloist.

Concerto for Piano and Percussion Orchestra
Ensemble: Solo Piano and Percussion Ensemble
Publisher: C. Alan Publications, 2003
Premiere: Nov. 12, 2002. University of North Carolina-Greensboro Percussion Ensemble, Cort McClaren, conductor. Andrew Willis, piano.

Concerto for Woodwind Quintet and Winds
Ensemble: Woodwind Quintet and Wind Ensemble
Publisher: C. Alan Publications (Pending)
Premiere: Jan. 13, 1995. MENC, Indianapolis, IN. Powers Quintet, Central Michigan University Wind Ensemble, John E. Williamson, conductor.

Double Star
Ensemble: Solo Piano, solo Clarinet and Chamber Winds
Publisher: C. Alan Publications, 2003
Premiere: Oct. 16, 2002. University of Miami Premiere Winds, Maggie Donaghue, clarinet. Ellen Rowe, piano. Gary Green, conductor.

Gate to Heaven
Ensemble: Solo Marimba and Percussion Ensemble
Publisher: C. Alan Publications, 1998
Premiere: Nov., 1998. Percussive Arts Society International Convention in Orlando, FL. University of North Carolina – Greensboro Percussion Ensemble, Cort McClaren, conductor. Nathan Daughtrey, soloist.

Interplay for Piano Four Hands and Orchestra
Ensemble: Piano, four Hands and Orchestra
Publisher: C. Alan Publications, 2002
Premiere: July 7, 1996. Czech Radio Symphony, Vladimir Valek, conductor; Daniel Koppelman/ Ruth Neville, pianists

Quintessence
Ensemble: Brass Quintet, Solo Percussion, and Band
Publisher: C. Alan Publications, 1997
Premiere: Feb., 1997. Illinois State University Wind Symphony, Stephen J. Steele, conductor. ISU Brass Quintet & Dave Collier, soloist.

Vintage
Ensemble: Solo Euphonium and Band
Publisher: T.U.B.A. Press, 1991
Premiere: Jan. 18, 1991. Ann Arbor, MI. Big Rapids High School Band, Kent Boulton, conductor. Ed. Mallet, euphonium soloist.

When Speaks the Signal-Trumpet Tone
Ensemble: Solo Trumpet and Wind Orchestra
Publisher: C. Alan Publications, 1999
Premiere: Mar. 30, 1999. University of Georgia Wind Ensemble, H. Dwight Satterwhite, conductor. Fred Mills, trumpet.

American Counterpoint
Ensemble: Flute, Clarinet and Alto Saxophone
Publisher: C. Alan Publications, 2002
Premiere: Feb. 18, 2003. Central Michigan University. Joanna White, flute. Kennen White, clarinet. John Nichol, Alto Saxophone.

Baker's Dozen
Ensemble: Horn and Piano
Publisher: C. Alan Publications, 2002
Premiere: June 7, 2001. International Horn Convention, Kalamazoo, MI. Bruce Bonnell, horn. Rebecca Wilt, piano.

Blue Lake Fantasies
Ensemble: Solo Euphonium
Publisher: TUBA Press, 1999
Premiere: Aug. 12, 1995. Blue Lake Fine Arts Camp (MI). Brian Bowman, Euphonium.

Dance of Redemption
Ensemble: Solo Marimba
Publisher: C. Alan Publications, 1998
Premiere: May, 1999. Jeff White, soloist.

Diversive Elements
Ensemble: Tuba, Euphonium and Piano
Publisher: TUBA Press, 1999
Premiere: Jan. 28, 1998. Michigan State University. Ed Mallett, euphonium. Philip Sinder, tuba. Jun Okada, piano.

Divertimento for Horn, Tuba and Piano
Ensemble: Horn, Tuba and Piano
Publisher: T.U.B.A. Press, 1994
Premiere: Oct. 3, 1993. Michigan State University. Janine Gaboury-Sly, horn. Philip Sinder, tuba. Deborah Moriarty, piano.

Echoes
Ensemble: Brass and Percussion
Publisher: C. Alan Publications, 2002
Premiere: Jan. 29, 1993. Central Michigan University Brass and Percussion, John Williamson, conductor.

Mindset
Ensemble: Solo Alto Saxophone
Publisher: Dorn Publications, 2000
Premiere: Sept. 26, 1996. Central Michigan University; John Nichol, alto saxophone.

Normandy Beach
Ensemble: Marimba Quartet and Percussion
Publisher: C. Alan Publications, 1995
Premiere: Dec. 15, 1994. Chicago, IL. North Farmington (MI) High School Percussion Ensemble, James Coviak, conductor.

Paschal Dances
Ensemble: Percussion Ensemble
Publisher: C. Alan Publications, 1994
Premiere: Apr. 15, 1986. Central Michigan University Percussion Ensemble, David Gillingham, conductor.

Ruffle and Flourish
Ensemble: Brass and Percussion
Publisher: C. Alan Publications, 2000
Premiere: Apr. 23, 1995. Michigan State University Wind Symphony, John L. Whitwell, conductor.

Sacrificial Rite
Ensemble: Percussion Ensemble
Publisher: C. Alan Publications, 1994
Premiere: Nov. 16, 1993. Central Michigan University Percussion Ensemble, Robert Hohner, conductor.

Saxophone Sonata
Ensemble: Alto Sax and Piano
Publisher: MMB Music, 1989
Premiere: Aug. 11, 1988. World Saxophone Congress, Japan. John Nichol, alto saxophone. David Gillingham, piano

Serenade for Winds and Percussion
Ensemble: Winds and Percussion
Publisher: Southern Music Co., 1996
Premiere: Mar. 1990. MENC Convention, Washington D.C. University of Georgia Wind and Percussion Faculty, Dwight Satterwhite, conductor.

Sonata for Bass Trombone and Piano
Ensemble: Bass Trombone with Piano
Publisher: ITA Press, 1999
Premiere: May 30, 1985. International Trombone Workshop, Nashville. Curtis Olson, bass trombone. Barry Scates, piano.

Sonata in F# Minor
Ensemble: Cello and Piano
Publisher: C. Alan Publications, 2002
Premiere: pending

Spiritual Dances
Ensemble: Oboe with Marimba Quartet
Publisher: C. Alan Publications, 2001
Premiere: April 20, 2001. Central Michigan University Marimba Quartet, Jennifer Morrison, soloist.

Stained Glass
Ensemble: Percussion Ensemble
Publisher: C. Alan Publications, 1994
Premiere: May 22, 1991. University of Utah Percussion Ensemble, Douglas Wolf, conductor.

Triplex
Ensemble: Brass and Percussion
Publisher: Music for Brass and Percussion, 1984 <OUT OF PRINT>
Premiere: Nov. 17, 1978. Michigan State University Brass and Percussion, Thad Hegerburg, conductor.

Visions
Ensemble: Saxophone Quartet
Publisher: Dorn Publications, 2000
Premiere: Mar. 10, 1992. Central Michigan University Student Saxophone Quartet

Waking Angels
Ensemble: Chamber Winds and Percussion
Publisher: C. Alan Publications
Premiere: Feb.26-Mar. 1, 1997. College Band Directors National Association National Convention, Athens, GA. Dave Collier, percussion soloist.

SUPPLEMENTAL BIBLIOGRAPHY

Batcheller, J. C. (2000). Waking Angels, A Light Unto the Darkness, and A Crescent Still Abides: the elegiac music of David R. Gillingham. (Doctoral dissertation, University of Oklahoma, 2000). *Dissertation Abstracts International*, 61, 416A.

Bradley, R. C. (2000). A study of the use of programmatic and liturgical themes in selected wind ensemble compositions of David Gillingham. (Doctoral dissertation, University of Washington, 2000). *Dissertation Abstracts International*, 61, 2093A.

Gillingham, D. R. (1981). Concerto for Bass Trombone and Wind Ensemble. (Doctoral dissertation, Michigan State University, 1981). *Dissertation Abstracts International*, 41, 3774A.

Schnoor, N. H., (1999). An analysis of David Gillingham's Prophecy of the Earth. *Journal of Band Research*, 34, 63–82.

John Harbison

by
Judson Scott

I am simply not interested in the projection of personal angst....Composition can be an escape from self-absorption, an actualization of something larger, and a whole lot more interesting than personality.—John Harbison[1]

Born in Orange, New Jersey, on December 20th, 1938, John Harbison grew up in the rarified air surrounding Princeton; his father was a professor of history at the local university, his mother wrote for magazines. Music was an integral part of the household and he received additional influence from his father's colleague, Roger Sessions, whose music remains an important influence on Harbison's compositional style. He studied several instruments throughout his youth, including violin, viola, piano, voice and tuba. Though he now performs rarely in public he can still occasionally be found at the piano or with a viola in his hands.[2]

Harbison graduated in 1960 from Harvard, where he studied with Walter Piston and with Boris Blacher in Berlin while on a Paine Traveling Fellowship. He received an MFA from Princeton in 1963, where he studied outside of the curriculum with Roger Sessions and Earl Kim. From 1963–68 he was a Fellow at Harvard and joined the faculty of the Massachusetts Institute of Technology in 1962 where he has taught ever since, interrupted only by residencies with the Pittsburgh Symphony from 1982–84 and the Los Angeles Philharmonic from 1985–1988.

His numerous awards include a Guggenheim Fellowship (1978), the Kennedy Center-Friedeim Award (1980), a Pulitzer Prize (1987) for his cantata, The Flight into Egypt, and a MacArthur Fellowship in 1989. He has received numerous commissions including one from the Fromm Foundation, the Koussevitsky Foundation, the Boston Symphony Orchestra and the Metropolitan Opera Company. During the 1999–2000 academic year he served as the Karel Husa Visiting Professor of Music at the Ithaca College School of Music.

In addition to composing, Mr. Harbison has committed considerable energy to conducting. As an undergraduate, he led the Harvard Bach Society Orchestra and later, while at Princeton, the Princeton University Orchestra. He has conducted many prestigious ensembles including the Boston Symphony Chamber Players, the San Francisco and Boston Symphony Orchestras, though perhaps more important to him and to his compositional life are the long-term relationships he has maintained with the Cantata Singers and Emmanuel Music, the ensemble in residence at Emmanuel Episcopal Church in Boston. His cantata, The Flight into Egypt was written for the Cantata Singers and he has written several vocal works for Emmanuel Music.

While the facts of Harbison's life are relatively easily to obtain, a sense of the man is somewhat more difficult to discover. He is an intensely private individual who nonetheless takes an active role in the world around him. It would be unfair to think of him as private in the sense of being reclusive; he simply has more important issues to address than the merely personal. He readily addresses societal concerns both through music and through direct action. He considers participating in the Freedom Summer Project in the early days of the civil rights movement as one of the few truly pivotal events of his life. More recently he addressed homelessness. Looking at the Christmas story from an unusual angle, his cantata, The Flight into Egypt, focuses not on the birth of Jesus, but rather on the subsequent flight from Herod. Not content to address the issue merely through music, Harbison took more direct action by donating his fee to a Boston homeless shelter.

Guiding young composers has also been a focus for Harbison. He serves on the board of directors of the American Academy in Rome, the Copland Fund (as president), and the Koussevitzky Foundation, as well as juries of the Fromm Foundation and the American Academy of Arts and Letters. During the composition of his cello concerto for Yo-Yo Ma, Harbison arranged an early reading with three of his students, one for each movement. Commenting on this rehearsal, Mr. Ma was quoted in the Boston Globe:

"I have always been impressed by John's sense of community and the selfless way he made this happen to benefit the music students at MIT." [3]

The essay by David St. George hosted at the Schirmer web site offers these insights regarding Mr. Harbison:

In the deepest sense of the word Harbison is a creator—as composer, as conductor, even in ordinary conversation, where an unremarkable question may well elicit the most thought-provoking of responses, as he typically brings together several seemingly unrelated ideas, thereby opening up an unforeseen path of thought. [4]

COMPOSITIONAL APPROACH

It may be a risk to make a complex shape but it is also a risk, and I believe a far greater one, to write a very direct and clear melody that you can absolutely stand behind.[5]

If one were to listen to the major works for winds by Joseph Schwantner, David Maslanka or Michael Colgrass, each composer's distinctive voice is easily discernable. However, upon listening to John Harbison's three major works for winds, *Music for Eighteen Winds* (1985), *Three City Blocks* (1993) and *Olympic Dances* (1997), one is perhaps more struck by their marked differences than their similarities. The diversity found in his music has led certain critics to label Harbison as an eclectic composer, a label that Harbison rejects. A more discriminating examination of his music reveals a composer with a consistent method who is simply not afraid to address a wide range of material.

Well I don't juxtapose within pieces, so I am always puzzled by [the label eclectic]. I go to some trouble to make the transitions between sections very smooth. In *Great Gatsby* people mention all the different styles, but the thing about that piece is that all the vocabulary is the same. Its really the opposite of what some composers are doing now with the sort of shock juxtapositions. Bill Bolcom does that very well, that's the whole basis of Bill's kind of music; the shocking change from one vocabulary to another, and Mike Daugherty does some of that. And that is interesting as one possible approach, but it is exactly the opposite of my intention. I create a vocabulary that can encompass everything in a work and then try to hide the distance between. In the *Gatsby* where there is period pop music going on which cycles right into the basic sound of the opera, and the only way I felt that I could do that would be if they share motives and chords.[6]

One of the hallmarks of this composer is in his formal approach, in which Harbison places blocks of differing thematic materials next to each other, not in a floating, passive Messiaenic sense, but rather with an active, sometimes confrontational approach. The differences among these works lie in the specifics of harmonic and melodic structure. This is not to say that there are no continuities in the harmonic or melodic approach in Harbison's works, but rather that he lets each work shape its own sound world from the broad pallet of compositional materials that he has at his disposal. He comments on the influences for the works for winds and the resultant distinctiveness of each piece:

I know some wind works pretty well. I know the Stravinsky *Symphonies*. I know Varese *Octandre* which is sort of almost a wind piece. They've tended—and the Mozart C minor serenade—to have served as my kind of anchors. But in the three wind pieces that I have written the idea was to work with a different ensemble each time. And to make a different sort of piece....[7]

In lectures given at Tanglewood and later published in *Perspectives of New Music* as *Six Tanglewood Talks*, Harbison divides the composing world into two categories: personality composers and philosophic composers, placing himself in the philosophic camp:

I want to be a composer of the philosophic mode, which I think requires a sophisticated harmonic language, an ability to re-imagine melody as a guiding force, an inventive formal sense, a willingness to be misunderstood, and much patience. [8]

This statement makes clear Harbison's priorities for composing music—priorities which can be clearly heard in *Olympic Dances* and are evident in *Three City Blocks* and *Music for Eighteen Winds* as well.

Harbison's admiration for the music of Heinrich Schutz also provides an insight into his compositional approach:

To me this is the music that gets the most expressive force from the least expenditure of surface energy. His notes just seem to come up very big...he never seems to over work, but completely gets it across. The difficulty with him...is [that this music] remains a music in which you have to hear the syntax. There is a context for it and when you achieve the context you are completely bowled over...but outside of it, I'm afraid, because it isn't graphic in a violent way at all, you might be just left outside. I think that it is the kind [of music] about which once you get the revelation of how it works, it becomes just as important as anything...for a long time that has been my experience of it.[9]

Though exuberant works such as the last movement of the *Concerto for Double Brass Choir and Orchestra* and *Three City Blocks* might not show this fascination to the fullest, *Music for Eighteen Winds* and especially *Olympic Dances* indeed succeed at achieving "...the most expressive force from the least expenditure of surface energy."

Three Works for Winds

It is beyond the scope of this short chapter to examine in detail Harbison's three works for winds, though a brief look at representative passages from *Music for Eighteen Winds* and *Three City Blocks* and a more extensive consideration of *Olympic Dances* should provide a starting point for approaching each work and give a larger sense of the composer's style. For a more complete analysis of each work the reader is referred to the article by Jerome Markoch (*Music for Eighteen Winds*) and the dissertations of Robert Spittal (*Three City Blocks*) and the author of this chapter (*Olympic Dances*).

In the *Music for Eighteen Winds*, Harbison approaches his material with a rather formalistic method: repetitions are exact and his pitch selection is governed by a clear system. Though the work is not serial, Harbison does utilize some twelve-tone methodology to create a consistent sound world. By contrast, in *Three City Blocks* he relies on traditional harmonic root motion; in *Olympic Dances*, while using traditionally rooted harmonies, he clouds their function with inversions and added tones.

Music for Eighteen Winds was composed in 1986 on a commission from the Massachusetts Institute of Technology

Council for the Arts. The commission stipulated that the work had to be composed for, and premiered by, one of the performing groups at MIT. Harbison's choice of eighteen winds was largely pragmatic:

> It was the ensemble that I felt I could assemble the strongest personnel for. In a way, sort of moving outside of the structures of MIT at the time. . .the MIT chamber music society, which is the group that initially put the piece on, was already at that time a sort of student/faculty group. And it was assembled ad hoc for each concert. We had about half students and half faculty for that concert and I was pretty sure of what kind of group we could get. Obviously eighteen winds is a piece where every player has to be able to play. [10]

Music for Eighteen Winds is in one movement that is clearly divided into two sections—a quick rhythmic section that Harbison characterizes as "urban" is followed by a more relaxed cantabile section which Harbison characterizes as "rural." The work requires strong players in every chair and poses sophisticated rhythmic challenges such as unison rhythms shifting among quarter notes, quarter note triplets, and quarter note quintuplets. *Olympic Dances* and *Music for Eighteen Winds* are similar in that the difficulties tend to be issues of ensemble as opposed to extreme technical demands on individual players.

The opening measures of *Music for Eighteen Winds* (see figure 1) set the atmosphere for the first half of the work.

The lack of a clear melodic idea, the static harmony and the irregular, shifting accents focus the listener's attention on the rhythmic energy in the music. This work's energy does not express a sense of driving motion so much as it sounds an alarm. Though he focuses initially on rhythm, Harbison does not neglect melody and harmony as structural elements in *Music for Eighteen Winds*. The quartal construction of the harmonies in the upper and lower choirs hints at the systematic approach to pitch selection that one finds elsewhere in this work. About the structure of *Music for Eighteen Winds*, Harbison states:

> [. . .in *Music for Eighteen Winds*], especially in the first movement, I was thinking in blocks of highly characterized, but not very differentiated material. There is also a rather curious thing going on; I had a basic shape, a model from which all of the material is derived, but it never appeared in the work so there is a sense in that piece of a circulation around material that you never hear in its original form. I think that is part of the reason that much of the repetition is literal. In order to make the form clear the identity of the material had to be not at all ambiguous...that goes to the source of the way I think about harmony. [11]

The second example (see figure 2) from *Music for Eighteen Winds* is the primary 'chorale' theme from the second section of the work. Here Harbison's attraction to a systemic approach is clearly visible. The soprano and alto voices are constructed from three pairs of pitches (E–C, Eb–Bb and

FIGURE 1. Music for Eighteen Winds, m. 1–6
Music for Eighteen Winds
Copyright © 1988 by Associated Music Publishers, Inc. (BMI)
International Copyright Secured. All Rights Reserved. Reprinted by Permission.

FIGURE 2. Music for Eighteen Winds, m. 180–184
Music for Eighteen Winds
Copyright © 1988 by Associated Music Publishers, Inc. (BMI)
International Copyright Secured. All Rights Reserved. Reprinted by Permission.

Db–Gb). The soprano line begins with the first note of each pair, subsequently continuing with the bottom pitch, while the alto voice uses the top pitches transposed down an octave. The tenor and bass voices are treated similarly though only using two pairs of pitches (D–Ab and B–F).[12] The use of these paired notes creates a consistent harmonic language without reference to traditional harmonic structures. These pairs of tones present 10 of the 12 available pitches; Harbison breaks the purity of this approach on the fourth eighth note in measure 182 to include the two missing pitches. In *Three City Blocks* and *Olympic Dances*, Harbison's approach is less systemic and more based in traditional functional harmony, albeit with his distinctive flavoring.

The wind ensembles of the New England Conservatory, the University of California, Florida State University, Ohio State University, the University of Michigan, the University of Southern California and the United States Air Force Band commissioned *Three City Blocks*. The work was completed in 1991 and was premiered on August 2, 1993 by the Air Force Band in Fort Smith, Arkansas. Steeped in the vernacular language of big band jazz, this must be considered Harbison's most approachable work for winds. Though formally a purely classical work, the language will seem familiar to most casual listeners. Scored for a full concert band, *Three City Blocks* will hide deficiencies of ensemble playing that *Music for Eighteen Winds* or *Olympic Dances* would ruthlessly expose. In fact, Harbison almost invites a certain roughness of approach:

> If *Three City Blocks* is played a little raw it sounds better…I've heard some really good performances of *Three City Blocks* where, in a sense, even the style of the piece welcomes a kind of roughness. [13]

In *Three City Blocks* Harbison clearly suggests the harmonic and rhythmic vocabulary of a swing orchestra. Harbison creates a rhythmic vocabulary that convincingly mimics the rhythmic inflections of swing, therefore the rhythms must be performed as strictly notated and not swung in the usual jazz manner. The progression II7–V7–I must be considered the most important progression in jazz; Harbison uses this as his starting point, though he extends this traditional progression almost completely around the circle of fifths (see figure 3). For the first three measures the root function is clearly articulated by the string bass and trombone. This strong movement defines the function of the harmonies, which often merely hint at traditional structures. Harbison comments on the formal construction of the work:

> *Three City Blocks* is much more concerned with very classical formal structure. The first movement is meant to be tonally and thematically a sonata structure. And the last movement is a rondo with very clearly differentiated material. In *Three City Blocks* the harmonic vocabulary is pretty consistently based on the seventh chord…I was very aware of making the chords quite clear as to root function and avoiding the kind of 'offshoot' function that goes on in *Olympic Dances*. But that had to do with the formal outline, because I needed that to clarify the sonata form.

Olympic Dances, completed in 1997, was commissioned by a College Band Directors National Association consortium of twelve wind ensembles. Harbison comments on the commission:

> When the College Band Directors asked me to do a piece for dancers and winds it immediately suggested something classical, not our musical eighteenth century, but an imaginative vision of ancient worlds. The clear, un-upholstered timbres of the winds—not colored by the throbbing emotive vibratos of our modern string players—playing in small, unconventional chamber subgroups, constituted my first musical images. Along with these I thought of an imagined harmony between dance, sport and sound that we can intuit from serene oranges and blacks on Greek vases, the celebration of bodies in motion that we see in the matchless sculpture of ancient times, and perhaps most important to this piece, the celebration of the ideal tableau, the moment frozen in time, that is present still in

FIGURE 3. City Blocks, m. 1–6
Three City Blocks
Copyright © 1993 by Associated Music Publishers, Inc. (BMI)
International Copyright Secured. All Rights Reserved. Reprinted by Permission.

the friezes that adorn the temples, and in the architecture of the temples themselves.[14]

The work is in four movements: *Prelude, Epithalamion, Variations,* and *Finale.* Though movements one, two, and four use contrasting themes to create structure, these themes are not used in opposition to create a dynamic form such as sonata-allegro, but rather exist next to each other in relative structural comfort. The variation movement is clearly framed—a twelve bar theme with six variations, each of which is exactly twelve bars.

When confronted with a large ensemble work in four movements it is impossible not to think of traditional symphonic form. Though the first movement is not an *allegro,* it does lay out the important arguments of the work as a whole by establishing the basic harmonic vocabulary and the primacy of a *cantus firmus* style of melody. The second movement easily takes the place of the traditional slow movement. It has a pastoral air that makes it the most relaxed of the movements; the harmonies, though structured from the same material as the first movement, are generally stripped of much of their dissonance and the melodic material is the most purely diatonic. Comparing the third movement to a *scherzo* may seem more of an analytical reach but in fact both serve a similar psychological function for the listener. A *scherzo* commonly offers relief from the rigor of the outer movements; the third movement's variations offer a framework within which the listener may puzzle out connections to the theme.

The finale is perhaps the most serious departure from the traditional symphonic framework; though fast and occasionally ebullient, it is by far the largest movement, not only the in number of measures and in duration, but also in terms of its scale. While the earlier movements have presented material, it is only in the fourth movement that Harbison develops this material, shifting important dramatic weight traditionally found in the first movement to the fourth movement.

Harbison declares that the idea of idealized Greek motion was key to his imagining the piece. Because this work has such strong formal construction, however, one may reasonably wonder about the suitability of the work for choreography. In fact the movement on the stage would seem to be a distraction from the work's subtle constructions. Harbison has said that the Pilobolus dance company was the perfect choice of dancers for this work in that their static human sculptures paralleled his image of Greek friezes. One must conclude that a more athletic choreography would be wholly inappropriate for the work. It is also easy to assume that the work would pose difficulties for the dancers that parallel those faced by the musicians.

The first movement is built on the alternation of two themes. Harbison refers to the first as a *cantus firmus* (first occurring in measures 1–3) and the second as a mono-linear theme (first occurring in measures 24–44).[15] The only additional material is a series of sustained harmonies which function as a *codetta* to the A theme. The *codetta* appears twice, in measures 6–11 and 84–89; although harmonically different, its use as a gesture is unmistakable.

The form of the movement may be described as: A A *codetta* A B A A A B A *codetta.* The *cantus firmus* appears completely seven times, though never twice in exactly the same form; the rhythms and harmonies are always slightly varied to create a subtly shifting effect. Through these changes to the *cantus,* Harbison is able to create the sense that the music is searching for its ideal presentation. This movement is not a discussion between two themes; the function of the mono-linear theme is to provide contrast to the *cantus.* For this reason the mono-linear theme has a texture and melodic shape that is clearly separate from the cantus, though the theme itself does not have a easily recognisable profile. The form of the movement is created not by motivic development, but rather by the transformation of the *cantus.* With the last statement of the *cantus* the listener is left with the sense that the it has not yet fully achieved its ideal potential. This final statement, which begins to fulfill the promise of the cantus, takes a chromatic turn away from the tonic, sinking a half step into dissonance.

This lack of conclusion is of course entirely intentional. While cyclical works have been around since the early romantics, Harbison may be creating a high-water mark for the concept. Many composers have used a return of a first movement theme to round out and unify a work; Harbison does not bring back the *cantus,* but rather creates in the listener a psychological need for the return of the *cantus* that is not fulfilled until the final movement where he provides a surrogate for the *cantus* by reworking his fundamental harmonic structure. In this way, Harbison propels the listener through the entire work to the last movement.

The harmonic language of *Olympic Dances* is certainly tonal and rests to a surprising degree on traditional harmonic function (or at least the implication of traditional harmonic function). Though employing harmonic structures beyond the scope of traditional harmony, Harbison nonetheless makes strong reference to traditional structures as the foundation for his more complex harmonies. When describing his harmonic language, Harbison makes reference to traditional structures in a somewhat oblique manner.

> In fact, all the way through the harmony of the first movement there are a lot of the triadic chords that have an added fourth. And the sense of that has a lot to do with the sense of everything tending to push toward the subdominant or to combine the subdominant with the tonic.[16]

Harbison identifies the tonic harmony of *Olympic Dances* as the chord in measures 3 and 6 (see figure 4 below).[17] A convenient way to conceive of this harmony is as a major chord and as a series of fourths built on the same root as the triad. Just as composers manipulating traditional harmonies used the different chord qualities available to them (i.e. major, minor, augmented, etc.), Harbison makes use of chromatic alteration to expand his palate of harmonic color. He also presents this sonority in incomplete forms. For example the Epithalamion begins with a harmonic construction built from the bass of root, fifth, fourth, root.

Analyzing the tonic harmony from traditional function reveals it to have a remarkably high degree of ambiguity. Harbison defines the root as C, though out of context one could easily wonder if F were the root. The addition of the minor seventh, B flat, suggests that this chord has a dominant function rather than a tonic function. Harbison describes the tonic harmony this way:

> . . .the governing sonority of the harmony in the first movement is just a kind of vocabulary which seems to be a complex triadic sonority with the lowered seventh and the added fourth as part of the assumption. For instance, the first big cadence chord in measure 6 could be considered the emblematic chord of that movement; it has the C notes in it, the B♭ and the F. But it becomes not the tendency chord in tonal terms, but stands for the conclusion chord in the vocabulary of this movement. [18]

A full harmonic analysis is beyond the scope of this chapter, though as the *cantus* is the primary material of the movement—not merely in being presented first, but as the home of the primary argument of the movement—it deserves detailed consideration. In the first three measures, Harbison has intentionally clouded his harmonic vocabulary with the addition of non-harmonic tones. His harmonic method is clearer in the second presentation of the *cantus firmus* (measures 4–6, see figure 4), which allows for a more straightforward analysis. The basic harmonic trajectory in the cantus is movement from a 'dominant' harmony in measure 4, repeated in measure 5 to the tonic harmony in measure 6. Both the dominant and tonic harmonies are pure presentations of the emblematic or tonic harmony.

The downbeat of measure four is the 'emblematic' sonority built on G. Harbison has placed the fourths in series from the bass note (i.e., G, C, F). This configuration is relatively stable, though less stable than when voiced with the fifth in the lowest two voices. The next chord could be built from the bass note as an A chord with an added second and added sixth, though it fits more comfortably into Harbison's vocabulary to think of it as rooted on 'F'—therefore it appears in first inver-

sion (IV$_{6532}$? Perhaps IV$_{62}$ for short?). Viewed this way we have an F triad (F, A, C) and a series of fourths built on F (F, B, E). The B natural is of course not a perfect fourth above the F, but rather an augmented fourth. Had Harbison used the B flat he would have moved this chord closer to the tonic; by using the B natural, he keeps the chord more in the sphere of the dominant. The last two chords of measure 4 make Harbison's intent clearer. Still fundamentally rooted on F, the final chord of measure 4 becomes an almost pure tertian harmony.

Measure 5 begins with the same chord that started this phrase. After the initial chord of the measure, Harbison introduces the B flat into the harmony and moves the music out of the sphere of the dominant and closer to the tonic. The second chord of measure 5 is the same as the second chord of measure 4, though now with the B flat instead of the B natural (i.e., in the sphere of the tonic rather than the dominant). Chord 3 of measure 5 is perfectly in line with Harbison's harmonic language, though a chord built on the flat seventh of the scale is little used in traditional harmony.

In the last chord of measure 5, Harbison uses a true dominant: the G chord includes a B natural and is therefore clearly in contrast to the tonic sonority. Though lacking the seventh commonly employed in a dominant harmony, Harbison's use of the B natural makes the function of this chord clear. The added fourth (C), though adding some ambiguity, keeps the harmonic color consistent with the harmonic language that Harbison is establishing. Measure 6 comes to rest on the tonic chord. Because Harbison has included the fourth scale degree, F, in his tonic harmony he avoids that pitch in his dominant harmony.

The harmonic similarities between these two presentations of the cantus are clearly evident. In both instances they begin with a dominant function chord on 'G' and move to the tonic, 'C', on the third bar of the phrase. Both presentations of the cantus use B natural for the first 5 chords and progress to B flat as they near the tonic, emphasizing the movement from the dominant to the tonic. In these first three bars Harbison clouds the harmonic vocabulary with the addition of non-harmonic tones. The 'A/G' combination can be considered a double pedal point; one of the notes is in the harmony, but usually not both. The harmonies are clarified in measures

FIGURE 4. Olympic Dances, m. 1–6
Olympic Dances

4–6 where Harbison removes these non-harmonic tones (see figure 4).

Though *Olympic Dances* is orchestrated for a large ensemble, Harbison rarely brings all of the players together for *tutti* expressions before the final movement. Instead, he utilizes the instruments as smaller chamber ensembles in various combinations. It is not uncommon for the musical thread to be carried by only two or three musicians for several phrases. In this regard *Olympic Dances* is similar to *Music for Eighteen Winds*, which Harbison describes as a piece of large chamber music:

> *Music for Eighteen Winds* is much more—even more so than this [*Olympic Dances*]—a big piece of chamber music, whereas this piece has a lot more homophonic music in it, sort of choral in the sense that I associated that with the kind of classic Greek presentation kind of mode that I see on the paintings and the sculpture. [19]

In *Three City Blocks*, Harbison was not afraid to draw on unusual instruments such as sirens, police-whistle, and a thunder-sheet. That he chose not to in this later work clearly shows that he was creating a different orchestration palette. In a somewhat unusual orchestrational choice, Harbison groups all of the instruments—except the horns—in threes. He chose groupings of three to help elucidate trio sonata-like texture that he employs throughout the work. This elucidation of form is especially clear in the variations where entire variations are carried by like instruments.

While the first movement has a few moments of large orchestral effect, most of the movement employs varying chamber combinations. The opening *fortissimo* of the winds is the largest dynamic of the movement—though it employs no brass, certainly an unusual choice for an intense dynamic moment. For the remainder of the movement Harbison demonstrates even greater orchestrational restraint. The second movement avoids the use of a full ensemble entirely, exploring chamber combinations of as few as five players for long periods of time. In the variations Harbison explores the leanest of textures, with as few as two players doubling one melodic line. In the variations, Harbison also employs larger textures, as if to admit the possibility of a full ensemble *forte*. At the opening of the fourth movement, though still eschewing a full *tutti*, he nonetheless makes a strong presentation of the first theme. In the finale, having previously explored the most transparent textures, Harbison reaches the full ensemble *tutti* that has been denied throughout the work.

PERFORMANCE CONSIDERATIONS

Harbison drew inspiration for *Olympic Dances* from the large amphorae of classic Greece. He is evoking a somewhat austere, classical world which should have an impact on the interpretation of the work, whether or not a performance makes any reference to the Greek images through dance.

Harbison states:

> I was marked at a very young listening age with an almost visual imagination of what ancient Greece was like, which was created for me by Stravinsky as much as the prairies were created by *Billy the Kid* or *Appalachian Spring*; and they're both imaginative constructs. I think that Copland's America is unbelievably convincing but it came out of his imagination, and he did it in Brooklyn, New York. I think that but for Stravinsky and other people who immersed themselves in the sort of evocation of the ancient world in the early part of the 20th century, we wouldn't necessarily imagine the ancient world in the way that we do. But when I think of it, I always think of Stravinsky's *Apollo* and *Oedipus* and something about his imagination has for me created something of that world. [20]

Harbison has taken care in his orchestration decisions to facilitate an objective approach to performance though the performers may need some direction in this regard. Most important melodic lines are doubled either at the unison or octave which makes overt or personal emotional display inappropriate. Passages where one performer has an extended melodic line that is not doubled tend to be too rapid for overt sentimentality, i.e. the triplet embellishments in the *Epithalamion*.

Similarly, Harbison divides up solo passages to avoid personal display and to further promote ensemble unity of purpose. In the *Prelude*, from measures 26–38, Harbison divides three phrases among the three trumpeters, giving one phrase to each player. This keeps all of the players involved in the performance and also promotes unity of purpose; one hopes that the performers will instinctively match styles. Also the extended mono-linear theme in the first movement (measures 24–44 and 64–80) is doubled at the octave which also helps to stave off inappropriate emotional display.

The music should not be presented in an artificially dry manner, but one cannot deny the objective quality of the music which begs for a clean presentation. Harbison states:

> One of the distractions of the piece might be that you do get wound up in trying to get it really, really clean and you can end up playing in a way that it is too segmented. Because part of the difficulty of the first movement, for instance, is to make the phrases under the cantus hold together as phrases; the melodic material is just so simple. [21]

Though Harbison has written music for student musicians, specifically *Fantasia on a Ground*, *Inventions for a Young Percussionist* and *Inventions for a Young Pianist*, his wind music requires mature players. Harbison takes some satisfaction in the knowledge that secondary school musicians have successfully performed the *Quintet for Winds* and *Three City Blocks*, though these performances must be considered something of an exception rather than an indication of the works' general accessibility. Upon opening the score to *Olympic Dances*, a conductor may imagine the work to be rather simple, as there are long passages of homophonic texture in whole, half and quarter notes, and few passages which have truly arduous technical demands. There are some passages of mixed meter, but tempi are moderate; here is seemingly a work of modest proportions. Upon more careful examination, however, one will notice the harmonies with complex additions to their tertian framework, or notice a solo passage for contra bassoon or some high *tessitura* trumpet writing—Yo-Yo Ma's words will begin to ring true: "When you first look, it [Harbison's music] looks very easy, but my God is it ever not." [22]

There are very few ensembles up to the challenge of performing John Harbison's *Olympic Dances*. With a very simple surface texture the work will ruthlessly expose every note or phrase that falls short of high-level playing. Harbison has stated that a little roughness can improve his largest work for winds, *Three City Blocks*, whereas a similar roughness in *Olympic Dances* destroys the voice of this work:

> I have heard wind ensembles play pieces that have required great agility and dexterity; they sounded great. My piece [*Olympic Dances*] requires more in the sense of control and being able to make the instrument speak in a certain way at a certain time. And that is the kind of thing that really the best players do master. And it is in some ways what we expect from the orchestral brass player who doesn't play much, but when they play they have to deliver it right on the mark. I've heard this piece when it wasn't really quite prepared and where the tunings and attacks weren't in great shape and it doesn't sound like the intention is coming through. It is pretty hard. . . On some recent occasions the piece has put ensembles to the test. It showed some weaknesses in their individual abilities that were not coming out in some of the other pieces they were playing. [23]

While *Three City Blocks* has quickly become a repertory staple, performances of *Olympic Dances* seem destined to remain more rare, appropriate for only those ensembles that possess the technical skill to perform Ingolf Dahl's *Sinfonietta* and the finesse needed for Stravinsky's *Symphonies of Wind Instruments*. Only elite ensembles will have *Olympic Dances* in their repertoires.

The crux of all the difficulties in the work lies in its need for mature performers. Every seat in the ensemble has exposed solo passages. These passages do not require extreme dexterity, but rather absolute control of execution even at extremes of dynamic and range. The performers must have the ability as well as the maturity to understand and accept each challenge, though there is little opportunity for personal showmanship. When asked about priorities for rehearsal, Harbison responded:

> My sense of it is that what is required of the kind of school ensembles that have been playing it is an unusual attention to tuning, to awareness of the doublings, to matching of the pitch in the doublings. Of getting the fifths in the chords very well in tune and attacking and releasing with even greater than the usual precision, because of the—what I would call—the objectivity of the first two movements or really of the first three. The whole sense of it being a precision and intonation kind of piece. [24]

Tuning proves to be one of the most difficult challenges. Harbison's harmonic structures are subtle and complex and will prove too great a challenge for most players to untangle on their own. Because many of the chords have a basis in traditional tertian harmonies, these intervals must take precedence and be tuned accurately. This is especially true when the root and fifth appear in the bass and tenor voices respectively.

The harmonic structure of the *cantus* has been examined previously (see figure 4). Because the harmonic function is clearer in measures 4–6, one may reasonably find that time spent in measures 4–6 will improve measures 1–3 more easily than the reverse. There simply isn't enough rehearsal time to tune and balance every chord, but time spent on these first six measures should translate to other areas of the work. One may want to focus on the emblematic sonority in measure 6. Helping the players to gain a genuine familiarity with this particular harmonic color could be most beneficial. The inverted harmonies (i.e., measure 1, beat 1, measure 2 beats 4, 5 and 6 etc.) may require more attention.

Identifying areas of harmonic tension should help clarify the purpose of those sections and therefore their quality as exceptions to the basic sonic palette of the work. The fundamentally augmented nature of the harmony in measure 11, for example; the flute and oboe section could readily come to agreement on their fourths without realizing that the A and C in the bass and tenor voices establish the fundamental augmented quality of the chord. Similarly, pure intonation of the augmented and minor/major chord qualities in 61–63 will not come naturally.

It is the rare work that features an unaccompanied duet by soprano and tenor saxophones (I, m24) and later the E flat and bass clarinets (I, m.64), or requires an unaccompanied unison line (III, var. 5) first by the contra bassoon and tuba, followed by the bass clarinet and third trombone and then finally the alto sax and the principal trombone (this final pair performing unison quintuplet rhythms). With little or no accompaniment, any imperfections stand out clearly. Ultimately one must rely on the instincts of the musicians: judicious use of rehearsal time will, however, establish both the basic sonic structures in the work as well as those structures' important exceptions.

Harbison has also edited his score with unusual precision of dynamics. In the first three bars the homophonic texture scored for winds rises from *forte* to *fortissimo*, relaxing first to *forte* then to *mezzoforte*. Each crescendo is marked at beginning and end with a precise dynamic indication. The 'answer' phrase performed by the brass in measures 4–6 is treated similarly, though marked one dynamic level lower. The cadential chords in measures 6–10 diminish in terraced steps from *mezzoforte*, through *mezzopiano* to *piano*. These are not passages that are vaguely louder or softer, but rather make structural use of precise dynamics.

The series of cadential chords in measures 6–10 offer another important example of Harbison's precise and even structural use of dynamics. The first appearance of these chords is harmonically static. The only motion comes from a terraced diminuendo from *mezzoforte* through *mezzo piano* to *piano*. In the second appearance at the end the first movement the upper harmony subtly shifts with each repetition and the dynamic remains fixed at *piano*. The motion supplied by the dynamics in measures 6–10 is here shifted to the harmony and Harbison asks for an even *piano* dynamic. *Olympic Dances* is filled with important dynamic details such as this.

Looking at an example in the *Epithalamion* one is struck again by Harbison's specificity of intent. In measures 10–13, Harbison briefly adds the saxophones and bassoons to reinforce the line; their four notes are given three dynamic markings, a diminuendo and two types of accent. These markings force the conductor to envision the important difference between a note marked *piano* with an accent, a note simply marked *mezzopiano*, and a note marked *sfortzando* within *mezzopiano*; these are subtle, though expressive, distinctions.

Building a program around *Olympic Dances* should prove to be a relatively easy task. Perhaps the only work to avoid would be the Stravinsky *Symphonies of Winds* which Harbison feels is too similar in aesthetic, though not in details, to his work. Though Harbison would be too modest to say so, *Olympic Dances* and *Three City Blocks* could share a program nicely, one before intermission and one after. Otherwise Harbison offers these compatible programming suggestions:

> I think *Mosaic* by Tippett—he made a wind arrangement out of the first movement of his *Concerto for Orchestra*. That would definitely fit. And then maybe not the *Symphonies of Winds* but perhaps something like the *Concertino* or the *Octet*. I think the *Octet* would be great because it has a variation movement of a really different cast. And of course I am very partial to anything by Varese. He is one of my absolute favorite 20th century composers and one of the great wind composers of all time. And then if there were a standard work, perhaps one of the Mozart serenades, or if it was possible to get a chorus, then Bach Cantata 118, *O Jesu Christ, meins Lebens Licht*. You can play it on whatever winds you've got really. It was written for cornetti and zink and all kinds of weird instruments that were really obsolete by the time he wrote it. Wind conductors should know that piece because it is the only Bach cantata which calls for a wind ensemble. And the piece is such a great piece and sounds so fine with modern brasses. . . it's a shame to not hear it because no one has the right zink player! [25]

DISCOGRAPHY

Battisti, Frank, conductor. (1996). New England Conservatory Wind Ensemble. *Three City Blocks, Music for Eighteen Winds*. Centaur, CD, CRC 2288.

Battisti, Frank, conductor. (1999). New England Conservatory Wind Ensemble. *Olympic Dances*. Albany, CD, Troy 340

Blomstedt, Herbert, conductor. (1994). San Francisco Symphony. *Oboe Concerto, Symphony No. 2*. London, CD, 443 376-2.

Boston Symphony Chamber Players. (1993). *Words from Patterson, Simple Daylight, Piano Quintet*. Elektra-Nonesuch, CD, 79189-2.

Corporon, Eugene, conductor. *Wind Dances*. The North Texas University Wind Ensemble. *Olympic Dances*. Klavier KCD 11084.

Corporon, Eugene, conductor. *Paradigm*. The Cincinnati College-Conservatory of Music Wind Symphony. *Three City Blocks*. Klavier, KCD 11059.

Harbison, John, conductor. Speculum Musicae. *The Flower-Fed Buffaloes*. Nonesuch, CD, 71366

Harbison, John, conductor. (1993). *The Bicentennial Collection*, Disc 9. "The Presidents Own" United States Marine Band. *Three City Blocks*.

Hoose, David, conductor. (1990). The Cantata Singers and Ensemble. *The Flight into Egypt*. New World Records, CD, 80395-2.

Levy, Robert, conductor. (1992). *American Music for Winds*. Lawrence University Wind Ensemble. *Music for Eighteen Winds*. Mark Records, CD, MCC-1302.

Lydian String Quartet. (1992). *String Quartet No. 1, String Quartet No. 2, November 19, 1828*. Harmonia Mundi, CD, 907057.

Lydian String Quartet. (2001) *The Rewaking, String Quartet no. 3, Fantaisa on a Ground, Thanks Victor*. Musica Omnia, CD, mo 0110.

Ozawa, Seiji, conductor. Boston Symphony Orchestra. *.Symphony No. 1*. New World Records, CD, 80331-2

Previn, Andre, conductor. (1990) Los Angeles Philharmonic Orchestra. *Concerto for Double Brass Choir and Orchestra*. New World Records 80395-2.

Schuller, Gunther, conductor. American Composers Orchestra. *Piano Concerto*. CRI S-440

Weisberg, Arthur, conductor. Contemporary Chamber Ensemble. *Confinement*. Nonesuch, CD, 71221.

Wolff, Hugh, conductor. New Jersey Symphony Orchestra. *Concerto for Viola and Orchestra*, Jaime Laredo, viola. New World Records, CD, 80404-2.

Zinman, David, conductor. (1995) *Dance Mix*. Baltimore Symphony Orchestra. *Remembering Gatsby*. Argo, CD, 444 454-2.

Zinman, David, conductor. Orchestra of St. Lukes. *Mirabai Songs*. Nonesuch, CD, 79187-2.

WORKS

OPERA

Full Moon In March (1977)
Duration: 33'
Opera in 1 act
Libretto (En) by the composer after the play by W. B. Yeats.
Cast: S, T, Ms, Bar; dancer
fl.ob.bcl/perc/pf(prpf)/vn.va.vc

The Great Gatsby (1999)
Duration: Full evening
Opera in 2 acts
Libretto (En) by the composer after the novel by F. Scott Fitzgerald with popular song lyrics by Murray Horwitz.
Cast: S, 2T, 2Mz, Bar, B; chorus
3(pic)2+ca.2(E♭cl)+bcl.ssx.2+cbn/4331/timp.3perc/pf.hp.bjo/str; stage band: solo violin; cl(ssx), tpt, tbn, tba, perc(trap set), pf, bjo

Remembering Gatsby (1985)
Duration: 8'
3(pic)3(ca)3(bcl,ssx)2+cbn/432+btbn.1/timp.perc.trap set/pf/str

Winter's Tale (1974, rev. 1991)
Duration: ca 90'
Libretto (En) by the composer after Shakespeare.
Cast: Bar, S, 2Mz, T, B, 6 male, 1 female; chorus
2(pic)2(ca)22(cbn)/2200/perc/str

ORCHESTRA

Concerto for Cello (1993)
Duration: ca 26'
Cello; 3(pic)23(bcl)3/4230/timp.4perc./hp.cel(pf)/str

Concerto for Double Brass Choir and Orchestra (1988)
Duration: 20'
Double Brass Choir (4431 total);2222(cbn)/0000/2timp/str

Concerto for Flute (1993)
Duration: 18'
Flute; 2222/2200/timp.perc/hp.cel/chamber str

Concerto for Oboe (1991)
Duration: 20'
Oboe; 2(pic).02+bcl(asx).3(cbn)/2221/timp.3perc.hp/str

Concerto for Oboe, Clarinet and Strings (1985)
Duration: 14'
Oboe and Clarinet; str(4.4.3.3.2) or str5t

Concerto for Piano (1978)
Duration: 24'
Piano; 2222/2221/perc/hp/str

Concerto for Viola (1989)
Duration: 20'
Viola; 2(pic)2(ca)1+bcl.2(cbn)/2200/timp.1perc/hp.cel/str(6.0.5.4.2 min; no second vns)

Concerto for Violin (1980/87)
Duration: 28'
Violin; 2222/2221/timp.vib/hp.pf/str

David's Fascinating Rhythm Method (1991)
Duration: 2'
2222/2200/timp.4perc.pf/str
certain restrictions apply

Diotima (1976)
Duration: 20'
3233/4331/timp.perc/cel.hp/str

Fanfare for Foley's (1986)
Duration: 2'
4hn.4tpt.3tbn.tba/timp.perc

The Most Often Used Chords (Gli Accordi Piu Usati) (1993)
Duration: ca 15'
2222/2200/timp.perc/hp.pf(cel)/str

I, II, III, IV, V: Fantasia on a Ground (1993)
Duration: ca 6'
str

Remembering Gatsby (Foxtrot for Orchestra) (1985, 1990)
Duration: 7'
3(pic)3(ca)3(bcl,ssx)2+cbn/432+btbn.1/timp.perc.trap set/pf/str or 2(pic)2(ca)2(ssx)2/2221/timp.perc/pf/str

Symphony No. 1 (1981)
Duration: 23'
3(pic,afl)3(ca)3(bcl)3(cbn)/4231/timp.6perc/hp/str

Symphony No. 2 (1987)
Duration: 23'
3(pic)2+ca.2+E♭cl+bcl.2+cbn/442+btbn.1/timp.3perc/hp.pf/str

Symphony No. 3 (1991)
Duration: 21'
3(pic)3(ca)3(bcl)3(cbn)/4331/timp.4perc/pf/str

Ulysses (1983)
Duration: 85'
3(pic)3(ca)3(ssx,E♭cl,bcl)3(cbn)/4231/timp.4perc/hp/str

Ulysses' Bow
Duration: 33'

Ulysses' Raft
Duration: 51'

Waltz—Passacaglia (in e minor) (1996)
Duration: ca 1'
2222+cbn /4230/timp/str

BAND

Music for 18 Winds (1986)
Duration: 10'
2(pic)22.asx.2(cbn)/40+2Ctpt.2(btbn)1

Olympic Dances (1996)
Duration: 17'
3(pic)3(ca)3(E♭cl+bcl).ssx.asx(tsx).3(cbn)/3331/2perc

Three City Blocks (1991)
Duration: 15'
4(2pic).2.4+2E♭cl+2bcl(cbcl).2(cbn)/2asx.2tsx/4442/
    5perc/hp.pf

CHAMBER

Bermuda Triangle (1970)
Duration: 9'
for ampified cello, tenor saxophone, and electric organ

Christmas Vespers (1988)
Duration: 27'
for brass quintet and reader (in movement II)

Confinement (1965)
Duration: 15'
fl, ob(ca), cl(bcl), asx, tpt, tbn, perc, pf, vn, va, vc, db

Duo (1961)
Duration: 18'
for flute and piano

Exequien for Calvin Simmons (1982)
Duration: 5'
afl, bcl, vib, pf, 2 va, vc

Fanfares and Reflection (1990)
Duration: 5'
for two violins

Fantasy Duo (1988)
Duration: 18'
for violin and piano

Fourteen Fabled Folksongs (1992)
Duration: 14'
for violin and marimba

Incidental Music (1971)
Duration: 12'
from 'The Merchant of Venice'
for string quintet

Die Kürze (1970)
Duration: 11'
fl, cl, pf, vn, vc

Little Fantasy (1988)
Duration: 4'
for brass quintet

November 19, 1828 (1988)
Duration: 16'
for piano quartet

Organum for Paul Fromm (1981)
Duration: 4'
for piano, marimba, vibes, cello, and harp

Overture: Michael Kohlhaas (1982)
Duration: 6'
for brass ensemble: 4hn, 4tpt, 3tbn(btbn), tba

Piano Quintet (1981)
Duration: 23'

Piano Trio (1969)
Duration: 9'

Quintet for Winds (1979)
Duration: 23'

San Antonio (1994)
Duration: 12'
for alto saxophone and piano

Serenade (1968)
Duration: 11'
for six players

Snow Country (1979)
Duration: 12'
for oboe and string quintet

String Quartet No. 1 (1985)
Duration: 11'

String Quartet No. 2 (1987)
Duration: 26'

String Quartet No. 3 (1993)
Duration: 22'

Thanks Victor (1994)
Duration: 6'
arrangement of four Victor Young tunes for string quartet

The Three Wise Men (1988)
Duration: 16'
for brass quintet and reader

Trio Sonata (1994)
Duration: ca 6'
for various combinations: String Trio (vn, va, vc); Single Reed Trio (cl, cl, bcl); Double Reed Trio (ob, ca, bn); Saxophone Trio (s, a, bar); or keyboard instrument

Twilight Music (1985)
Duration: 17'
for horn, violin, and piano

Two Chorale Preludes for Advent (1987)
Duration: 8'
for brass quintet

Variations (1982)
Duration: 23'
for clarinet, violin, and piano

Variations (1992)
Duration: ca 5'
for string quartet

VOCAL

Ave Maria (1959)
Duration: 2'
for women's chorus a cappella

Ave Verum Corpus (1990)
Duration: 5'
for SSATB choir and optional string quintet/string orch

Between Two Worlds (1991)
Duration: 29'
for soprano, 2 cellos, and 2 pianos

Book of Hours and Seasons (1975)
Duration: 20'
for mezzo-soprano; fl, vc, pf

Chorale Cantata (1995)
Duration: 10'
Martin Luther (Aus Tiefer Not [1523]), Michael Fried (A Block of Ice, [1991] In A New Apartment, [1992])
S; ob, 2vn, va, vc, cb

Communion Words (1994)
Duration: 3'
Text (En): Bible, I Corinthians II, 23–25 for SATB chorus a cappella

Concerning Them Which Are Asleep (1994)
Duration: 7'
Text (En): Bible, I Thessalonians 4, 13–18 for SSATBB chorus

Due Libri (1981, rev. 1991)
Duration: 23'
Mz; fl, ob, cl/bcl, hn, cel, vn, va, vc, db (orchestral version of "Motetti di Montale" Books 3,4)

Elegiac Songs (1974)
Duration: 20'
Text: Emily Dickinson
Mezzo Soprano; 2(pic)22(ssx)2/2000/perc/str

Emerson (1995)
Duration: 14'
for SATB double chorus

Five Songs of Experience on Poems of William Blake (1971)
Duration: 19'
SATB chorus; 2 perc, 2 vn, va, vc
Vocal score 50231780 for sale

Flashes and Illuminations (1995)
Duration: 16'
for baritone and piano

The Flight into Egypt, Sacred Ricercar (1986)
Duration: 14'
Soprano & Baritone; Chorus; 2ob+ca.bn/3tbn(btbn)/ch org/str

The Flower-Fed Buffaloes (1976)
Duration: 19'
Bar; chorus, fl/vn, cl, tsx, perc, vib/pf, vc, db

The Flute of Interior Time (1992)
Duration: 2'
for baritone or mezzo-soprano and piano

Four Psalms (1999)
Duration: 40'
Text: Hebrew, English
S, Mz, T, B; SATB; 2(pic)2(ca)2(bcl)2(cbn)/4220/timp.2perc/hp/pf/str

Gatsby Songs (1999)
for voice and piano
Fourteen popular songs, with lyrics by Murray Horwitz, from the opera

He Shall Not Cry (1959)
Duration: 2'
for women's chorus and organ

"I remember long ago" (2000)
arranged by the composer for baritone and piano from the opera "The Great Gatsby"

Im Spiegel (1988)
Duration: 3'
for voice, violin, and piano

Mirabai Songs (1982)
Duration: 17'
Text: selected poems of Mirabai, trans. by Robert Bly
S; afl, bcl, perc, hp, vn, va, vc, db

Moments of Vision (1975)
Duration: 15'
for soprano, tenor, and Renaissance consort
alto rec(sopranino,bass rec,alto crumhorn)/lute(hurdy
gurdy,dulcimer)/viola da gamba

Mottetti di Montale (1980)
Duration: 55'
for soprano and piano

Mottetti di Montale (1980, arr. 2000)
Duration: 55'
for mezzo-soprano and strings

Music When Soft Voices Die (1966)
Duration: 3'
for mixed chorus and harpsichord or organ

The Natural World (1987)
Duration: 15'
S/Mz; fl, cl, pf, vn, vc

Nunc Dimittis (1975)
Duration: 9'
for men's chorus

O Magnum Mysterium (1992)
Duration: ca 3'
for chorus a cappella

La primavera de Sottoripa (1998)
Duration: 15'
Soprano; 1(pic)1(ca)1(bcl)0/1000/hpd/str (orchestral
version of "Motetti di Montale," Book 1)

Recordare (1995)
Duration: ca 8'
SATB Soloists; 2(pic)222/222+btbn.0/2perc/hp.pf(cel)/
str

The Rewaking (1991)
Duration: 19'
for soprano and string quartet

Rot und Weiss (1987)
Duration: 3'
vo; fl, vn, vc, pf

Samuel Chapter (1978)
Duration: 12'
S/T; fl, cl, vc, pf, perc (incl vib, bells)

Simple Daylight (1988)
Duration: 16'
for soprano and piano

Three Harp Songs (1975)
Duration: 10'
for tenor and harp

Two Emmanuel Motets (1990)
Duration: 10'
for a cappella chorus

Veni Creator Spiritus (1996)
Duration: 2'
for men's chorus a cappella

Words from Paterson (1989)
Duration: 28'
for baritone and ensemble
Bar; fl(afl), ob(ca), va, vc, hp, pf

SOLO

Amazing Grace (1972)
Duration: 8'
for oboe

Four More Occasional Pieces (1987–90)
Duration: 15'
for piano

Four Songs of Solitude (1985)
Duration: 15'
for violin

Gatsby Etudes (1999)
for piano
Three etudes based on music from the opera

Inventions for a Young Percussionist (1992)
Duration: 4'

Inventions for a Young Pianist (1992)
Duration: ca 5'

On an Unwritten Letter (2000)
Duration: 7' 30"
for piano

Parody Fantasia (1968)
Duration: 8'
for piano

Sonata No. 1 (1987)
Duration: 15'
for piano

Suite (1993)
Duration: 8'
for solo cello

Three Occasional Pieces (1978)
Duration: 10'
for piano

ADDITIONAL RESOURCES

MONOGRAPHS

Spittal, Robert Joseph. *Three City Blocks* by John Harbison. D.M.A. dissertation, University of Cincinnati, College-Conservatory of Music, 1995.

Scott, Judson J. *Olympic Dances* by John Harbison. D.M.A. dissertation, University of Washington, 2003.

ARTICLES

Bond, Victoria. "Towards Creating A Composer-Friendly Environment." *Journal of the Conductors' Guild* 11, no. 3–4 (summer–fall 1990): 89–95.

Harbison, John. "Six Tanglewood Talks (1,2,3)." *Perspectives of New Music* 23, no. 2 (Spring–Summer 1985): 12–22.

Harbison, John. "Six Tanglewood Talks (4,5,6)." Perspectives of New Music, 24, no.1 (Autumn–Winter 1985): 46–60.

Harbison, John. "Symmetries and the New Tonality." *Contemporary Music Review* 6, no. 2 (1992): 71–79.

Isenberg, Barbara. "Courting the Muse in the 20th Century." *Los Angeles Times*, April 22, 1990, Home Edition, Calendar; 5.

Manning, Michael. "Harbison Premiere Falls Short of its Lofty Promise." Boston Globe, October 24, 1997, City Edition: C 12.

Markoch, Jerome R. "Analysis: '*Music for Eighteen Winds*,' by John Harbison." Journal of Band Research, 30/2 (Spring 1995):1–26.

Peyser, Joan. "Harbison's Continuing Ascent." *New York Times*, August 16, 1981, Late City Final Edition: sec. 2, 17.

Seabrook, Mike. "John Harbison and his music." *Tempo: A quarterly review of modern music*, 197; (July 1996): 7–11.

WEB PAGE

Feder, Susan, Ed Matthew, et al. "John Harbison." [article on-line] (New York, NY.: G. Schirmer, Inc., 15 May 2001, accessed 1, Jan. 2002); available from http://www.schirmer com/composers/harbison_bio.html; internet.

Feder, Susan, Ed Matthew, et al. "John Harbison—Works published by Associated Music Publishers, Inc." [article on-line] (New York, NY.: G. Schirmer, Inc., 11 May 2001, accessed 1, Jan. 2002); available from http://www.schirmer com/composers/harbison_works.html; internet.

St. George, David. "John Harbison—Composer Essay." [article on-line] (New York, NY.: G. Schirmer, Inc.,16 Oct. 1997, accessed 1, Jan. 2002); available from http://www.schirmer.com/composers/harbison_essay.html; Internet.

NOTES

1. Mike Seabrook, "John Harbison and his music," *Tempo: A quarterly review of modern music*, 197 (July 1996): 9.
2. Biographical data comes from the Schirmer web site and the New Groves Dictionary of Music and Musicians.
3. Richard Dyer, "John Harbison, local hero," *The Boston Globe*, April 3, 1994, City Edition, p. B15.
4. David St. George, "John Harbison—Composer Essay," [article on-line] (New York, NY.: G. Schirmer, Inc., 16 Oct. 1997, accessed 1, Jan. 2002); available from http://www.schirmer.com/composers/harbison_essay.html; Internet.
5. Peyser, sec. 2, p. 17.
6. John Harbison, telephone interview by author, tape recording, July, 2001.
7. Ibid.
8. John Harbison Harbison, John, "Six Tanglewood Talks (1,2,3)." Perspectives of New Music, 23/2 (Spring–Summer 1985): 12–22.
9. John Harbison, telephone interview by author, tape recording, July, 2001.
10. Ibid.
11. Ibid.
12. Jerome R. Markoch, "Analysis: *Music for Eighteen Winds*, by John Harbison," *Journal of Band Research*, 30/2 (Spring 1995): 1–26.
13. John Harbison, telephone interview by author, tape recording, July, 2001.
14. Battisti, Frank, conductor, New England Conservatory Wind Ensemble, (1999), Albany, CD, Troy 340.
15. John Harbison, telephone interview by author, tape recording, July, 2001.
16. Ibid.
17. Ibid.
18. Ibid.
19. Ibid.
20. Ibid.
21. Ibid.
22. Barbara Isenberg, "Courting the Muse in the 20th Century," *Los Angeles Times*, April 22, 1990, Home Edition, Calendar, p. 5.
23. John Harbison, telephone interview by author, tape recording, July, 2001.
24. Ibid.
25. Ibid.

Karel Husa

by
David Fullmer

Karel Husa, internationally known conductor, composer and Pulitzer Prize winner, has had a uniquely 20th-century career: exiled for 40 years from his native country of Czechoslovakia, he has prevailed over the tyranny which disrupted his life by summoning a quiet determination and fortitude that he has drawn upon to create a body of inimitable and imperishable music. This music, which by its originality and authenticity transcends the composer's own time and personal experience, inspires performers and listeners throughout the world and will continue to instruct and sustain succeeding generations. It is clear that Karel Husa is an artist whose compassionate voice will resonate well into the next century and beyond.[1]

BIOGRAPHICAL INFORMATION

Karel Husa was born August 7, 1921 in Prague, Czechoslovakia. Although his parents wanted their son to become an engineer, they insisted that Karel learn to play a musical instrument. In 1929 he began taking two violin lessons a week with Antonin Svejnoha. These lessons were a significant financial sacrifice for the Husa family, but the parents deemed it important that their children receive a musical education. Over time Husa displayed remarkable musical abilities causing Svejnoha to encourage him to consider application to the Prague Conservatory. However, his parents' wishes prevailed and he soon began his engineering studies.[2]

Husa came face-to-face with oppression at an early age and his reactions to these experiences would serve as a major creative catalyst throughout his life. Just before his graduation in the spring of 1939, the German army occupied Czechoslovakia. Shortly after Husa enrolled for further education at the technical institute the Nazis closed all the universities in Prague in reaction to a student protest. Husa was then drafted to work in a Dresden munitions factory but was miraculously granted a last-minute exemption due to his job at his father's shoe store.[3]

While working with his father Husa began studying privately with Jaroslav Ridky, a composition teacher at the Prague Conservatory. Ridky, impressed with his student's rapid progress, convinced Husa's parents to permit their son's enrollment at the conservatory in 1941. Concurrent with his composition studies Husa also studied conducting with Pavel Dedecek and enjoyed a successful professional debut with the Czechoslovak Radio Orchestra in 1945. By the time he graduated in that same year Husa was already receiving considerable public acclaim for his compositions.[4]

After Czechoslovakia was liberated Husa was granted a fellowship to continue his studies in Paris with Arthur Honegger, Nadia Boulanger and Darius Milhaud. Even though his early compositional output led one Czech music critic to consider Husa "one of the greatest hopes of Czech music," the government revoked his passport in 1949. Reluctantly choosing not to return to his homeland, he forfeited his Czechoslovak citizenship and remained in Paris as a refugee under the protection of the French government. Despite the discouraging circumstances Husa developed a plan based upon his desire to compose:

> My main reasons for not returning when ordered to were artistic, not only political. I would study for two to four years in Paris, go to the United States, travel, conduct and become a known composer. It was not mainly politics; I wanted to prove that I was a composer.[5]

He ultimately received his conducting diploma in 1949 from the Conservatoire Nationale de Musique. His compositions continued to attract attention in Paris and he conducted the first recording of Bartok's ballet *The Miraculous Mandarin* with the Centi Soli Orchestra in 1953.[6]

In 1954 Husa moved to America and accepted a teaching position at Cornell University where he was Kappa Alpha Professor until his retirement in 1992. He was also a lecturer at Ithaca College from 1967 to 1986. Husa has achieved considerable acclaim for his compositional output and has received numerous awards. He was elected Associate member of Royal Belgian Academy of Arts and Sciences in 1974 and he has received numerous honorary doctorates from institutions including Coe College, the Cleveland Institute of Music, Ithaca College, and Baldwin Wallace College. The New York Philharmonic has commissioned two works from Husa: *Concerto for Orchestra*, premiered by Zubin Mehta and *Concerto for Violin and Orchestra* premiered by Kurt Masur and concertmaster Glen Dicterow.

Through his compositions, Husa has earned the label of humanitarian. His response: "I like it. Any epitaph I can get, I take it."[7] His relationship with his home country of Czechoslovakia came full circle when the November 1989 Velvet Revolution, led by Vaclav Havel's Civic Forum, began; by the end of the month, Prague was free. Havel was elected president in December 1989 after helping to inspire the massive public protests that peacefully toppled the country's Communist rulers. Husa recalls the remarkable events that followed.

> In December of 1989, I received a fax from a Schirmer Music agent in Berlin which read, "Mr. Husa, We have just received an order to send *Music for Prague 1968* to Prague." On February 13, 1990 I received the invitation to guest conduct *Music for Prague*. My visit to Prague was amazing. Everything looked like there had been no problem...the same as it had 30 or 40 years earlier.[8]

Husa did conduct the State Symphony Orchestra in a performance of *Music for Prague 1968* for the first time in Prague. On a program featuring works about past oppression, Husa received a tumultuous response by both the orchestra and audience. He also learned that recordings of his works had circulated underground during his absence from his homeland, just as in his youth the forbidden scores of Bartok, Honegger, and Stravinsky were distributed in quiet defiance of the Nazis. Husa reflects on the lessons of Prague:

> My native city is free now, which I didn't think I would see in my lifetime. I hope some day it will be an additional thousand years old, still majestic and beautiful, although marked by its tragedies, sadness, and joy. It is free now, and this all depends on people, not Czechs only but also those around them, to keep it so. Freedom is, however, very fragile and can be easily destroyed. This is what I would compose about Prague today. And I would write the work also for the wind ensemble, because of its conductors and performers, who have always had a great interest in my music.[9]

In 1995 Husa was awarded the Czech Republic's highest civilian honor—the State Medal of Merit, First Class. On June 2, 1997, *Music for Prague 1968* was programmed with the Beethoven 9th Symphony as the finale of the 52nd International Spring Music Festival in Prague. Czech exile conductor Zdenek Macal conducted the Czech Philharmonic in the closing concert that had the "character of an exceptional event." Husa felt deep satisfaction with the music critic who wrote, "The substantial feature of Husa's work rang precisely in a similar way with Beethoven's dream for the freedom of the human race."[10]

COMPOSITIONAL OVERVIEW

Until the end of the 1950s, Husa's compositions were influenced by the neo-classicism of Honegger and Stravinsky and by the folkloric idioms of Janacek and Bartok. His first published composition for winds, *Divertimento for brass and percussion* (an arrangement of four of his *Eight Czech Duets* for four

hand piano, 1955), is a modern setting of Czech folk music representative of his interest in writing music for young people.[11]

When *Divertimento* premiered on February 17th, 1960, in Ithaca, New York, Husa had already begun to move away from tonality toward serialism. *Mosaiques for orchestra* (1961) is a prominent work that was written in his newly adopted serialistic style. This period of experimental serialism was followed by a period of reflection and stylistic consolidation during the mid-1960s.

With the composition of his first work for concert band, the *Concerto for Alto Saxophone and Concert Band* in 1967, Husa synthesized all of the disparate elements of his previous styles and experiments. He retained the clarity and formal logic of neo-classicism, the expressive qualities and intervallic contours of the folkloric idiom, the intricate motivic interrelationships derived from serialism, and an ongoing fascination with new and unusual instrumental techniques and orchestrations.[12]

One of the unusual compositional techniques employed in the *Concerto for Alto Saxophone and Concert Band* is the use of extreme ranges and dynamics required of the soloist as well as the ensemble. His assessment of the technique required of soloist and ensemble is clear:

> The soloist must have complete control of the entire 3 1/2 octave range of the instrument at all dynamic levels, and must be well versed in contemporary techniques. The ensemble needs to have strong players throughout who are equally capable of playing contemporary notation and techniques.[13]

In the spring of 1968, Husa received an invitation from his sister to return to Prague for a visit. She told him of the political excitement surrounding the new freedoms of Alexander Dubcek's reforms known as the "Prague Spring." Husa had already accepted a prior invitation to teach summer courses as a visiting professor at Northwestern University in Chicago and was unable to make the trip. On August 21, Soviet led Warsaw Pact troops invaded Prague and put an end to Dubcek's reforms. These disturbing events compelled Husa to compose his powerful commemoration, *Music for Prague 1968.*

> It was in late August of 1968, when I decided to write a composition dedicated to the city in which I was born. I had thought about writing for Prague for some time because the longer I am far away from this city (I left Czechoslovakia in 1946) the more I remember the beauty of it. I can even say that in my idealization, I actually see Prague even more beautiful. During those tragic and dark moments....I suddenly felt the necessity to write this piece for so long meditated....I was sure that the music I would write for Prague would be scored for the concert band, a medium that I have admired for a long time. The combination of wind and brass instruments with percussion fascinated me; the unexplored possibilities of new sounds and combinations of instruments had attracted me for some time. I am not speaking here against the orchestra for this is a medium I have written much for and in addition to begin an orchestral conductor, I used to play the violin. However, so much great music

has been written for orchestras and strings in the past that it is difficult to produce new works in which orchestral musicians would be interested....[14]

Eleven days after the invasion, Husa learned that the Ithaca College Concert Band would definitely be commissioning a piece for their performance at the Music Educators National Conference in Washington. Within two months Husa had completed the work that would bring him his greatest notoriety. This composition has been described as more than a memorial to a tragic episode in the history of one city; its cries of anguish and indignation are relevant wherever the innocent are crushed and victimized by the strong.[15] *Music for Prague 1968* received its premiere on January 31, 1969. In the forward to the score Husa writes;

Three main ideas bind the composition together. The first and most important is an old Hussite war song from the 15th century, "Ye Warriors of God and His Law," a symbol of resistance and hope for hundreds of years, whenever fate lay heavy on the Czech nation. It has been utilized also by many Czech composers, including Smetana in *My Country*. The beginning of this religious song is announced very softly in the first movement by the timpani and concludes in a strong unison (chorale).

The second idea is the sound of bells throughout; Prague, named the "City of One Hundred Spires," has used its magnificently sounding church bells as calls of distress as well as to signal victory.

The last idea is a motif of three chords, first appearing very softly under the piccolo solo at the beginning of the piece, then in flutes, clarinets, and horns. Later it reappears at extremely strong dynamic levels—for example, in the middle of the *Aria*.

Different techniques of composing as well as orchestrating have been used in *Music for Prague 1968* and some new sounds explored, such as the percussion section in the *Interlude*, the ending of the work, etc. Much symbolism also appears: in addition to the distress calls in the first movement (*Fanfares*), the unbroken hope of the Hussite song, sound of bells, or the tragedy (*Aria*), there is also the bird call at the beginning (piccolo solo), symbol of the liberty which the city of Prague has seen only for moments during its thousand years of existence.[16]

Husa has utilized several innovative compositional techniques in the creation of this work. The experimental use of extreme ranges in his saxophone concerto continued in *Prague* with the opening piccolo solo:

In that frustration or anger over the Soviet invasion, I had the idea that the piece would start with two measures of the "War Song," in the beginning pianissimo, and then it would all finish fortissimo with five measures of the song. This drama of the fifteenth century, when the Hussites went into their war, I imagined this just as a symbol. And then I thought, "Yes, as a symbol of freedom—like a bird song." I could have put flute, but I thought so many pieces have started with flute, but not with piccolo. Piccolo would make a more unusual beginning...the uneasy quietness before the storm. I knew that the piccolo has a 'D' low note, but I didn't know how it would sound. It's sort of unusual. I'm sure that the flute would have sounded beautiful in that register, but that is maybe why I didn't want it.[17]

Many of the Husa's unconventional orchestrations were a result of his deliberate intention to write in a way that would maximize the coloristic potential of the large choirs of instruments available in the contemporary wind band. He based many of his orchestrational choices on his aural 'glossary' of sounds, a sound memory based upon the symphony orchestra. In applying the same techniques to his scoring for the wind band he was, admittedly, stepping into unfamiliar orchestrational territory. His experimentation resulted in many wonderful new sounds. He writes the following about his scoring of the saxophone section:

At the time when I wrote *Prague*, I didn't have very much experience with instruments that normally play a leading role in a wind band. For instance, had I had more knowledge, I may not have written the *Aria* for saxophones. At that time, the saxophones were not used to having melodic ideas in the music. I really didn't know, so I mostly put instruments together merely like I was used to doing for a symphony orchestra, except now I had only winds. Maybe the deduction I made was; because I don't have strings, it will be up to the clarinets and saxophones to replace them. I thought the saxophones would be great for the lower beginning in the *Aria*, but I didn't realize that the saxophones were not used the same way as cellos and violas in a string section. I was always amazed by the saxophones when I conducted Gershwin. Grofe put them in (*Rhapsody in Blue* and *An American in Paris*), and it is a rich and powerful sound in a symphony orchestra. Maybe that's where I got that idea to use them in the *Aria*. I like the several-octaves sound in saxophones.

The title of *Aria* might be a little surprising; it is, of course, not an 'aria' in an operatic sense, the word may be a little sarcastic for that occasion: it is not a happy aria. I have given it to the saxophones purposely: they have the tremendous ability to sing, sound strong and loud, and yet expressive at all times; also by their vibrating quality, it may be close to what we call vox humana on the organ. And this is what this melodic line was about: to say the anguish, fear and desolation in awaiting what will come next.[18]

One of the more important innovations found in Husa's compositions is the expanded role of the percussion section. He was satisfied with the color and contrast of his percussion movement in his *Mosaiques* for orchestra, which included percussion, piano, celesta and harp. With virtually no precedent in band literature, *Music for Prague 1968* raised the importance of the percussion section to be equal with brass and woodwinds. This trend culminated in 1971 with his *Concerto for Percussion and Wind Ensemble*, which was commissioned by the Ludwig Industries and premiered in 1972.

As I look at the development of the symphony orchestra...the development of the sections was about similar. I mean, the string body at first was involved constantly. Then in symphonies, you go to Haydn, Mozart—and the woodwinds, except for soli, were not yet fully explored....later they grew in Beethoven's and Brahms' music. Then in Debussy and composers at the turn of the century, the woodwinds were, we could say, fairly equal to the strings. But the brasses still weren't and then, suddenly, the brass instruments were coming, and now this section is equal in the symphony orchestra to the other two. Percussion has developed in the second half of the century into the fourth prominent instrumental section. I try to treat each of the four sections equally.[19]

Music for Prague 1968 has become a standard in the band repertoire with over 10,000 performances worldwide. A few months after the premiere, Husa was notified that he was the winner of the 1969 Pulitzer Prize in music for his *String Quartet No. 3* (1967). These two events—the premiere of *Prague* and winning the Pulitzer Prize, created a tremendous demand for Husa's music. The resultant increase of commissions combined with the Cornell University music department's demands for Husa to teach graduate composition and his numerous guest-conducting invitations convinced Husa to resign from conducting the university orchestra in 1975.

Music for Prague 1968 was the first of a compositional triptych that Husa has named his three "manifests"; scores intended to address serious issues of international concern. The second work of the triptych, *Apotheosis of this Earth*, was composed in 1971 as a prophetic warning about the dire consequences of humanity's abuse of the environment. This three-movement work was commissioned by the Michigan School Band and Orchestra Association and dedicated to Dr. William D. Revelli upon his retirement as Director of Bands at the University of Michigan. Husa offers the following programmatic explanation in the forward to the score:

> In the first movement, *Apotheosis*, the Earth first appears as a point of light in the universe. Our memory and imagination approach it in perhaps the same way as it appeared to the astronauts returning from the moon. The Earth grows larger and larger, and we can even remember some of its tragic moments (as struck by the xylophone near the end of the movement).
>
> The second movement, *Tragedy of Destruction*, deals with the actual brutalities of man against nature, leading to the destruction of our planet, perhaps by radioactive explosion. The Earth dies as a savagely, mortally wounded creature.
>
> The last movement is a *Postscript*, full of the realization that so little is left to be said: The Earth has been pulverized into the universe, the voices scattered into space. Toward the end, these voices—at first computer-like and mechanical—unite into the words of *this beautiful Earth*, simply said, warm and filled with regret…and one of so many questions comes to our minds: "Why have we let it happen?"[20]

Husa continued writing for the wind ensemble in 1973 with the 14-minute *Concerto for Trumpet and Wind Orchestra* that is to be performed by an orchestral wind section. This somewhat experimental work is not to be confused with Husa's *Concerto for Trumpet* (1987) written for Adolph Herseth of the Chicago Symphony.

Al Fresco, also written in 1973, was the first in a series of commissions in memory of Walter Beeler who conducted the Ithaca College Concert Band for over forty years. The Ithaca College Concert Band gave its premiere at the MENC Con-

vention in Philadelphia on April 19, 1975, with the composer as guest conductor.[21] Husa, with only a short time in which to complete this commission, based the work on his 1963 orchestral work *Fresque* that was based on a 1947 orchestral work entitled *Three Fresques*. Husa included the following explanation in the forward of the *Al Fresco* score:

> *Al Fresco* has no programmatic content. However, the title indicates my admiration for the art of painting, especially mural painting on wet plaster. And I have always been greatly moved by the forceful, even grandiose and rough, mysterious pictures dealing with primitive life, war and pageantry.[22]

Coe College in Cedar Rapids, Iowa commissioned Husa in 1976 to commemorate the American Bicentennial and the 125th anniversary of the founding of the college. An *American Te Deum* is an exploration of Husa's American experience, an immigrant composer who became a U.S. citizen in 1959. It is a lengthy, intricate work for baritone voice, mixed chorus and wind ensemble. Husa selected texts illustrating the diversity of American culture, folk and traditional liturgical sources alternate with passages drawn from the writings of Thoreau, Engle, Brezina and others. Husa comments on his compositional perspective for this work:

> An *American Te Deum* is the way I look at the U.S.: from an immigrant's point of view. Everybody wanted to work in this country.[23]

During the late 1970s, Husa wrote three chamber pieces for winds and percussion. The Western Brass Quintet of Kalamazoo, Michigan commissioned *Landscapes* in 1977. *Three Dance Sketches* is a percussion quartet composed in 1979 using three percussion 'families' in three movements. Later that same year, a commission by the International Trumpet Guild *Intradas and Interludes* for 7 trumpets and percussion was completed.

The *Concerto for Wind Ensemble* was intended to be a virtuosic showpiece for band. Husa wanted to write a wind composition like Bartok's *Malipiero's* or Tippett's *Concertos* for orchestra. The work, commissioned by Michigan State University in 1982, is a brilliant technical challenge for soloists and small groups within the ensemble and earned Husa the first Sudler prize in 1983. The *Concertino for Piano and Wind Ensemble*, premiered at the 1983 College Band Directors National Association and the National Band Association combined convention in Florida, is a reworked version of the 1947 orchestral work.

Smetana Fanfare was commissioned by San Diego State University for the 1984 International Musicological Conference and Festival of Czechoslovak Music honoring the Czech composer Bedrich Smetana (1824–1884). The San Diego State University Wind Ensemble, on the occasion of the centennial celebration of Smetana's death, premiered it on April 3, 1984. This short, declamatory work uses two excerpts from Smetana's symphonic poem *Wallenstein's Camp*, a work completed in 1859 in Goteberg, Sweden, during his exile from Prague.[24] Smetana's greatest influence on Husa was "his sincerity of feeling and his expression of the struggle for national identity and freedom in Czechoslovakia."[25] *Smetana Fanfare* is undeniably Husa; massive fanfare-like textures with multiple divisis (8 trumpet parts); driving ostinati, rhythmically unison woodwind choir dissonant textures and emphatic percussion are hallmarks of this composition. Throughout the work there is a sense of intensifying dissonance via the use of "Renaissance thirds" or the simultaneous sounding of major and minor thirds. A forceful culmination is achieved through increased volume and instrumental texture by layering in lower voices in reverse score order.[26]

ANALYSIS OF *LES COULEURS FAUVES*

In 1995 Husa completed *Les Couleurs Fauves* (The Vivid Colors), a commission by alumni and friends of the Northwestern University School of Music written in honor of the 40th anniversary of John P. Paynter's appointment to the faculty. Husa became acquainted with Paynter when he drove his family to Northwestern for a one-month summer teaching appointment in July of 1968, the same appointment that prevented him from visiting his sister during the "Prague Spring". Paynter had rented a home for the Husas which, at the last minute, did not become available until after July 4th. Husa and his family stayed for a few days in Paynter's home. In Husa's estimation John Paynter "was a wonderful friend and man; very gentle, and very powerful, monumental in front of the band. These two sides of Paynter are represented in the two movements of *Les Couleurs Fauves*."[27] Regarding the composition of the work Husa writes:

I have always been fascinated by colors, not only in music but also in art and nature. The paintings of the impressionists and Fauvists have been particularly attractive to me, and their French origin accounts for the title of my piece. The two movements (*Persistent Bells* and *Ritual Dance Masks*) gave me a chance to experiment with colors…sometimes gentle, sometimes raw…of the wind ensemble, something that John (Paynter) liked to do. John has been a wonderful friend since we met for the first time in 1968, when we both taught summer courses at Northwestern University. At that time I had written only one work for band, the *Saxophone Concerto*. John's devotion to wind ensemble made a great impression on me and certainly influenced me to write more for these instrument combinations. His honesty and dedication to the art of music and to teaching was exemplary. He had first-class baton technique and communicated to the players, as well as to the audiences, in a very moving way: powerful, passionate, or delicate and gentle, as the score required. I was reminded of those French painters whom I admired as young student in Paris. They called themselves fauvists (vivid, wild), for they used bold, often powerful strokes of brushes with unmixed colors. Their paintings, though, breathe with sensitivity, serenity, and gentleness, John's transcriptions as well as his conducting had these characteristics and hopefully *Les Couleurs Fauves* will remind you of them.[28]

Paynter postponed his retirement scheduled for the fall of 1995. Even though he passed away unexpectedly in January of 1996, ten months before the premiere, he was able to see the score and discuss it with Husa. One of Paynter's ideas was to add extra balcony brasses for the end of the piece.

The first of the two continuous movements, *The Persistent Bells*, opens with a delicate oboe solo in the first seven measures. The long notes of the oboe solo are decorated with soft sextuplet fragments in the glockenspiel (fig. 1).

FIGURE 1: Measures 1–7, oboe and glockenspiel
Les Couleurs Fauves

In measure eight, the second oboe enters to create the first of many inventive woodwind duets. The rhythmic interaction is at times imitative, at times unison. Sextuplet fragments added by the vibraphone to the bells creates an interesting rhythmic interplay (fig. 2).

Beginning in measure twenty, the initial oboe duet becomes a trio with the addition of the English Horn. The melodic percussion answers the woodwinds during long note values. This "call and response" provides forward motion and a sense of persistent tension to the first movement. Husa also begins to add other supportive voices, which remain rhythmically static, but harmonically impor-

tant. In order to maintain interest, it is imperative that all lines have an involving sense of contour.

In measure twenty-eight Husa combines all upper woodwind voices in unison rhythm and contrary melodic motion. The percussion section continues to answer during woodwind rhythmic inactivity, but the sextuplet fragments are noticeably longer in duration and stronger dynamically. The addition of marimba and xylophone creates a thicker texture and heightened tension (fig. 3).

Measure 34 marks the entrance of the lower reeds to the woodwind choir. Beginning with a high solo voice, Husa gradually adds layers of voices in reverse score order to build

FIGURE 2: Measures 8–12, oboes and percussion
Les Couleurs Fauves
Copyright © 1996 by Associated Music Publishers, Inc. (BMI)
International Copyright Secured. All Rights Reserved. Reprinted by Permission.

tension. The addition of the low woodwinds completes this classic Husa compositional technique. This time the percussion answer to the woodwinds contains no additional frag-

ments. All four-mallet voices are playing nearly continuous sextuplets, increasing in volume until the arrival point at measure 40 (fig. 4).

FIGURE 3: Measure 28–33, woodwinds and percussion
Les Couleurs Fauves
Copyright © 1996 by Associated Music Publishers, Inc. (BMI)
International Copyright Secured. All Rights Reserved. Reprinted by Permission.

In this movement, as in previous Husa compositions, the saxophone section provides prominent color. The movement ends with interesting combinations of bassoon and bass clarinet, upper woodwinds and percussion and, ultimately, a piccolo solo.

The second movement, *Ritual Dance Masks*, features intense brass punctuations alternating with dancing temple blocks in six-eight meter (fig. 5).

Sustained voices increase volume and harmonic dissonance to create tremendous dramatic tension. The section concludes abruptly with driving fanfare-like accents in duple meter (fig. 6).

Mallory Thompson, Director of Bands at Northwestern University conducted the premiere and has described the second half of the second movement as a "bolero."[29] The snare drum begins softly on the 'bolero' rhythmic pattern, which continues to the end of the work. Solo piccolo eventually joins solo clarinet for some of Husa's most inventive duet interplay (fig. 7).

The clarinet and saxophone sections begin to interact in a "call and response" fashion. The brasses interject sextuplet figures, which increase in length, volume, frequency and breadth of sonority by the expansion of lower tessitura instruments in reverse score order (as in *Persistent Bells*). The woodwinds add increased complexity to a homophonic line, which, with the brass, plays out over the incessant rhythmic ostinato of the "bolero" rhythm. The tension builds slowly and steadily to the *exaltando* for the dramatic climax. "Players need to pace themselves and not get too excited. Piano, mezzo-forte, forte are not fortissimo. They should stay reserved until the last twelve measures. Also, don't slow down in the last section or the players become tired."[30]

In December 1996 at the Mid-West Clinics 50th anniversary in Chicago, Husa premiered his latest work for brass and percussion entitled *Mid-West Celebration*. The event marked the 50th anniversary of Husa's departure from his homeland and beginning of his international career. His contribution to the wind band repertoire is unique and significant. It could

FIGURE 4: Measure 35–39, mallet percussion
Les Couleurs Fauves

FIGURE 5: Measures 11–19, temple blocks
Les Couleurs Fauves
Copyright © 1996 by Associated Music Publishers, Inc. (BMI)
International Copyright Secured. All Rights Reserved. Reprinted by Permission.

FIGURE 6: Measures 252–256, trumpets
Les Couleurs Fauves
Copyright © 1996 by Associated Music Publishers, Inc. (BMI)
International Copyright Secured. All Rights Reserved. Reprinted by Permission.

FIGURE 7: Measure 274–276, piccolo and clarinet
Les Couleurs Fauves
Copyright © 1996 by Associated Music Publishers, Inc. (BMI)
International Copyright Secured. All Rights Reserved. Reprinted by Permission.

be reasonably argued that perhaps no one of his stature in the world of serious contemporary music has devoted so much energy to writing for the wind band.[31] When asked if he has ever been criticized for writing for bands, Husa replied:

> I don't care. I write for those who like to play my music. I'm a violinist, but I like to write for woodwinds, brass and percussion, too. Composers should be able to write for any ensemble. I won a Pulitzer Prize for a string quartet that hardly gets played. I received a Pulitzer Prize in 1969 for the string quartet, the same year *Music for Prague* premiered at the National MENC. *Music for Prague* has received over 10,000 performances while the string work less than 800. The universities have very good bands with conductors interested in playing new music. The orchestra conductors cannot. They have such extended repertoire with so many masterpieces and are not interested in new music as much. Composers must look for ensembles that will play their music. I don't want my compositions to sit on the shelf.[32]

In November of 2000 Husa donated his archive to Ithaca College in Ithaca, New York. That archive now exceeds in scope and volume the Husa documents in the Library of Congress. In addition to the original manuscripts of several of his works the archive contains many personal letters to composers regarding matters of the interpretation of their music. Due to the nature and chronology of Husa's international career the archive is a remarkable display of musical life during the last half of the 20th century.

CONDUCTING APPROACH

Karel Husa has enjoyed a distinguished career as a conductor. His ideas for conductors who are engaged in the study and performance of his music are informed by his own experiences on the podium:

> My music has roots in the music of the past, i.e. in the classic-romantic tradition. It is though different, because of additions of new techniques, ideas and a desire to create music of today, and hopefully a personal one. The conductor should approach it the same way as studying Beethoven's or Mahler's symphonies or Debussy's *La Mer*: analyze the form, phrasing (very important!), orchestration, establish contrasts, climaxes, melodic lines, rhythmical pulses, learn the music so well as not to look constantly in the score, distinguish between the most important, somewhat important and less important lines, colorings and sustained sounds. Prepare in advance the different phrases, measure, stops (including fermatas), rehearse these several times with the ensemble explaining clearly your intentions. Music has intensity, tension and release, these have to be known precisely to the conductor and first communicated in rehearsal to the players. The "intensity" exists in every work: Debussy's first movement of *La Mer* or *Nocturnes* are as "intense" as Beethoven's first movement of the *Fifth Symphony*, although the intensity is an inner one. Despite the lack of precise notations (and in the modern music very precise), still, one cannot notate all, the same way a poem or play is written: the actor has to bring the written text into "life". The musicians do the same. The conductor has to know how to teach the interpretation

to them...he can see "all the notes" in the score. And they all present the work to the audiences. In case of new works, which they do not know, it is imperative, that the preparation is as best as possible; if not, it is always the composer who is blamed for the result. It is impossible that Bartok's Quartets would not be appreciated by the audiences if played excellently; but it is very probable, that they will not be if not played well. Stravinsky said (I paraphrase) that out of ten performances of a work of his, only one or two are really good. Our duties as conductors are to present every work as best we can. The future will be the judge of what is valuable and what is not. The conductors (and all performers) are composer's advocates and have to do so at their best abilities. I am sure all composers are grateful for their help; they bring notes to life.

> I think it also important—for some of my compositions—to know why they were written; for example, what happened in Prague during the year 1968, when I wrote it, or why have I written such a piece as *Apotheosis of this Earth*. One understands Janacek better, when one learns about the "realistic" life of his country, or the magic colors of Debussy, when one learns about his time in the sophistically artistic Paris around 1900.

Husa's listing of his own compositions that conductors of his music should be familiar with is as follows:[33]

Orchestral works:	*Symphony No. 1* (1953)
	Mosaiques (1961)
	Serenade (1963)
	Landscapes (brass quintet, 1977)
	CRI CD 592
Chamber works:	*String Quartet No. 1* (1948)
	Variations for Piano Quartet (1984)
	Five Poems for Wind Quintet (1994)
	Panton-Supraphon 81 9009-2 131
	(Distributed in U.S. by Qualiton)
	Landscapes (brass quintet, 1977)
	CRI CD 592

He recommends the following recorded interpretations of his music:

Music for Prague 1968	Albany/Troy CD 271 Temple University Wind Symphony Karel Husa, guest conductor Sony/CBS Masterworks MS 44916 CD Eastman Wind Ensemble Donald Hunsberger, conductor
Concerto for Percussion and Wind Ensemble	Sheffield Salon Series SLS 506CD Moscow Philharmonic Dmitri Kitaenko, conductor
Concerto for Wind Ensemble Smetana Fanfare	Summit DCD 192 Cincinnati Wind Symphony Mallory Thompson, conductor

Les Couleurs Fauves	Albany/Troy 340 CD New England Conservatory Wind Ensemble Frank Battisti, conductor
Apotheosis of This Earth	(first edition. orchestra/chorus version) LCD 005 Louisville Orchestra Karel Husa, guest conductor Mark C.R.S. 3182 CD Arkansas State University Wind Ensemble Karel Husa, guest conductor
Apotheosis of This Earth	Golden Crest LP only/CRS-4134
Music for Prague 1968	University of Michigan Symphony Band Karel Husa, guest conductor
Al Fresco	Golden Crest LP only/CRS-4134
Concerto for Saxophone	Michigan State University Symphony Band
Concerto for Percussion	Karel Husa, guest conductor (Stanley De Rusha, conductor in the Concerto for Percussion)

APPENDIX

EDUCATION

Conservatory of Music in Prague, 1941–1945:
    composition with Jaroslav Ridky
conducting with Pavel Dedecek
Academy of Music in Prague, 1945–1947:
    composition with Jaroslav Ridky
Ecole normale de musique de Paris, 1946–1948:
    composition with Arthur Honegger
conducting with Jean Fournet
Conservatoire de musique de Paris, 1948–1949:
    conducting with Eugene Bigot privately in Paris
1946–1949: composition with Nadia Boulanger conducting
    with Andre Cluytens

BRIEF SUMMARY OF ACTIVITIES

Secretary of Czech Section for the International Society for
    Contermporary Music, Prague, 1946
Guest conductor for Czechoslovak Radio Prague, 1945–1946
Member of the Jury at the Paris National Conservatory,
    1952–1953
Member of the Jury at the Fountainebleau School of Music
    and Arts, 1953

Conductor of Cento Soli Orchestra, Paris, 1953–1954:
    Recordings of Bartok and Brahms
Member of the Music Department, Cornell University,
    1954 to 1992: (Assistant Professor 1954, Associate Professor 1957, Full Professor 1961, Kappa Alpha Professor
    1973) Taught Composition, Theory, Conducting, and
    Orchestration, Retired in 1992 as Kappa Alpha Professor
    Emeritus
Lecturer in composition, Ithaca College, School of Music,
    1967–1986
Director of the Cornell University Orchestra, 1956–1975
Ithaca Chamber Orchestra, 1951–1961
Cayuga Chamber Orchestra, 1978–1984
Guest Conductor with many orchestras including: Orchestre National de France, Orchestre des Cento Soli, Hamburg Radio (NDR), Symphony Orchestras in Prague,
    Paris, Stockholm, Oslo, Brussels, London, Manchester,
    Munich, Basel, Lausanne, Geneva, New York, Boston,
    Buffalo, Rochester, Baltimore, Cincinnati, Denver, San
    Diego, Syracuse, Hong Kong, Puerto Rico, Singapore,
    and Tokyo.

AWARDS AND PRIZES

Czech Academy of Art and Sciences Prize, Prague for Sinfonietta for Orchestra in 1948
Lili Boulanger Foundation Prize, Boston, Massachusetts, for
    String Quartet No. 1 in 1950
Bilthoven Contemporary Music Festival, Holland for String
    Quartet No. 1 in 1951
Guggenheim Fellowship in 1964 and 1965
Pulitzer Prize in 1969 for String Quartet No. 3
"Orpheus" Award from Phi Mu Alpha, Musiscal Fraternity:
    1972, 1974, and 1980
Associated Member of the Royal Belgian Academy of Arts
    and Sciences, Brussels, 1974
Honorary degree of Doctor of Music, Coe College, 1976
Friedheim Award, Washington D. C. for Recollections in
    1983
Sudler International Award, Chicago, Illinois for Concerto
    for Wind Ensemble in 1984
Honorary degree of Doctor of Music, Cleveland Institute of
    Music, 1985
Sterling Silver Bicentennial Medallion, University of Georgia, 1984
Sousa Order of Merit, J.F. Kennedy Center, Washington D.
    C., 1985
Honorary degree of Doctor of Music, Ithaca College, 1986
Honorary membership: Association of French Saxophonists, 1986
Karel Husa Professor in composition established in honor of
    Husa by Ithaca College, 1986
Honorary membership: ARDESA (Society of German
    Saxophonists), 1988

Master Teacher Award by the Music Teachers National Association, 1989

American Academy and Institute of Arts and Letter Award, 1989

Honorary degree of Doctor of Music, Baldwin-Wallace College, 1991

Citation, National Federation of Music Clubs, 1993

Grawemeyer Award 1993 for the Concerto for Violoncello and Orchestra

Member of the American Academy of Arts and Letters, New York, 1994

Czech Republic State Medal of Merit, 1st Class Gold granted by President Vaclav Havel, 1995

Honorary member of the American Bandmasters Association (ABA), 1995

Honorary member of the club of Moravian Composers (founded by Leos Janacek), 1995

Honorary doctor of Humane Letters, St. Vincent College, New York, 1995

Medal of Honor, Midwest International Clinic, 50th Anniversary, Chicago, 1996

Honorary degree of Doctor of Music, Hartwick College, New York, 1997

Honorary degree of Doctor of Music, New England Conservatory, 1998

Honorary degree of Doctor of Music, Masaryk University (Brno, Czech Republic), 2000

Honorary degree of Doctor of Music, Academy of Musical Arts (Prague, Czech Republic), 2000

COMMISSIONS

Smetana Quartet, 1947 (String Quartet No.1)

UNESCO, Paris, 1952 (Music for Band)

Donaueschingen Festival, 1953 (Portrait for String Orchestra)

Friends of Music at Cornell, 1957 (Fantasies for Orchestra)

Radio Hamburg, 1961 (Mosaiques for Orchestra)

Fine Arts Quartet, 1968 (String Quartet No. 3)

Cornell University Wind Ensemble, 1967 (Concerto for Saxophone)

Ithaca College, 1968 (Music for Prague) and 1973 (Al Fresco)

University of Michigan, 1970 (Apotheosis of this Earth)

Ludwig Percussion for Baylor University, 1971 (Concerto for Percussion and Wind Ensemble)

Evanston Symphony, 25th anniversary, 1971 (Two Sonnets from Michelangelo)

Koussevitsky Foundation, 1972 (Sonata for Violin and Piano)

Kappa Kappa Psi Biennial Convention, 1973 (Concerto for Trumpet and Wind Orchestra)

John E. Fowler Foundation, 1974 (The Steadfast Tin Soldier)

Washington Performing Arts Society Bicentennial Celebration, 1953(Sonata for Piano#2)

National Endowment for the Arts Bicentennial Celebration, 1975 (Monodrama, Ballet for Orchestra)

Coe College Bicentennial Celebration, 1976 (Landscapes)

Portland Opera, 1980 (Fanfare for Brass and Timpani)

American String Teachers Association (ASTA) National Convention, 1980 (Pastoral for String Orchestra)

National Association for College Wind and Percussion Instructors, 1980 (Intradas and Interludes)

Holland-Michigan Choir Festival, 1981 (Three Moravian Songs)

University of Louisville, Louisville Ballet and Orchestra, 1981 (The Trojan Women)

Ithaca College Choral Festival, 1981 (Every Day)

Verdehr Trio, 1982 (Sonata a Tre)

Holland-America, 200th anniversary of friendly relations, 1982 (Recollections)

Michigan State University for the opening of the Warton Center, 1982 (Concerto for Wind Ensemble)

Wabash College, 1983 (Cantata)

Eastern Music Festival, 1983 (Reflections/Symphony No.2)

San Diego State University, 1983 (Smetana Fanfare)

University of Central Florida for 1984 CBDNA Convention, 1983 (Concertino for Piano)

National Endowment for the Arts for the consortium of Altanta Virtuosi, Rowe Quartet, and New England Quartette, 1984 (Variations for Piano Quartette)

University of Georgia Bicentennial Celebration, 1984 (Symphonic Suite)

New York Philharmonic and Zubin Mehta, 1986 (Concerto for Orchestra)

Michelson-Morley Centennial Celebration, 1987 (Concerto for Organ and Orchestra)

Chicago Symphony Orchestra, Adolph Herseth, and Sir Georg Solti, 1987 (Concerto for Trumpet and Orchestra)

University of Southern California, 1988 (Concerto for Violoncello and Orchestra)

National Endowment for the Arts for the consortium of Colorado, Alard, and Blair Quartets, 1988 (String Quartet NO. 4)

SeattleYouth Symphony Orchestra Centennial Celebration, 1991 (Ouverture for "Youth" Orchestra)

Ithaca College Centennial Celebration, 1992 (Cayuga Lake, for chamber ensemble)

New York Philharmonic Orchestra, 150th Anniversary, 1993 (Violin Concerto)

Koussevitzky Foundation commission, 1994 (Five Poems for Wood-wind Quintet)

Northwestern University, 1995 (Les Couleurs Fauves)

Mid-West International 50th Anniversary Clinic, 1996 (Midwest Celebration)

Orquesta Sinfonica de Galicia, 1997 (Celebracion)

Appendix

CHRONOLOGICAL LIST OF WORKS

Sonatina for Piano Op.1	1943
String Quartet No O.	1943
Ouverture for Orchestra	1944
Sonatina for Violin and Piano	1944
Suite for Viola and Piano	1945
Sinfonietta for Orchestra	1946
Three Frescoes for Orchestra	1946–7
String Quartet No.1	1948
Divertimento (String Orchestra)	1948
Sonata (Piano)	1949
Concertino (Piano and Orchestra)	1949
Evocations of Slovakia (Clarinet, Viola and Violoncello)	1951
Symphony No.1 (Orchestra)	1953
String Quartet No.2	1953
Portrait (String Orchestra)	1953
Four Little Pieces for Strings (Orchestra or Soloistic)	1955
Eight Czech Duets (Piano Four-Hands)	1955
Twelve Moravian Songs (Voice and Piano)	1956
Fantasies (Orchestra)	1956
Elegie (Piano)	1957
Divertimento (Brass and Percussion)	1958
Poem (Viola and Chamber Orchestra)	1959
Elegie et Rondeau (Alto Saxophone and Orchestra)	1960
Mosaiques (Orchestra)	1961
Serenade (Woodwind Quintet and String Orch w/ harp,xylo.)	1963
Fresque (Orchestra)	1963
Festive Ode (Chorus and Orchestra or Band)	1964
Concerto for Brass Quintet (and String Orchestra)	1965
Two Preludes (Flute, Clarinet and Bassoon)	1966
Concerto (Alto Saxophone and Concert Band)	1967
String Quartet No.3	1968
Divertimento (Brass Quintet)	1968
Music for Prague 1968 (Band)	1968
Music for Prague 1968 (Orchestra)	1969
Apotheosis of this Earth (Band)	1970
Concerto for Percussion (and Wind Ensemble)	1971
Two Sonnets from Michelangelo (Orchestra)	1971
Apotheosis of this Earth (Orchestra and Chorus)	1972
Al Fresco (Band)	1973
Sonata for Violin and Piano	1973
Concerto for Trumpet (and Wind Orchestra)	1973
The Steadfast Tin Soldier (Narrator and Orchestra)	1974
Sonata for Piano No.2	1975
Monodrama (Ballet for Orchestra)	1975
An American Te Deum (Baritone, Chorus, and Wind Ensemble)	1976
An American Te Deum (Baritone, Chorus, and Orchestra)	1977
Landscapes (Brass Quintet)	1977
Pastoral (String Orchestra)	1979
Three Dance Sketches (Four Percussionists)	1979
The Trojan Women (Ballet for Orchestra)	1980
Intradas and Interludes (Seven Trumpets and Timpani)	1980
Three Moravian Songs (A'Cappella Chorus)	1981
Every Day (A'Cappella Chorus)	1981
Fanfare (Brass and Percussion Ensemble)	1981
Recollections (Woodwind Quintet and Piano)	1981
Sonata a Tre (Clarinet, Violin and Piano)	1981
Concerto for Wind Ensemble	1982
Cantata (Men's Chorus and Brass Quintet)	1983
Concertino (Piano and Wind Ensemble, Version of 1949)	1983
Reflections/Symphony No.2 (Orchestra)	1983
Smetana Fanfare (Band)	1984
Variations (Violin, Viola, Violoncello and Piano)	1984
Symphonic Suite (Orchestra)	1984
Intrada (Brass Quintet)	1984
Concerto for Orchestra	1986
Concerto for Organ and Orchestra	1987
Frammenti (Organ Solo)	1987
Concerto for Trumpet and Orchestra	1987
Scenes from "The Trojan Women" for Orchestra	1988
Concerto for Violoncello and Orchestra	1988
String Quartet No.4	1990
Overture "Youth" (Orchestra)	1991
Cayuga Lake "Memories" (Chamber Orchestra)	1992
Tubafest Celebration Fanfare (Four Tubas)	1992
Concerto for Violin and Orchestra	1993
Five Poems for Woodwind Quintet	1994
Les Couleurs Fauves (Wind Ensemble)	1995
Celebration Fanfare (Orchestra)	1996
Midwest Celebration (Three Brass Choirs and Percussion)	1996
Celebracion (Orchestra)	1997
Postcard from Home (Saxophone and Piano)	1997
Song (Chorus a cappella)	2000

CATEGORICAL LIST OF WORKS

ARRANGEMENTS

Herschel, William, 1738–1822. *Sinfonia no.XIV in D major.*
[arr. 1962] For orchestra
Premiere: 28 August, 1962, Cornell University, Ithaca, New York
Performers: Rochester Chamber Orchestra; conducted by Karel Husa
Unpublished

Lully, Jean-Baptiste, 1632–1687. *Carnaval, a masquerade.*
[arr.1961]
For orchestra 18 min.
Premiere: 24 November, 1963, Cornell University Ithaca, New York
Performers: Cornell Chamber Orchestra; conducted by Karel Husa
Kassel [W. German]: Barenreiter Verlag, 1968

Lully, Jean-Baptiste, 1632–1687. *Le ballet des muses.* [arr.1961]
Excerpts, transcribed and arranged for orchestra 18 min.
Premiere: 13 May, 1979, Cornell University, Ithaca, New York
Performers: Cayuga Chamber Orchestra; conducted by Karel Husa
New York: Associated Music Publisher, 1978

Delalande, Michel, 1739–1812. *Cantemus Domino.* [arr.1961]
Motet for soli, chorus and orchestra 23 min.
Premiere: 5 March, 1967, Cornell University, Ithaca, New York
Performers: John Ferrante, countertenor; John Burns, tenor; Arthur Neal, bass; Cornell
Chorus and Chamber Chorus; Cornell Chamber Orchestra; conducted by Karel Husa
New York: Lawson-Gould Music Publishers, 1971

BALLET

Monodrama: Portrait of an Artist (1976) 23 min.
Commissioned by the National Endowment for the Arts for the Jordan College of Music of Butler University and the Bicentennial of the United States
Premiere: 26 March, 1976, Indianapolis, Indiana
Performers: The Butler Ballet; the Indianapolis Symphony Orchestra; conducted by Oleg Kovalenko
New York: Associated Music Publishers, 1979

The Steadfast Tin Soldier (1974) 27 min.
Commissioned by the John Ernest Fowler Memorial Fund
Text from the Hans Christian Andersen fairy tale (narration is omitted when performed as a ballet)
Premiere: 10 May, 1975, Boulder, Colorado
Performer: John Paton, narrator; Boulder Philharmonic Orchestra; conducted by the composer
New York: Associated Music Publishers, 1975

The Trojan Women, ballet (1980) 45 min.
Commissioned by the University of Louisville School of Music
Premiere: 28 March, 1981, Louisville, Kentucky
Performers: Louisville Ballet; University of Louisville Orchestra; conducted by the composer
New York: Associated Music Publishers, 1981

BAND/WIND ENSEMBLE

Al Fresco (1974) 12 min.
Derived from the first movement of *Three fresques*
Commissioned by Ithaca College
Premiere: 19 April, 1975, Ithaca College, Ithaca, New York
Performers: Ithaca College Concert band; conducted by the composer
New York: Associated Music Publishers, 1975

An American Te Deum (1976) 45 min.
For baritone solo, mixed chorus and wind ensemble
Text complied from the writings of Henry David Thoreau, Ole E. Rolvaag, Otokar Brezina, folk, traditional and liturgical sources Commissioned by Louie J., Ella, and Joanne Pochobradsky, to commemorate the125th anniversary of Coe College and the Bicentennial of the United States
Premiere: 5 December, 1976, Cedar Rapids, Iowa
Performers: Allan D. Kellar, bartione, Coe College Wind Ensemble; Coe Concert Chorale, Cedar Rapids concert chorale; conducted by the composer
New York: Associated Music Publishers, 1976

Apotheosis of this Earth (1971) 25 min. (optional mixed chorus)
Commissioned by the Michigan Band and Orchestra Association, and dedicated to William D. Revelli on the occasion of his retirement
Premiere: 1 April, 1971, Ann Arbor, Michigan
Performers: University of Michigan Symphonic band; conducted by Karel Husa
New York: Associated Music Publishers, 1971

Concertino (1983) 16 min.
For piano and wind ensemble
Commissioned by the University of Central Florida Department of Music, Jerry Gardner, director
Premiere: 27 January, 1984, at the combined meetings of the College Band Directors National Association and the National Band Association, Southern Divisions, Orlando, Florida
Performer: Gary Wolf, piano; University of Central Florida Wind Ensemble; conducted by Karel Husa
Mainz: Schott, 2001

Concerto for Alto Saxophone and Concert Band (1967) 20 min.
  Commissioned by the Cornell University Wind Ensemble, Maurice Stith, director
  Premiere: 17 March, 1968, Ithaca, New York
  Performer: Sigurd Rascher, saxophone; Cornell University Wind Ensemble; conducted by the composer
  New York: Associated Music Publishers, 1972

Concerto for Percussion and Wind Ensemble (1971) 18 min.
  Commissioned by Ludwig Industries
  Premiere: 7 February, 1972, Waco, Texas
  Performer: Baylor University Symphonic Wind Ensemble; conducted by Gene C. Smith and Larry Vanlandingham
  New York: Associated Music Publishers, 1973

Concerto for Trumpet and Wind Orchestra (1973) 14 min.
  Commissioned by Kappa Kappa Psi and Tau Beta Sigma
  Premiere: 9 August, 1973, at the biennial convention of Kappa Kappa Psi and Tau Beta Sigma, University of Connecticut, Storrs, Connecticut
  Performer: Raymond Crisara, trumpet, National Intercollegiate Band; conducted by Arnold Gabriel
  The composer notes that this work can also be performed by the wind sections of symphony orchestras.
  New York: Associated Music Publishers, 1980

Concerto for Wind Ensemble (1982) 19 min.
  Commissioned by Michigan State University Alumni Band, for the opening of the Wharton Center for the Performing Arts
  Premiere: 3 December, 1982, East Lansing, Michigan
  Performers: Michigan State University Wind Symphony; conducted by Karel Husa
  Winning composition in the first biennial Sudler International Wind Band Composition Competition
  New York: Associated Music Publishers, 1982

Midwest Celebration Fanfare (1996) 6 min.
  For three brass choirs and percussion
  Written for the 50th anniversary of the Midwest Clinic
  Premiere: 17 December, 1996, Chicago
  Performers: Northshore Brass Ensemble, conducted by Karel Husa
  New York: Associated Music Publishers, 1999

Les Couleurs Fauves (1996) 17 min.
  Commissioned by Northwestern University and dedicated to John P. Paynter on the occasion of his retirement
  Premiere: 16 November, 1996, Evanston, Illinois
  Performers: Northwestern University Wind Ensemble, conducted by the composer
  Unpublished

Music for Prague 1968 (1968) 19 min.
  Commissioned by the Ithaca College Band, Kenneth Snapp, director
  Premiere: 31 January, 1969, at the national convention of the Music Educators National Conference, Washington, D.C.
  Performers: Ithaca College Concert Band; conducted by Kenneth Snapp
  New York: Associated Music Publishers, 1969

Musique pour harmonie (1951) 15 min.
  Commissioned by UNESCO
  No known public performance
  Unpublished

Smetana Fanfare (1984) 4 min.
  Commissioned by San Diego State Univesity Wind Ensemble; Charles Yates, dir.
  Premiere: 3 April, 1984, San Diego, California, commemorating the 100th anniversary of Smetana's death
  Performers: SDSU Wind Ensemble; conducted by Charles Yates
  New York: Associated Music Publishers, 1989

CHAMBER/SOLO

Cantata (1982) 18 min.
  For male chorus and brass quintet
  Commissioned by the Wabash College Glee Club, Dr. Stanley Malinowski, director
  Texts compiled from the writings of E.A. Robinson, Emily Dickinson and Walt Whitman
  Premiere: 20 April, 1983, Wabash College Chapel, Crawfordsville, Indiana
  Performers: Wabash College Glee Club and student brass quintet; conducted by the composer
  New York: Associated Music Publishers, 1982

Cayuga Lake "Memories" (1992) 21 min.
  For chamber orchestra
  Premiere: 4 April 1992, Ithaca College Centennial, Ithaca College Chamber Ensemble, Karel Husa conducting, Ithaca, NY,
  New York: Associates Music Publishers, 1996

Concerto for Brass Quintet and Piano (1965) 24.5 min.
  Paris: Leduc, 1965

Concerto for Alto Saxophone (1967) 20 min., saxophone-piano version
  Premiere: 1972, Evanston, Illinois
  Performers: Fred Hemke, saxophone; Milton Granger, piano
  New York: Associated Music Publishers, 1972

Deux Preludes (1966) 12 min.
  For flute, clarinet, and bassoon
  Premiere: 21 April, 1966, Ithaca, New York
  Performers: Ithaca College
  Paris: Leduc, 1968

Divertimento (1958) 15 min.
  For brass ensemble and percussion
  Expansion of movements from *Eight Czech Duets*
  Premiere: 17 February, 1960, Ithaca, New York
  Performers: Ithaca College Brass Ensemble; conducted
    by Robert Prins
  New York: Associated Music Publishers, 1970

Divertimento (1968) 16 min.
  For brass quintet
  Expansion of movements from *Eight Czech Duets*
  Premiere: 20 November, 1968, Ithaca College, Ithaca,
    New York
  Performers: Ithaca Brass Quintet
  New York: Associated Music Publishers, 1968

Drum Ceremony (1977) 2 min.
  For five percussionists (timpani, tom-toms, woodblocks)
  Introductory movement to *An American Te Deum*
  New York: Associated Music Publishers, 1982

Elegie et rondeau (1960) 10 min.
  For alto saxophone and piano
  Elegie is from piano solo; *Rondeau* is new material
  Premiere: July 29, 1960, at the Eastman School of Music
    Summer Saxophone Symposium, Rochester, New York
  Performers: Sigurd Rascher saxophone; William Krevis,
    piano
  Paris: Leduc, 1961

Evocations de Slovaquie (1951) 15 min.
  For clarinet, viola and violoncello
  Premiere: 4 May, 1952, Paris
  Performers: Maurice Cliquenois, clarinet; Micheline
    Lemoine, viola; Jacques Neiltz, violoncello
  Mainz: Schott, 1970

Fanfare (1981) 6 min.
  For brass ensemble and percussion
  Commissioned by the Portland (Oregon) Opera
  Premiere: 7 March, 1981, Portland, Oregon
  Performers: Portland Opera Brass Ensemble; conducted
    by Fred Sautter
  New York: Associated Music Publishers, 1984

Five Poems (1994) 19 min.
  For woodwind quintet
  Premiere: 10 February 1995, Carnegie Hall, New York,
    New York
  Performers: Quintet of the Americas

Four Little Pieces for Strings (1955) 14.5 min.
  For single string (quartet or quintet)
  Mainz: Schott, 1955

Intrada (1984) 3 min.
  For brass quintet
  Commissioned by the Brass Menagerie and the National

Endowment for the Arts
  Premiere: 15 November, 1984, Festival of the Arts, Balti-
    more, Maryland
  Performer: The Brass Menagerie
  Unpublished

Intradas and Interludes (1980) 17 min.
  For 7 trumpets and percussion
  Commissioned by the International Trumpet Guild
  Premiere: 21 June, 1980, at Ohio State University, for
    the International Trumpet Guild annual convention,
    Columbus, Ohio
  Performers: International Trumpet Guild Ensemble; con-
    ducted by Marshall Haddock
  New York: Associated Music Publishers, 1985

Landscapes (1977) 22 min.
  For brass quintet
  Commissioned by the Western Brass Quintet for the
    Bicentennial of the United States
  Premiere: 17 October, 1977, Kalamazoo, Michigan
  Performers: Western Brass Quintet
  New York: Associated Music Publishers, 1978

Poem (1959) 13 min.
  For viola and piano, reduction of the original work with
    orchestra
  Mainz: Schott, 1963

Postcard from Home (1997) 5 min.
  For alto saxophone and piano
  Premiere: 1 August 1997, National Concert Hall, Taipei,
    Taiwan
  Performers: John Sampen, alto saxophone; Marilyn
    Schrude, piano
  New York: Associated Music Publishers, 2000

Recollections (1982) 21 min.
  For woodwind quintet and piano
  Commissioned by the Grenadilla Enterprises to celebrate
    the bicentennial of Dutch-American diplomatic rela-
    tions
  Premiere: 28 October, 1982, The Library of Congress,
    Washington, D.C.
  Performers: New Amsterdam Ensemble; Walter Ponce,
    piano
  New York: Associated Music Publishers, 1985

Sonata (1973) 30 min.
  For violin and piano
  Commissioned by the Koussevitzky Foundation
  Premiere: 30 March, 1974, New York City, New York
  Performers: Ani Kavafian, violin; Richard Goode, piano
  New York: Associated Music Publishers, 1979

Sonata a Tre (1981) 20 min.
  For violin, clarinet and piano
  Commissioned by the Verdehr Trio

Premiere: 23 March, 1982, Hong Kong
Performers: Verdehr Trio
New York: Associated Music Publishers, 1987

Sonatina (1945) 15 min.
    For violin and piano
    Premiere: 27 September, 1945, Prague
    Performers: Spytihnev Sorm, violin; Otakar Parik, piano
    New York: Associated Music Publishers, 1985

String quartet, op. 2 (1943) 20 min.
    Premiere: private performance in Prague, March 1944
    Performers: Prague Quartet
    Unpublished

String quartet, no. 1 (1948) 24 min.
    Commissioned by the Smetana Quartet
    Premiere: 23 May, 1948, Prague
    Performer: Smetana Quartet
    Mainz: Schott, 1948
    Lili Boulanger Foundation Prize, 1950; Bilthoven (Gaudeamus) Festival Prize, 1952

String quartet, no. 2 (1953) 20 min.
    Commissioned by the Parrenin String Quartet of Paris
    Premiere: 23 October, 1954, Paris
    Performers: Parrenin String Quartet
    Mainz: Schott, 1953

String quartet, no. 3 (1968) 19 min.
    Commissioned by the Fne Arts Foundation of Chicago
    Premiere: 14 October, 1968, Chicago, Illinois
    Performers: Fine Arts String Quartet
    New York: Associated Music Publishers, 1970
    Pulitzer Prize for Music, 1969

String quartet "Poems," no. 4 (1990) 20 min.
    Commissioned by the National Endowment for the Arts for the Colorado Quartet
    Premiere: 12 October, 1991, International Brno Festival, Brno, Czechoslovakia
    Performers: Colorado Quartet
    New York: Associated Music Publishers, 2002

Suite (1943) 15 min.
    For viola and piano
    Premiere: 26 November, 1946, Prague
    Performers: Antonin Hyksa, viola; Jiri Berkovec, piano
    New York: Associated Music Publishers

Three Dance Sketches (1979) 18 min.
    For four percussionists
    Commissioned by the National Association of College Wind and Percussion Instructors
    Premiere: 12 April, 1980, at the 27th National Music Educators National Conference Biennial Convention, Miami, Florida
    Performers: University Tennessee Percussion Ensemble;

conducted by H. Michael Comb
New York: Associated Music Publishers, 1982

Two Preludes (1966) 12 min.
    For flute, clarinet and bassoon
    Commissioned by the Iota (Ithaca College) chapter of Kappa Kappa Psi
    Premiere: 22 April, 1966, Ithaca College, Ithaca, New York
    Performers: William Hoff, flute; Joseph Amisano, clarinet; Donald Winch, bassoon
    Paris: Leduc, 1968

Tubafest Celebration Fanfare (1992) 3 min
    For tuba quartet
    Premiere: 9 October 1992, Bloomington, IN
    Performers: Tuba Quartet of Indiana University

Variations (1984) 21 min.
    For violin, viola, violoncello and piano
    Commissioned by the National Endowment for the Arts for the consortium of the Atlanta Virtuosi, the Rowe Quartet and the New England Piano Quartette
    Premiere: 20 May 1984, Atlanta, Georgia
    Performers: Atlanta Virtuosi
    New York: Associated Music Publishers, [NYP]

CHORAL/VOCAL

An American Te Deum (1976) 45 min.
    For baritone solo, mixed chorus and wind ensemble
    Text complied from the writings of Henry David Thoreau, Ole E. Rolvaag, Otokar Brezina, folk, traditional and liturgical sources
    Commissioned by Louie J., Ella, and Joanne Pochobradsky, to commemorate the 125th anniversary of Coe College and the Bicentennial of the United States
    Premiere: 5 December, 1976, Cedar Rapids, Iowa
    Performers: Allan D. Kellar, baritone, Coe College Wind Ensemble; Coe Concert Chorale, Cedar Rapids concert chorale; conducted by the composer
    New York: Associated Music Publishers, 1976

An American Te Deum [orchestral version] (1977) 45 min.
    For baritone solo, mixed chorus and orchestra
    Premiere: 10 May, 1978, Inter-American Festival of Music, Washington, D.C.
    Performers: Carl Gerbrandt, baritone; The Festival Orchestra; Peabody Conservatory Chorus; Morgan State University Choir; conducted by the composer
    New York: Associated Music Publishers, 1986

Apotheosis of this Earth (1972) 27 min.
    For mixed chorus and orchestra
    Text by the composer
    Premiere: 12 April, 1973, Cornell University, Ithaca, New York

Performers: Cornell University Orchestra, Chorus and Glee Club; conducted by the composer
New York: Associated Music Publishers, 1974

Cantata (1982) 18 min.
For male chorus and brass quintet
Commissioned by the Wabash College Glee Club, Dr. Stanley Malinowski, director
Texts compiled from the writings of E.A. Robinson, Emily Dickinson and Walt Whitman
Premiere: 20 April, 1983, Wabash College Chapel, Crawfordsville, Indiana
Performers: Wabash College Glee Club and student brass quintet; conducted by the composer
New York: Associated Music Publishers, 1982

Every Day (1981) 7 min.
For mixed chorus a cappella
Commissioned by the Ithaca College Concert Choir for the Ithaca College Choir Fesival
Text by Henry David Thoreau
Premiere: 14 November, 1981, Ithaca, New York
Performers: Ithaca College Concert Choir; conducted by Lawrence Doebler
New York: Associated Music Publishers, 1983

Festive Ode (1964) 4 min.
For mixed chorus and orchestra (also for chorus and band, brass or organ)
Text by Eric Blackall
Premiere: 9 October, 1964, Cornell University Centennial Convocation, Ithaca, New York
Performers: Cornell University Symphony Orchestra, Chorus and Glee club; conducted by Thomas A. Sokol
New York: Highgate Press, 1977; Boston: E.C. Schirmer, 2000

There Are From Time to Time Mornings (1976) 6 min.
For mixed chorus a cappella (extracted from *An American Te Deum*)
Text from Henry David Thoreau
Commissioned by Louie J., Ella, and Joanne Pochobradsky, to commemorate the 125th anniversary of Coe College and the Bicentennial of the United States
Premiere: 5 December, 1976, Cedar Rapids, Iowa
Performers: Allan D. Kellar, baritone, Coe College Wind Ensemble; Coe Concert Chorale, Cedar Rapids Concert Chorale; conducted by the composer
New York: Associated Music Publishers, 1982

Three Moravian Songs (1981) 10 min.
For mixed chorus a cappella
Folk texts. English text by Ruth Martin
Commissioned by the Holland [Michigan] Community Choir

Premiere: 14 March, 1981, Holland, Michigan
Performers: The Holland Community Choir (Calvin Langejans, director); conducted by the composer
New York: Associated Music Publishers, 1982

Twelve Moravian Songs (1956)
For voice and piano
Folk texts. English text by Ruth Martin
Premiere: April 1968, Brno, Czechoslovakia
Performer: Unknown singer and pianist for the Czechoslovak Radio-TV of Brno
New York: Associated Music Publishers, 1977

KEYBOARD

Eight Czech Duets (1955) 20 min.
For piano (4 hands)
Premiere: 28 April, 1956, Cornell University Festival of Contemporary Arts, Ithaca, New York
Performers: Bruce Archibald and Charles McClain
Mainz: Schott, 1958

Elegie (1957) 5 min.
For piano
Premiere: 15 November, 1967, Ithaca College, Ithaca, New York
Performer: Elaine Merrey
Paris: Leduc, 1968; Merion Music, 1994

Frammenti (1987) 6 min.
For organ
Excerpts for solo organ, from the *Concerto*, for organ and orchestra
Premiere: 6 November, 1987, Northwestern University, Evanston, Illinois
Performer: Karel Paukert
New York: Associated Music Publishers, [NYP]

Sonata, no. 1 (1949) 26 min.
For piano
Premiere: 19 April, 1950, Paris, France
Performer: Luise Vosgerchian
Mainz: Schott, 1952

Sonata, no. 2 (1975) 18 min.
For piano
Commissioned by the Edyth Bush Charitable Foundation for the Bicentennial Piano Series of the Washington Performing Arts Society
Premiere: 4 October, 1975, Washington, D.C.
Performer: Andre-Michel Schub
New York: Associated Music Publishers, 1978

Sonatina (1943) 12 min.
For piano
Premiere: 20 April, 1945, Prague

Performer: Jiri Berkovec
Prague: Fr. Urbanek, 1947 [dist. by Boosey & Hawkes]
New York: Associated Music Publishers, 1947 [new engraving of Urbanek ed., 1980]

ORCHESTRA

Celebracion (1997) 6 min.
  Premiere: October 1997, La Coruna, Spain
  Performers: Orquesta Sinfonica de Galicia; Victor Pablo Perez, conductor

Celebration Fanfare (1996) 2 min.
  Premiere: 7 July 1996, Oneonta, NY
  Performers: Summer Festival and Institute, Hartwick Festival Orchestra, Charles Schneider, conductor
  New York: Associated Music Publishers, 1998

Concertino (1949) 15 min.
  For piano and orchestra
  Premiere: 6 June, 1952, Brussels, Belgium
  Performers: Helene Boschi, piano; Belgian Radio and Television Orchestra; conducted by Daniel Sternfeld
  Mainz: Schott, 1952

Concerto for Brass Quintet and Strings (1965) 24 min.
  (also available for brass quintet and piano)
  Premiere: 15 February, 1970, Buffalo, New York
  Performers: New England Conservatory Student Brass Quintet; Buffalo Philharmonic Orchestra; conducted by Lukas Foss
  Paris: Leduc, 1971

Concerto for Orchestra (1987) 39 min.
  Commissioned by the New York Philharmonic and Zubin Mehta
  Premiere: 25 September, 1986, New York City, New York
  Performers: The New York Philharmonic; conducted by Zubin Mehta
  New York: Associated Music Publishers, [NYP]

Concerto for Organ and Orchestra (1987) 21 min.
  Commissioned by the Michelson-Morley Centennial Celebration, 1987
  Premiere: 28 October, 1987, Cleveland Museum of Art, Cleveland, Ohio
  Performers: Karel Paukert, organ; The Cleveland Institute of Music Orchestra; conducted by the composer
  New York: Associated Music Publihsers, 1994

Concerto for Trumpet and Orchestra (1987) 20 min.
  Commissioned by the Chicago Symphony Orchestra
  Premiere: 11 February, 1988, Chicago, Illinois
  Performers: Adolph Herseth, trumpet; the Chicago Symphony Orchestra; conducted by Sir Georg Solti
  New York: Associated Music Publishers, 1994

Concerto for Violin and Orchestra (1993) 28 min.
  Premiere: 27 May 1993
  Performers: Glenn Dicterow, violin, New York Philharmonic, Kurt Masur, conductor
  New York: Associated Music Publishers, 1994

Concerto for Violoncello and Orchestra (1988) 27 min.
  Commissioned by the University of Southern California, for the Frank Kerze Jr. Memorial Fund (the commission and world premiere performance is dedicated, in memorial, to Frank Kerze Jr. by his sisters Terese Kerze Cheyovich and Florence Kerze)
  Premiere: 2 March, 1989
  Performers: Lynn Harrell, violoncello; the University of Southern California Symphony; conducted by Daniel Lewis
  New York: Associated Music Publishers, 1997

Divertimento (1948) 15 min.
  For string orchestra
  Premiere: 30 October, 1949, Paris
  Performers: Club d'essai Paris Orchestra; conducted by Stanislaw Skrowacewski
  Mainz: Schott, 1977

Elegie et Rondeau (1961) 10 min.
  For alto saxophone and orchestra (originally for alto saxophone and piano)
  Premiere: 6 May, 1962, Cornell University Festival of Contemporary Arts, Ithaca, New York
  Performers: Sigurd Rascher, saxophone; Cornell Symphony Orchestra; conducted by the composer
  Paris: Leduc, 1963

Fantasies (1956) 19 min.
  Commissioned by the Friends of Music at Cornell University
  Premiere: 28 April, 1957, Cornell University Festival of Contemporary Arts, Ithaca, New York
  Performers: Cornell University Orchestra; conducted by the composer
  Mainz: Schott, 1961

Four Little Pieces (1955) 16 min.
  For string orchestra
  Premiere: 17 March, 1957, at the Youth Music Festival, Fürsteneck Castle, West Germany
  Performers: Ensemble of the Youth Music Festival, conducted by Hilmar Hockner
  Mainz: Schott, 1955

Fresque (1963) 11 min.
  Revision of first movement of *Three fresques*
  Premiere: 5 May, 1963, Syracuse, New York
  Performers: Syracuse University Orchestra; conducted by the composer
  New York: Associated Music Publishers, 1976

Monodrama: Portrait of an Artist (1976) 23 min.
> Commissioned by the National Endowment for the Arts for the Jordan College of Music of Butler University and the Bicentennial of the United States
> Premiere: 26 March, 1976, Indianapolis, Indiana
> Performers: The Butler Ballet; the Indianapolis Symphony Orchestra; conducted by Oleg Kovalenko
> New York: Associated Music Publishers, 1979

Mosaïques (1961) 15 min.
> Commissioned by the Hamburg Radio Corporation
> Premiere: 7 November, 1961, Hamburg, W. Germany
> Performers: Nord-Deutscher Rundfunk Orchestrer; conducted by the composer
> Mainz: Schott, 1977

Musique d'amateurs (1953) 15 min.
> Commissioned by UNESCO
> Premiere: 1954, Castle Frubeck, W. Germany
> Performance: UNESCO chamber orchestra; conducted by Hilmar Hockner
> Mainz: Schott, 1977

Music for Prague, 1968 (1969) 19 min.
> For orchestra (Originally for band)
> Premiere: 31 January, 1970, Munich, West Germany
> Performers: Munich Philharmonic Orchestra; conducted by the composer
> New York: Associated Music Publishers, 1969

Nocturne from Fantasies 7 min.
> Mainz: Schott, 1961

Overture (1944) 8 min.
> Premiere: 20 January, 1945, Prague (broadcast); 18 June, 1946, Prague (concert)
> Performers: Czechoslovak Radio Orchestra (broadcast); Prague Symphony orchestra (concert); both performances conducted by the composer
> Unpublished

Overture "Youth" (1990) 5 min.
> Premiere: 24 November 1991, Seattle, Washington
> Performers: Seattle Youth Symphony Orchestra, Ruben Gurewich, conductor
> New York: Associated Music Publishers, 1996

Pastoral (1979) 7 min.
> For string orchestra (derived from the 2nd movement of the *Sonatina*, for Violin and Piano)
> Commissioned by the American String Teachers Association
> Premiere: 12 April, 1980, at the 27th Music Educators National Conference biennial Convention, Miami, Florida
> Performers: ASTA National String Orchestra
> New York: Associated Music Publishers, 1982

Poeme (1959) 13 min.
> For viola and chamber orchestra
> Premiere: 12 June, 1960, World Music Festival of the International Society for Contemporary Music, Cologne, West Germany
> Performers: Ulrich Koch, viola; Süd-Westfunk Radio Orchestra; conducted by Hans Rosbaud
> Mainz: Schott, 1963

Postcard from Home (1997) 5 min.
> For saxophone and piano
> Premiere: 1 August 1997, Taipei, Taiwan
> Performers: John Sampen, saxophone, Marilyn Schrude, piano
> New York: Associated Music Publishers, 1999

Portrait (1953) 12 min.
> For string orchestra
> Commissioned by the Donaueschingen Musiktage
> Premiere: 10 October, 1953, Donaueschingen, W. Germany
> Performers: Süd-Westfunk Radio Orchestra; conducted by Hans Rosbaud
> Mainz: Schott, 1977

Serenade (1963) 15 min.
> For woodwind quintet, strings, harp and xylophone (Expansion of Evocations de Slovaquie)
> Commissioned by the Baltimore Symphony Orchestra
> Premiere: 7 January, 1964, Baltimore, Maryland
> Performers: Baltimore Symphony Orchestra; conducted by Peter Herman Adler
> Paris: Leduc, 1965

Sinfonietta for orchestra (1944) 20 min.
> Premiere: 25 April, 1947, Prague
> Performers: Czechoslovak Radio Orchestra; conducted by Karel Ancerl
> Prague: Czech Musical Fun, [n.d.]
> Awarded Prague Academy of Arts and Sciences Prize, 1948

Song for mixed chorus (2000)
> Premiere: 3 May, 2000. Oneonta, New York
> Performers: Hartwick College Choir; conducted by J. Kratochvil
> New York: Associated Music Publishers, 2000

Symphonic Suite for orchestra (1984) 19 min.
> Commissioned by the University of Georgia for the Bicentennial Celebration of its charter
> Premiere: 1 October, 1984, Athens, Georgia
> Performers: University of Georgia Festival Orchestra; conducted by the composer
> New York: Associated Music Publishers, 1984

Symphony, no.1 for orchestra (1953) 27 min.
> Premiere: 4 March, 1954, Brussels, Belgium

Performers: Belgian Radio and Television Orchestra;
conducted by Daniel Sternfeld
Mainz: Schott, 1953

Symphony, no.2 "Reflections" for orchestra (1983) 20 min.
Commissioned for the Eastern Music Festival
Premiere: 16 July, 1983, Greensboro, North Carolina
Performers: Eastern Philharmonic Orchestra; conducted
by the composer
New York: Associated Music Publishers, 1983

The Steadfast Tin Soldier for narrator and orchestra (1974) 26 min.
Commissioned by the John Ernest Fowler Memorial Fund
Text from the Hans Christian Andersen fairy tale
Premiere: 10 May, 1975, Boulder, Colorado
Performers: John Paton, narrator; Boulder Philharmonic
Orchestra; conducted by the composer
New York: Associated Music Publishers, 1974

The Trojan Women, (scenes from..) (1984) 22 min.
Premiere: 28 October, 1988, Metropolitan Museum of
Art, New York City, New York
Performers: Orchestra of St. Luke's; conducted by the
composer
New York: Associated Music Publishers, 1986

Three Fresques for orchestra (1947) 27 min.
Premiere: 27 April, 1949, Prague
Performers: Prague Radio Orchestra; conducted by
Vaclav Smetacek
Prague: Czech Musical Fund, [n d]

Two Sonnets by Michelangelo for orchestra (1971) 16 min.
Commissioned by the Evanston (Illinois) Symphony
Orchestra Association
Premiere: 28 April, 1972, Evanston, Illinois
Performer: Evanston Symphony Orchestra; conducted
by Frank Miller
New York: Associated Music Publishers, 1975

DISCOGRAPHY

(recordings are compact discs unless otherwise noted)

Al Fresco
Golden Crest Records ATH-5066. 1979 33 1/3 LP
James Forger, saxophone; Michigan State University
Wind Symphony and Symphony Band; Karel Husa,
conductor.
In: *Compositions of Karel Husa.*
Includes his *Concerto,* for saxophone and concert band,
Concerto, for percussion and wind ensemble.

Mark MC-5405. 1976 33 1/3 LP
Western Illinois University Wind Ensemble; Harry
Begian, conductor

In: *The Breaded Leaf.*
Includes works by Robert Linn, Warren Benson, and William Hill.

Mas DDD 330
Sinfonisches Jugenblasorchester, Felix Hauswirth, conductor

Clarton CQ 0016-2 4,3,1
Czech Army Centra Band; K Belohoubek, conductor

Mark MCD 1202
Sam Houston U.Wind Ensemble; Gary Sousa, conductor

ARS MUSICI AMP 5068-2 (Germany)
Stadtkapelle Wangen; Alfred Gross, conductor

Apotheosis of this Earth (band)
Golden Crest Records CRS 4134. 1974 33 1/3 LP
University of Michigan Symphony Band; Karel Husa,
conductor.
Includes his *Music for Prague, 1968*

Mark Custom Recording Service 3182 MCD
Arkansas State Univeristy Wind Ensemble; Karel Husa,
conductor.
Includes his *Concertino for Piano and Wind Ensemble*

Mirasound BV, WWM 500.075 Banda Sinfonica La
Artistica, Bunol, Spain; Henrie Adams, conductor.

Apotheosis of this Earth (orchestra)
Louisville Orchestra LS799. 1991.
University of Louisville Concert Choir and Louisville
Orchestra; Karel Husa, conductor.
Louisville Orchestra first edition records.

Cayuga Lake
Live from Ithaca College—Centennial Premieres
Ithaca College, Ithaca NY 14850
Ithaca College Faculty Chamber Orchestra
Karel Husa, conductor

Concertino for Piano
Mark 2568 MCD
Akiko Sakai, piano: California St. University-Northridge
Karel Husa, guest conductor

Concerto for Alto Saxophone and Concert Band
Golden Crest 4124. 1970 33 1/3 LP
Tim Timmons, saxophone; Ithaca College Concert Band;
Edward Gobrecht, conductor.
Includes Ingolf Dahl's *Concerto,* for saxophone and wind
ensemble.

Cornell University Records CUWE-3 [n.d.] 33 1/3 LP
Sigurd Rascher, saxophone; Cornell University Wind
Ensemble; Karel Husa, conductor.
Includes his *Music for Prague, 1968*

Golden Crest Records ATH-5066. 1979 33 1/3 LP
James Forger, saxophone; Michigan State University
    Wind Symphony and Symphony Band; Karel Husa,
    conductor.
In: *Compositions of Karel Husa.*
Includes his *Al Fresco* and *Concerto*, for percussion and
    wind ensemble.

Concerto for Alto Saxophone and Concert Band (piano reduction)
Brewster 1203. [1971] 33 1/3 LP
Frederick Hemke, saxophone; Milton Granger, piano.
In : *The American saxophone.*
Includes works by Ingolf Dahl and Warren Benson.

Brewster 1216. 1976 33 1/3 LP
Robert Black, saxophone; Patricia Black, piano
In: *Concert repertoire for saxophone.*
Includes works by Henry Cowell and Jacques Ibert.

Concerto for Percussion and Wind Ensemble
Golden Crest Records ATH-5066. 1979 33 1/3 LP
James Forger, saxophone; Michigan State University
    Wind Symphony and Symphony Band; Stanley E.
    DeRusha, conductor.
In: *Compositions of Karel Husa.*
Includes his *Concerto*, for saxophone and concert band,
    and *Al Fresco*

Sheffield Salon Series SLS506
The Moscow Philharmonic, Dmitri Kitayenko, conductor

Concerto for Orchestra
St. Louis CD 1995 Slatkin Years
St. Louis Symphony Orchestra; Leonard Slatkin, con-
    ductor

Concerto for Wind Ensemble
Summit DCD 192
Cincinnati Wind Symphony; Mallory Thompson, con-
    ductor

Divertimento, for Brass Ensemble
Phoenix PHCD 128
New York Brass Ensemble, Lawrence Sobol, conductor

Divertimento, for Brass Quintet
University of Iowa Press. 1976 33 1/3 LP
Iowa Brass Quintet.
In: *Sounding Brass*
Includes works by Eugene Bozza, J.S. Bach, Paul Smoker,
    Michel Leclerc, Jean Mouret and John Wilbye.

Golden Crest 4114. [n.d.] 33 1/3 LP
Ithaca Brass Quintet.
Includes works by Verne Reynolds, Mikolaj Zielenski and
    Andreas Berger.

Divertimento for Band (arr. John Boyd)
BRAIN BOCD 7507

Indiana State U. Symphonic Band; John Boyd, conductor
Drum Ceremony
WORE 970007-2CD
Dama-Dama 3 Ensemble, Brno

Eight Czech Duets, for piano, 4-hands.
Orion 81412. 1981 33 1/3 LP
Frederic Schoettler and Theresa Dye, pianists.
Recorded in the Carl F.W. Ludwig Recital Hall, Kent
    State University.
Includes works by Aaron Copland and Robert Starer.

Elegie
Golden Crest CRS 4175. 1978 33 1/3 LP
Mary Ann Covert, piano.
Includes his *Sonatina*, op.1, and *Sonata*, no.1 and 2

Elegie et Rondeau, for saxophone and piano.
Brewster 1295. [n.d.] 33 1/3 LP
Joseph Wytko, saxophone; Madeline Williamson, piano.
In: *Recital music for saxophone*
Includes works by Ryo Noda, Tommy Joe Anderson, Les-
    lie Bassett, and Hermann Reutter.

Roncorp EMS-031. 1984 cassette
Michael Jacobson, saxophone; Paul Borg, piano
Includes works by Ingolf Dahl, Warren Benson, and Paul
    Arma.

Open loop "Vintage Flora" CD007
Lyn Kock, saxophone, Nadine Shank, piano

Crystal Records DCD 652
Lawrence Gwozdz, saxophone; David Evenson, piano

Music Contrasts NSS-CD 36931
Due Boemi di Praga; J. Horak-E. Kovarnova
(version for bass-clarinet and piano)

Vanguard Classic DDD 99092
A. Bornkamp, Ivo Janssen

Albany – Troy 331
L. Gwozdz, B. Martinu Philharmonic, K. Trevor, con-
    ductor

Evocations de Slovaquie
Grenadilla Records QS1008. 1976 33 1/3 LP
Lawrence Sobol, clarinet; Louise Schulamn, viola; Timo-
    thy Eddy, violoncello.
Includes Alan Hovanhess' *Firdausi.*

Phoenix PHCD 113. 1990
The Long Island Chamber Ensemble
Includes his *String quartet no. 2* and *String quartet no. 3*

Fantasies for Orchestra
Grenadilla GSC 1054. 1984 cassette
Orchestres de Solistes de Paris, Karel Husa, conductor
Includes Sidney Hodkinson's *The edge of the olde one.*

Phoenix PHCD 128
Les Solistes de Paris and Brno Philharmonic
Karel Husa, conductor

Five Poems
SUPRAPHON-PANTON 819009-2131
Prague Wind Quintet

Fresque
Marco Polo DDD 8.223640
Slovak Radio Symphony Orchestra, Barry Kolman, conductor

Four Little Pieces, for chamber orchestra.
Opus One 51. 1979? 33 1/3 LP
Chamber Orchestra of Albuquerque; David Oberg, conductor.
Includes works by Michael Mauldin and John Robb.

Landscapes
Composers Recordings CRI SD 192(78). 1978 33 1/3 LP
Western Brass Quintet.
In: *Brass Etcetera.*
Includes Herbert Haufrecht's *Symphony for brass and timpani*

Composers Recordings CRI SD 261. 1971
Western Brass Quintet.
Includes his *Serenade* for woodwind quintet, with strings, harp and xylophone, and *Nocturne,* from *Fantasies,* for orchestra

Monodrama
Louisville Orchestra LS799. 1991.
University of Louisville Concert Choir and Louisville Orchestra; Karel Husa, conductor.
Louisville Orchestra first edition records.

Mosaïques
Composers Recordings CRI USD 221. 1968 33 1/3 LP
Stockholm Radio Symphony Orchestra; Karel Husa, conductor.
Includes works by Alan Hovhaness and Willard Straight.

Composers Recordings CRI SD 261.
Stockholm Radio Symphony Orchestra; Karel Husa, conductor.

Music for Prague, 1968 (band)
Cornell University Records CUWE-3 [n.d.] 33 1/3 LP
Cornell University Wind Ensemble; Karel Husa, conductor.
Includes his *Concerto for Alto Saxophone and Concert Band*

Mark Records UMC 2389. 1970 33 1/3 LP
Ohio State University Symphonic Band; Gene Thrailkill, conductor.
Includes works by Vaclav Nelhybel, Alfred H. Barles and Dmitri Shostakovich.

Golden Crest Records CRS 4134. 1974 33 1/3 LP
University of Michigan Symphony Band; Karel Husa, conductor.
Includes his *Apotheosis of this Earth.*

Franco Columbo Publications BP 136. 197? 33 1/3 LP
University of Texas Symphonic Band; William J. Moody, conductor.
Includes works by Vaclav Nelhybel and Edward J. Madden.

Educational record reference library series.
Mark Custom Recording Division MC 20379. 198?
University of Illinois Symphonic Band #106.
Includes works by Kenneth J. Alford, Roger Nixon, and Ralph Vaughan Williams

CBS MK 44916 DDD. 1989
Eastman Wind Ensemble; Donald Hunsberger, conductor.
Includes works by Ralph Vaughan Williams, Paul Hindemith and Aaron Copland

Mark Custom Recording Service MCD-1866. 1995
University of Illinois Symphonic Band; James F. Keene, conductor.
Recorded in the Foellinger Great Hall, Krannert Center for the Performing Arts, Urbana, Illinois. Recording #129
Includes works by Percy Grainger, David Stanhope and Ron Nelson

Obrasso 8265
Texas All-State Symphonic Band and Concert Band
Larry Rachleff, conductor

CBDNA CD1991
St. F. Austin S.U. Symphonic Band
John L. Whitwell, conductor

Albany TRO 271
Temple University Wind Symphony
Karel Husa, guest conductor
Includes works by Rimsky-Korsakov.

ARS MUSICI AMP 5049-2 (Germany)
Stadtkapelle Wangen; Alfred Gross, conductor

WASBE CD5820 AMOS (Switzerland)
International Y.W. Orchestra, Karel Husa, conductor

Klavier K 11126
University of North Texas Band, Eugene Corporon, conductor

Klavier 11124.
University of North Texas Wind Symphony, Eugene Corporon, conductor.
Includes works by Ellerby, Grainger, Gillingham, Persichetti, Finney.

KAREL HUSA

Music for Prague, 1968 (orchestra)
Louisville LS 722. 1972
Louisville Orchestra; Jorge Mester, conductor.
Includes works by Krzysztof Penderecki and Gene Gutche.

Vienna Modern Masters, Music from Six continents DDD V MN 3023
B. Martinu Philharmonic Orchestra, Milos Machek, conductor
Marco Polo DDD 8.223640
Slovak Radio Symphony Orchestra, Barry Koman, conductor

Recollections for woodwind quintet and piano
Lodenice DDD L10150-2131
Czech Woodwind Quintet and D. Weisner, piano

Serenade, for woodwind quintet, with strings, harp and xylophone
Composers Recordings CRI SD 261. 1971
Prague Symphony Orchestra; Karel Husa, conductor.
Includes his *Symphony*, no. 1, and *Nocturne*, from *Fantasies*, for orchestra

Serenade for Woodwind Quintet and Piano
Crystal Records 751
Westwood Quintet; Lisa Bergman, piano

Smetana Fanfare
Obrasso 8265
Texas All State Symphonic Band and Concert Band
Mallory Thompson, conductor

Summit DCD 192
Cincinnati Wind Symphony; Mallory Thompson, conductor

Sonata a Tre, for violin, clarinet and piano
Crystal Records S648. 1986
The Verdehr Trio.
Includes Jospeh Haydn's *Three trios*, Hob. IV.

Sonata a Tre
Crystal Records DCD 744
Verdehr Trio.
Sinfonietta 0006 2 231
Sonata a Tre Ensemble, Brno Czech Republic

Sonata for Violin and Piano
New World Records 80493-2
Elmar Oliveira, violin; David Oei, piano

Sonata, no. 1.
Golden Crest CRS 4175. 1978
Mary Ann Covert, piano.
Includes his *Elegie, Sonatina*, op.1, and *Sonata*, no.2

Sonata, no. 2.
Grenadilla Records 1025. 1978
Peter Basquin, piano
Includes works by Ingolf Dahl and Dave Diamond.

Golden Crest CRS 4175. 1978
Mary Ann Covert, piano.
Includes his *Elegie, Sonatina*, op.1, and *Sonata*, no.1

New World Records 80493-2. 1995
Peter Basquin, piano; Recorded at Rutgers Presbyterian Church, NYC
Originally released on Grenadilla Records
Includes his *Twelve Moravian songs* and *Sonata*, for violin and piano

Sonatina, for piano
Golden Crest CRS 4175. 1978
Mary Ann Covert, piano.
Includes his *Elegie, Sonata*, no.1, and *Sonata*, no.2

String quartet, no.1.
Leonarda LPI 117. 1983
The Alard Quartet.
Includes Priaulx Rainier's *Quartet for strings*.

PANTON 819009-2131
Suk Quartet
Includes his *Five Poems and Variations*

String quartet, no.2.
Everest SDBR 3200. 1971
Fine Arts Quartet.
Includes his *String quartet*, no.3

Phoenix PHCD 113. 1990
The Fine Arts Quartet
Includes his *Evocations de Slovaquie* and *String quartet no. 3*

String quartet, no.3.
Everest SDBR 3200. 1971
Fine Arts Quartet.
Includes his *String quartet*, no.2

Phoenix PHCD 113. 1990
The Fine Arts Quartet
Includes his *Evocations de Slovaquie* and *String quartet no. 2*

String Quartet, no.4 "Poems"
Albany TROY 259
Colorado Quartet

Symphony, no.1.
Composers Recordings CRI SD 261. 1971
Prague Symphony Orchestra; Karel Husa, conductor.
Includes his *Serenade* for woodwind quintet, with strings, harp and xylophone, and *Nocturne*, from *Fantasies*, for orchestra

Symphony, no.2. "Reflections"
Marco Polo DDD 8.223640
Slovak Radio Symphony Orchestra, Barry Koman, conductor
Includes his *Fresque* and *Music for Prague 1968*

The Trojan Women
Louisville orchestra Records LS 775. 1981
Louisville Orchestra; Akira Endo, conductor.

Scenes from The Trojan Women
Phoenix PHCD 128
Les Solistes de Paris and Brno Philharmonic
Karel Husa, conductor

Three Dance Sketches for Percussion
Rotag RG 0019-2131 DDD
Prague Percussion Project, Lynn A. Barber, artistic director
"Contemporary Czech Music for Percussion"

Twelve Moravian Songs
Grenadilla GSC 1073 [cassette]. 1988
Barbara Ann Martin, soprano; Elizabeth Rodgers, piano.
Includes works by Walter Piston and Alan Hovhaness

New World Records 80493-2. 1995
Barbara Ann Martin, soprano; Elizabeth Rodgers, piano
Recorded at Sorcerer Sounds, NYC
Originally released on Grenadilla Records
Includes his *Sonata* no. 2 for piano and *Sonata*, for violin and piano

Two Preludes, for flute, clarinet and bassoon
Vox SVBX 5307. 1977
The Dorian Quintet.
In: *The avant garde woodwind quintet in the U.S.A.*
Includes works by Samuel Barber, Arthur Berger, Elliott Carter, Luciano Berio, Irving Fine, Lukas Foss, Mario Davidovsky, Jacob Druckman, and Gunther Schuller.

Two Sonnets from Michelangelo
Louisville Orchestra LS 725. 1972
Louisville Orchestra, Jorge Mester, conductor.
Includes Matthias Bamert's *Septuria lunaris.*

Variations, for violin, viola, violoncello and piano
Orion ORS 86498. 1986
The New England Piano Quartette.
Includes Werner Torkanowsky's *Piano Quartet.*

PANTON 819009-2131
Prague Trio and J.Klepac

ENDNOTES

1. Byron Adams, *Karel Husa* (New York: Associated Music Publishers, 1997), 8.
2. Susan Hayes Hitchens, *Karel Husa: A Bio-Bibliography* (Westport, CT: Greenwood Press, (1991), 4.
3. Karel Husa, phone conversation with author (February 14, 1998).
4. S. Hitchens, p. 5.
5. Ibid, p. 7.
6. B. Adams, p.8.
7. K. Husa, phone.
8. Ibid.
9. K. Husa, *Wind Works*, p. 10.
10. Petr Zapletal, "The Most Remarkable from Prague Festival." *Rozhlas, Weekly magazine of the Czech Broadcasting Corp.* (July 15, 1997).
11. Husa, phone.
12. B. Adams, p. 3.
13. Paul Cohen, "Vintage saxophones revisited: 'classic' band music for the saxophone soloist." *Saxophone Journal* (March/April, 1989): 8–10.
14. Richard Miles, *Teaching Music through Performance in Band* (Chicago: GIA Publications, Inc., 1997), 422–23.
15. B. Adams, p. 4.
16. R. Miles, p. 421.
17. Karel Husa, "A Talk with Karel Husa." *Wind Works: A Journal for the Contemporary Wind Band* (Fall, 1997): 10.
18. Ibid, pp. 8–9.
19. Ibid, p. 9.
20. K. Husa, *Apotheosis of this Earth* (New York: Associated Music Publishers, Inc., 1971).
21. Mark Scatterday, "Karel Husa's *Al Fresco*: An Analysis and Performance Practice Guide." *College Band Directors National Association Journal* (Fall, 2001): 3.
22. K. Husa, *Al Fresco* (New York: Associated Music Publishers, 1975).
23. S. Hitchens, p. 13.
24. K. Husa, *Smetana Fanfare* (New York: Associated Music Publishers, 1984).
25. Mark Scatterday, "Karel Husa's *Smetana Fanfare*: An Analysis and Discussion of Performance Issues." *College Band Directors National Association Journal* (Spring, 1998): 39.
26. Ibid, p. 40.
27. K. Husa, phone.
28. K. Husa, program notes, Northwestern University Symphonic Wind Ensemble Concert, Evanston, Illinois, November 16, 1996.
29. K. Husa, phone.
30. Ibid.
31. M. Scatterday, p. 38.
32. K. Husa, phone.
33. Karel Husa, Letter to Tim Salzman, February 2, 2001.

Yasuhide Ito

by
Miho Takekawa

Yasuhide Ito is a member of the faculties at Tokyo Geijutsu Daigaku (Tokyo National University of Fine Arts), Senzoku Gakuen College, and serves as the wind band conductor at Kurashiki Sakuyou College and Tokyo Music and Media Arts Shobi. Ito has written fifty-one compositions for the wind band which have been played by numerous organizations throughout the world including the Tokyo Kosei Wind Orchestra and many collegiate bands in the United States. His most popular band composition is *Gloriosa* (1990) a work that has received many performances throughout Asia, Europe and the United States. He has also written ten pieces for saxophone, a variety of pieces for string quartet, piano, sixty art songs, a piece for string orchestra, a piece for chamber orchestra and an opera entitled *Mr. Cinderella*. He is a member of the board of directors of the Japanese Band Directors Association and the Academic Society of Japan for Winds, Percussion and Band (ACSJWB). In 1997 Ito presented a comprehensive lecture about Japanese wind ensemble compositions at the World Association for Symphonic Bands and Ensembles (WASBE) in Schladming, Austria and has subsequently been named to the WASBE board of directors.

BIOGRAPHICAL INFORMATION

Yasuhide Ito was born on December 7th, 1960 in Hamamatsu, Shizuoka, Japan located in the approximate center of the main island of Honshu, facing the Pacific to the south. He started learning piano when he was six years old and began composing during his middle school years with his first formal composition lessons taking place in high school under the tutelage of composition teacher Noda Teruyuki. His early experiences with the piano led to his initial interest in composing:

> ... I didn't enjoy playing from written notation; instead, I liked to create my own arrangements of simple folk songs I had heard from various parts of the world. When I learned a classical piece I would often create my own song in the style of that piece.

He was a member of his middle and high schools' wind ensembles as a percussionist, student conductor and arranger. Regarding his choice of percussion as an instrument Ito says:

> When I was in my first year of middle school, I started playing percussion because I was physically weak. As people know, the job of a percussionist is to count the rests. During the long rests,

> I listened to the other instruments playing and [frequently] thought 'how boring!'. Of course the middle school band at that time did not play much great music and I did not have the technique to play much great music either. It just seemed that my band played very boring music all the time.[1]

The lack of artistic repertoire sparked Ito's interest in writing for the wind band:

> ... although there are many pieces for wind ensemble many are, unfortunately, very typical, written within a certain conservative compositional style; ordinary rhythms, poor harmony, typical orchestration, predictable form... there are, of course, some good works... and even the more typical kinds of pieces work as educational music.

While a student at Hamamatsu Kita High School, Ito arranged the last movement of *Symphony No.2* by Sibelius and the finale from the *Firebird Suite* by Stravinsky. According to Ito's high school friend Kenichiro Isoda, a composer and musical director:

> Ito seemed like an advanced music student... however, the ideas for his music, while very traditional in some ways were still fresh and even humorous. Today, even though he has become a famous composer his style is still centered in Western traditional music and is marked by a certain humorous originality.[2]

When he was in his third year of high school, he sent his composition *On The March* (1978) to the All Japan Wind Ensemble Composition Contest; however, the piece was rejected. Ironically, in 1993 *On The March* was published by the TRN Music Publishing Company (Ruidoso, New Mexico) in the United States. Ito does not feel that this work is his first 'serious' composition; in his view it is merely a short march. In 1979 he composed *"Progress"*, a work he does consider to be his first serious effort for the wind band idiom. Ito entered Tokyo National University of Fine Arts as a composition major in 1979 and completed his Master's degree in 1983. He has been the recipient of numerous prizes including first place at the 5th Shizuoka Piano Competition (1980), third place at the 51st Japan Composition Competition (1982), the best composition prize in the Japan Composition Competition for Saxophone (1987), the All Japan Band Association Academy Composition Prize (1994), and the Hamamatsu Prefectural Artists Prize (1997). Ito appeared as guest conductor at the joint convention of the Japan Bandmasters Association and the American Bandmasters Association at the University of Tennessee in 1987 conducting *Jojoteki Matsuri* (1986) (*Festal Scenes for Band*) in its America premier with the University of Illinois Symphonic Band.

As an author Ito has regularly submitted series articles such as *Kangakugassou Meikyoku Hyakka* (Analysis of Works for Wind Ensemble) and *Suigaku 18 ban* (Favorite Wind Ensemble Works) to the *Japan Band Journal* in which he has also written about composers from Mozart and Handel to Husa and Messiaen. The *Kyouiku Ongaku*, a music education periodical published by Shinan, has published another article entitled *Kangakugassou Henkyoku* (Arranging for the Wind Instruments). He is the author of one book, *Kangakki no Meikyoku Meiensou* (The Masterpieces and Great Performances of Wind Instruments), published by Ongaku no Tomo Sha (1998) and has translated from English into Japanese Frank Erickson's book *Arranging for the Band*, published by Toa Ongaku Sha (1990). Ito, in collaboration with the author/poet Nozomi Hayashi, has written the songs for a CD ROM guide published by Shogakukan entitled *Ankoma Pan*.

In addition to Ito's compositional activities he frequently performs as a piano soloist and accompanist.

COMPOSITIONAL APPROACH

As is the case with other contemporary Japanese wind band composers, Yasuhide Ito's compositional style is marked by an intriguing combination of European classical tradition laced with traditional Japanese folk music atmospheres. He has successfully forged a musical alliance built upon western harmonic structures and classical formal development imbued with a strong pentatonic melodic sense and driving taiko drumming-influenced rhythmic stylings. Ito talks about his 'East meets West' compositional style:

> It has been 100 years since Western music came to Japan. I grew up with Western music and I like [its compositional characteristics] so I compose in a Western way. Personally, I think that the western compositional approach is 'to compose particular time within a logical framework, which is called music.' Composers build their personal [sense of] time; this [is individual] and differs from ethnic music. Because of these ideas, there are multiple kinds of music(s), which have clear structural principals such as serial music. Many of those structural principals have the aesthetic of western form. My compositional style is to interweave the Japanese sense of music into western music from my particular perspective as a Japanese composer. It is not only the use of Japanese traditional instruments or Japanese traditional scales; I also would like to treasure [in my music] the differences between Japan and other countries. For example, the Japanese feeling of rhythm is different...it is best explained as the understanding that a Japanese person would have of the concept of 'ma' or space. In America a blues singer or a great jazz ensemble playing American jazz swing rhythms have a sense of 'ma' born of their culture; in Japan it is the same. Although it is very difficult to explain I have attempted to include that feeling in my music.

When one listens to the music of Yasuhide Ito it is clear that he has spent considerable time studying the craftsmanship of certain composers. He elaborates:

> I like many composers...first I will mention Mozart and Bach; their music is always safe! I don't really like Beethoven, but I want to learn from his technique. I am attracted to the music of Shostakovich because his music is very powerful, and Gershwin and Bernstein (especially their musicals) because of their attitude and style.

GURURIYOZA (GLORIOSA)

With his composition *Gloriosa* (subtitled 'Symphonic Poem'), Ito has attempted to compose a work that embodies his view of the musical and philosophical combination of Japanese and western culture. In a general sense, the composer had three clear goals in the construction of this particular work:

> First, I tried to achieve a balance between the music I would like to create and the level of band education present in the country; secondly a balance between music that is simply enjoyable to perform and music that has more of a depth of artistry; and thirdly, a balance between Japanese traditions and Western styles. There are many great aspects to this piece and I would like to compose more pieces like it. It is one of my favorites among my creations and I believe it has genuine lasting value.[3]

The commission to write the work was initiated by the Sasebo Band of the Maritime Self-Defense Force, Shoji Iwashita, conductor, and was premiered by that organization in 1990. The band is stationed in the city of Sasebo, located in Nagasaki prefecture[4] on the southern island of Kyushu, an area rich in the fascinating history of feudal Japan. Understanding the historical background of the work is critical to informed performance as it was Ito's intent to musically portray this turbulent time in Japanese history.

During the Edo Period (1603–1867), Japan was closed to all foreigners largely due to the isolationist national leaders' concerns that outside influences had so permeated Japanese society that the culture was eroding. One of these influences was Christianity, a religion initially introduced to Japan by Jesuit missionaries in the mid-sixteenth century. The missionaries had particular influence in the southern island of Kyushu and it has been estimated that nearly 300,000 people (including six regional military lords) had converted in approximately fifty years. Christianity, with its' tenet of individual freedom over obedience to one's superiors in matters of conscience, began to be viewed by the Edo government as subversive and in 1614 persecution became systematized; some 3,000 believers are estimated to have been martyred, some by crucifixion, and many were forced to renounce their faith as a result of torture. All missionaries were either executed or forced to leave the country. In 1638 the country completely severed ties with all outsiders and the only point of governmentally allowed contact was with Dutch traders on the small island of Dejima very near Nagasaki. However, some 60,000 *kakure* (hidden) Christians continued to practice their faith in secret for some three hundred years. *Gloriosa* is intended to portray their hidden worship as well as the dramatic events surrounding this era in Japanese history.

Ito became quite intrigued with the history of Nagasaki and the music of the Hidden Christians after receiving the commission and subsequently beginning his personal study of the subject matter of the work. Through his research efforts he began to view Nagasaki as an important intersection for European and Japanese music:

> During the mid-sixteenth century, western music was imported to Japan. In fact, there is proof that Shogun Nobunaga Oda appreciated western music. Thus, today's Hogaku (Japanese traditional music) had very possibly been influenced by western music. For example, one of the most well known pieces for koto, *Rokudan* might have a western influence by using the variation form as a basis for its composition; in Japanese traditional music, variation is rarely employed as a formal structure. So, in this piece, it became clear to me that Japanese traditional music and western music have met a long time ago. After the proscription of Christianity, the faith was preserved and handed down in secret in the Nagasaki and Shimabara areas of Kyushu. My interest in the *kakure* Christians was particularly piqued by the way in which the Latin words of Gregorian chants were gradually 'Japanized' during the two hundred years of hidden practice. For example, the word 'Orasho' which the hidden Christians still recite, was formed from the Latin word, 'Oratio'; 'Gloriosa' equals 'Gururiyoza.' Their music forms the basis of *Gloriosa*. I was also interested in answering the philosophical question; did the hidden Christians really win; in other words, did they finally become free?

His fascination with the subject matter became so intense that he barely finished the composition in time for its première:

> I finally finished the piece two weeks before the world première concert; my research led to so much interesting information about the hidden Christians in Nagasaki that I could not even think about composing! I felt that this research was just like solving a mystery....

Ito comments on the formal structure that he chose for the composition as a whole and the first movement specifically:

> Even though 'Symphonic Poem' is the subtitle of the piece, this is more clearly a symphony in three movements rather than a symphonic poem. The first movement is based on thirteen variations (see appendix)[5] of a hymn that was probably brought to Japan at that time by the missionaries. Because of the strict prohibition against Christianity, the melodies and lyrics were deliberately disguised, probably several times, through the years that followed. Therefore I decided to employ a Chaconne-based variation form. I was asked to compose with the elements of folk songs in Sasebo and Nagasaki; Nagasaki is the place where much continental culture landed, Christianity came, and European music became popular before the Meiji period. Because I gradually had growing interest [in the subject matter], the compositional style is very mixed up between European and Japanese music.

The first movement of *Gloriosa*, 'Oratio,' opens with glockenspiel, vibraphone and chimes rendering the hymn's initial phrases at the pianississimo dynamic level. An obvious orchestrational attempt at imitating the sounds of church bells serves to introduce both the initial gregorian chant motif while foreshadowing the second movement theme. (see figure 1)

Ito suggests that this part should be played very quietly and conducted with small gestures.[6] The Gregorian chant, sung in Latin by members of the ensemble in dorian mode, makes its elegaic first entrance at #11. The text is as follows:

O gloriosa Domina	O Heaven's glorious mistress,
excelsa super sidera.	enthron'd above the starry sky,
Qui te creavit provide	thou feedest with thy sacred breast
lactasti sacro ubere.	thy own Creator, Lord most high.

(see figure 2. quarter note = 50 bpm):

FIGURE 1.
Gloriosa
© 1990 by ONGAKU NO TOMO SHA CORP. Used by permission.

FIGURE 2. Quarter note = 50 bpm
Gloriosa
© 1990 by ONGAKU NO TOMO SHA CORP. Used by permission.

The fermatas indicated on the last note of each phrase of the chorale function as interpretive clues and, in the manner of Gregorian chant, the singers should linger for a significant time. Phrasing is an obvious antecedent and consequent. Following the singing, the first variation begins quietly in the brass section at #11; at #32 the woodwind section follows with its variation in a new meter (3/2) at a slightly quicker tempo. Ito's contrapuntal craftsmanship is immediately apparent particularly in the elegant independence of lines scored in the clarinet section.

In measure #34 an interruptive fanfare motif introduced by the trumpet serves as recurrent and highly significant compositional 'signal' in the dramatic development of the work. With each occurrence, this 'danger motif', through its jarring syncopation and, at times, additive dissonance (see #57), a foreboding sense of dread becomes increasingly apparent. Regardless of the musical context, the motif appears with an unrelenting regularity throughout the remaining variations in a compositional attempt to portray the always-immediate sense of danger that the Hidden Christians experienced during their worship. Further, this motif is used as a foreshadowing element as it is taken from the principal theme of the second movement. (see figure 3)

The serene, alto-voiced variation found at #47 is contrasted with a darker, pesante brass choir variation written in canon at #61. The fiery allegro at #75 introduces a new, three-part brass choir canon at #89 accompanied by an militant triplet ostinato found in the woodwind choir, timpani, tubas and bass trombone. The triplets build important

density leading to a free variation technique, written in 2/4 meter, at #103. Seemingly, this variation is unrelated to the original chant, but a closer examination reveals a remarkable allusion to the earlier material. (see figure 4)

After an urgent and technically challenging stringendo, the music momentarily pauses via the use of overlapping fermata between trumpets and oboe at #118. In the subsequent material, (see #120), Ito again demonstrates his understanding of the Baroque with a serene two-part chorale featuring solo oboe. Woodwind texture is characteristically additive even though the trumpet section once again sounds the 'danger motif' at #132. At #145, a piu mosso (144 bpm), the ensemble outlines the theme with staccato chordal structures accompanied by tom-tom and snare drum, instruments also scored in thematic variation. (see figure 5)

Measure #139 is marked by a new, chromatically altered two part brass canon based on thematic material and accompanied by urgently strident, high-register woodwind tone clusters. The end of the movement (#181) is shocking in its rhythmic and dramatic effect; the ensemble plays a syncopated tutti variation of the first four notes of the theme leading to a shrieking high woodwind unison clearly intended to be the scream of desperate victims. Xylophone is the punctuating instrument on the last note of the 'scream' and a solo fortississimo tam-tam note follows. This should be allowed to fade for some time before melding into the glockenspiel, vibraphone and chimes that close the movement as it began. Ito explains his concern for the correct percussion sounds at this particular moment in the music:

FIGURE 3
Gloriosa
© 1990 by ONGAKU NO TOMO SHA CORP. Used by permission.

FIGURE 4
Gloriosa
© 1990 by ONGAKU NO TOMO SHA CORP. Used by permission.

Compositional Approach

When I wrote the one tam-tam hit, it is just one hit; however, there is more to that moment. It is my preference that the percussionists be concerned about all details. For example, what kind of bass drum and tam-tam would be the perfect choice; the tuning of the instruments; the mallet selection; where the instrument should be struck…it is fun to think about one particular note. The bass drum hit, the xylophone's E, and the tam-tam hit take the responsibility for the sense of space ('ma') that is needed at that moment. This is the perfect job for percussion. I also think that this is one of the Japanese ways to treat the sound. Thus, the tam-tam changes the thought for that moment, creating a true sense of 'ma'. (see figure 6). I was also able to bring a Japanese instrument, the ryuteki, to further the Japanese-like space at the beginning of the second movement. (see figure 7)

The second movement, 'Cantus', a brilliant blend of Gregorian chant infused with Japanese elements, opens with an initially unaccompanied thirty-four measure solo passage for the ryuteki, a kind of Japanese flute.[7] The commissioning conductor, Shoji Iwashita, had asked Ito specifically to utilize the ryuteki in the second movement. A piccolo can be substituted although the bending of pitches and portamenti required in the solo are somewhat more difficult to emulate. (see figure 7)

FIGURE 5
Gloriosa
© 1990 by ONGAKU NO TOMO SHA CORP. Used by permission.

FIGURE 6
Gloriosa
© 1990 by ONGAKU NO TOMO SHA CORP. Used by permission.

FIGURE 7
Gloriosa
© 1990 by ONGAKU NO TOMO SHA CORP. Used by permission.

The theme is based on 'San Juan-sama no Uta' (The Song of San Juan), a seventeenth-century folk song commemorating the martyrdom of the Kyushu Christians, including two whose baptismal name was Juan, one killed in 1622 and the other in 1623. There were many martyrs at Nakaeno shima, a small, rocky island near Nagasaki, which was called "San Juan Island" by the hidden Christians. During persecution and concealment, this song was born when hidden Christians watched the martyrdoms taking place on San Juan Island from across the water. The small amount of water streaming from slits in the rocks on this island was treated as "holy water" and 'San Juan Sama no Uta' was sung with great reverence for those martyred hidden Christians. In its original form, this Gregorian chant was a paean for the Virgin Mary, sung throughout Spain and Portugal in the middle of the sixteenth century. Missionaries brought the melody to Japan from Portugal where it underwent its linguistic metamorphosis to a Japanized language version rendered in Nagasaki regional dialect. (see fig.8)

In measure #16 the ryuteki is joined by an ethereal accompaniment of sleigh bells, lightly struck bass drum and bowed vibraphone; the resultant haunting atmosphere is coloristically supported by the addition of a dynamically subdued clarinet choir at #26. The horn-led Piu Mosso at measure #35 more forcefully presents the thematic material and ultimately builds to an intense, tutti, rubato section at #69. The 'danger motif' from the first movement is ever-present during *Cantus*; however, given its context as a principal theme begun by the plaintive ryuteki, the overall sense of the motivic development is decidedly more elegaic in nature. The ryuteki returns (#67) in a slightly altered restatement of the opening theme again accompanied by a texturally sparse percussion and clarinet choir backdrop. The movement concludes with the sound of a gyoban, a type of wooden plate gong in the shape of a fish being violently struck. It should be noted that the gyoban is an instrument occasionally utilized to accompany the chanting of Buddhist monks—perhaps this is the indication of the finality of the Christians' end? Ito mentions, in his forward to the score, that a 'relatively hard, wooden, rectangular board' can be substituted for the gyoban.

The third and final movement, *'Dies Festus,'* takes as its theme the Nagasaki folk song *'Nagasaki Bura Bura Bushi,'* (The Wandering Song of Nagasaki) a folk tune from the early Edo period re-introduced to 20th Japan by way of a famous 1930 Victor recording by Aihachi (1874–1933) a Nagasaki geisha. (see fig.9)

FIGURE 8. 'San Juan no Uta'
Gloriosa
© 1990 by ONGAKU NO TOMO SHA CORP. Used by permission.

FIGURE 9. Nagasaki Bura Bura Bushi
Gloriosa
© 1990 by ONGAKU NO TOMO SHA CORP. Used by permission.

The movement opens with a tutti, highly syncopated, fortissimo declaration of a motivic variation of the folk song. Requiring absolute ensemble concentration and a forcefully dry conducting style, the opening measures, if performed with rhythmic exactness, will serve as a strident alarm, a violent contrast to the end of the preceding movement. (see fig. 10)

Immediately following the opening a driving taiko-influenced percussion trio (timpani, three toms and bass drum) propels the movement forward from #3. (see fig. 11)

An incisive war-like interaction in parallel fourths between trombones (initially), upper woodwinds, trumpets, horns and, subsequently, the full ensemble from #11 to #42 is perhaps the most militant Japanese 'feudal' expression in the work; deeply dramatic and confrontational, it easily conjures images of samurai warriors in full battle.

Ito again displays a wonderful sensitivity in his understanding of woodwind chorale writing with an espressivo section beginning at #46. Line is important through these particular phrases with direction and contour being somewhat obvious given the thoughtful orchestration. Textural

tension is gradually released through thinning orchestrations leading to a 'moderato religioso' (#63), a beautiful four-part brass choir retelling of the woodwind chorale found in the first movement at #120. Texture is quietly added and, at #84, the entire ensemble is engaged in the most 'singing' moment of the work, a truly glorious statement of the main theme in F major.

At #101 a startling return to the opening taiko drumming section (#11) leads to a rapid fugue at #132. The abrupt tempo shift (quarter = 160 bpm) and subsequent technical requirements, especially in the woodwind section, are concerning and require intense concentration. The conductor will best serve the ensemble by conducting in a dry, waltz-like manner with secure emphasis on each downbeat. The texture and technical challenges increase; dissonance is added, particularly through the high horn writing and a dramatic allargando leads to a tutti, fortissimo closing recapitulation of the opening Gregorian chant at #166. Dynamics need to be managed somewhat carefully here as the ensemble may over-extend before their full power is most needed, the 'meno mosso' at #181.

FIGURE 10
Gloriosa
© 1990 by ONGAKU NO TOMO SHA CORP. Used by permission.

FIGURE 11
Gloriosa
© 1990 by ONGAKU NO TOMO SHA CORP. Used by permission.

Gloriosa, fusing Gregorian chant and Japanese folk music, displays some of the most sophisticated counterpoint yet found in any Japanese composition for wind orchestra and is considered by many (including Frederick Fennell) to be at the forefront of a newly emerging Japanese wind band repertoire. Ito has successfully crafted a work that truly evokes the fervent prayers and the suffering of the Hidden Christians of Kyushu.

CONDUCTING APPROACH

Ito's *Gloriosa* contains several conducting challenges. Pacing within each movement is critical as the dynamic and articulative editing may elicit overly aggressive sounds from players (particularly the brass and percussion) before the apex of each movement is actually reached. An overactive conductor could add to that particular dilemma which will unfortunately obscure much of Ito's most imaginative woodwind counterpoint. Sudden changes of tempi and texture throughout the work require a relaxed anticipation particularly in the third movement when the fugue suddenly emerges at a very rapid tempo. There are many beautiful moments of linear beauty in the chorale sections of the composition and the conductor must always demonstrate a thorough understanding of line direction. Obviously, the conductor needs to be sensitive to the programmatic inspiration for the piece as a fully informed ensemble will have a much greater probability of rendering a true musical portrayal of the religious persecution experienced during this fascinating time in Japanese history.

Ito feels that there is a certain uninformed performance practice that is brought about by a lack of ensemble awareness on the part of the players in bands today. His solution, while costly, is effective:

> I strongly recommend reading from the score when there is a performance of band music. The score is the tool that shows the clearest ideas of composers. People might say, "We don't know how to read the score"; however, there are a few obvious things a player can gain from just looking at the score. For example, what kind of part you are playing in the whole band, whom you are doubled with, you are playing solo. By the way, orchestra players often carry the score of the piece that they are working on…it is very common to see the score when there are some questions about the piece at an orchestra rehearsal. However, at the band rehearsals almost all players tend to practice only their parts and not to see what their musical 'duties' are with respect to the whole band. Players often ask many small questions to the conductor; those questions wouldn't need to be asked if the performers had consulted the score. Thus, when band players play my pieces, I recommend buying many scores. I wish every single player were able to buy a score and use it along with his or her own part.

The composer has heard his music played many times as he has frequently served as a guest conductor and adjudica-

tor in Japan. He comments on the Japanese band world and what he views to be important performance practice:

> In Japan there are enormous band competitions and winning these competitions becomes the entire focus of many band programs. Most Japanese band compositions are designed especially for these competitions and most decisions about which pieces are (and aren't) good result from performances at these competitions. Currently, this is the biggest problem for Japanese wind bands. When I listen to my pieces played in live performance, it is very obvious if that band has read the score carefully or not. It is sad to notice that a band plays in a certain imitative way that other bands have played in. On the other hand, even though the style of performance differs from composer's idea, it is always fun to listen to see if that band has done the basic score reading very carefully and understands the music. However, it is also very important to study the background of the piece. For example, there are many pieces by Japanese composers that utilize Japanese traditional folk songs. I wouldn't say that performers and conductors should know the meaning of every single folk song but it is necessary to have some knowledge of them. All of my compositions are not programmatic necessarily but if some works include a dramatic or historical background it is very important to understand the specific nature of the story behind the music.

ADDITIONAL RESOURCES

WEBSITES

http://www.itomusic.com
http://www.keller.co.jp
http://www.wizvax.net/abe/winds/cd/ito.html
http://www.net.jp/asahi/music/takamasa/review/wind.html

MAJOR WORKS FOR WIND BAND

Year	Title	Publisher
1978	On the March	TRN
1979	Progress for Band	
1982	Evocation for Band	
	Concerto Fantastique pour Alto Saxophone et Orchestre d'Harmonie	
	Liturgia Sinfonica for Band	
	Rag-Time-March	TRN
1985	Sinfonia for Band	
1986	Piano Concerto	
1986	Festal Scenes for Band	TRN
1986	Prelude a un Opera inacheve	
	Tableau for Band	
	Gloriosa, Symphonic Poem for Band	Ongaku no Tomosha
	Fantasy Variations for Euphonium and Band Symphony	

1991	Variations from the Northern Sea for Band	TRN
	Interlude a un Opera inacheve	
	Rapsodia Formosa for Band	
1992	Overture for Wind Ensemble	Ludwig
1992	'Fuji' Symphonic Sketch for Band	
1992	'Fantasia Classica' for Wind Ensemble	Yamaha
1992	Soma Festival March	
1993	Soma Festival March No. 2	
	Remembrance II for Wind Ensemble	
1993	Funa-Uta (Boat Song) for Band	
	Fanfare for Hamamatsu City	
1994	A Jubilee Symphony	
1994	Three Scenes from Soma	
1994	Chopin Fantasy	
	Preludio Celebrativo for Band	
1995	'Melodies' for Wind Ensemble	
1995	Hamamatsu Overture	
1995	'Sonata Classica' for Wind Ensemble	Japan Community Band Association
	A la Suite Classique for Wind Ensemble	Ongaku no Tomosha
	Meguru kisetsu Ni for Wind Ensemble	
1998	Ryukuan Fantacy	
1998	Maiko Spring Mach	
1998	Tsudoe, Iwae, Utae, Festival song for Wind Ensemble	Brain
1998	La Vita, Symphony in Three Scenes	
1999	Kokiriko March	
	Ryukuan Fantacy for Piano and Band	
2000	Go For Broke, Symphony Poem for Wind Ensemble	
2000	As Time is Passing On	
2001	Pacem et Gloriam Pro Nobis	

WORKS OF PARTICULAR INTEREST

Rag-Time-March duration: 3'

Ito was attracted by rhythms and typical chord changes of ragtime music and was specifically inspired by Scott Joplin's music in the composition of this work. However, to apply for the march category of the All Japan Wind Ensemble Competition he had to insert a Trio, which features a chalameau register clarinet melody.

Festal Scenes for Band (Jojoteki Matsuri): duration: 6'

This piece is based on four folksongs ('bushi') from the Aomori Prefecture. The rhythm patterns are from shamisen[8] of 'Tsugaru Jongara Bushi'. The yodel-like sound 'Ho-Hai' is from 'Tsugaru Ho-Hai Bushi' and the Japanese flute and taiko drum of the Nebuta festival. The Nebuta festival is one of the largest and most famous festivals in all of Japan and their Taiko drumming is considered to be very powerful and energetic.

Variations from the Northern Sea for Band duration: 6'
Commissioned by the Ominato Band of the Japan Maritime Self Defense Force.

This piece is an arrangement of 'Soran Bushi', which is one of the most well known folk songs in Japan. Usually a work that is a theme and variations begins with a straightforward presentation of the theme; however, in this composition the theme does not appear until after the last variation.

SELECTED DISCOGRAPHY

Hiroyuki Odano, conductor. (1990) **Subliminal Festa.** Tokyo Kosei Wind Orchestra. *"Concerto Fantastique"* KOCD-0401

Hiroyuki Odano, conductor. (1991) **Gloriosa.** Tokyo Kosei Wind Orchestra. *"Gloriosa"/"Symphonic Poem for Band"* KOCD-2902

Nobutaka Masui, conductor. (1994) **Ritual Fire.** Tokyo Kosei Wind Orchestra. *"Festal Scenes"* KOCD-2904

Kim Hong Jae, conductor. (1995) **Procession Fantasy.** Tokyo Kosei Wind Orchestra. *"Melodies"* KOCD-2905

Yoshihiro Kimura, conductor. (1995). **WASBE Concerts.** Osaka Municipal Symphonic Band. *"Hamamatsu Overture"* KOCD-4551

Yasuhide Ito, conductor. (1995). **WASBE Concerts.** WASBE International Youth Wind Orchestra. *"Cantus"* from *"Gloriosa"* / *"Symphonic Poem for Band"* KOCD-4553

Eugene Corporon, conductor. (1995). **Luminaries.** University of North Texas Wind Symphony. *"Gloriosa"* Klavier CD-11077

Yoshihiro Kimura, conductor. (1996–1998) **Gloriosa-Works of Yasuhide Ito.** Osaka Municipal Symphonic Band. *"Gloriosa"* / *"Interlude to an Unfinished Opera"* / *"A Jubilee Symphony"* / *"Funa-Uta for Band"* / *"La Vita" Symphony in 3 Scenes* / *"Japanese Soccer Anthem"* (Sakamoto, arr. Ito) Brain BOCD-7402

various conductors. (2000). **As Time is Passing On: Band Works by Yasuhide Ito.** various Japanese bands. *"Ryukuan Fantasy for Piano and Band"* / *"Liturgia Sinfonica for Band"* / *"As Time is Passing On"* Goodlife, Inc. CACG-0015

Kazufumi Yamashita, conductor (2002) (untitled as of this writing). Tokyo Kosei Wind Orchestra. *"Symphony"* KOCD-2908

various conductors. **Festivals.** Tokyo Kosei Wind Orchestra. *"Festal Scenes: Jojoteki Matsuri"* KOCD-2410

END NOTES

1. From a preface, Japanese composers and their composition series No. 1.
2. From a preface, Japanese composers and their composition series No. 1.
3. Yasuhide Ito, Interviewed by David Hebert, e-mail and fax exchange, February 28–March 3, 1999.
4. A prefecture is a division of the country based upon geography. There are 47 prefectures in Japan.
5. Japanese Composers and Their Composition Series No.1.
6. Made of bamboo, the ryuteki is also called 'youjou' or 'outeki', meaning seven-holed transverse flute. The instrument was used in traditional Imperial Court music (gagaku) and dance and was initially introduced to Japan from ancient China.
7. Shiro Amakusa, who was baptized, rose in rebellion with twenty thousand farmers.
8. The three string shamisen is one of Japan's most popular classical musical instruments. Another Chinese import, it came to Japan by way of Okinawa in the middle of the sixteenth-century. Shamisen of varying sizes are used to play different forms of music, and they are plucked with a large "pick," which is gripped in the palm of one's hand.

APPENDIX

Ito explains the symbolism and formal architecture of the number '13' as follows:

'13' is not only the symbol of ordeals in Christianity, but it is also the meaning of 'The Golden Section' or 'Fibonacci Sequence', a system I utilized in composing the section from rehearsal #6 to #10. Named after Italian mathematician Leonardo Fibonacci this sequence follows the pattern 1, 1, 2, 3, 5, 8, 13, 21, 34, 55, 89, etc. Each term in the sequence is the sum of the previous two, i.e., 21=13+8.

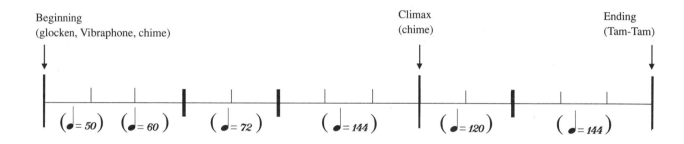

Cindy McTee

by
David Fullmer

Dr. Cindy McTee is Professor of Music Composition at the University of North Texas in Denton. She has received numerous awards for her music, most significantly a Guggenheim Fellowship, a Fulbright Senior Lecturer Fellowship, a Goddard Lieberson Fellowship from the American Academy of Arts and Letters, and a Composers Fellowship from the National Endowment for the Arts. She was also winner of the 2001 Louisville Orchestra Composition Competition. Her work has been commissioned by the National Symphony Orchestra, the Dallas Symphony Orchestra, the American Guild of Organists, the Barlow Endowment, and the College Band Directors National Association.

McTee's compositions have received performances by leading orchestras, bands, and chamber ensembles in the United States, Japan, South America, and Europe. Her music is published by MMB Music, Inc. in St. Louis.[1]

BIOGRAPHICAL INFORMATION

Cindy McTee was born February 20, 1953 in Tacoma, Washington and grew up in the nearby town of Eatonville, located between Tacoma and Mt. Rainier National Park. McTee was raised in a musical family. Both of her parents played in the University of Washington Concert Band under the direction of Walter Welke.[2] Her mother, a clarinetist and tenor saxophonist and her father, a trumpeter, formed their own small dance band that also included a drummer, an alto saxophone player, and a pianist. She has vivid memories of her musical upbringing:

> I was often taken to rehearsals in lieu of being left with a baby sitter, and I have fond memories of hearing tunes like *Night and Day, Misty*, and *Autumn Leaves*. My mother gave me my first saxophone lessons. She taught me to transpose from sheet music, and when I attended my first band rehearsal in fifth grade, I continued to transpose. You can imagine the result! I began my piano studies at age five with Mrs. Melvin, a teacher who encouraged improvisation by requiring that I play a small number of pieces differently each time I returned for a lesson. I now realize the importance of this and credit her with having given me my first opportunity to compose, although it wasn't until much later that I actually put notes to paper.
>
> Actually, throughout my childhood, I thought I would grow up to be a visual artist. As a youngster, I spent much more time drawing and painting than practicing the piano. But looking back, I recognize early signs of my fascination with sound. I remember quite vividly some experiments that got me into trouble, for example, playing inside my grandmother's grand piano and improvising piano accompaniments during high school choir concerts. I wasn't considered to be an ideal music student because I found it very difficult to play exactly what other composers wrote. Improvising, that is, composing spontaneously, was much more interesting to me.[3]

Cindy McTee received a BM (1975) from Pacific Lutheran University in Tacoma where her principal teacher was David Robbins; an M.M. (1978) studying with Krzysztof Penderecki, Jacob Druckman, and Bruce MacCombie at the Yale School of Music; and a PhD (1981) under the direction of Richard Hervig at the University of Iowa. She also completed one year of study in Poland with composers Penderecki, Marek Stachowski and Krystyna Moszumanska-Nazar at the Higher School of Music in Cracow.

McTee describes her studies with Penderecki as being most influential in her development as a composer:

> I first met Krzysztof Penderecki in the spring of 1974 at Pacific Lutheran University in Tacoma, Washington. I was a junior, majoring in composition, and he was the featured guest composer at our festival of contemporary music. Following a concert of works by PLU students, Mr. Penderecki invited me to spend a year with his family in Poland where he proposed I would teach his children English in return for composition lessons. Several months later, at the age of 21, I flew to London, took the train to Paris for a few days of sightseeing, and continued the journey by train to Cracow. Lessons with Penderecki were conducted informally, generally at the family dining room table. I studied orchestration, twentieth-century techniques, and sixteenth and eighteenth-century counterpoint at the Cracow Academy of Music. Penderecki insisted I devote a large portion of my time to writing counterpoint exercises because, as he put it, "American schools don't require enough counterpoint." Most of my instruction was given in the form of private lessons and conducted in English, an arrangement that suited everyone since I spoke very little Polish and the Academy's professors were more than happy to practice their English. In those days, of course, there were relatively few foreigners behind the Iron Curtain.
>
> Penderecki taught me much more than music — he taught me a way of life. I learned about commitment, professionalism, and the benefits of hard work. I learned the value of having a supportive teacher—his frequent encouragement of my work did much to bolster my confidence. He also taught me an appreciation for old things: antique clocks, Renaissance painting, medieval architecture, and Gregorian chant.

I know of no one more musically courageous than Krzysztof Penderecki. He has always composed exactly what his muse dictates, writing with honesty, conviction, and integrity. I will be forever indebted to Mr. Penderecki for having provided me the opportunity to witness his work firsthand.[4]

Dr. McTee returned to Pacific Lutheran University in Tacoma, Washington to teach composition from 1981 to 1984, and subsequently joined the faculty of the University of North Texas in Denton, Texas where she is Regents Professor of Music Composition.

COMPOSITIONAL PHILOSOPHY

McTee believes that composers today are faced with more options than ever before due to the explosion of technology as well as the emphasis that educators now place on aesthetic and cultural diversity. The problems of sorting through the many options, finding one's muse and organizing disparate musical materials are among the daunting challenges facing young composers. She explains her specific passion for composing in beautifully simple terms:

> I write music because I enjoy the process. I enjoy exercising my imagination and hearing the result. I feel changed by the process and invigorated by a positive response from persons who are touched by my music. I write music because sound fascinates me. But I also find delight in the more intellectual parts of composing, in creating intricate patterns of pitch and rhythm. Creating art is, for me, not unlike a religious experience. It is a profound human response to living, and provides a path for spiritual renewal. It celebrates life and sharing.[5]

McTee has experienced many of the difficulties that a composer of new music typically encounters. Shortly after finishing graduate school, she took a position with the Washington State Arts Commission, a job that required her to visit several elementary and junior high schools each week. When she was introduced as a composer the students would frequently respond with exclamations of surprise and say, "You're alive"! Composers of new music are misunderstood, in part, because they are thought to not even exist.

Another difficulty in the understanding and acceptance of new music is a lack of exposure due to the enormous expense involved in performing new music. The standard repertoire generally costs far less to perform for a number of reasons not the least of which is a lack of rehearsal time. Most musicians in a symphony orchestra will have played all of the Beethoven symphonies many times, but a new piece, usually rife with fairly formidable technical demands, typically requires additional rehearsal. The acceptance of new music by the general public is another issue:

> The taste for new music can be acquired, as can so many good things. It is not enough to hear a piece once, or to hear new music only occasionally. The language of new music is for most people like Chinese is to me. I don't understand Chinese because I haven't studied it and because I haven't heard it very much. But of course, Chinese communicates meaningful things. Likewise, new music can communicate in a meaningful way to those who understand its language.[6]

McTee believes that another reason for the lack of acceptance of new music is that there is so much artistically inferior new music, which she concedes would include some of her work. However, she contends that composers, as is the case with all artists, must risk failure if they are to discover and develop their craft to a higher level. McTee explains that this is not a new development:

> There was a lot of bad music in the 18th and 19th centuries too. But most of the old bad music has been discarded or is collecting dust in the basement of a library somewhere. In the case of new music, too little time has passed for us to know which new music is good. We must be patient. We must be willing to give new music a hearing. We must support the creation and performance of new music in order to discover the next Beethoven.[7]

Cindy McTee belongs to an automobile club and participates in amateur auto-racing on occasion. She explains her own compositional risks and compares the philosophical similarities between auto racing and composing music:

> Racing is about taking risks—it is about testing one's limitations as well as the limitations of one's vehicle. Likewise, writing music requires concentration and the willingness to explore new territory. When I am poised at the start-finish line, the adrenaline is flowing. I might crash and burn. I might embarrass myself and run over a cone or miss a turn. I feel the same way especially before the first performance of a new piece. The piece could fall apart and there is always the possibility for embarrassment. But ultimately, I become a better driver/composer.[8]

Her "rules" for racing and composing are remarkably parallel:

Racing Rules	Composing Rules
Wear a helmet. Protect yourself.	Shield yourself by belonging to a community of like-minded creative people.
Prevent injury.	Seek out those who can and will support you.
In a race, one is better off when entering a corner relatively slowly, turning in late, and then exiting as quickly as possible. Lengthen the straight-away. Create a late apex.	Approach a creative project with some caution. Do your homework. Then, go for it.
Stay on the brakes or on the accelerator pedal. Never coast.	Pursue knowledge as if there were no tomorrow.

Given the fact that bands typically have more time to rehearse, McTee finds great freedom in composing for the wind band, especially in writing challenging music that requires ultimate rhythmic precision. In addition to the additional rehearsal hours, wind conductors seem to have more freedom to try out new ideas than do their orchestral counterparts. She has compared college bands with professional orchestras; in both cases expertise and virtuosity create clarity and precision. McTee views college wind conductors as heroes because of the numerous opportunities they provide composers, and she expresses great enthusiasm about organizations such as the College Band Directors National Association which commissions and premieres many new compositions each year.[9] McTee advocates a long-term view in gaining acceptance of a new wind repertoire.

> Wind bands are performing the repertoire of the future. It would seem that a medium is only as successful as its literature. Therefore, the future depends upon a close collaboration between wind players, conductors, and composers. I think the seeds of this collaboration have already begun to grow in a very important way. For example, CBDNA conferences are about new music—about premieres. What could be more exciting![10]

She expresses similar hope when speaking to the issue of artistic community:

> Let's pretend for a moment that composers initiate musical ideas by putting pen to paper. Those black marks are then studied, practiced, and synthesized into a polished performance for presentation by a wind ensemble, for example. The vast amount of coordinated, skilled, artistic effort required to bring that entire process to completion is truly the stuff magic is made of. The conductor creates an environment that allows each person involved to make his or her own personal contribution. The conductor/composer relationship works this way too. The opportunities conductors provide composers stimulate artistic expression in a very important way. It could be argued that conductors and performers are actually the persons who initiate musical ideas by providing the vehicle—the means. The pen goes to paper because the composer has heard great playing—because the composer has experienced passionate music making by a particular ensemble—because enthusiastic conductors and performers have encouraged the composer. The MAGIC exists in the collaboration between composers, performers, conductors, dancers, funding agencies, performing rights organizations, publishers, and others. Music making will flourish as long as we all work together.[11]

COMPOSITIONAL STYLE

McTee believes that concert music has entered a renewed age of tonality. She describes tonal music as including any or all of the following features: a persistent and discernible pulse, clear rhythmic patterns, consonant sonorities, lyrical melodic phrasing, and diatonic scale relationships. She identifies three major recent tonal styles or techniques: 1) mini-malism 2) neo-romanticism and 3) appropriation.[12] McTee notes that these styles are in constant flux and are frequently used interchangeably in that a single composition can include all three of these approaches.

A description of McTee's compositional style would include humor, expectation denied, unexpected silences and rhythmic displacement, jazz textures, and post minimalism. She believes, as Stravinsky, that music either sings or it dances. She characterizes her music as intentionally playful and humorous:[13]

> As far as specific musical influences are concerned, I can say that my current interest in expressing humor through music may be attributable to Penderecki. When thinking of Penderecki's music, most people probably recall *Threnody*, the *St. Luke Passion*, the *Dies Irae*, and other solemn works. However, there are also several capriccios and a comic opera. I think Penderecki may have given me the courage to break away from the notion that modern music need always express serious modes of thinking and feeling.[14]

Structurally her music embraces traditional forms that are unified through unrelenting 'chains of ostinati' which, via clever asymmetrical variations, run counter to predictable strong beat/weak beat relationships. Those variations in typical accent structures draw the listener into a deeper mode of concentration, as one is never sure where the next rhythmic displacement will occur.

There is a pervasive jazz influence in her music rhythmically, harmonically and melodically. Her technically complex melodic fragments comprised of a step-wise chromaticism as well as disjunct leaps are clearly references to the be-bop jazz era. Rhythmically, many of those melodic fragments conclude on an offbeat and are frequently broken up by brief, syncopated tutti statements. Driving bass lines, snare drum rim shots and the use of ride cymbal and hi-hat percussive effects are also hallmarks of her composition's jazz textures.

ANALYSIS OF *CALIFORNIA COUNTERPOINT: THE TWITTERING MACHINE*

California Counterpoint: The Twittering Machine is evidence that McTee has found a unique compositional voice in creating modern music of a fanciful and light-hearted nature. This whimsical exercise of the imagination is energetically animated throughout its approximate eight-minute length. Humor is created, in part, through musical surprises of denied rhythmic expectation and the abrupt, mechanistic interplay between sound and silence. The effects of this interplay can be diminished by inaccurate attacks and releases. McTee has stated that the marked tempo of 144 may be slowed slightly if increased ensemble clarity results.

The work consists of several sections of seemingly unrelated material usually connected by brief transitions. The only recurrence of material occurs during the coda when the introduction and first section are briefly restated.

The introduction (M 1–16) begins with the piano playing major sevenths in displaced octaves (see fig. 1).

The eighth note wind fragments and sixteenth note runs leading to the forte downbeat of measure five are primarily comprised of major sevenths. McTee's extensive use of this interval is one of the unifying compositional threads found throughout the work. In measures fifteen and sixteen, McTee offers the first of many surprises to follow. The forte down-beat following the second set of sixteenth notes has been postponed by one count (see fig. 2).

These performance "traps", which represent a certain element of danger in Paul Klee's painting entitled *Twittering Machine*, are scattered throughout the work and require a high level of concentration from the performers.

The first section (M 17–71) is a marvelous study in the layering of textures. Since each layered voice remains repeti-

tive and brief, musical interest is sustained by the juxtaposition of each voice in varied rhythmic patterns. The opening statement of the introduction, now stated with the piano and vibraphone, are accompanied by a rhythmic ostinato on the temple blocks. The temple block ostinato is the only rhythmic constant throughout this section. Much of the variation in sound and texture comes from the voice displacement in relationship to the fixed ostinato as demonstrated in the first four measures of this section (see fig. 3).

The upper woodwinds in measure 21 have added the next layer of melodic fragments that are constructed mainly of major sevenths and minor seconds. Low woodwinds add counter-melodic fragments four measures later followed by a brief tutti rhythmic statement in measure 33. It appears in measure 35 that there will be a direct repeat of the previous material. However, when the melodic fragments reappear in measure 39, McTee includes additional voices playing an exact canon displaced by two beats (see fig. 4).

FIGURE 1. Measures 1–3, piano
California Counterpoint
© 1993 MMB Music, Inc. Saint Louis
Used by Permission. All Rights Reserved.

FIGURE 2. Measures 4–5 and 15–16, woodwinds
California Counterpoint
© 1993 MMB Music, Inc. Saint Louis
Used by Permission. All Rights Reserved.

FIGURE 3. Measures 17–20, piano and percussion
California Counterpoint
© 1993 MMB Music, Inc. Saint Louis
Used by Permission. All Rights Reserved.

FIGURE 4. Measures 43–45, woodwinds
California Counterpoint
© 1993 MMB Music, Inc. Saint Louis
Used by Permission. All Rights Reserved.

In measure 55 the brass, in the form of a sort of lyrical fanfare, contribute an additional layer to the texture. The fanfare does not, however, begin immediately after its four-measure statement. Four beats (one measure and one beat in 3/4 time) are added before commencing the next fanfare. This displacement creates additional interest in the colorful flourish of sound. The independence of the lines and rhythms comes abruptly to an end in measure 69–71 with a sudden tutti syncopation. A piccolo 'recitative' is utilized as a transition into the next section (see fig. 5).

A driving staccato chromatic line of eighth notes in the low voices characterizes the second section, beginning in measure 83 (see fig. 6).

The mechanistic angularity of this line with its abrupt starts and stops is reminiscent of factory scenes found in animated cartoons. Each appearance of this 'walking bass' is slightly rhythmically varied and the length of rest between each presentation is also altered. The spaces are at times in odd meter and up to seven beats in length. The attempt at humor is obvious and successful. The lines are accompanied by the inclusion of sixteenth note fragments marked 'jazz like' in the upper woodwinds and piano (see fig. 7).

Many of the statements' endings arrive at the metered silences with a snare drum rim shot, trombone glissando and short forte chord of major sevenths in the upper brass. These elements are used in measure 134 as a transition into the next section (see fig. 8).

The third section, beginning in measure 139, continues the use of the minor second (major seventh) but adds repeated notes to the motif (see fig. 9).

The combination of breath weight on the first of the sixteenth notes and the bass notes on beats 1, 3 and 4 creates a tremendous sense of momentum in the music. The 5/4 feel is so well established that the sudden appearance of 3/4 in measures 165–166 is unexpected and highly effective. McTee adds fresh interest by sudden transpositions of a half step (see fig. 10).

Ascending sixteenth notes in the brass are occasionally utilized as a textural and coloristic relief throughout this section. The ascending sixteenth notes followed by silence are used as transitory material into the next section.

The fourth section, beginning in measure 187, employs a simulated jazz rhythm section that is driven by a light jazz ride cymbal. The percussion part instructs the performer to

FIGURE 5. Measures 74–81, piccolo
California Counterpoint
© 1993 MMB Music, Inc. Saint Louis
Used by Permission. All Rights Reserved.

FIGURE 6. Measures 83–84, euphonium
California Counterpoint
© 1993 MMB Music, Inc. Saint Louis
Used by Permission. All Rights Reserved.

FIGURE 7. Measure 84, piano
California Counterpoint
© 1993 MMB Music, Inc. Saint Louis
Used by Permission. All Rights Reserved.

FIGURE 8. Measures 134–136, brass and percussion
California Counterpoint

FIGURE 9. Measure 139, E♭ clarinet
California Counterpoint

FIGURE 10. Measures 173–174, E♭ clarinet, bass clarinet, tuba
California Counterpoint

113

improvise the eighth note pattern in the manner of a jazz drummer. The walking bass line is covered by the double bass and bass clef piano which play connected, driving eighth notes (see fig. 11).

This line, just like lines played by jazz bassists, is accompaniment to an imagined soloist, primarily comprised of notes hinting at the jazz harmonic ambiguity of this particular segment of the music. The piano adds 'comping' chord patterns in the right hand while the upper woodwinds play virtuosic and complex be-bop melodies. This section concludes with the same tutti rhythmic syncopation that concluded the first section followed by a brief larghetto fanfare in the horn and trumpet (see fig. 12).

McTee borrows an obscure, decorative rhythmic idea from the third section and develops it as the main theme of the fifth section. This agitated rhythmic pattern is stated, in whole or in part, in virtually every measure of this section (see fig. 13).

The use of silence of varying lengths is utilized as it was earlier in the second section. A brief, lyrical statement by the upper woodwinds in measure 247 adds contrast and mystery to the punctuated section (see fig. 14).

The transition material used between the third and fourth sections is utilized again after the fifth section. The sustained piccolo, a voice utilized as an aria-like unifying element, is again sounded. At measure 286 there is a brief reprise of material from the end of the first section, functioning in the manner of an informal coda. This section of the music contains many of the elements that have contributed to the interest of the entire piece; repeated structures, denied expectation, displaced rhythms and juxtaposed textures. The fact that the last note is displaced by one beat is not as surprising as its construction. McTee saves one of her more unique and humorous surprises for the very end: a C major chord.

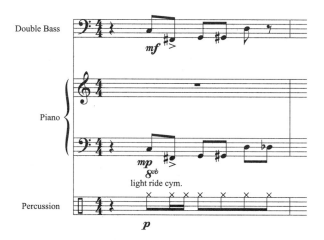

FIGURE 11. Measure 187, bass, piano and cymbal
California Counterpoint
© 1993 MMB Music, Inc. Saint Louis
Used by Permission. All Rights Reserved.

FIGURE 12. Measures 220–222, horn and trumpet
California Counterpoint
© 1993 MMB Music, Inc. Saint Louis
Used by Permission. All Rights Reserved.

FIGURE 13. Measures 223–224, flute 3
California Counterpoint
© 1993 MMB Music, Inc. Saint Louis
Used by Permission. All Rights Reserved.

FIGURE 14. Measures 246–254, clarinet
California Counterpoint
© 1993 MMB Music, Inc. Saint Louis
Used by Permission. All Rights Reserved.

CONDUCTING APPROACH

The music of Cindy McTee requires both the conductor and ensemble to maintain a concentrated devotion to a 'razor-sharp' subdivision of the pulse. This subdivision becomes quite critical during those moments of metered silence, a silence that is not meant to be broken! The transmission of that subdivision coupled with the chamber-like transparency of each score demands a thorough knowledge of all of the various 'rhythmic gears' that the composer has set in synchronous motion. Due to the pervading jazz harmonic language a sensitive attention to the balance of the various vertical harmonic structures is also of paramount importance. As so much of her dance-like music is based upon motivic interplay, textures are clear enough for melody to be easily discerned. However, much of the 'bebop' influence in the melodic writing involves doubled major or minor seconds. At times, preserving that particular melodic balance between the dissonant voices demands a more careful layering due to certain orchestrational choices that the composer has made.

Dr. McTee offers three practical considerations in her advice to conductors who are contemplating the rehearsal and performance of her music.

Take whatever steps are necessary to correct problems with the scoring. Conductors, by virtue of the fact that they spend countless hours in rehearsal with their ensembles, know more than many composers about what makes good sound. If I've created balance problems, I would like the conductor to fix them. If I've made unreasonable demands upon a performer, I would like the conductor to solve that problem too if possible. I believe the score provides a set of instructions that should be interpreted with some liberty. Rather than dictate all things, it initiates a process or team effort that benefits from the individual contributions of conductor and performers.

Clarity is important to me. Sometimes exaggerated articulations can help. Rhythmic precision is also a must. I would rather the tempo be too slow than the texture cloudy from inaccurate placement of events.

Listen for the humor. I have often said that I would like listeners and performers to take my music very seriously while smiling! Sure, some pieces aren't humorous, but many are and I want the playfulness of this music to be heard.

When asked about 'reference' music for a conductor contemplating a performance of her music, McTee referred to a recent review published in the Houston Chronicle (7/10/2000) by Charles Ward.

A recent review that helped me understand my own music.

"*Circuits* . . . was a charging, churning celebration of the musical and cultural energy of modern-day America. From repetitive ideas reminiscent of Steve Reich to walking bass lines straight from jazz, *Circuits* refracted important American musical styles of this century. Similarly, the kaleidoscope of melodies, musical "licks" and fragmented form aptly illustrated the electric, almost convulsive nature of American society near the start of the 21st century."

So in answer to your question . . . listen to jazz, listen to the repetitive sounds of finely crafted machinery, and listen to the *Rite of Spring*. I too want to write a ballet some day, but in the mean time, I must settle for making my other music dance. I feel a very strong physical connection to the music I write.

115

Dr. McTee enthusiastically recommends all of the recordings issued by the University of North Texas Wind Ensemble, Eugene Corporon, conductor, identifying them as "first-rate" interpretations of her music.

For additional information, interviews, etc., visit the following web sites:

> http://www.newmusicnow.org/frameset.cfm?navnum=7&
>   bodyframe=/works/bio.cfm&id_work=40341473
> http://american-music.org/bulletn/McTee.html
> http://courses.unt.edu/cmctee/

COMPOSITIONS FOR WIND ENSEMBLE

Circuits (1990) 5:20 Difficult. Recorded on CD: KCD 11042. Klavier Records, 1992.

Circuits was written in 1990 for the Denton Chamber Orchestra of Denton, Texas. The composer's intention was to write a short orchestral piece that could be programmed along with a standard concerto and symphony. It has also received performances by the San Antonio Symphony, Symphony II, the Rhode Island Philharmonic Orchestra, the Houston Symphony, the Sydney Symphony Orchestra, the Orquesta Sinfonica Bahia Blanca (Argentina), the Rhode Island Philharmonic Orchestra, the Buffalo Philharmonic Orchestra, the Honolulu Symphony, the Memphis Symphony, the National Repertory Orchestra, the Cleveland Chamber Symphony, the American Composers Orchestra with Dennis Russell Davies conducting at Carnegie Hall, and the Sydney, Saint Louis, Cleveland, NHK, and the London Philharmonia Symphony Orchestras under the direction of Leonard Slatkin. One of McTee's colleagues, Martin Mailman, heard the first orchestral performance of the work and suggested that she arrange the piece for wind ensemble. Of *Circuits* McTee writes:

> The title, *Circuits,* is meant to characterize several important aspects of the works musical language: a strong reliance upon circuitous structures such as ostinatos; the use of a formal design, incorporating numerous, recurring short sections; and the presence of an unrelenting, kinetic energy achieved through the use of 16th notes at a constant tempo of 152 beats per minute.[15]

California Counterpoint: The Twittering Machine (1993) 8:00 Difficult. Recorded on CD: KCD 11070. Klavier Records, 1995.

California Counterpoint: The Twittering Machine was adapted for wind ensemble with a commission from the College Band Directors National Association (Western and Northwestern Divisions), and was premiered by Tim Salzman conducting the University of Washington Wind Ensemble in Reno, Nevada, March 19, 1994, at the Regional Conference of the CBDNA's Western and Northwestern Divisions. The wind ensemble version is based on McTee's 1993 commission from the Barlow Endowment for Music Composition, *The Twittering Machine* for chamber orchestra. David Stock conducting the Pittsburgh New Music Ensemble in November of 1993 first performed *The Twittering Machine.* The musical language is similar to *Circuits* and therefore was easily translated to wind ensemble. McTee writes:

> Like my earlier work, *Circuits, California Counterpoint: The Twittering Machine* was originally written for orchestra and later adapted for wind ensemble. The title is intended to recognize California conductor, Mitch Fennell, for having organized the commission to adapt the piece for winds, and is also meant to express my life-long fascination with the work of painter Paul Klee.
>
> Klee's Twittering Machine is both a drawing and a painting of four birds perched on a crank shaft. The images are whimsical, puppet-like, mechanistic, ironic, and playful. I was especially drawn to the paintings biting humor (imagine what would happen to the birds if the crank shaft were turned). In my piece, I make attempts at humor through the use of repeated structures and denied expectation — rhythms are displaced, passages are suddenly transposed or textures juxtaposed.
>
> There are elements of danger in Klee's painting: arrows piercing some of the birds, a gaping hole or ditch the birds might fall into, and the presence of an exclamation mark which is a recurring symbol in Klee's work meant to suggest impending doom. The danger elements in my piece consist of many large silences, or musical holes, that the players risk falling into if they're not attentive.
>
> But most important is my intention that the works, like Klee's Twittering Machine, convey movement—that it engages the body as well as the mind—that it dance![16]

Soundings (1995) 15:20 Moderately difficult

I. Fanfare
II. Gizmo
III. Waves
IV. Transmission

Soundings is a four-movement work for band of approximately fifteen minutes' duration. It was commissioned in 1995 by the Big Eight Band Directors Association whose affiliates include the University of Colorado, Iowa State University, the University of Kansas, Kansas State University, the University of Missouri, the University of Nebraska, the University of Oklahoma, and Oklahoma State University. *Soundings,* unlike McTee's first two compositions for wind ensemble, was conceived as a piece for band.

> In writing *Soundings* for band, I did not have to concern myself with length or with difficulty because I knew that, 1) I would probably not be competing with Beethoven and Brahms for a spot on the program, and, 2) the piece would be given many hours of rehearsal. *Soundings* was written with specific colors in mind, often similar to the colors of a large jazz ensemble with its brass and saxophone sections playing parallel melodies in unison rhythm.

The third movement of the work, *Waves,* was inspired by sounds McTee had created in her home computer studio. She believes that orchestral strings could not have duplicated those overtone-rich sounds with the same capabilities that oboes, bassoons, and saxophones can. McTee's further comments on *Soundings*:

> Several composers and authors, most recently Glen Watkins for his book about music in the twentieth century, have used the title, Soundings. I chose the title quite literally for its "sound", but also because its relatively abstract definition—"the making or giving forth of sounds"—complements the more descriptive titles of the individual movements: *"Fanfare"*, *"Gizmo"*, *"Waves"*, and *"Transmission"*.
>
> Each of the four movements explores different musical territory. *"Fanfare"* employs familiar musical materials such as quartal harmony and imitative counterpoint, but departs from traditional fanfares in its use of woodwind as well as brass instruments. *"Gizmo"* reflects my fascination with gadgets, motoric rhythms, and the sound of major sevenths. *"Waves"* was born out of my experience in the computer music studio and my preference for sounds whose shapes slowly expand and contract. In *"Waves"*, four musical layers are presented: (1) a steady tremolo in the percussion serves to anchor as well as animate the music; (2) waves of sound through the lower brass and woodwinds are supported by timpani and tamtam; (3) scattered, freely-moving solos in the upper winds are complemented by; (4) a repeated melody played by trumpets, oboe, flute, and piccolo. *"Transmission"* is not unlike *"Gizmo"* in its reliance upon a quickly-moving, steady pulse and sonorities employing major sevenths. The title, *"Transmission"*, was chosen for its double meaning: (1) information from a transmitter and (2) an assembly of gears and associated parts by which power is transmitted from the engine to the gearbox. In *"Transmission"* I have "transmitted" musical information using "metric or temporal modulation", a process analogous to that executed by the driver of an automobile smoothly shifting gears to change engine speed.[17]

Timepiece (2001) 8:00 Moderately difficult. Recorded on CD: K11122. Klavier Records, 2001.

Premiered on February 17, 2000 under the direction of Andrew Litton, the original version of *Timepiece* was commissioned by the Dallas Symphony Orchestra for its 100th Anniversary Season. A transcription for winds was subsequently commissioned by a consortium of ensembles affiliated with the College Band Directors National Association and premiered on February 22, 2001 with Eugene Migliaro Corporon conducting the North Texas Wind Symphony.

> I have dedicated this transcription to the memory of Martin Mailman (1932–2000), friend and colleague for many years at the University of North Texas, without whose encouragement I might never have transcribed an earlier work, *Circuits*, for wind ensemble.
>
> I entitled the work, *Timepiece*, not only for its connection to the celebration of special events marking the Dallas Symphony Orchestra's one hundredth anniversary and the beginning of a new millennium, but also for the manner in which musical time shapes the work. The piece begins slowly, "before" time, in a womb-like, subjective, holding place. And then a clock-like pulse emerges, takes control, and provides the driving force behind a sustained, highly energized second section of about six minutes.

Much of my recent thinking about music is informed by the writings of Carl G. Jung who, in the words of Anthony Storr, "felt that the whole energy of mental functioning" sprang from the tension between the oppositions of conscious and unconscious, of thought and feeling, of mind and body, of objectivity and subjectivity. So too have the integration and reconciliation of opposing elements become important aspects of my work: the frequent use of circular patterns, or ostinatos, offer both the possibility of suspended time and the opportunity for continuous forward movement; carefully controlled pitch systems and thematic manipulations provide a measure of objectivity and reason, while kinetic rhythmic structures inspire bodily motion; discipline yields to improvisation; and perhaps most importantly, humor takes its place comfortably along side the grave and earnest. I wish both to enlighten and to entertain, to communicate wholeness, and above all, to celebrate life!

CHRONOLOGICAL LIST OF WORKS

Year	Title	Instrumentation
2002	Symphony No. 1: Ballet for Orchestra	orchestra
2001	Timepiece	wind symphony
2000	Timepiece	orchestra
1999	Pathfinder	orchestra
1998	Agnus Dei	organ
1996	Einstein's Dreams	chamber ensemble
1996	Changes	violoncello and double bass
1995	Soundings	band
1994	Elegy	string orchestra
1993	Stepping Out	flute accompanied by hand claps or claves
1993	Fantasia	organ and percussion
1993	Capriccio per Krzysztof Penderecki	solo violin
1993	California Counterpoint: The Twittering Machine	wind ensemble
1993	The Twittering Machine	chamber ensemble or chamber orchestra
1992	"M" Music	computer generated tape
1992	Etudes	alto saxophone and tape
1992	Circle Music V	trombone and tape
1991	Eight Etudes	four instruments and tape
1990	Circuits	wind ensemble or orchestra
1989	Metal Music	computer music on tape
1988	Circle Music IV	horn and piano
1988	Circle Music III	bassoon and piano
1988	Circle Music II	flute and piano

1988	Circle Music I	viola and piano
1987	Images	horn and piano
1985	On Wings of Infinite Night	orchestra
1985	Octonal Escalade	20 trumpets
1984	Psalm 142: Threnody	medium voice and organ
1984	A Mighty Fortress, arr.	A cappella chorus
1983	Frau Musica	chorus, orchestra, and mezzo soprano
1983	Songs of Spring and the Moon	soprano and 8 instruments
1982	Psalm 100	a cappella chorus
1981	Wind Quintet No. 1	wind quintet
1981	Gloria	chorus and instrumental accompaniment
1980	King Lear Fragments	baritone, bass flute, and percussion
1979	A Bird Came Down the Walk	contralto and piano
1979	Capriccio	piano or harpsichord
1979	Piano Percussion Piece	piano, marimba/vibraphone
1978	Unisonance	orchestra
1977	Sonic Shades	concert band
1977	Chord	solo flute
1976	Eatonville	jazz band
1976	String Quartet No. 1	string quartet
1976	Dialogue	soprano and male vocalist
1975	Music for 48 Strings, Percussion, and Piano	strings, percussion, and piano
1975	Organism	organ
1975	Trio	flute, cello, harpsichord
1974	Two Blind Mice	flute and piano
1973	Three Miniatures	solo clarinet

APPENDIX

Minimalism is an idiom that was born in America in the 1960's, although it was heavily influenced by the music of other cultures, including those of West Africa, Bali and Java. The unifying features of this music include a steady pulse, repetition (hence the term "minimal"), consonance, a lack of sharply articulated contrasts, and the gradual transformation of musical ideas. Steve Reich is one of minimalism's most famous composers. Others include Philip Glass and John Adams.

Neo-romanticism or new-romanticism is a term generally applied to recent music that emulates nineteenth-century harmonic practice. The 3rd Symphony of Polish composer, Henryk Gorecki might be considered neo-romantic. In this piece one hears elongated modal melodies and gently shimmering tonal clusters. Other composers working in a neo-romantic idiom include George Rochberg and Krzysztof Penderecki.

Appropriation in music is characterized by a mixture of styles and frequent borrowings, especially from tonal music of the seventeenth and eighteenth centuries. Appropriation is, of course, by no means new to music. Composers of the 15th and 16th centuries borrowed secular as well as sacred music to create so-called parody masses. Bach rearranged his own and other composers' music extensively. Handel "stole" from Scarlatti, Telemann, and others. Mozart borrowed from Beethoven and the list goes on. Appropriation became less popular in the late 19th century as composers strove to assert their individuality and independence. But the pendulum has swung back again to the point where appropriation has been accepted as a natural part of "conventional" concert music.[18]

ENDNOTES

1. Letter from McTee to the author, June 5, 1998.
2. Walter Welke was the Director of Bands at the University of Washington from 1929–1974 and was an original founding member of the College Band Directors National Association (CBDNA).
3. McTee letter, June 5, 1998.
4. Ibid.
5. Ibid.
6. Ibid.
7. Ibid.
8. Ibid.
9. McTee, phone conversation, June 1, 1998.
10. McTee, letter.
11. Ibid.
12. See Appendix A.
13. Composers Session: NOTES from CBDNA Journal Number 11 Fall, 1997 Proceeding of the 29th National Conference of the College Band Directors' National Association, p. 38.
14. McTee letter, June 5, 1998.
15. Cincinnati Conservatory Wind Ensemble liner notes, KCD 11042. Klavier Records, 1992.
16. Cindy McTee, composer notes, California Counterpoint: The Twittering Machine score, Norruth Music, Inc., St. Louis, MO, 1993.
17. McTee letter, June 1, 1998.
18. McTee letter, June 5, 1998.

Alfred Reed

by
David Waltman

It is virtually impossible to participate in a scholastic instrumental music program in the United States, Europe or Japan without encountering the music of Alfred Reed. Throughout his 60-year professional career, Reed's work as a composer and arranger has had a profound influence on the development of school music programs around the world. With over 250 original works, transcriptions and arrangements to his credit, Reed is among the most prolific of American composers.

The enduring popularity of Alfred Reed's music stems from several readily identifiable factors, the most notable of which are accessibility and orchestration. Reed's music is accessible to both players and audiences, written with memorable lyric melodies while remaining firmly grounded in traditional 19th century western harmonic structures. Thoughtfully crafted with the clear intention of capitalizing on the strengths of each instrumental family, Alfred Reed's warm, sonorous orchestrations are perhaps the most recognizable hallmark of his music.

In spite of—and perhaps because of—its widespread popularity, Reed's music is not without critics. During the past thirty years, as 'serious art music' composers have intensified their commitment to write for the wind band medium, collegiate wind bands have less frequently scheduled performances of Reed's music. With players of almost limitless virtuosity in the top American college music programs, conductors are gravitating toward challenging works from composers who regularly redraw the boundaries of form, style, structure and technique defining western music.

Even as his popularity has somewhat declined in this relatively small segment of wind music performance, Alfred Reed is enjoying skyrocketing popularity in music programs overseas, most notably in Japan. For the past twenty years, beginning with his association with the Tokyo Kosei Wind Orchestra in 1980, Reed has regularly traveled to Japan to conduct professional and academic ensembles throughout the country. During the past ten years, Japanese patrons, including the city of Takasaki, the Shimoneseki Wind Orchestra, the Senzoku Gakuen Wind Orchestra, the Yokohama Kounan Jr. High School and the Kuwana Community Band, have commissioned a significant number of Reed's new compositions.[1]

BIOGRAPHICAL INFORMATION

Alfred Reed was born Alfred Friedman on January 25th, 1921 to Carl and Elizabeth Friedman in the Chelsea neighborhood of New York City. Alfred's parents were first generation Viennese Austrian immigrants, his mother emigrating around 1899 and his father in 1910. At the time of his arrival, Carl Friedemann von Mark worked as a singing waiter in such renowned New York venues as Little Hungary and the Café Royale. During World War I, Carl changed the family name to Friedman in light of anti-German sentiment.[2] Alfred also had a half brother from his mother's first marriage, but before the war his father took the child to Italy, and Alfred never knew what became of him. Alfred was the only child of Carl and Elizabeth.

Alfred Reed's musical career began with his enrollment in the New York Schools of Music in 1931 where he took only three cornet lessons. At this time, his father made the acquaintance of Abraham Nussbaum, a trumpet player and conductor of stage music at the Metropolitan Opera. Carl made the necessary arrangements and Alfred began studying trumpet with Nussbaum until the age of 13.[3] After working with several other teachers, Alfred began playing professionally at about age 14 and soon retained an agent to represent him and his small dance band. The agent suggested Alfred change his last name to Reed since this name carried no particular religious or ethnic connotations. Alfred Reed has been known professionally by his adopted name ever since, although he did not legally make the change until 1955.[4]

After graduating from high school Reed worked several summer jobs as a dance band musician in the Catskills of New York. On one occasion his band was asked to play some Irish music for a visiting New York City politician of some importance, but the band had no Irish arrangements available. Reed recalls telling his fellow band members, "Don't worry, I'll write us something",[5] which he did. The politician was suitably impressed and gave the band a memorable tip. Reed realized after this experience that writing music was his true calling and he began to pursue compositional studies with considerable diligence. When he returned to the city however, he found his mother in poor health. She had been diagnosed with cancer and subsequently passed away when Alfred was only 16. He and his mother had always been very close and losing her was quite difficult for him.[6]

After his mother died, Alfred made the acquaintance of composition teacher Paul Yartin. Yartin was educated in Vienna and Paris and had studied with Saint-Säens. Through an arrangement made by his father Alfred was able to study with Yartin on what essentially amounted to a full scholarship. Reed credits much of his success as a composer to Yartin's early influence, particularly his insistence that Alfred thoroughly learn the harmonic and contrapuntal techniques of the Viennese masters.[7]

Alfred's first public success as a composer came with performances of his work *Country Night* by the National Youth Administration Sinfonietta and subsequently by the NBC Symphony. The piece was later renamed *Interludium* and became Reed's first published work in 1953. The Charles H. Hansen Music Company published the work in an arrangement for Hammond Organ as part of a series of organ publications for the Ethel Smith Organ Company.[8]

After marrying Marjorie Delay in 1941 Reed was inducted into the Army Air Corps in 1942. Stationed in Atlantic City and Denver, he completed numerous original compositions and arrangements for band during his three years of military service. It was during the war that Reed's career as a composer of wind music was launched with his composition *Russian Christmas Music*, which was nationally broadcast during a joint military band Christmas concert in Denver.[9]

Before the war Reed had made the acquaintance of Vittorio Giannini who agreed to take him as a composition student. Upon returning to New York City after the war Reed accepted his offer and enrolled in the Juilliard School where Giannini served as a member of the composition faculty.[10] Like Reed's former mentor Paul Yartin, Giannini was also grounded in the traditional 19th century German compositional style. A pupil of composer Reuben Goldmark, Giannini encouraged Reed's continued development along the lines of the European masters insisting that, "music could not stand the test of time unless it was grounded in Italian melodic form and German symphonic craftsmanship".[11]

Reed, with Giannini's blessing, left Juilliard without a degree in 1948 in order to work for composer Morris Mamorsky.[12] Mamorsky, a former NBC staff music writer, was a free-lance composer very much in demand for television and radio. Most of Reed's work for Mamorsky between 1948 and 1950 was ultimately broadcast on the NBC network.

In 1950 Alfred Reed replaced Richard Maltby as staff arranger and composer at ABC and began to focus on composing for television. Between 1948 and 1950 Reed also composed music for several full-length motion pictures including "Wings Over France" and "The Inner Man Steps Out". While working for ABC Reed was contacted by Bernard Kalban of the Charles H. Hansen Music Corporation who asked him to write music for young wind players. At that time Alfred had no particular inclinations toward writing wind music but agreed to meet with Kalban. This meeting was an important turning point in Alfred's career and began his long association with the school band movement with which he is so closely associated.[13]

In 1952 the Reeds' first child died at the age of three months from congenital heart defects. This was a difficult time for the couple, and in 1953 Alfred accepted a position as conductor of the University Orchestra at Baylor University in Waco, Texas, hoping to make a new start. Prior to his departure for Texas, Reed signed a contract with Hansen, whose company earned right of first publication for any music Reed produced while at Baylor. While teaching at Baylor, Reed completed his undergraduate work at that institution and received his Bachelor of Music degree, Cum Laude, in 1955. In 1956 Reed was awarded a Master of Music degree, also from Baylor. After two years in Texas the Reeds were ready to return to New York with their newly adopted son, Richard. In the summer of 1956 Reed went to work for Hansen full time as a senior editor and was released from his earlier contract with the company. Reed's new contract gave him the right to have his works published with any publisher he desired, even while employed by Hansen.[14]

While Reed enjoyed his work at Hansen he found he did not have sufficient time to devote to his own writing and in 1966 accepted a position on the faculty at the University of Miami. Over the next 27 years of his association with this school Reed composed most of his well-known works for bands. During his tenure at Miami Reed also became acquainted with Toshio Akiyama of the Sony Corporation in Japan. In 1981 Akiyama invited Reed to Japan to conduct a concert and produce a recording with the Tokyo Kosei Wind Orchestra. This visit led to a long association with the Tokyo Kosei Wind Orchestra and other Japanese music organizations that continues to the present day.

COMPOSITIONAL STYLE

Reed's sense of musical craftsmanship, instilled by his early teachers, has resulted in a body of repertoire that is universally appealing. Although he has composed numerous works based on original melodies, many of his most outstanding and popular works are in fact masterful arrangements and orchestrations of material borrowed from a variety of sources; a myriad of musics ranging from sacred Orthodox Christian hymns to traditional flamenco dance rhythms. Regardless of the original source material, Reed consistently draws upon his considerable skills as an orchestrator in crafting well-balanced and playable works for ensembles of varying ability and instrumentation. Important melodic and harmonic lines are frequently doubled across complementary families of instruments permitting a conductor with limited instrumental resources the opportunity to perform a satisfactory concert of Reed's music.

The sonorities in Reed's orchestrations are achieved

through a thoughtful blending of instrumental textures that draw upon the full range of the instrumental families for which they are scored. Although most of Reed's compositions are playable by ensembles with more limited instrumentation (thanks to liberal cross cueing and doubling), his work is heard at its greatest advantage when performed with the composer's intended scoring. Reed is particularly fond of the sound produced by the complete woodwind section; E♭ and B♭ clarinets, alto clarinet, bass and contrabass clarinets, oboes, English horn, bassoons and contrabassoon, the complete saxophone family, piccolos and flutes.[15] Rather than 'one on a part' instrumentation, Reed prefers multiple players on section clarinet parts, considering these instruments 'the string section of the band'.[16] While many modern composers also rely on special instrumental effects in their compositions, such as gongs dipped in water or extended wind instrument techniques, Reed generally stays within the realm of more traditional orchestration.

In many respects Reed's orchestration is reminiscent of techniques perfected by such 19th century masters as Berlioz and Rimsky-Korsakov. In Reed's compositions, instruments are generally employed in their most effective ranges, blending and balancing to create timbres no single voice alone could project.

These techniques of orchestration serve as a palette upon which Reed skillfully mixes melody and rhythm of his own with borrowed material to create original compositions unique in the literature. One of Reed's most popular works, *Armenian Dances* (parts I and II) is an excellent example. Originally conceived as a single work in two movements, the decision was made to publish the 30 minute long *Armenian Dances* in two parts to facilitate distribution and marketing.

Parts I and II of the *Armenian Dances* were both written at the suggestion of Harry Begian, a prominent American wind conductor of Armenian descent.[17] When Reed asked Begian why he thought he should write such a piece, Reed recalls:

Harry Begian first proposed to me the idea of doing a major instrumental work for winds based on some of the collected folk music by the great Armenian musicologist Gomidas Vartabed. At the time that he spoke with me he said that he felt in my *Russian Christmas Music* I had captured so faithfully the color, the emotion, the feeling of this derivative folk music that he felt I might be able to do a decent job with this Armenian material. Well (I said to him) but we already have Armenian music—Hovhanness, Chobanian, Katchaturian, and one or two others. Yes, Harry said, they are Armenian, but my feeling is they are not representative of the true Armenian folk music— they are too Kurdish—too much belly dancing...Harry felt that the true Armenian folk music was more Western rather than Eastern oriented, and he told me about this Gomidas Vartabed, who devoted his entire life to collecting the native folk music of Armenia. He collected over 4000 different pieces. He annotated it, he purified it, he gave it definitive musical as well as literary form in the lyrics, and without his having done so, all of this music might today have simply perished...however, the problem was that Vartabed's definitive editions were all left in

vocal form—there were no instrumental works. And that was what Harry wanted me to do, to make use of this material in large-scale instrumental forms...so it would have a chance to be heard in America. Employing a number of Vartabed's collected Armenian folk tunes, Reed went on to write what is perhaps his most popular work throughout the world, originally published in 1974 (Part I) and 1978 (Part II).

COMPOSITIONAL PROCESS

Among his over 250 works Alfred Reed has completed 15 well-received arrangements of J.S.Bach's music, the most recent being the *Arioso* from Cantata No. 157, published by C.L. Barnhouse in 1998. Representative of the many arrangements Reed has scored for winds, the *Arioso* is exemplary of Reed's conception of an arrangement as opposed to a transcription. Reed considers an arrangement to be different from a transcription in that the latter is essentially a re-orchestration of material for an ensemble with instrumentation different from that originally intended by the composer, while an arrangement may require the addition of new material. According to Reed, this addition of material, whether just a few notes or entire passages, requires the arranger to become essentially a 'recomposer' of the original work. The *Arioso*, by Reed's definition is an arrangement, about which he says the following:

The *Arioso* puzzled me a bit when I first thought of doing it, because of what it is and how I thought it could be best handled in a full-scale arrangement—by which I mean developing the original material to a certain extent. Some of the arrangements in this Bach series are really transcriptions, in other words, I've not added anything to the basic musical texture that Bach left us. For example, the *Jesu, Joy of Man's Desiring* and the *Komm Susser Tod* I have merely orchestrated in as fitting a manner as that music called for. In other arrangements I've had to add a good deal of my own material; always, of course, with the hope that the listener would accept this as being in keeping with the original chorale melody as Bach left it to us.

The *Arioso*, however, presented a rather interesting challenge...it is the only one of (the 15 Bach arrangements) that is not built on a chorale melody. All the other 14 are adaptations of standard Protestant chorales. With the *Arioso* we are dealing with a known instrumental piece; it is the introduction to one of the almost 280 church cantatas Bach turned out in the course of his employment for the church he was working for. And, this [*Arioso*] is purely instrumental which sets it aside from all the other cantatas we know of, because in all of them, all the movements are for voices with orchestra. But here we have an absolutely independent orchestral composition, with the entire melody throughout played by a solo oboe with nothing but a small string choir playing 'oom-pa-pa, oom-oom-pa-pa, oom-oom-pa-pa' continuously throughout the piece. The melody is never used again in the course of that cantata, or, so far as we know, in any other works of Bach. But it is, without question, one of the most glorious melodies that Bach ever wrote.

Now, how do you take something like this and develop it into a work for a large ensemble? This is what puzzled me for quite a while before I decided to tackle it. The problem here is you simply cannot, in a large orchestra, give such a long melody to just one instrument or one section. The listener will expect variety of color. What we may put up with as part of a church service...the oboe playing this long melody...would not work very well in the concert hall. We would feel there was a lack of variety; and working this out...to create this variety, and still maintain the calm feeling of this long, beautifully developing line, I assure you was not a problem that was too easily solved! But once I had worked out this one aspect—variation and color in the melodic line—the rest of it fell pretty well into place."[18]

ANALYTICAL OVERVIEW AND CONDUCTING CONSIDERATIONS FOR *ARIOSO*

Reed's solution to his 'problem' of orchestration consisted of developing the lyrical oboe melody from the original work in the woodwinds and saxophones, accompanied by brass instruments with cup mutes, and occasionally, flutes. Reed's arrangement retains the original key of F Major, and employs the harp (or piano) to provide warmth and linear continuity to support the more stylistically separated eighth note figures in the brass.

Consistent voice doubling and liberal cross cues, hallmarks of Alfred Reed's lush orchestration, provide adequate support for long phrases required by the slow Adagio (ca. 48 to the quarter) tempo. Typical of his style, Reed scores instruments well within the limits of their ranges, a significant contributing factor to the overall sense of serenity and sonority in this work.

Modern wind band works often pose significant challenges for the conductor in terms of metric and rhythmic analysis, special instrumental techniques or technical problems associated with ensemble logistics and special effects. In conducting a work such as the *Arioso*, the conductor is spared these concerns and given the opportunity to concentrate on the supremely important issues of phrasing, balance and style which, in this work, is quite simple from an analytical standpoint, but very difficult in terms of essential musicality for many ensembles.

It is not uncommon to hear conductors discuss a work in terms of being simple 'technically', but difficult 'musically'. Although this may be a somewhat imprecise statement, the general meaning is readily understood by most conductors approaching a work like the *Arioso*— specifically, maintaining sustained lines and phrases with a wind band can be as difficult as working with complex rhythms and meter changes which present more formidable mathematical challenges for the conductor and ensemble.

In order to effectively conduct the *Arioso*, or any Alfred Reed work, the conductor must take sufficient time to thoroughly understand the phrasing in the piece.

In Reed's music, articulations, dynamic markings— even ornamentation—are all directed toward shaping phrases. To conduct the *Arioso* in a strictly metrical fashion would destroy the subtleties of texture and color the composer felt were so important in this arrangement. Significant rubato, a challenging concept for many modern wind bands, is not only acceptable in a work of this nature, but necessary. The slow tempo and long phrases in this piece make it impossible for most wind players to complete an entire phrase without a breath, and the conductor must be prepared to provide opportunities for them to breathe without interrupting the line. One obvious solution to this problem is to stagger breathing among players on a particular part.

SUMMARY

Alfred Reed has been one of the most frequently performed composers of the 20th and 21st centuries and the wind band repertoire would not be the same without his contributions. He has not earned his place among the world's great composers as a result of bold experimentation, startling new directions or innovative approaches to form; however, for over 60 years Alfred Reed has written music people enjoy playing and audiences enjoy hearing—which to him, is the most important point.[19]

SELECTED DISCOGRAPHY

Begian, Dr. Harry, conductor. University of Illinois Symphonic Band. "Armenian Dances" (complete) UI Bands 1001

Reed, Alfred, conductor. **Alfred Reed and the Tokyo Kosei Wind Orchestra**. *"Second Suite for Band"* / *"The Enchanted Island"* / *"The Music-Makers"* / *"Russian Christmas Music"* / *"Ballade"* / *"A Festival Prelude"* / *"Armenian Dances (Part I)"* KOCD 2301

Reed, Alfred, conductor. **Othello**. Tokyo Kosei Wind Orchestra. *"Othello"* / *"Second Century"* / *"A Symphonic Prelude"* / *"Danza Caribe"* / *"Rushmore"* KOCD 3006 -

Reed, Alfred, conductor. **Hamlet**. Tokyo Kosei Wind Orchestra. *"Music for Hamlet"*/ *"Pro Texana"* / *"Prelude and Capriccio"* / *"The Garden of Proserpine"* KOCD 3007

Reed, Alfred, conductor. **Salutations!** Tokyo Kosei Wind Orchestra. *"Salutations!"* / *"A Northern Legend"* / *"El Camino Real"* / *"Might and Majesty"* / *"Praise Jerusalem!"* KOCD 3009

Reed, Alfred, conductor. **Symphony No. 3**. Tokyo Kosei Wind Orchestra. *"Symphony No. 3"* / *"A Celebration Fanfare"* / *"Wapawekka"* KOCD 3010

Reed, Alfred, conductor. **March: Golden Eagle / Symphony for Brass and Percussion**. Tokyo Kosei Wind Orchestra. *"March: Golden Eagle"* / *"Symphony for Brass and Percussion"* / *"A Little Concert Suite"* / *"Eventide"* / *"Seascape"* / *"Third Suite for Band"* Johann Sebastian Bach: *"Who Will But Let Himself Be*

Guided" / Anonymous: "Greensleeves" KOCD 3012

Reed, Alfred, conductor. **Armenian Dances**. Tokyo Kosei Wind Orchestra. *"Armenian Dances (Part I)"* / *"Armenian Dances (Part II)"* / *"A Jubilant Overture"* / *"Song of the High Cascades"* / Johann Sebastian Bach: Sleepers, Awake!" / Cesar Franck: "Panis Angelicus" KOCD 3016

Reed, Alfred, conductor. **The Marimba Concertino**. Tokyo Kosei Wind Orchestra. *"Concertino for Marimba and Winds"* / *"A Springtime Celebration"* / *"Serenade"* / *"Hymn Variants"* / *"A Festive Overture"* / *"Passacaglia"* KOCD 3019

Akiyama, Kazuyoshi, conductor. **The Lotus Sutra**. Tokyo Kosei Wind Orchestra. *"Three Revelations from the Lotus Sutra"* / *"Passacaglia"* / *"First Suite for Band"* KOCD 3071

Reed, Alfred, conductor. **Second Symphony**. Tokyo Kosei Wind Orchestra. *"Second Symphony"* / *"Punchinello"* / *"The Hounds of Spring"* / *"Three Revelations from the Lotus Sutra"* / Antonio Vivaldi: *"Concerto in C for Piccolo"* KOCD 3312

Reed, Alfred, conductor. **The Wind Music of Alfred Reed**. Tokyo Kosei Wind Orchestra. *"Second Symphony"* / *"Symphony No. 3"* / *"Fourth Symphony"* KOCD 3550

Reed, Alfred, conductor. **The Wind Music of Alfred Reed**. Tokyo Kosei Wind Orchestra. *"Viva Musica!"* / *"The Hounds of Spring"* / *"Evolutions"* / *"Golden Jubilee"* / *"The Music-Makers"* / *"A Jubilant Overture"* / *"A Springtime Celebration"* / *Curtain Up!"* / *"Punchinello"* KOCD 3551

Reed, Alfred, conductor. **The Wind Music of Alfred Reed**. Tokyo Kosei Wind Orchestra. *"First Suite for Band"* / *"Second Suite for Band"* / *"Third Suite for Band"* / *"Fourth Suite for Band"* / *"A Little Concert Suite"* KOCD 3552

Reed, Alfred, conductor. **The Wind Music of Alfred Reed**. Tokyo Kosei Wind Orchestra. *"Music for "Hamlet"* / *"Othello"* / *"The Enchanted Island"* / *"Praise Jerusalem!"* KOCD 3553

Reed, Alfred, conductor. **Alfred Reed— Live!**. Senzoku Gakuen Symphonic Wind Orchestra & Otonowa Wind Symphonica. *"El Camino Real"* / *"Divertimento for Flute and Winds"* / *"Armenian Dances Part I"* / *"Praise Jerusalem!"* Reed-1462. (West Coast Music Service, North Ft. Meyers, Florida)

Reed, Alfred, conductor. **Russian Christmas Music: Alfred Reed—Live! Volume 2**. Senzoku Gakuen Symphonic Wind Orchestra & Otonowa Wind Symphonica. *"First Suite"* / *"Marimba Concertino"* / *"Russian Christmas Music"* / *"Fourth Symphony"* Reed-1555 (West Coast Music Service, North Ft. Meyers, Florida)

Reed, Alfred, conductor. **Russian Christmas Music: Alfred Reed—Live! Volume 3: Giligia**. Senzoku Gakuen Symphonic Wind Orchestra & Otonowa Wind Symphonica. *"Sixth Suite"* / *"Three Revelations from the Lotus Sutra"* / *"Giligia: A Song of Rememberance"* / *"Fifth Symphony"* Reed-1616 (West Coast Music Service, North Ft. Meyers, Florida)

SELECTED LISTING OF PUBLISHED MUSIC

A. ORIGINAL WORKS FOR WIND ENSEMBLE, WIND ORCHESTRA AND CONCERT BAND

Slavonic Folk Suite	MMP/Kalmus	1953
Choral Prelude in E Minor	Southern Music Co.	1953
Lumberjack Overture	MMP/Kalmus	1954
The Crowning Glory, (Processional March)	Southern Music Co.	1956
Ode for Trumpet (Solo Trumpet and Band)	Southern Music Co.	1956
Ballade (Solo Alto Saxophone and Band)	Southern Music Co.	1956
Serenade (Solo B♭ Clarinet and Band)	Southern Music Co.	1957
Might and Majesty, Biblical Suite for Band)	MMP/Kalmus	1958
Greensleeves (Fantasy for Band)	E.F. Kalmus/ Barnhouse	1962
A Festival Prelude	Piedmont/Marks/ HLPC	1962
Seascape (Solo Baritone/ Trombone and Band)	Piedmont/Marks/ HLPC	1962
A Sacred Suite	Piedmont/Marks/ HLPC	1962
A Symphonic Prelude (Based on "Black Is the Color of My True Love's Hair")	Piedmont/Marks/ HLPC	1963
Ceremony of Flourishes	Bourne Music Co.	1963
Song of Threnos	Bourne Music Co.	1964
A Festive Overture	Frank/HLPC	1964
Rahoon (Rhapsody for Solo B♭ Clarinet and Band)	E.F. Kalmus and Co.	1966
Poetry and Power (Ceremonial March)	Southern Music Co.	1966
War March and Battle Hymn of the Vikings (A Nordic Trilogy)	Belwin/Warner	1967
Passacaglia	Frank/HLPC	1968
The Music-Makers (Concert Overture)	Frank/HLPC	1968
Wapawekka (Symphonic Rhapsody on Canadian Indian Themes)	E.F. Kalmus and Co.	1968
Intrada Drammatica	E.F. Kalmus and Co.	1968
Symphony for Brass and Percussion	Sam Fox Publ.Co.	1968
Russian Christmas Music	Sam Fox Publ. Co.	1968

A Jubilant Overture	C.L. Barnhouse Co.	1969
The Pledge of Allegiance	Piedmont/Marks/ Kalmus	1970
A Ceremonial Fanfare	E.F. Kalmus and Co.	1971
in Memoriam (An Elegy for the Fallen)	E.F. Kalmus and Co.	1972
A Northern Legend	E.F. Kalmus and Co.	1972
Imperatrix (A Concert Overture)	Piedmont/Marks/ HLPC	1972
Music for "Hamlet"	Theodore Presser Co.	1973
Alleluia! Laudamus Te (A Celebration Hymn for Winds and Optional Organ)	Piedmont/Marks/ HLPC	1973
Armenian Dances (Part I)	Sam Fox Publ.Co.	1974
Punchinello (Overture to a Romantic)	C.L. Barnhouse Co.	1974
A Northern Nocturne	UMMP/Plymouth	1974
Testament of an American	Warner/Belwin	1974
First Suite for Band	Piedmont/Marks/ HLPC	1976
Othello (A Symphonic Portrait for Band)	Piedmont/Marks/ HLPC	1977
Armenian Dances (Part II)	C.L. Barnhouse Co.	1978
Prelude and Capriccio	Piedmont/Marks/ HLPC	1978
Second Symphony	Piedmont/Marks/ HLPC	1979
Second Suite for Band	Piedmont/Marks/ HLPC	1980
The Enchanted Island	Piedmont/Marks/ HLPC	1980
The Hounds of Spring (A Concert Overture for Winds)	Piedmont/Marks/ HLPC	1981
A Christmas intrada (Concert Band with Antiphonal Brass Choirs)	Piedmont/Marks/ HLPC	1981
Rushmore, A Symphonic Prologue for Winds	C. L. Barnhouse Co.	1981
Third Suite for Band	Piedmont/Marks/ HLPC	1982
The Garden of Prosperpine (A Symphonic Pastorale for Winds)	E.F. Kalmus and Co.	1982
Queenston Overture	Piedmont/Marks/ HLPC	1983
Viva Musica! (A Concert Overture for Winds)	Piedmont/Marks/ HLPC	1984
A Little Concert Suite	Piedmont/Marks/ HLPC	1984
Pro Texana (Concert March)	Southern Music Co.	1984
Three Revelations from The Lotus Sutra (Part I: Awakening)	E.F. Kalmus and Co.	1985
Three Revelations from The Lotus Sutra (Part II: Contemplation, Rejoicing)	Piedmont/Marks/ HLPC	1985
Song of the High Cascades	Piedmont/Marks/ HLPC	1985
El Camino Real	Piedmont/Marks/ HLPC	1986
Danza Caribe (Caribbean Dance)	Piedmont/Marks/ HLPC	1986
Centennial! (A Celebration Hymn for Winds)	Piedmont/Marks/ HLPC	1986
A Christmas Celebration (for Winds with Mixed Voices, Brass Choir and Optional Organ)	Piedmont/Marks/ HLPC	1987
Golden Jubilee (Concert Overture)	Piedmont/Marks/ HLPC	1987
Praise Jerusalem! (Variations on an Armenian Easter Hymn)	C.L. Barnhouse and Co.	1988
Symphony No. 3	Jenson/HLPC	1988
Salutations! (Fanfares and intradas)	Molenaar Edition BV	1989
A Celebration Fanfare	C.L. Barnhouse Co.	1989
Mr. Music! (Concert March)	C.L. Barnhouse Co.	1990
Golden Eagle, Concert March	API/Molenaar Edition BV	1990/ 1994
Russian Christmas Music (arr. James Curnow)	Jenson/HLPC	1990
Curtain Up! A Theatre Overture for Winds	Jenson/HLPC	1991
A Springtime Celebration, Overture	C.L. Barnhouse Co.	1991
A Festival Prelude (arr. James Curnow)	Jenson/HLPC	1991
Hymn Variants (Lasst Uns Erfreuen)	C.L. Barnhouse and Co.	1992
with Trumpets and Drums (A Northern Salute!)	Hal Leonard Publ. Corp	1992

Concertino for Marimba and Winds	C.L. Barnhouse and Co.	1993
Fourth Symphony	Molenaar Edition BV	1993
Evolutions, A Concert Overture for Winds	Molenaar Edition BV	1993
Fourth Suite for Band ("City of Music")	C.L. Barnhouse Co.	1994
The King of Love My Shepherd Is	C.L. Barnhouse Co..	1995
The Ramparts of Courage	C.L. Barnhouse Co.	1995
Fifth Suite for Band (international Dances)	Piedmont/Marks/ HLPC	1996
Two Bagatelles for Concert Band	C.L. Barnhouse and Co.	1997
Concerto for Trumpet (Cornet, Fluegelhorn and Winds)	Molenaar Edition BV	1997
Divertimento for Flute and Winds	Molenaar Edition BV	1998
Sixth Suite for Band	Piedmont/Marks/ HLPC	1998
The Golden Year, an Anniversary Celebration	C.L. Barnhouse and Co.	1998
Sumus Futuro (We Are the Future!)	C.L. Barnhouse and Co.	1999
Silver Shadow (Concert March)	Piedmont/Marks/ HLPC	1999
Millenium III, a Concert Overture	C.L. Barnhouse and Co.	1999
Canto E Camdombe	Neil A. Kjos Co.	1999
Jidai (Year of Years!)	Neil A. Kjos Co.	2001
Children's Suite, Solo E♭ Alto Saxophone and Winds	MMP/Kalmus	2001
Acclamation! A Global Greeting for Winds	Piedmont/Marks/ HLPC	2001

B. ARRANGEMENTS/TRANSCRIPTIONS FOR WIND ENSEMBLE, WIND ORCHESTRA, AND CONCERT BAND

Bolero (from "Sicilian Vespers") Verdi	Golden Bell Songs	1956
Gymnopedies (Satie/ Debussy)	Editions Salabert	1960
Concerto in C Major (Piccolo and Winds)	E.F. Kalmus and Company	1962
La Procesion Du Rocio (Joaquin Turina)	Editions Salabert	1962

Concertino (B♭ Clarinet and Winds) Weber	Kendor Music, inc.	1962
Serenade (B♭ Clarinet(s) and Winds) Pierne	E.F. Kalmus and Co.	1963
Prelude and Dance (from "Bachianas Brasileras, No. 4")	Warner/Belwin	1964
Air De Sarabande (Handel)	Marks/HLPC	1965
Suite in A Minor (Flute(s) and Winds) Parts I, II, and III (Telemann)	Southern Music Company	1965
Nimrod (from "Enigma Variations") Elgar	Warner/Belwin	1966
March "Grandioso" (Seitz)	Southern Music Company	1969
in Dulci Jubilo (J.S. Bach)	Sam Fox Pub. Company	1969
Vilabella (Concert March) with Kenneth Williams	UMMP/Plymouth	1970
Eighteenth Variation (Piano and Winds) (from "Rhapsodie on A Theme of Paganini) Rachmaninoff")	Warner/Belwin	1971
Severn Suite (Elgar)	Sam Fox Publ. Co	1973
The Entertainer (Scott Joplin)	Theodore Presser Co.	1974
The Strenuous Life (Scott Joplin)	Theodore Presser Co.	1974
Nocturne, Op. 9, No. 2 (Scriabin)	Piedmont/Marks/ HLPC	1975
The Barnhouse Bach Series		
My Jesus! Oh, What Anguish!	C.L. Barnhouse Co.	1975
Come, Sweet Death	C.L. Barnhouse Co.	1976
Thus Do You Fare, My Jesus	C.L. Barnhouse Co.	1978
Jesu, Joy of Man's Desiring	C.L. Barnhouse Co.	1980
Sheep May Safely Graze	C.L. Barnhouse Co.	1981
Prelude No. 4 (Well Tempered Clavier)	C.L. Barnhouse Co.	1983
Sleepers, Awake!	C.L. Barnhouse Co.	1984
If Thou Be Near	C.L. Barnhouse Co.	1984
forget Me Not, O Dearest Lord	C.L. Barnhouse Co.	1985
God Still Lives!	C.L. Barnhouse Co.	1985
My Heart Is Filled with Longing	C.L. Barnhouse Co.	1986
Our Father Who Art in Heaven	C.L. Barnhouse Co.	1988

Who Will But Let Himself Be Guided	C.L. Barnhouse Co.	1989
Deck Thyself, My Soul, with Gladness	C.L. Barnhouse Co.	1990
Arioso (from Cantata No. 157)	C.L. Barnhouse Co.	1998
Sine Nomine (Ralph Vaughn Williams)	Warner/Belwin	1976
Azrael (from "Crucifixus") Antonio Lotti	Warner/Belwin	1977
Cantata De Chiesa (Karg-Elert)	Piedmont/Marks/HLPC	1979
March of the Little Tin Soldiers (Pierne)	E.F. Kalmus and Co.	1981
Prelude, Op. 9, No. 1 (Scriabin)	Piedmont/Marks/HLPC	1985
Pavane (Maurice Ravel)	MMP/Kalmus	1988
Three Symphonic Preludes (Shostakovich)	MMP/Kalmus	1988
Presentation of the Silver Rose (from Act II—"Der Rosenkavalier") Richard Strauss	MMP/Kalmus	1988

The Barnhouse Classics Series

Chanson Triste (Tchaikovsky)	C.L. Barnhouse Co.	1989
Vilia (from "The Merry Widow") Franz Lehar	C.L. Barnhouse Co.	1990
The Pilgrim's Chorus (from "Tannhauser")	C.L. Barnhouse Co.	1991
Macarena ("Le Virgen De La Macarena")	C.L. Barnhouse Co.	1992
Radetzky March (Johann Strauss, Father)	C.L. Barnhouse Co.	1993
Funiculi Funicula (Luigi Denza)	C.L. Barnhouse Co.	1994
Tarantella (Traditional)	C.L. Barnhouse Co.	1996
Gypsy Dance (from Act II—"Carmen") Bizet	C.L. Barnhouse Co.	1997
Panis Angelicus (Cesar Franck)	C. L. Barnhouse Co.	1988
Tritsch-Tratsch Polka (Johann Strauss)	C.L. Barnhouse Co.	1998
Thunder and Lightning Polka	C.L. Barnhouse Co.	1999
Clear Track Polka (Eduard Strauss)	C.L. Barnhouse Co.	2000
Pomp and Circumstance, No. 1 (Elgar)	MMP/Kalmus	2000
Pomp and Circumstance, No. 2 (Elgar)	MMP/Kalmus	2001
Pomp and Circumstance, No. 3 (Elgar)	MMP/Kalmus	2000
Pomp and Circumstance, No.4 (Elgar)	MMP/Kalmus	2001

C. BROADWAY MUSICAL SHOWS

Frank Loesser's Showtime Concert Band Book	Frank/HLPC	1954
Li'l Abner, Overture	Hansen Publications	1957
Take Me Along, Overture	Hansen Publications	1959
The Music Man, Highlights	Frank/HLPC	1959
Greenwillow, Selections	Frank/HLPC	1960
The Unsinkable Molly Brown, Highlights	Frank/HLPC	1961
The Fantasticks, Overture	Chappell/HLPC	1966

D. MOTION PICTURE SCORES

Cinderella, Overture	Walt Disney Music	1955
Peter Pan, Overture	Walt Disney Music	1955
The Man with the Golden Arm	Dena Music Company	1956
The Wonderful World of the Brothers Grimm	Golden Bell Songs	1962
Exodus, Highlights	Chappell/HLPC	1962
The Valiant Years	Chappell/HLPC	1962
Lawrence of Arabia	Gower Music, inc.	1963
Mary Poppins, Highlights	Walt Disney Music	1965
Mancini! A Concert Medley	Famous Music Co.	1965
Rodgers and Hart, A Concert Medley	Famous Music Co.	1965

E. ORIGINAL WORKS FOR ORCHESTRA AND STRING ORCHESTRA

Rhapsody for Viola and Orchestra	Boosey and Hawkes	1966
A Festival Prelude	Piedmont/Marks/HLPC	1968
Titania's Nocture (String Orchestra)	Piedmont/Marks/HLPC	1968
The Pledge of Allegiance (with Narrator and Chorus)	Piedmont/Marks/HLPC	1970
Testament of An American (with Narrator and Chorus)	Warner/Cpp/Belwin	1974

Siciliana Notturno (String Orchestra)	Piedmont/Marks/ HLPC	1977
Greensleeves (Fantasy for Orchestra)	E.F. Kalmus and Co.	1979
Suite Concertante (String Orchestra)	E.F. Kalmus and Company	1982
American Sketches, Series I		
Strings 'N' Things	E.F. Kalmus and Co.	1988
Fashion Show	E.F. Kalmus and Co.	1988
Country Night	E.F. Kalmus and Co.	1988
By the Lagoon	E.F. Kalmus and Co.	1988
The Mechanical Doll	E.F. Kalmus and Co.	1988

F. TRANSCRIPTIONS AND ARRANGEMENTS FOR ORCHESTRA AND STRING ORCHESTRA

Selections from "Oliver" (Lionel Bart)	Richmond Organization	1970
Jesu, Joy of Man's Desiring (J.S. Bach)	E.F. Kalmus and Co.	1981
Sheep May Safely Graze (J.S. Bach)	E.F. Kalmus and Co.	1981
in Dulci Jubilo (J.S. Bach)	E.F. Kalmus and Co	1981
Come, Sweet Death (J.S. Bach)	E.F. Kalmus and Co.	1981
My Jesus! Oh, What Anguish! (J.S. Bach)	E.F. Kalmus and Co.	1981
Thus Do You Fare, My Jesus (J.S. Bach)	E.F. Kalmus and Co.	1981
Claire De Lune (Claude Debussy)	E.F. Kalmus and Co.	1981

G. COMPOSITIONS/ARRANGEMENTS FOR INSTRUMENTAL SOLO AND ENSEMBLES

Havana Moon (Clarinet Choir with Percussion)	E.F. Kalmus and Co.	1955
Seventy-Six Trombones (Brass Ensemble with Percussion)	Frank/HLPC	1958
Clarinette Valsante	Kendor Music inc.	1961
Sarabande and Double (from English Suite No. 6, J.S. Bach) Woodwind Quartet	Kendor Music inc.	1963

Intermezzo (Eb Alto Clarinet and Piano)	Carl Fischer inc.	1964
Hoe-Down (Eb Clarinet and Piano)	Piedmont/Marks/ HLPC	1966
Sarabande (Eb Alto Clarinet and Piano)	Piedmont/Marks/ HLPC	1966
Guaracha (Bb Bass Clarinet and Piano)	Piedmont/Marks/ HLPC	1966
Afro (Eb/Bb Contrabass Clarinet and Piano)	Piedmont/Marks/ HLPC	1966
Hora (Bb Clarinet and Piano)	Piedmont/Marks/ HLPC	1966
March Variations (Eb Clarinet and Piano)	Piedmont/Marks/ HLPC	1966
Serenata (Eb Alto Clarinet and Piano)	Piedmont/Marks/ HLPC	1966
Haitian Dance (Bb Bass Clarinet and Piano)	Piedmont/Marks/ HLPC	1966
Pastorale (Bb Clarinet and Piano)	Piedmont/Marks/ HLPC	1966
Scherzo Fantastique (Eb Contrabass Clarinet and Piano)	Piedmont/Marks/ HLPC	1966
Ode for Trumpet (Bb Trumpet and Piano)	Southern Music Co.	1966
Ballade (Eb Alto Saxophone and Piano)	Southern Music Co.	1966
Concertino (Oboe and Piano)	Carl Fischer, inc.	1968
Variations on L.B.I.F.D. ("London Bridge Is Falling Down") Brass Quintet	UMMP/Plymouth	1970
Fantasy on "Black Is the Color of My True Love's Hair" (Woodwind Choir)	Piedmont/Marks/ HLPC	1973
A Christmas Suite (Brass, Bells, Chimes and Percussion)	Piedmont/Marks/ HLPC	1974
Double Wind Quintet	Piedmont/Marks/ HLPC	1975
Nun Komm', Der Heiden Heiland (Solo Oboe, Celli and Double Bass) After J.S. Bach	E.F. Kalmus and Co.	1978
Wenn Wir in Hoechsten Nothen Sein (English Horn, Celli and Double Bass) After J.S. Bach	E.F. Kalmus and Co.	1978

Suite Concertante (Four-Part Cello Orchestra and Double Bass)	E.F. Kalmus and Co.	1978
Siciliana Notturno (E♭ Alto Saxophone and Piano)	Piedmont/Marks/HLPC	1978
Fantasia A Due (Tuba and Piano)	Piedmont/Marks/HLPC	1979
Two Bagatelles for Four Trombones	C.L. Barnhouse Co.	1983
Two Bagatelles for Brass Ensemble and Percussion	C.L. Barnhouse Co.	1995
French Suite for Four French Horns	MMP/Kalmus	1998
Joyeux Noel (Brass Ensemble and Percussion)	MMP/Kalmus	1999
Laid-Back Rag (Brass Quintet)	MMP/Kalmus	1999

H. COMPOSITIONS AND ARRANGEMENTS FOR CHORUS

The Prophecy	Ethel Smith Music Corp.	1955
Cathedral Chorus	Hansen Publications	1955
Tears, Idle Tears	Hansen Publications	1956
Seek Ye First the Kingdom of God	Piedmont/Marks/HLPC	1963
A Sea Dirge	Frank/HLPC	1963
Choric Song	Boosey and Hawkes	1966
The Pledge of Allegiance	Piedmont/Marks/HLPC	1970
Testament of An American (with Narrator)	Warner/Belwin	1974
Requiescat	Piedmont/Marks/HLPC	1977
The Willow Song ("Othello")	Piedmont/Marks/HLPC	1977
Come Live with Me and Be My Love	Piedmont/Marks/HLPC	1977
The Moon Shines Bright	Piedmont/Marks/HLPC	1977
All Hail to the Days!	E.F. Kalmus and Co.	1979
Prologue (Song for St. Cecilia's Day)	Piedmont/Marks/HLPC	1983

I. MARCHING BAND

101 for Band	Hansen Publications	1963
102 for Band	Hansen Publications	1964
103 for Band	Hansen Publications	1965
104 for Band	Hansen Publications	1966
The Pledge of Allegiance	Piedmont/Marks/HLPC	1970
Russian Christmas Music	C.L. Barnhouse Co.	1980
Russian Christmas Music	Jenson/HLPC	1981
Acalarado (3rd Movement from "Symphony for Brass and Percussion")	C.L. Barnhouse Co.	1981
A Festival Prelude	Piedmont/Marks/HLPC	1984

ADDITIONAL RESOURCES

BOOK

Jordan, Douglas M. Alfred Reed A Bio-Bibliography. Greenwood Press, 1999. First Edition. Near Fine / No Jacket. No. 72 of the Bio-Bibliographies in Music series. Contains biography, works and premieres, discography. index. 282 pp.

ARTICLES

Author(s): Jordan, Douglas Michael
Title: The Russian Christmas That took 24 Years to Arrive.
Journal Name: The Instrumentalist
Volume: 50
Date: Oct 1995
Page(s)/Issue: 26–9+

Author(s): Mcalister, Clark
Title: Transcriptions in Reverse: Rescoring Russian Christmas Music for Orchestra.
Journal Name: The Instrumentalist
Volume: 50
Date: Oct 1995
Page(s)/Issue: 29–30+

Author(s): Reed, Alfred
Title: The Miracle of Music.
Journal Name: The Instrumentalist

Volume: 45
Date: Mar 1991
Page(s)/Issue: 96

Author(s): Reed, Alfred
Title: Some Thoughts on Band instrumentation: Wind
    Ensembles and Concert
Bands.
Journal Name: The Instrumentalist
Volume: 45
Date: Sep 1990
Page(s)/Issue: 12–16

Author(s): Reed, Alfred
Title: How A Composer Works.
Journal Name: The Instrumentalist
Volume: 44
Date: Jun 1990
Page(s)/Issue: 48–9

Author(s): Reed, Alfred
Title: Friendly Advice on Friendly Advice.
Journal Name: The Instrumentalist
Volume: 45
Date: Oct 1990
Page(s)/Issue: 4+

Author(s): Begian, Harry
Title: Alfred Reed's Armenian Dances (Part II), A Rehearsal
    Analysis.
Journal Name: The Instrumentalist
Volume: 42
Date: Feb 1988
Page(s)/Issue: 24–30
Author(s): Reed, Alfred
Title: The Making of Praise Jerusalem.
Notes: (Kovia Yeroosaghem!)
Journal Name: The Instrumentalist
Volume: 42
Date: Jun 1988
Page(s)/Issue: 18–19

Author(s): Reed, Alfred
Title: Composer—Performer—Publisher—Audience: A
    Quadraphonic
Relationship.
Journal Name: The Instrumentalist
Volume: 41
Date: Jul 1987
Page(s)/Issue: 22–4+

Author(s): Norberg, John
Title: Praise Jerusalem!
Journal Name: The Instrumentalist

Volume: 41
Date: Jul 1987
Page(s)/Issue: 58–60

Author(s): Reed, Alfred
Title: Careers in the Music industry.
Journal Name: Clavier
Volume: 28
Date: 1989
Page(s)/Issue: 38–40 N9

Author(s): Reed, Alfred
Title: Careers in the Music industry.
Journal Name: The Instrumentalist
Volume: 44
Date: Sep 1989
Page(s)/Issue: 98+

Author(s): Reed, Alfred
Title: The String Bass in a Wind Group.
Journal Name: American String Teacher
Volume: 38
Date: 1988
Page(s)/Issue: 66–9 N2

Author(s): Begian, H.
Title: A Rehearsal Analysis of Praise Jerusalem!
Journal Name: The Instrumentalist
Volume: 42
Date: Jun 1988
Page(s)/Issue: 20–23

Author(s): Reed, Alfred
Title: Personal insights on the Music Scene in Japan.
Journal Name: The School Musician
Volume: 53
Date: Nov 1981
Page(s)/Issue: 32–3

Author(s): Begian, Harry
Title: Alfred Reed's Armenian Dances: A Rehearsal Analy-
    sis.
Journal Name: The Instrumentalist
Volume: 40
Date: Oct 1985
Page(s)/Issue: 27–30+

Author(s): Decarbo, N.
Title: Alfred Reed: Composer of Our Time.
Notes: (interview)
Journal Name: The Instrumentalist
Volume: 40
Date: Oct 1985
Page(s)/Issue: 20–22+

Author(s): Reed, Alfred
Title: A Composer–Conductor's View: Russian Christmas
    Music.
Journal Name: The Instrumentalist
Volume: 34
Date: Oct 1979
Page(s)/Issue: 36–41

Author(s): Reed, Alfred
Title: Viva Musica! A Celebration of the Joys of Teaching
    Music.
Journal Name: The School Musician
Volume: 55
Date: Dec 1983
Page(s)/Issue: 18

END NOTES

1. Douglas Jordan, *Alfred Reed*, a Bio-Bibliography. P. 83–85
2. ibid, p.2
3. ibid., p. 6
4. ibid., p.7
5. Interview with the author, Dec. 1999
6. ibid
7. ibid
8. Jordan, p. 12
9. Interview with the author, March 2000
10. ibid
11. ibid
12. Jordan, p.22
13. ibid, p.28
14. ibid, p.28
15. Interview with the author, March, 2000
16. ibid
17. ibid
18. ibid
19. ibid

Joseph Schwantner

by
Scott Higbee

Joseph Schwantner's wind ensemble compositions stand as three of the more important additions to the repertoire in the last twenty-five years of the twentieth century. The vast landscapes of sonority generated by his unusual grasp of the sonic potential of wind and percussion instruments create a world of sound that is distinctive and dramatic. Successful performances of these works require the utmost in technical proficiency and musical understanding from both players and conductor. The challenges are formidable but the artistic growth available to those ensembles who experience this music is invaluable.

BIOGRAPHICAL INFORMATION

Born in Chicago on March 22, 1943, Joseph Schwantner began learning music by studying classical guitar and, in grade school, also played the tuba. When he reached high school, his guitar teacher, concerned about Schwantner's tendency to "elaborate" on the music he was practicing, suggested that Schwantner take one or two of his ideas and write his own piece. "What I thought was advancing my technique on the guitar was actually composing," Schwantner recalls. "Eventually I became more interested in creating instead of re-creating."

Schwantner attended Chicago's American Conservatory where he studied composition with Bernard Dieter and became familiar with the music of Debussy, Bartók and Messiaen. He graduated in 1964 with a Bachelor of Music degree and went on to Northwestern University for graduate studies. It was at Northwestern where he felt he was truly introduced to the "vast panoply" of music in the world. Studying with Alan Stout and Anthony Donato, he earned a Master of Music degree in 1966 and a Doctor of Music degree in 1968. He would later be influenced by the work of Berio and Rochberg. Of Berio, he cites the *Sinfonia* as a seminal work of the 1960's, re-engaging as it did the music of Mahler and opening a "startling" new door through which composers could engage the past. Similarly, Schwantner noted how George Rochberg—considered by many to be the pre-eminent North American serialist of the 1950's—suddenly veered in the direction of Beethoven's late quartets with his *String Quartet No. 3* in 1972.

In 1968 Schwantner took the position of assistant professor at Pacific Lutheran University and in 1969 took a similar position at Ball State University. He joined the faculty of the Eastman School of Music in 1970. A leave of absence from 1982 to 1984 allowed him to serve as Composer in Residence for the Saint Louis Symphony Orchestra through the Exxon Corporation's "Meet the Composer" program. In 1986 he taught at the Juilliard School, and joined the faculty of Yale University in 1999, where he is currently Professor of Composition (Adjunct). He retired from the Eastman faculty in 2000.

Schwantner's many awards include the Charles Ives Scholarship from the American Academy of Arts and Letters in 1970, four National Endowment for the Arts grants between 1974 and 1979, first prize in the 1981 Kennedy Center Friedheim Competition for his chamber piece *Music of Amber*, and the 1970 Pulitzer Prize for his orchestral work *Aftertones of Infinity*. His work *Magabunda "Four Poems of Agueda Pizarro,"* recorded on Nonesuch Records by the Saint Louis Symphony, was nominated for a 1985 Grammy Award in the category "Best New Classical Composition," and his *A Sudden Rainbow*, also recorded on Nonesuch by the Saint Louis Symphony, received a 1987 Grammy nomination for "Best Classical Composition." He has also been a subject on the television series *Soundings* produced by WGBH of Boston.

COMPOSITIONAL STYLE

With the 1997 premiere of *"In evening's stillness..."* Joseph Schwantner has completed what he envisions as a trilogy of wind compositions, a project that began with *and the mountains rising nowhere* in 1977, and followed by *From a Dark Millennium*, completed in 1980. As with most of his compositions, each piece was inspired by poetry; *From a Dark Millennium* and *In evening's stillness...* after his own poems, *and the mountains rising nowhere* after a poem by children's author Carol Adler. Schwantner notes that most artists are inspired in some way or another by the work of other artists. About himself he says, "I respond to images of poetry... poetry can be a kind of trigger for musical ideas. I can get very excited by spending an evening reading poetry. It can be such a wellspring of ideas." As these three related works were composed over a period of twenty years, the evolution of the composer's style during that time span deserves a brief examination.

Schwantner left college practicing composition in a strict serialist style which he then abandoned around 1975 in favor of "a freer, more eclectic idiom characterized by lyrical gestures, impressionist sound colors, and clearly defined tone centers." At the heart of this idiom lies "a strong interest in sonority for its own sake," which the composer attributes to his early experiences with the guitar and its ringing, sustained chords. In his compositions this interest is worked out in part by what he calls "static pillars of harmonies," or long periods of unchanged pitch clusters which undulate through small manipulations of orchestration or registration. The more unusual aspects of his instrumentation also evidence his interest in color.

All three compositions find their organic root in material introduced by an amplified piano, the central instrument in each work. This material is also the basis of the sonorities and harmonic "pillars" that follow. Also common to all three works is Schwantner's "shared monody" approach to melodic material, namely a single linear idea shared by different voices. Over the twenty-year span of the trilogy, this ultimately manifests itself as each voice entering on and sustaining a different pitch of the theme, in order. As with the characteristics noted above, these will be more closely detailed as each piece of the trilogy is examined individually.

COMPOSITIONAL OVERVIEW

…and the mountains rising nowhere…—(1977, 12')
Copyright by Helicon Music Corporation
Sole agent: European American Music Distributors Corporation

6 flutes (4 doubling piccolo), 2 B♭ clarinets, 4 oboes (2 doubling english horn), 4 bassoons, 4 B♭ trumpets, 4 horns, 4 trombones (4th is bass trombone), tuba, amplified piano, 5 percussion, timpani, contrabass

Commissioned by Donald Hunsberger and the Eastman School of Music through a grant from the National Endowment for the Arts, *and the mountains rising nowhere* was premiered by the Eastman Wind Ensemble in 1977. The work is dedicated to Carol Adler and the title is taken from her poem, "Arioso":

> arioso bells
> sepia
> moon-beams
> an afternoon sun blanked by rains
> and the mountains rising nowhere
> the sound returns
> the sound and the silence chimes

Although obviously somewhat experimental, Schwantner describes *and the mountains rising nowhere* as Baroque in character, given its ornamental nature and complexity. As it contains so many different elements—tonality, atonality, serialism, aleatory—Schwantner acknowledges the influence especially of Rochberg, taking the opportunity to point "in many different directions within one piece of work."

All of the harmonic material of *and the mountains rising nowhere* is found in the piano's arpeggiated tone clusters in the first full measure, the most important of which is the cluster doubled by the fingered crystal glasses (see fig. 1).

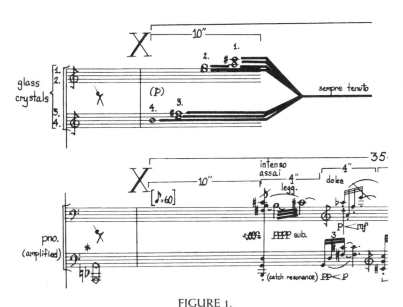

FIGURE 1.
…and the mountains rising nowhere…
© 1977 Helicon Music Corp.
All Rights Reserved. Used by Permission of Helicon Music Corp.

This cluster forms the static harmonic pillar of measures 2–35, therefore the perfect intonation of the glasses is of paramount importance. Although the pitch cluster of the crystal glasses serves to open and close the piece, the work cannot be said to have any formal structure in the traditional sense; it is a through-composed work that takes its form and programmatic influence from Adler's poem.

One characteristic of *and the mountains rising nowhere* that is unique among Schwantner's wind compositions is the frequent use of clock time and aleatory instead of time-signatured measures. The first full measure is divided into timed sections totaling 35 seconds (see fig. 2).

This use of aleatory, especially when combined with clock-time mensuration, is one way in which shared monody is utilized in this piece. At measure 13, each member of Schwantner's "celestial choir" (the wind instrumentalists who are frequently called upon to sing and whistle) vocalizes two pitches of the glasses' tone cluster on the syllable "ah." This line, later augmented by whistling, grows to include all the pitches of the cluster being audibilized at any given moment (see fig. 3).

This also serves to amplify the title of the poem, as well as its first word, "Arioso," one definition of which includes "a recitative of the more melodious type" (Oxford Dictionary of Music, second edition).

Another form of shared monody is present in measures 36–84. This a germinal form of Schwantner monody that will be fully realized in the latter two works of the trilogy. Specifically mensurated in the high woodwinds, it involves the upper woodwinds sustaining the penultimate note of a cluster while others sound the final note; in the bassoons and brass it involves the simultaneous playing of two or three notes of the cluster. Throughout this section the piano and the pitched percussion play the entire cluster, sometimes playing each pitch individually and sometimes sounding the pitches simultaneously (see fig. 4).

Reflecting his interest in impressionist sound colors and "sonority for its own sake," *and the mountains rising nowhere* contains the most unusual instrumentation of Schwantner's three wind compositions. While all three works call for amplified piano, and both *and the mountains rising nowhere* and *From a Dark Millennium* require the instrumentalists to sing and whistle, it is only in *and the mountains rising nowhere* that the use of crystal glasses is required. This piece also requires the largest wind and percussion sections. Unusually large sections are six flutes, four doubling piccolo; four oboes, two doubling english horn; four bassoons; four trombones; the largest percussion section (six players) as well as an extensive inventory of percussion instruments, including two water gongs. In all

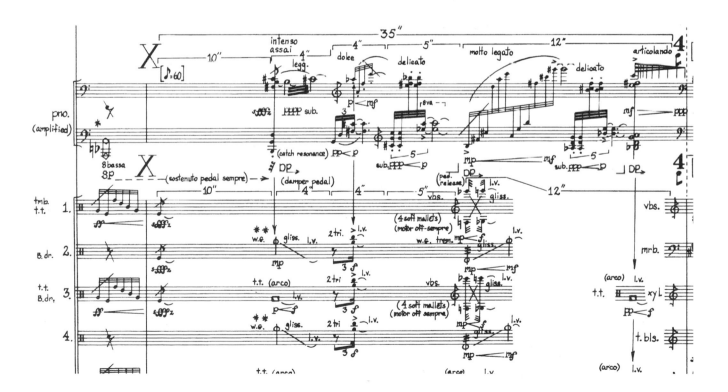

FIGURE 2.
. . . and the mountains rising nowhere . . .
© 1977 Helicon Music Corp.
All Rights Reserved. Used by Permission of Helicon Music Corp.

three works the percussionists are required to bow mallet instruments with contrabass bows. Schwantner comments:

> When I first started writing for wind ensemble there wasn't much to look at other than Hindemith and Schoenberg. My whole band experience in the public schools had been mostly third-rate music and transcriptions. I grew up with a certain envy of my colleagues who were in orchestra: they got great music to play and we got bad transcriptions and this third-rate "educational" music.
>
> You'll notice in *and the mountains rising nowhere* that I go a long way to avoid typical band sounds. I had to overcome my school experience. For example, I have this horde of clarinets, this sea of anonymous clarinets.

The hurdles to be leapt in rehearsing *and the mountains rising nowhere* are formidable, not the least of which is visually encountered when the conductor first opens the score and discovers Schwantner's open scoring. This method of scoring only gives measures for an instrument when it is actually playing. Any full-measure absence and the scoring for that instrument disappears, without, however, compressing the staves in use on the page. This means that a staff can appear in the middle of the page for as little as one measure and then vanish, creating huge gaps throughout the score which can be very distracting to a conductor unfamiliar with this technique.

Although he abandoned this method around 1990 due to time constraints, the use of open scoring is a favorite technique of Schwantner's. He comments,

> George Crumb always drew his scores by hand. His publisher, C.F. Peters, eventually asked him if they could take charge of the copying. Absolutely not, he said. He felt that how the music looked was a key part of the art. He once said to me, "Music that looks beautiful often sounds beautiful."

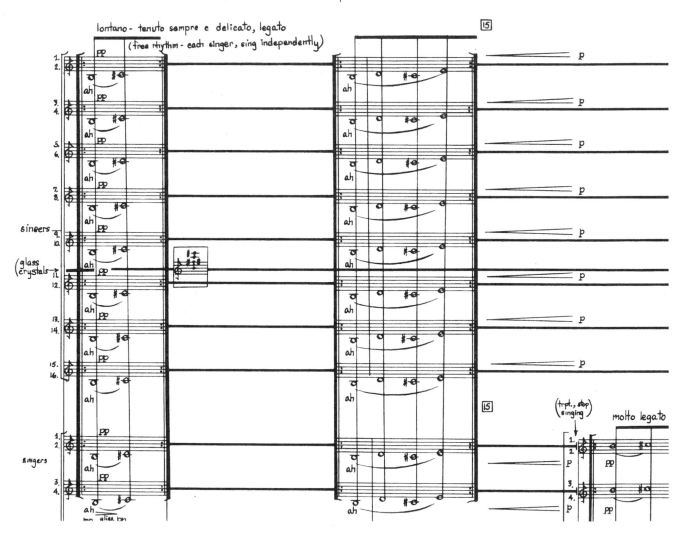

FIGURE 3.
. . . and the mountains rising nowhere . . .
© 1977 Helicon Music Corp.

134

FIGURE 4.

. . . and the mountains rising nowhere . . .

I like the look of the open score. Eventually, though, it began to take longer to copy a piece than to compose it! I would still use open scoring if I could, but in this day, with computers and copyists, it's a matter of practicality.

Schwantner's method of mensuration may be unfamiliar to the instrumentalists in that traditional time signatures are not employed. Instead, the time signature appears with the number of beats in a bar on top and the beat-duration *symbol* (instead of the corresponding number) underneath. This may seem innocuous enough until measure 59 when the symbol ♪. appears as the beat duration, which can be a metric and visual obstacle to instrumentalists and conductor alike.

Because of the shared monody that permeates the piece, precise rhythm is key to a successful performance. This burden falls particularly to the pianist and the percussionists, the latter frequently doubling the piano.

Precise rhythm is also the key to the long *brutale* section, dominated by a sort of "groove" in the timpani and nonpitched percussion from measures 91–119. The percussion rhythm is strictly notated, originating in a four-beat bar, the eighth note equaling 108 m.m./sec. The second measure of the section switches to a sixteenth-note marking, thus equaling 216 m.m./sec., which continues through the end of the section, alternating between five- and six-beat measures (see fig. 5).

Additionally, forearm clusters to the piano keyboard that punctuate this section occur simultaneously with *sffp* brass clusters. The last half of this section involves the winds in the germinal form of shared monody. All of this complexity is set at a breakneck tempo in unusual meters.

There are some unusual intonation concerns in *and the mountains rising nowhere*. As noted earlier, the intonation of the crystal glasses must be perfect as their doubling with the mallet instruments and the piano could otherwise create problems. Per Schwantner's instructions on the instrumentation page of the score, the fingers and glasses need to be free of oils in order to maximize the glass's response and projection. As it is the oboists who are called upon to finger the glasses, the presence of key oils on the fingers is of concern in accomplishing this (it is also common practice to use an ensemble's saxophonists as there are no saxophone parts in the score). Filling the glasses with cider vinegar instead of water, and having the players moisten their fingers with the vinegar eliminates oils on the fingers, guaranteeing the friction needed to generate immediate response from the glasses.

Further exacerbating the issue of intonation is the use of singing instrumentalists who may not have had any vocal training and may be singing *falsetto*, as well as the tremendous difficulty of whistling in tune. Coaching by a choral instructor would undoubtedly be helpful.

The score indicates that the whistling in measures 120A–120D should follow the notated descent of the flutes and water gongs. Unfortunately, in a large ensemble the

FIGURE 5.
. . . and the mountains rising nowhere . . .
© 1977 Helicon Music Corp.
All Rights Reserved. Used by Permission of Helicon Music Corp.

water gongs are difficult to hear, as are the flutes, who are asked to play *ppp*, *lontano* (distant), and *bisbigliato* (whispering). Compounding this difficulty is Schwantner's use of clock-time mensuration over relatively long periods of time (15–25 seconds), during which the instrumentalists often find it difficult to keep track of their places. Clear direction is required from the conductor, perhaps by giving obvious downbeats every fifth second.

From a Dark Millennium—(1981, 11')
Copyright by Helicon Music Corporation
Sole agent: European American Music Distributors Corporation
3 flutes (2 doubling piccolo), 3 Bb clarinets (2nd and 3rd clarinets double bass clarinet, 1st clarinet doubles Eb clarinet), 2 oboes, english horn, 3 bassoons, 3 Bb trumpets, 4 horns, 4 trombones (4th is bass trombone), tuba, amplified piano, amplified celeste, 4 percussion, timpani, 2 contrabasses

From a Dark Millennium was commissioned by the Mid-American Band Directors Association and given its premiere by the University of Northern Illinois Wind Ensemble in 1981. The music is drawn from the second movement of Schwantner's 1980 chamber work, *Music of Amber*, which was based on his poem "Sanctuary":

SANCTUARY…
 deep forests
a play of Shadows,
 most ancient murmurings
from a dark millennium
 the trembling fragrance
of the music of amber

The octatonic pitch set in the piano and vibraphones that opens the piece is the springboard for all that follows. The center of the set—descending half step, descending perfect fourth, ascending whole step—is the motivic core of the work (see fig. 6).

Because of its brevity as compared to the whole set, the motivic core is more readily discerned and retained by the listener's ear; therefore, having been frequently reiterated early in the piece (measures 20–34), it is instantly identifiable when it returns at the conclusion. Nonetheless, as with the first piece, *From a Dark Millennium* is a through-composed work, albeit with a more clearly heard organic unity than *and the mountains rising nowhere*.

The opening of the piece is an excellent example of Schwantner's idea of "static pillars of harmony." While each pitch set is sounded individually by the amplified piano, amplified celeste, and vibraphones, the first ten measures emphasize F by its constant presence in the "celestial choir," stopped horns, and tubular bells (see fig. 7).

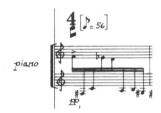

FIGURE 6.
© 1981 Helicon Music Corp.
All Rights Reserved. Used by Permission of Helicon Music Corp.

FIGURE 7.
From a Dark Millenium
© 1981 Helicon Music Corp.
All Rights Reserved. Used by Permission of Helicon Music Corp.

In the eleventh measure more pitches of the set are added and sustained by the brass, serving to outline the construction of this pillar and leading to the simultaneous sounding of all the pitches of the set at measure 17 (see fig. 8).

Introduced in its nascent form in *and the mountains rising nowhere*, shared monody has three distinct, more fully realized appearances in *From a Dark Millennium*. From measures 54–64, while an altered version of the pitch set is delineated in the keyboards and mallet percussion, the individual upper woodwinds enter on different notes of the set. Each note is sounded by a woodwind instrument at the same time that it is played by the keyboards and mallets. The note is repeated or sustained until that instrument is called upon to play another note (see fig. 9).

In perhaps the purest form of shared monody, from measures 92–109 the brass intermittently play as the woodwinds did in measure 54–64, but without the underlying establishment of the whole pitch set being played by any single instrument (see fig. 10).

The third appearance of shared monody coincides with another marvelous example of a static pillar of harmony, one that slowly evolves through a repeated section of twelve bars, measures 121–132, which are played a total of four times (see fig. 11).

At first, the nonpitched percussion play the 3+3+3+2 pulse that has become the rhythmic core of the piece. As the section is without pitch, and is at a modest tempo of ♪ = 64 m.m./sec., what may seem like a brief period on paper is in fact quite static to the listener, especially with the incessant, unchanging rhythm of the percussion.

At the first repeat the low voices of the ensemble present a more sustained line characterized by occasional rests which frequently occupy the strong subdivisions of the beat. This particular line serves to keep the original stasis of the harmonic pillar firmly present while providing continued clear aural development.

The rests in the low voice line are filled on the second repeat by a new rhythm in the upper brass, a line that is characterized by only slightly more rapid rhythmic motion than that of the low voices, thereby developing the harmonic pillar rather than disrupting it.

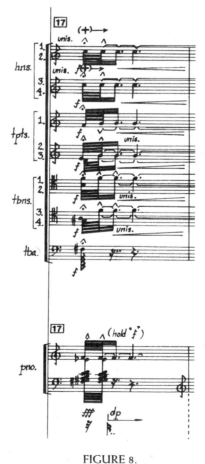

FIGURE 8.
From a Dark Millenium
© 1981 Helicon Music Corp.
All Rights Reserved. Used by Permission of Helicon Music Corp.

FIGURE 9.
© 1981 Helicon Music Corp.
All Rights Reserved. Used by Permission of Helicon Music Corp.

FIGURE 10.
From a Dark Millenium
© 1981 Helicon Music Corp.
All Rights Reserved. Used by Permission of Helicon Music Corp.

FIGURE 11.

From a Dark Millenium

© 1981 Helicon Music Corp.

All Rights Reserved. Used by Permission of Helicon Music Corp.

The final repeat of this section calls for the remaining instruments to play a line quite similar to that of the upper brass but usually displaced from the brass by a sixteenth note, sometimes ahead and sometimes after. The conglomeration of all four lines creates a very dense homophony that juxtaposes comfortably with the development of the harmonic pillar.

As with the previous work, unusual colors in *From a Dark Millennium* include celestial choir, whistlers, amplified piano and bowed percussion. While crystal glasses and water gong are not used, and one less percussionist is needed, an amplified celeste is required.

In evening's stillness... — (1996, 11')
Copyright by Helicon Music Corporation
Sole agent: European American Music Distributors Corporation

piccolo, 3 flutes, 3 B♭ clarinets, bass clarinet, 3 oboes, english horn, 3 bassoons, contrabassoon, 3 B♭ trumpets, 4 horns, 3 trombones, tuba, amplified piano, 4 percussion, timpani

The last piece of the trilogy to be composed, *In evening's stillness...* was commissioned by the Illinois College Band Directors Association in 1996 and premiered in January 1997 at the Midwest MENC convention in Peoria. Donald Hunsberger conducted an ensemble made up of students selected from ten universities in the consortium that participated in the commission. Again, Schwantner's own poetry provided the title:

> In evening's stillness,
>   a gentle breeze,
>   distant thunder,
>   encircles the silence.

The instrumentation for *In evening's stillness...* is much more traditional than the earlier works; however the stage set-up, as specified by the composer's diagram in the score, utilizes non-traditional "columns" of wind players and is critical to the sonic success of the work. As with the other pieces, amplified "lidless" piano is utilized, located in the center of the ensemble. There is a fairly extensive percussion section requiring five players. In this work, however, singing and whistling are not called for.

Unlike the previous works, *In evening's stillness...* has a formal ternary structure; the ABA structure breaks down as *aabbcbbc/d/aabccb*. As with the previous works, all of the melodic and harmonic materials on which it is based are introduced by the piano in the first *a* section. A septatonic scale unfolds, triadically and slowly, across two octaves as a static pillar of harmony (see fig. 12).

It is immediately repeated, transposed up a fourth, foreshadowing the shifting harmonic character of the work as a whole; while each section has a definite tonal center, the character of that center will change as sections are repeated, most notably the *b* sections. The scale is then played by the winds in a shared monody of the sort seen previously in *From a Dark Millennium* (see fig. 13).

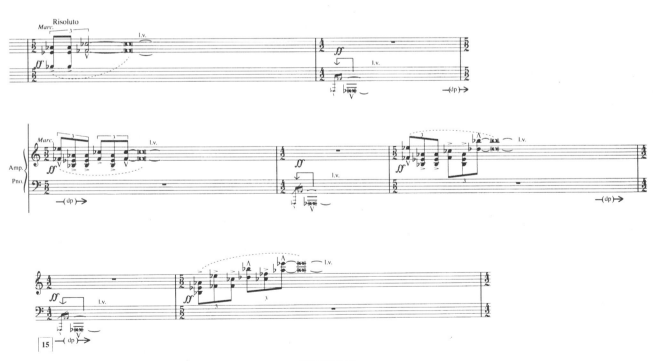

FIGURE 12.
In evening's stillness...
© 1996 Helicon Music Corp.
All Rights Reserved. Used by Permission of Helicon Music Corp.

141

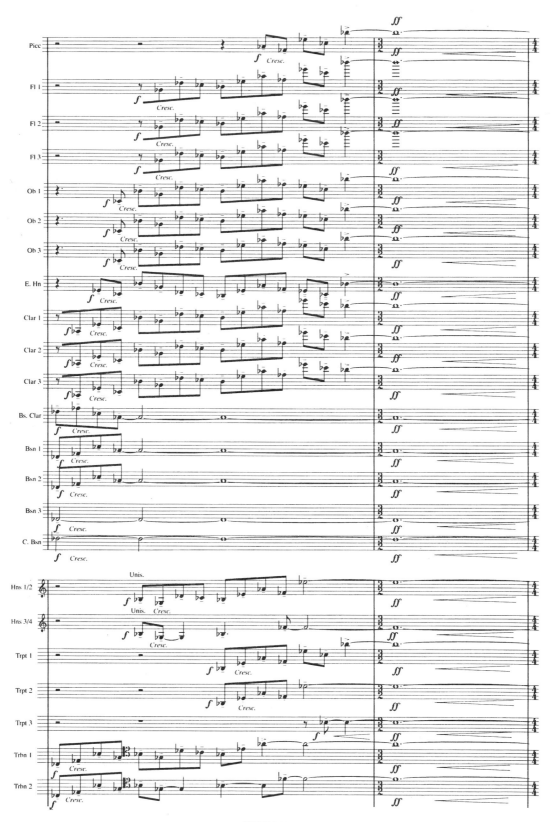

FIGURE 13.
In evening's stillness . . .

Shared monody and harmonic pillar come together to form the *b* section, beginning at measure 36. Built on eight repetitions of the septatonic scale, each repetition is comprised of a four measure construction, 5+6+5+7 in eighth-note time. (In addition to normal scoring, Schwantner also uses traditional key signatures in this work.) The seventh note of the scale is not heard until the final (23rd) beat of the four-bar section (see fig. 14).

The harmonic stasis is underscored by the addition of sustained triads (each one held for 20 beats) in the muted trumpets.

A repeat of the *b* section brings in the horns and trombones with chordal statements of the scale and also introduces the greatest rhythmic difficulty encountered in the piece. As noted, each four-bar section is constructed 5+6+5+7, which Schwantner indicates should be broken down to (3+2)(3+3)(3+2)(3+2+2). However, the emphases of the brass rhythms frequently fall differently than the emphases of the shared monody rhythm; for example, brass

entrances are often on the second beat of the 5/8 measure. The tempo is a brisk ♩ = 88 m.m./sec. (♪ = 264), making for a formidable subdivision task for the brass who, at the same time, need to sustain the atmosphere of flowing lyricism created by the piano and woodwinds.

Each appearance of the *c* section, with its repeated, staccato sixteenth-note rhythms, serves to move the harmony of the piece up or down a whole step. This sets the stage for the tonal center to develop a new, bitonal character in the return of the *b* section, where the piano plays the septatonic scale in parallel sixths.

The center of the large ternary form returns to lyricism with a slower presentation of the scale in shared monody among solo woodwinds. The slower tempo of ♩ = 66 m.m./sec. magnifies the stasis of the section, which in turn magnifies the importance of intonation among the solo winds, a situation further exacerbated as the piano's use of the scale is rapid, brief, and restricted to the extremes of the instrument into which the woodwinds must fit their pitches.

FIGURE 14.
In evening's stillness . . .
© 1996 Helicon Music Corp.
All Rights Reserved. Used by Permission of Helicon Music Corp.

Not surprisingly, given that it is separated by over fifteen years from the previous work, *In evening's stillness…* stands in contrast to its predecessors in Schwantner's wind trilogy. The colors used are fairly standard in wind ensemble usage (especially as whistling and singing are absent), and its relatively formal architecture makes its cohesive unity much more easily discerned.

Nonetheless, there are enough similarities among the three pieces to support the notion of a trilogy. Foremost among them is the central role of the amplified piano, which Schwantner refers to as the "spine" running through each of the three works. Also, each work is nearly equal in duration, approximately eleven to twelve minutes. Schwantner comments that after *From a Dark Millennium* turned out to have the same length as *and the mountains rising nowhere*, he thought that *In evening's stillness…* should be of similar length. "I didn't want to be too ambitious in the scope of any of the three."

The composer noted it was when he was working on *From a Dark Millennium* that it first occurred to him that, with the composition of a third piece, his wind compositions could be part of a greater whole. "They would still be individual pieces, but with an arc of sonic landscapes over a greater period." As such, he originally envisioned *In evening's stillness…* as the middle movement of the trilogy, its uniqueness from the earlier works acting as the keystone to the arcing form. Since its premiere, however, a number of people have approached Schwantner and suggested it as the third movement, and Schwantner has subsequently decided that he would leave it up to the conductor to choose the order of the movements (an approach not without precedent, as in the individual songs from Mahler's *Des Knaben Wunderhorn*). He even concedes that, "Maybe, now, it doesn't work. As far as I know, no one has performed it as a trilogy."

CONDUCTING APPROACH

Discussing his use of open scoring, Schwantner drew the analogy of crafting furniture. Although a craftsman can build a chair that has magnificent proportions and terrific lines, he noted that the chair isn't finished until the final stain is applied. He went on to say, "I really think compositions are like furniture. They're very utilitarian. People use the music, so you want it to be strong and sturdy." He observed that often, when he turns a new work over to a conductor or ensemble, "the sonic reality of the piece is quite different than what I had imagined. Of course, I always imagine a piece as perfectly played, with no intonation problems." He therefore finds it time well spent when he can work with a group as it prepares for a premiere performance.

> It is very satisfying when in some cases the reality is even more than I had imagined. I really enjoy it when a piece is made better by the sensitivity and skills of the musicians. They can illuminate the music in a way that I might not have imagined.

I hope that they will understand my ideas and bring them to life; in turn they can help me understand better what music is all about. This is especially true when I can think about for whom I am writing when I am writing.

[When it was premiered] *In evening's stillness…* was the only piece this group performed at the concert. It was fun to have Donald Hunsberger there, sort of an old, steadfast, trusted colleague. I came to the rehearsals with ideas about seating arrangements and such, but a lot came together during the three days of rehearsals.

Schwantner offers this advice for those conductors intent on rehearsing and performing his music for wind ensemble:

> I am especially concerned that conductors remain sensitive to the expanded timbral qualities of my work. In my wind ensemble works, I have attempted to create a sense of directed musical motion through the use of carefully controlled and constantly changing timbral landscapes, as opposed to those typical developmental techniques that are usually employed in more traditional works.
>
> Also, in my wind pieces, larger gestural statements [shared monody, for example], may be articulated by large instrumental combinations that frequently engage and span the entire ensemble. It is important that conductors seek to unite these disparate and fragmented instrumental strata into a cohesive and singular whole.
>
> In my three works for wind ensemble, I employ the percussion choir as a fully independent instrumental unit, clearly equal to the winds and the brass. The piano—usually amplified—also becomes an integral member of this expanded percussion section, as well.

He further notes that conductors interested in expanding their awareness and perspective of his music could become more fully informed by listening to these additional works:

Concerto for Percussion and Orchestra
From Afar, "Fantasy for Guitar and Orchestra"
New Morning for the World, for narrator and orchestra

He also recommends the recent recordings of his wind ensemble works by the University of North Texas Wind Symphony.

Joseph Schwantner is in the rare and enviable composer's position of being able to choose what commissions he accepts. Presently no more wind works are planned although he remains interested in writing for the idiom. When Donald Hunsberger first came to him with the commission for what became *and the mountains rising nowhere*, Schwantner accepted it because, as he says, "I thought it would be fun," in part because many of his composition and orchestration students were in the Eastman Wind Ensemble and he thought it would be enjoyable to work with them in a different capacity. The commission also came at a time when all of his works were for chamber groups and the wind ensemble gave him an opportunity to try his sonic ideas with a large and flexible ensemble. He wryly notes, "Can you imagine asking the members of the Boston Symphony Orchestra to whistle and sing? Professional musicians are very reluctant to do anything more than that for which they've been trained."

He also notes that the work was, at the time, quite difficult for the Eastman Wind Ensemble.

Someone later told me it was a "grade six" composition, and I said, "What's that all about?" I had no idea that there was a grading system for band compositions. I never expected the piece to be played by high school bands. Now, of course, it's played quite frequently. That's due to the increased competence of today's musicians.

Refreshingly, Schwantner feels that the college wind ensemble is an instrument greatly underappreciated by many composers.

I really encourage my composition students to explore the wind ensemble as an outlet for their ideas. Where else are you going to get that kind of flexibility, both sonically and from the individual players?

The non-professional environment can be very conducive for composers. Some of the best performances of my compositions have been by university wind ensembles, where they really get the time to know a piece over a protracted period of time. That doesn't happen with a professional orchestra where they get three rehearsals and then it's performed. And if the music is rather difficult, often the [professional] performances are quite poor.

Schwantner also notes that collegiate wind ensembles can be a very exciting source of commissions: "Every time a college group goes to a regional or national convention, they always want to bring a new work with them. Can you imagine if professional orchestras did that?"

From a pedagogical standpoint it may be easiest to introduce an ensemble to the music of Joseph Schwantner by using *In evening's stillness...* The instrumentalists are not required to do anything unusual (such as singing or whistling), and the notation is standard. Unfortunately, for the reasons noted above, it is not what most people perceive to be a typical Schwantner composition while the other two works are. But while *and the mountains rising nowhere* is certainly the most well-known of his wind works and has earned its way into the staple repertoire of the wind ensemble, *From a Dark Millennium* may be a more useful teaching tool in explaining the harmonic and melodic concepts of Schwantner's style, for in that piece, as opposed to its predecessor, can be found the principles of shared monody and static pillars of harmony used by a composer who had matured greatly in the intervening years. *and the mountains rising nowhere* announces the early forms of these ideas, but they are fully developed in the later compositions. After students have grasped those concepts, the genesis of their development then becomes more apparent in the first work.

END NOTES

1. Joseph Schwantner, telephone interview with the author, 28 January 1998.
2. Schwantner, telephone interview.
3. James Wierzbicki, "Schwantner, Joseph," in *New Grove Dictionary of American Music* 4:171–172.
4. quoted in Jeffrey Renshaw, "From a Dark Millennium: An Interpretive Analysis," *The Instrumentalist* (September 1989): 22
5. Schwantner telephone interview. All subsequent quotations are from the author's interview with the composer.

DISCOGRAPHY

From a Dark Millennium (1981)
"Dream Catchers"
North Texas Wind Symphony
Eugene Corporon—conductor
Klavier Records KCD-11089

In Evening's Stillness... (1996)
"Wind Dances"
North Texas Wind Symphony
Eugene Corporon—conductor
Klavier Records KCD-11084

...and the mountains rising nowhere... (1977)
"Wild Flowers"
North Texas Wind Symphony
Eugene Corporon—conductor
Adam Wodnicki—piano soloist
Klavier Records KCD-11079

...and the mountains rising nowhere... (1977)
The Eastman Wind Ensemble
Donald Hunsberger—music director
Sony Records SK 47198

From a Dark Millennium for Wind Ensemble (1981)
Ithaca College Wind Ensemble
Rodney Winther—conductor
Ithaca College School of Music
Mark Records, Inc MCBS-35891

...and the mountains rising nowhere... (1977)
The Eastman Wind Ensemble
Donald Hunsberger—music director
Mercury Golden Imports SRI-75132

ADDITIONAL LISTENING

The Music of Joseph Schwantner
Velocities
Concerto for Percussion and Wind Orchestra
New Morning for the World

The National Symphony Orchestra
Evelyn Glennie—percussion & solo marimba
Leonard Slatkin—conductor
Vernon Jordan—narrator
BMG Classics/RCA Red Seal CD 09026-68692-2

From Afar... "A Fantasy for Guitar" (1987)
"American Landscapes"
Saint Paul Chamber Orchestra
Sharon Isbin—guitar
Hugh Wolf—conductor
Virgin Classics CDC-7243-5-55083-2-4

New Morning for the World for narrator & orchestra (1982)
The Eastman Philharmonia Orchestra
Willie Stargell—narrator
David Effron—music director
Mercury 2890411 031-1

New Morning for the World
"Daybreak of Freedom"
Oregon Symphony
Raymond Bazemore—narrator
James DePreist—narrator
Koch International Classics CD 3-7293-2H1

David Stanhope

by
Timothy Salzman

I started composing really just as a hobby with no thought of doing anything terribly serious...it's really only been the wind band, by its enthusiasm, that has drawn me on more and more.
David Stanhope

It is difficult to imagine a musician whose life would encompass a broader range of professional experience than David Stanhope. Conductor, composer, pianist, hornist, trombonist, and fortunately for the world of wind band music, a composer of significant merit, Stanhope is the contemporary archetype of the musically multi-gifted Renaissance man.

BIOGRAPHICAL INFORMATION

David Stanhope was born December 19th, 1952, in Sutton Coldfield located in the English midlands on the outskirts of Birmingham. In 1958 his parents, both teachers, took the family and left England by boat arriving in Melbourne, Australia in 1959. Stanhope grew up in a musically supportive environment as both of his parents were quite interested in music and played at an amateur level. At the age of four Stanhope began piano lessons, a course of study he pursued until his final year of high school. Early in his piano training he studied with Norman Kaye, a Melbourne-based organist and composer to whom Stanhope attributes much of his early musical inspiration. Kaye is also a multi-talented individual; in addition to his professional musical life he is also a noted actor and has appeared frequently in Australian feature films, television, and on the stages of major theatre companies in Melbourne and Sydney.

Stanhope has always continued to play the piano to some degree, but did not develop a strong technique until the mid-1970s when he was able to purchase a grand piano.

Stanhope initially played the trumpet as a schoolboy but left that instrument for the horn during his last year of high school. He experienced a higher degree of success as a hornist and, upon graduation from high school, went to Monash University in Victoria, Australia with the idea of becoming a professional horn player. However, he left after one year describing his university matriculation as a "complete flop."

Shortly after leaving the university he was invited to become a member of a training orchestra sponsored by the Australian Broadcasting Commission (now referred to as the Australian Broadcasting Corporation). This orchestra was formed with the intention of providing young players with the type of repertory experience needed to ultimately move into vacant positions as they developed in the various professional symphony orchestras found throughout Australia. A fourth horn vacancy in the Adelaide Symphony came open not long after Stanhope joined the ABC training orchestra. He was initially sent there as a temporary replacement but eventually won the formal audition and, from the age of 18, for a period of 14 years, earned a living as a professional horn player. In 1979, after six years in Adelaide and two years in London, Stanhope moved to Sydney and has been based there ever since. As a hornist he has held the position of principal horn, The Australian Opera and principal horn, Australian Chamber Orchestra. While in London he freelanced with several ensembles including the Royal Opera House Covent Garden, the English National Opera, the Royal Philharmonic Orchestra and the London Sinfonietta.

1984 was a significant year in Stanhope's life on a variety of fronts. He moved to London with the intentions of developing his career; unfortunately things did not go as he wished:

Many things that I was hoping would happen that year didn't happen; I had certain vague ideas of trying to do some conducting and composing but those ideas went nowhere.

He had grown tired of the horn and was somewhat frustrated with certain technical issues he faced in his playing. He was quite aware of the necessary work involved in addressing those issues but lacked the necessary motivation to work through the obstacles:

I didn't really have the interest or the energy to practice the instrument to get to the very top level even though I was playing principal horn in Sydney in a number of professional orchestras.

Stanhope determined that he would not go back to Australia to continue playing the horn professionally, a pivotal decision that ultimately benefited his playing future as well as the wind band repertoire.

At about this time Stanhope's friend Brett Kelly, principal trombonist in the Melbourne Symphony Orchestra, visited him in London. They happened to visit a music shop where Stanhope noticed a used Bach 36 trombone on display which he purchased for a few hundred pounds. For the next six months he spent five or six hours a day practicing the trombone in tenacious pursuit of his goal of returning to Australia in a different musical capacity. Although the change-over was exhausting he was decidedly much more content believing that the trombone suited him far better in terms of his own physical capabilities. After six months of extremely hard work he felt comfortable enough to join a London repertory orchestra as a trombonist. The familiarity of participation in an orchestra was somewhat offset by the sensation of experiencing that environment in an entirely new way:

> ...it felt quite strange to go back into an orchestra, sit on the other side blowing forwards instead of backwards!

Stanhope never played the horn again. He sold his old Yamaha double horn in London and bought two more Bach trombones, a 42c tenor and 50b bass. In late December of 1984 he returned to Australia and, to the surprise of many of his friends and colleagues, was immediately hired to temporarily replace the second trombonist in the Sydney Symphony Orchestra who had taken extended leave for health reasons and ultimately retired. He auditioned as bass trombonist with the West Australia Symphony Orchestra and was offered the position but, not wanting to leave Sydney, declined it. He continued as a freelance player with the Sydney, Melbourne and Adelaide Symphony Orchestras until about 1995.

During his year in London and concurrent with his transformation from hornist to trombonist Stanhope dabbled in composition, a long-held interest that had been stymied by a problem sadly familiar to many young composers; the lack of any reciprocal interest in new music expressed by various orchestras:

> It's very difficult to get orchestral music played unless one has powerful friends in high places. Certainly, I turned to the wind band initially because I thought it would be an opportunity to get my music played.

Stanhope hadn't written any wind band music prior to 1984 but, while in London, made a number of contacts with American wind conductors through his friendship with the noted Grainger scholar John Bird. Bird suggested that he write music for wind band and introduced him to a few helpful American wind band conductors, Frank Battisti (New England Conservatory) and James Croft (Florida State University) among others. They, in turn, provided Stanhope with a suggested wind band instrumentation list. It was during that year that Stanhope wrote his first two folksong suites which he ultimately sent to James Croft who promptly premièred both works.

Upon his return to Australia Stanhope continued to pursue composition as well as his career as a trombonist continuing to play off and on for several years. However, his interest in the trombone soon waned and he found himself contemplating the pursuit of one of his life-long dreams—conducting:

> I really enjoyed [the trombone] but, after a year or two I began to be restless again and thought well, if I'm ever to conduct perhaps now is the time. Even as a child I was always much more interested in orchestral texture, or many-voiced music.

In 1986 an opening was announced for the position of repetiteur with the Australian Opera (now Opera Australia). Once again Stanhope successfully auditioned for this new position and spent the next few years coaching singers, understudying scores, conducting chamber operas as well as continuing to freelance as a trombonist in various orchestras. In 1992 his operatic conducting career took flight when, on short notice (due to the cancellation of an appearance by another conductor), he was asked to conduct several performances of Benjamin Britten's great 20th century opera, *Peter Grimes*. The resultant critical acclaim led to numerous engagements for Stanhope as one of the principal conductors of 20th century opera for Opera Australia. He has subsequently conducted seasons of *Albert Herring, Turn of the Screw, The Pearlfishers, Peter Grimes, Hansel and Gretel, Salome, Lulu, Ariadne Auf Naxos, Eugene Onegin, La Traviata, Jenufa, Fidelio* and *The Makropoulos Secret*. In addition to conducting major productions at the Sydney Opera House, he is guest conductor with the Australian Broadcasting Corporation and a regular guest conductor of the Melbourne, West Australian, Queensland, Adelaide and Tasmanian Symphony Orchestras. He is also a regular guest conductor with Australia's leading contemporary group, Sydney Alpha Ensemble and The Australian Ballet.

In addition to his compositions for the wind band he has composed for a variety of other idioms, ranging from songs and chamber music to numerous works for large orchestra. The Australian Opera gave the first performances of excerpts from his 3 act opera "*The Un-Dead*" in November of 1990, but he subsequently withdrew the work. Some of the music of the opera was revised and included in a later symphony. Wind band and brass band works of his have been competition test pieces in Britain and Australia and in 1979 he won the ensemble section of the International Horn Society composition contest with a horn octet entitled *Hornplayers' Retreat and Pumping Song*. His most recent compositions include a suite for string orchestra, *String Songs*, the *Symphony No. 1* for large wind band and *Songs Without Words* for solo saxophone quartet and wind band. Publishers of his works include Novello & Co., Tezak, The Hornists' Nest, Action Music and H.L. Music, but the majority of his works, especially those for wind band and brass ensembles, are now available from Southern Music Company.

David Stanhope has conducted the soundtracks of *Babe, Children of the Revolution, Paradise Road* and *Passion*. For the last-named film based upon a year in the life of Percy Grainger, he also recorded the entire solo piano repertoire for the soundtrack and is the on-screen hand 'double' for actor Richard Roxburgh.

As a concert pianist, he has performed concerti with all

major Australian symphony orchestras, including the Rachmaninoff 3rd Concerto in D minor. He has made a number of recordings with EMI, and in 1980 toured throughout Australia in a concerto tour featuring the Grieg and Schumann concertos for the Australian Broadcasting Corporation. Tall Poppies Records released his CD, *Virtuoso Transcriptions*, in 1996 and *"David Stanhope plays"* in 1999, the latter receiving high praise from Gramophone magazine and the noted American critic, Harold Schonberg.

In 2000 Stanhope conducted the Sydney Symphony Orchestra in several items for the opening ceremony of the Sydney Olympic Games. He also wrote fanfares and fireworks music for both the opening and closing ceremonies. He subsequently was commissioned to write the music for Australia's New Year Celebrations adapting some of his earlier Olympic Games music for the soundtrack recording session on which he conducted and played pipe organ.

He is currently preparing some new compositions for wind band including some international commissions.

COMPOSITIONAL APPROACH

The wind band compositions of David Stanhope can be roughly divided into two broad categories; music written within a familiar folksong tradition and a more adventuresome compositional style that is technically and harmonically more complex frequently marked by a strong sense of bitonality. Of the former, the listener will quickly identify the musical influence of another Australian, Percy Grainger. Stanhope first encountered Grainger's music via a 1960s Decca recording of the English Chamber Orchestra, Benjamin Britten conducting, entitled "Salute to Percy Grainger." He subsequently came upon the legendary Eastman Wind Ensemble/Frederick Fennell Mercury LP and, through the years, has heard and admired numerous recordings of various wind bands' performances of Grainger's music. He particularly has high regard for the fine Mark Hindsley and Dr. Harry Begian University of Illinois Grainger recordings. Although Stanhope has never played in a wind band he was immediately fascinated by the texture, color and brightness of the sound generated by the aggregate group of wind and percussion musicians.

The influence of Grainger's music on Stanhope's band works is heard most predominantly in the three brilliant folksong suites that Stanhope wrote between 1984 and 1991. Each unique setting reveals Stanhope's emotional and compositional affinity for the music of the Australian master:

> Percy Grainger, was, and perhaps still is, the single most important influence in my music. At first it was his harmony that fascinated me; he wrote that he had always tried to "wrench the listener's heart with my chords", but made the point that mere discords were not the key to creating "agonizing" music—"it is the contrast between the sweet & the harsh that is heart-rend-

ing". I think such contrasts can easily be found in my compositions. Later I took ideas from his "democratic" scoring.

Initially Stanhope was especially engaged by Grainger's harmonic schemes, admiring the way in which harmony is employed as a variation technique in support of a repeated folksong melody. This compositional device is a hallmark of Stanhope's folksong suites which were written in tribute to Grainger:

> The three Folksong Suites for Band are all dedicated to the memory of Grainger, each setting usually following the variation or passacaglia-like form that he commonly used. I like the rich variety of harmony that he used particularly in the folk tune settings like *Lincolnshire Posy*. In *The Lost Lady Found* [for example] his harmonic scheme follows a kind of variation pattern, a passacaglia pattern...it's not just a matter of [harmonic] variety, it's a matter of the growth and development of the harmonies from the beginning to the end. That was [my] initial attraction to his music...

After a time he began to investigate other attributes of Grainger's work soon recognizing the genius of his 'free polyphony', a compositional attribute that Stanhope amplified to some degree in his own works, most definitively in the third movement of *Folksongs for Band Suite No. 2*:

> The first writing of any lasting significance of mine is probably the first verse of *Rufford Park Poachers* (about 1973), which rather imitates Graingerian sliding harmonies, and the following two verses (written some years afterward) perhaps reflect a growing control over a kind of free polyphony. Nevertheless it is the harmonies that occur through that polyphony that appeal to me, and the fact that they happen by apparent accident seems to increase their power.

Stanhope also professes a love of Russian music, particularly Tchaikovsky's output, and is struck by the emotive, vocal atmosphere that Grainger's compositions seem to share with Russian music:

> Later on I began to appreciate the polyphonic aspects of [Grainger's] music and the genius he had for choral writing; not just writing for vocal choirs but for instrumental choirs...that's what comes through...you can't hear *Harkstow Grange* without thinking that it sounds like a Russian choir. Grainger himself said that he thought that his music had a lot in common with Russian music. It comes back to my love of Tchaikovsky...there are aspects of Grainger's music, particularly the melancholy aspects, which are Russian-sounding. Grainger might have said that it's one long heroic moan...there's a mournfulness; it's not a weaklings moan...it's the heroes' moan of centuries of oppression and suffering. There's a flavor in Russian and other Slavonic music that comes from that kind of oppression. There's something in Grainger which is attune to that.

The other side of Stanhope's compositional personality is most clearly manifest in two works, *E.G.B.D.S.* and the more recent *Symphony No. 1*. These are darker works, marked by a textural density and dissonance borne of the composer's predilection for the utilization of simultaneous keys. More extreme technically and more complex to conduct due to the frequency of meter change and the occasional metric modulation, both works satisfy what Stanhope views as a need to express the darker side of his personality:

> I like writing melodies, and I like writing accessible music but there are other pieces I've written which are less accessible and may never be embraced by as many audiences or performers—but those things are just a valuable to me. They may be a little more cerebral. It's probably more the twisted part of me...there's a great deal of me in that music. It's not easy for the players or the conductor to understand because it's densely harmonized [and frequently] bitonal. But with perseverance the clouds should lift!

Stanhope is responsive to commissions from a broad range of organizations and has the creative flexibility to 'tailor' his works to the specific desires of the commissioning agencies. He is pragmatic about the commercial aspects of composition while maintaining a strong pursuit of the satisfaction of both sides of his compositional psyche:

> The popular nature of a work like *Olympic Fireworks* comes at least as much from the commission requirements as anything else. Of course popular pieces lead to more commissions of the popular-type. If I ever become so well-off that I can do whatever I like, maybe I will reject some! [However] I am conscious of what will readily be understood and hence performed. The tuneful thematic nature of folksongs encouraged a very tonal approach for the suites, but this fitted well with what I wanted to write at the time. I have not written any folksong-based music since *Bold Benjamin* (1996). Complex pieces like *E.G.B.D.S.* and the *Symphony* will not be performed much, and would not have been written for wind band without the commissions. I am delighted that those willing to take the time to get into them have appreciated these last two works, but I know most directors or ensembles will immediately put them in the "too difficult" basket. I also doubt if I would write such works unless I really wanted to write them anyway (i.e. without commission), but the commission allows me to make the time.

Stanhope's considerable compositional skills are even more impressive in light of the fact that he came to the practice of composition without formalized study:

> Yes, [I'm] mostly self-taught I think, based on a bit of school theory and harmony. Studying innumerable instrumental scores by other composers together with studying the piano (not with composition in mind at the time) gave me a few clues. Being a conductor has also helped enormously in knowing what will work or is practical.

CONDUCTING APPROACH

In order to preserve the independence of ideas inherent in Stanhope's wind band music, a careful approach to balance coupled with an ear for transparency are paramount. The challenges presented by the tonal density and multi-layered "free polyphony" of his scores are moderated by the composer's strong sense of the capabilities of the instruments of the wind band. His obvious knowledge of the coloristic contributions and technical boundaries of each instrument and their respective families facilitates a greater ease in presenting each musical idea in a clear fashion. Stanhope's background as a player and conductor are the chief contributing factors to the orchestrational clarity that is a hallmark of his work:

> I'm sure that [background] has helped a lot. We're talking about twenty-five years of experience with large ensembles, half of that time as a player, half of it "out front". Without that experience I'd be floundering.

His folksong settings require a conductor to maintain an unwavering dedication to textural transparency as the true brilliance of the writing will only be apparent to the listener if the various themes that are frequently written in a sort of Ivesian juxtaposition are clearly discernable. At times the conductor will be required to spend rehearsal time in the clarification of articulations with a special emphasis on pointed enunciations. Stanhope is attracted to the wind band's capacity for a true 'point' to articulation, particularly in the lower register, and regards that as an advantage when compared to the symphony orchestra:

> Obviously both ensembles have plusses and minuses. The wind band has that clarity in the lower register which an orchestra just doesn't have. That comes [not only] from the extra brass but in particular, the saxophone section. When it's well-balanced a band is a better balanced ensemble, rather like a perfect organ with all those different voices but with a more sharply defined tone color than an organ has. One of the things that I like (which Grainger also liked) is the ability of a wind ensemble to play with a fierceness, an attack, that isn't so easy to get from a string section. One of my criticisms of the wind band is that too often [the players] try to make such a wonderful, mellow sound they lose that ferocity of which they are capable. Particularly with young players who often are just trying to play notes with a nice sound...the articulation is often something that is neglected. Whenever I conduct a wind band I often insist on those things because it is the articulation which is so important.

As is the case in the performance of all folksong-based music, phrase lengths as well as melodic and harmonic contour must be fully explored and creatively performed. Stanhope's editing is quite helpful in this regard particularly in the lyric moments; a pervasive sense of a vocally-based rubato approach to performance is underscored by a metric resourcefulness as he occasionally utilizes asymmetric meters in an effort to approach certain cadence points with a more heightened musical sensitivity. Again, he points to Grainger as a model:

> Grainger wanted to 'wrench people's hearts'...if you're not faithful in your attempts to wrench people's hearts as a performer you're not playing music. At least in the better moments of the better pieces of mine I feel that applies as well.

Stanhope's more compositionally adventuresome works (*E.G.B.D.S.; Symphony No. 1; Endpiece*) frequently utilize bitonality and will require discipline on the part of each member of the 'opposing' tonal forces who must work to match dynamic intensities in their efforts to preserve the harmonic effect of the music.

WIND BAND MUSIC

Folksongs for Band Suite No. 2 (1985) duration:16'30" (Novello)
Premièred by the Florida State University Wind Orchestra, James Croft, conductor.
I. *The Jolly Sailor*
II. *O Shepherd, O Shepherd, Won't You Come Home?*
III. *Rufford Park Poachers*
IV. *The Keel Row*

My three wind-band suites of British folksong settings are dedicated to the memory of Percy Grainger. Grainger used folk melodies as vehicles for his own expression, and I try to follow his example. Each suite consists of four settings; three of the eight melodies [employed] were also used by the Australian master.

Subtitled *A Leadsman, Landsmen and Dancers* the *Folksongs for Band Suite No. 2* begins with *The Jolly Sailor*, a boisterous portrait of the subject. The third movement, *Rufford Park Poachers*, is my most heart-felt tribute to Grainger, who once said somewhat bitterly that the true worth of his own music would never be gauged until it was understood to be 'a pilgrimage to sorrows'. Grainger often spoke of rhythm as a tyranny, and the regular pounding in my last verse is a reference to that tyranny. But the percussion breaks off at the moment when I quote a few bars from Grainger's setting. My coda is bleaker than the one in the "Posy", although it ends with one of Grainger's favorite finishing chords, minor with added major sixth. The deliberately chaotic finale, *The Keel Row*, is an attempt to depict a spontaneous folkdance for the musical and the not-so-musical, and has the following program:

"After a couple of fits and starts, the bagpipes get going, and the dance begins smoothly; after a few verses a very large gentleman attempts to join in. He cannot keep up; he staggers and tumbles over. The dance carries on merrily until some over-enthusiastic jumping on the stage causes it to break. The dancers keep going, but the musicians are thrown off balance—none of them can find the key, although many are prepared to try. This is inconclusive, whereupon a small party of troublesome individuals (who have indulged in too much liquid refreshment) bursts into the main area, singing loudly. This draws whistles, boos and even punches from the crowd, who roughly bundle the intruders out of the way. Fortunately the barrel-organ has kept turning, and a whistler takes up the melody. The dancers are catching their breath, and the village virtuoso seizes his chance to show off, being rewarded with murmurs of admiration. His final flourish starts the dance again. More and more people join in, faster and faster until, suddenly, all are dancing or playing at, or over, the limit. The dancers spread out into a vast circle and join hands for a final verse, leaping high together. The dance is apparently over, but the joker smacks his tambourine, jerking everybody off their feet."

Folksongs for Band Suite No. 1 (1986) duration: 16'15" (Southern Music Company)
Premièred by the Florida State University Wind Orchestra, James Croft, conductor.
I. *Good Morning, Good Morning, My Pretty Little Miss*
II. *Lovely Joan*
III. *The Blacksmith*
IV. *Irish Tune*

Each of the folksong suites is based on tunes from Great Britain, and all are dedicated to the memory of Percy Grainger. Like the folk-music settings of that composer, they use the original melodies in a variation or passacaglia-like form as a means for harmonic and contrapuntal invention.

The first suite contains four movements: *Good Morning, Good Morning, My Pretty Little Miss*, a fast-moving passacaglia; *Lovely Joan*, a melody worked into multiple canons; *The Blacksmith*, a vigorous portrait of the man at work; and *Irish Tune*, which depicts a nostalgic seascape, with waves finally crashing onto the shore. A structural element developed in *Lovely Joan* and *Irish Tune* is the use of multiple canons in different keys; this creates expansiveness in the first, and staggered waves of sound in the second.

Concerto for Band (1988) duration: 16'19" (Southern Music Company)
I. *Theme–Variation 3*
II. *Variation 4–6*
III. *Presto (Variation 7–Coda)*
Commissioned by the Sydney Brass & Woodwind Society. Premièred by the Florida State University Wind Orchestra, James Croft, conductor.

The *Concerto for Band* is an affectionate parody of several composers, written as a set of variations, but loosely cast in the shape of three movements. All the players get a chance to show off their virtuosity, with each variation favoring one or more instrumental groups. The opening theme (which is not the real theme!) is given by the oboe, variation 1 features the horns and trombones, variation 2 the trumpets, cornets, euphonium and tuba, and variation 3 is dominated by the saxophones. The next two variations are not so clearly defined, but favour the upper winds—oboes, flutes and upper clarinets in variation 4, flutes, piccolo and high E♭ clarinet in variation 5. Variation 6 features marimba, vibraphone and glockenspiel, and variation 7 the entire clarinet family. The coda gives the (well-known *Country Gardens*) theme at last, with a canon thrown in.

The Little Ripper (1989) duration: 3'21" (Southern Music Company)
A rollicking 6/8 march that reminds the listener of Grainger's "Children's March: Over the Hills and Far Away", the work contains an interesting trio written for mallet percussion and timpani only.

The Little Ripper was written after I was approached to write a march for the Australian bi-centenary (1988). Although the commission failed to come through, I wrote the march anyway a year or so later. The title is quintessentially Australian, being a recognition of achievement (particularly when shouted at sporting events). Good is "You Beaut!" better is "You Beautyyyy!" but best of all is "you Little Ripper!".

Folksongs for Band Suite No. 3 (1991) duration: 14' (Southern Music Company)
I. *Droylsden Wakes*
II. *Lord Bateman*
III. *Three Ships and Lisbon*
Commissioned and premièred by the Florida State University Wind Orchestra, James Croft, conductor.

Droylsden Wakes is one of the more heart-rending folksong expressions in the wind repertoire and stands as equal lyric partner to the well-known Grainger folk tune settings. (Stanhope has recently composed an independent setting of this movement for young band.) *Lord Bateman* opens with a startling brass and percussion fanfare that announces the beginning of an amazing canon construct. *Three Ships and Lisbon* could be subtitled "Percy Grainger meets Charles Ives" with a confrontational setting of the two familiar folksongs. Stanhope provides the following commentary on the 2nd and 3rd movements:

> Canons of a more conventional sort appear towards the end of *Lord Bateman*, where a canon at half-speed is in conjunction with the same tune at normal speed. The picture drawn in *Three Ships and Lisbon*, which also includes a tune of my own, requires some explanation. My idea was to imagine a group of dancers approaching a seaside town where bells are chiming; when the dancers enter the town they are gradually overwhelmed by the bells and the three ships melody, but continue to try and whistle their own tunes over the top.

E.G.B.D.S. (1996) duration: 13'37" (Southern Music Company)
Commissioned and premièred by the Elder Conservatorium Wind Ensemble, Bob Hower, conductor.

E.G.B.D.S. is a rather different world, being largely bi-tonal and bi-metrical. There is another tribute here, the title standing for "Edvard Grieg By David Stanhope". Inspired by Grieg's piano minature "Students' Serenade", the piece pits the various families of the band against each other in an often violent manner; but the final elegaic section reconciles the two meters, with the Serenade music shifting constantly back and forth between the two keys.

The Demon Fanfare (1995) duration: 2' (Southern Music Company)
Commissioned and premièred by the Australian Wind Orchestra, Russell Hammond, conductor.

The Demon Fanfare is a violent, bitonal fanfare dedicated to Russell Hammond and the Australian Wind Orchestra, who gave the first performance. The two keys can be clearly heard in the second statement where the brass play in canon—G major followed closely by B♭ major. The third verse switches to B♭ major and D♭ major in alternation, before returning to the original two keys in a very densely scored final section.

The Bold Benjamin (1996) duration: 5' (Southern Music Company)

Written for solo baritone voice (or euphonium/trombone solo), optional male chorus and wind band, the *Bold Benjamin* (subtitled Sea Chantey) is a beautifully scored work recounting the legend of an English ship, the Bold Benjamin, and the disastrous loss of life experienced by its crew after a battle with the Spanish Armada during one of the English/Spanish conflicts of the 16th or 17th centuries. An emotional folksong setting that displays the composer's ability to successfully integrate solo voice and chorus with wind band, this work is distinguished by moments of haunting transparency and opportunities for sensitive rubato interpretation.

Retreat and Pumping Song (1997) duration: 7' (Southern Music Company)

The slow *"Retreat"* is richly scored; gentle chords are gradually transformed into an evocative cascading effect before a muted brass conclusion. The *"Pumping Song"* is an extrovert number that builds from the opening melody in a solo trumpet (offstage if desired) to a fortissimo finish.

Grand Fanfare (1999) duration: 5' (Southern Music Company)
Commissioned and premièred by the University of Georgia Wind Symphony, Dwight Satterwhite, conductor.

Bold, ceremonial fanfare music written for traditional band instrumentation as well as sixteen antiphonal trumpets, organ, piano, six percussionists and timpani.

Endpiece (1999) duration: 5' (Southern Music Company)
Commissioned and premièred by the Florida State University Wind Orchestra, James Croft, conductor.

Subtitled "Folk-Elegy", *Endpiece* is an atmospherically haunting setting of three familiar folktunes; *Lovely Joan, The Sussex Mummer's Christmas Carol* and *Rufford Park Poachers*. Endpiece was the formal term Percy Grainger used to describe his musical codas. Extremely slow, with thin textures, the work requires a special attention to melodic contour as well as musicians capable of reproducing true pianissimo dynamic levels in transparent settings. Stanhope looks at this work as a sort of bridge between his two compositional personalities:

> *Endpiece* stands somewhere between the folksong suites and the more complex, bitonal works (*E.G.B.D.S.* and the *Symphony No. 1*). I call it a "folk-elegy", and it is perhaps the most personal of my folksettings; as ever, with a nod towards Grainger and especially his anguished side. Two of the folksongs I had already used in the suites.

152

Olympic Fireworks (2000) duration: 4'30" (Southern Music Company)

Olympic Fireworks was given its première by the Sydney Symphony Orchestra, with the composer conducting, at the closing ceremony of the Sydney 2000 Olympics. As well as being played during the final fireworks, it was also played during the entrance of the athletes. The wind band version, (premièred by the University of Missouri-Columbia Symphonic Wind Ensemble, Dale Lonis, conductor), was written at the same time, and both versions along with a new brass/percussion choir arrangement are available as concert works. The work is made up of four main sections. The first begins with sparkling sixteenth-note patterns followed by a rising theme in triplets. The second (announced by the horns) introduces a new triplet theme with rising and falling duplets answering; these themes are developed to some extent before the third section, a chorale-like melody with the original sixteenth-note patterns dancing over the top. The fourth section repeats much of the opening part, adding a majestic coda.

Symphony No. 1 (2001) duration: 34' (Southern Music Company)
I. *Dreams*
II. *Desires*
III. *Devils*
IV. *Irish Tune*
Premièred by the University of Georgia Wind Symphony, Dwight Satterwhite, conductor.

Elegaic in nature, *The Symphony No. 1* is Stanhope's most ambitious work and is representative of that side of his compositional nature that finds voice in a more densely textured, harmonically bitonal and rhythmically aggressive style. The symphony was developed out of musical material found in his opera *The Un-Dead* a work that was inspired by Bram Stoker's *Dracula*. The opera had never been performed beyond certain workshopped excerpts and Stanhope was interested in using it as the basis for a purely instrumental work:

> …I certainly drew on the opera extensively, but also wrote quite a bit of new material (e.g. most of the 1st half of the 1st movement, sections of the slow movement etc.), as well as revising and recasting, not to mention rescoring. The fact that much of the music was originally inspired by the *Dracula* noveletta in no way detracts from the personal emotions of the symphony. The titles of the movements indicate human feelings and thoughts—my response to those titles. The reason Dracula has had such a long success (and why it once appealed to me as a subject, as it has appealed to many) is that it taps into emotions that are already there in the reader. Of course I do not mind if the history of the symphony is known, but one should not try and understand it in terms of the old opera. I no longer think of it that way, and (for better or worse) what I am trying to say in the music comes from me, whatever the original inspiration may have been. It is perhaps nevertheless a valid point to make that my attempt to write an opera "developed" my writing in a cer-

tain way. EGBDS has a similar "dark" quality, tortuous perhaps, [but] the technical aspect of the bitonality and the rather rigid structure make it different from the more rhapsodic nature of the symphony.

Southern Cross (2001) (Southern Music Company)

Southern Cross fanfare was commissioned by the Waverley Bondi Beach Band and premièred by the New South Wales Public Schools Symphonic Wind Ensemble with the composer conducting at the opening ceremony of the 40th New South Wales School Band Festival, University of New South Wales, Australia.

The *Southern Cross* fanfare is based on material from a short fanfare written for the opening ceremony of the 2000 Sydney Olympics.

Songs Without Words (2002) (Southern Music Company)
I. *Questions*
II. *Innocence*
III. *Acceptance*
Commissioned by a consortium of twenty United States universities and colleges and premièred by the College Band Directors National Association Western/Northwestern Division Intercollegiate Band, composer conducting.

> In 1983 I wrote a work for soprano and string orchestra using texts from three poems by the Australian poet Gwen Harwood. This did receive a workshop performance, but, as I was not happy with the composition as a whole, I withdrew it. A few sections from one movement were subsequently used in another composition for trombone quartet. Several years later I decided much of the original "Three Poems" could be salvaged if I made a complete revision of it, this time expanding the solo aspect to four "voices" together with a richer accompaniment. The result is a new work with which I am very pleased, one where the lyrical qualities of the saxophone quartet are to the fore, with a wide range of timbre in the accompaniment. Although *Songs Without Words* is largely an introspective work, there are a few moments when the full power of the ensemble is released, particularly the ecstatic section near the end. The titles I have given reflect the general mood of each movement.

NEW WORKS

Promenade commissioned by Andrew Dale, band director at Ballarat High School in Victoria, Australia was premiered on August 3rd, 2002 with the composer conducting. He describes the work as:

> …a tuneful, medium-level work in three sections (ABA) featuring an opening trumpet solo and an intense and more-sustained middle section. The recapitulation introduces two countermelodies to the main theme, one developed from the middle section, the other a descant featuring sixteenth note patterns. I was somewhat inspired by Hansen's *Valdres*, which has a charming predictability and the work is similarly built around an opening arpeggio.

Australian Fantasia is a four-movement level 3 to 4 work based partly upon music that Stanhope wrote for the Sydney Olympic Games as well as the 2001 Sydney New Year's fireworks celebration. The work incorporates traditional Australian tunes including *Waltzing Matilda*, *The Road to Gundagai* and *Advance Australia Fair*. The third movement is a fanfare entitled *Southern Cross* which can be performed separately (see above).

All works published by Southern Music Company with the exception of *Folksongs for Band Suite No. 2* which is published by Novello.

WORKS LISTING

Orchestra Music	**Publisher**
Olympic Fireworks	Stanhope Music
Games 2000 Fanfares 1, 2, 3	Stanhope Music
Olympic Fanfare	Stanhope Music
Fireworks Sydney 2001	Stanhope Music
Two Folk-Elegies	Stanhope Music
Grand Fanfare	Stanhope Music
E.G.B.D.S.	Stanhope Music

Opera	**Publisher**
The Un-Dead (3 act chamber opera; 10 voices, 10 players)	Stanhope Music

Brass Band	**Publisher**
Droylsden Wakes	Stanhope Music
The Little Ripper	Stanhope Music
A Leadsman, a Lady and a Lord	Novello

String Orchestra	**Publisher**
String Songs	Stanhope Music

Chamber Works For Brass	**Publisher**
Endpiece (brass decet)	Stanhope Music
4-Concert Studies (trombone quartet)	Stanhope Music
Hornplayers' Retreat and Pumping Song (horn octet)	Hornists' Nest
Cortettes (horn quartet)	Hornists' Nest
The Australian Fanfare (9 trumpets)	Southern Music Company
Three Folksongs for Quintet (brass quintet)	Southern Music Company
A Day in the Life of Jim Dempsey (brass quintet)	Southern Music Company
Ceremonial Fanfares (brass quintet)	Southern Music Company

Songs	**Publisher**
Felix Randal (voice and piano)	Stanhope Music
Jolly, Geordie, Jane (voice and piano)	Stanhope Music
In Brisbane (voice and piano)	Stanhope Music

Other Chamber Works
Three Folksongs for Pianola

Piano Transcriptions	**Publisher**
Scherzo Prestissimo (Borodin)	Stanhope Music
The Tryst (Sibelius)	Stanhope Music
March of the Toys (Hebert)	Stanhope Music
The Little Ripper March (Stanhope)	Stanhope Music

DISCOGRAPHY

Keene, James F., conductor. (1995) "**In Concert #129.**" University of Illinois Symphonic Band. *"Folksongs for Band, Set II"* / *"The Little Ripper, Australian March"* Clarence, N.Y. MCD-1866 Mark Custom Recording Service

Hammond, Russell, conductor. (1995) **Music for winds II.** The Australian Wind Orchestra. *"Folksongs for band, Suite No. 3"* Quest Records. AMC Library number: CD 257 c.1

Hammond, Russell; Rob McWilliams, Rob; Williams, Stephen; conductors. (1995) Australian Wind Orchestra. **WASBE Concerts.** *"The Demon Fanfare"* / *"Folk Songs for Band, Suite No. 1"* KOCD 4552

Hower, Robert, conductor. (1996) **Little Ripper! Wind Band Music by David Stanhope.** Elder Conservatorium Wind Ensemble. *"The Little Ripper"* / *"Folksongs for Band, Suite No. 3"* / *"E.G.B.D.S."* / *"Folksongs for Band, Suite No. 1"* / *"Concerto for Band"* / *"Folksongs for Band, Suite No. 2"* (recorded over a two year period; David Stanhope was present for all recording sessions) UISB-808 $15.00/CD

Middleton, Arthur, conductor. (1995) **Fantasy variations.** Queensland Conservatorium of Music Wind Symphony. *"Folksongs for band, Suite No. 3"* Australian Music Center (AMC) Library number: CD 265 c.1

Lichtenwalter, Ray, conductor. **Postcard.** University of Texas at Arlington Wind Ensemble. *"Folksongs for band, Suite No. 3* West Coast Music Service. VAWB-1276

Corporan, Eugene, conductor. (1998) **Teaching Music Through Performance in Band, Volume II.** University of North Texas Wind Symphony. "Retreat and Pumping Song" GIA Publications.

ADDITIONAL RESOURCES

"The utilization of folk song elements in selected works by Ralph Vaughan Williams and Percy Grainger with subsequent treatment exemplified in the wind band music of David Stanhope", John Cody Birdwell. Dissertation: Thesis (D.M.A.)—University of North Texas, May, 1996. Reproduction: Microfiche./ Ann Arbor, MI. :/ University Microfilms International,/ 1996./ 2 microfiches. Website ordering information can be found at: http://www.umi.com/hp/Products/Dissertations.html

Additional information regarding the music of David Stanhope can be found at his frequently updated website: http://www.davidstanhope.com/

James Syler

by
Miriam Krueger and Timothy Salzman

The most anguishing and inspiring moment for me is hearing the pencil move across the page as the first measure is written. —(J.S.)

James Syler (b.1961, Hyde Park, New York) was raised in New York and Florida. He completed his Bachelor's of Music Education degree at Northern Illinois University and his Master of Music degree from the University of Miami in studio writing and production. He continued his education for one year as a doctoral student at the University of Texas at Austin and has studied composition privately with Alfred Reed, Karl Korte and Michael Colgrass. His awards include the 1993 Colonel Arnald D. Gabriel Composition Award, sponsored by the United States Air Force Band; the 17th Annual National Band Association Composition Contest; two grants from the American Music Center in New York, two artist residencies at the Hambidge Center for the Creative Arts in Rabun Gap, Georgia—one as a composer, the other as a writer, as well as numerous commissions.

BIOGRAPHICAL INFORMATION

James Syler came from a supportive but nonmusical family and began percussion lessons at the age of nine through the Ralph R. Smith Elementary School band program in Hyde Park, New York. He continued in band programs throughout middle school and high school, but feels that he learned the most in private lessons.

> Janice Holloway was my first band director in the fourth grade. I would get out of class once a week to go have a lesson in the band room with her and another student. We all strapped on big field drums and she proceeded to teach us how to read music from Rubank's "Easy Steps to the Band". I think that's called the good 'ole fashioned way . . .

His family moved to Boca Raton, Florida in 1972 where he completed his middle school and high school years. As is the case with many aspiring percussionists, jazz was his first serious interest and he slowly began to discover other forms of music during his high school years.

> I can remember when I was 12 or 13 going to hear the Buddy Rich Big Band as they came through South Florida. I was completely and totally knocked out. All through high school, jazz was my musical world. When I was 17 I remember flipping on my little black and white TV and catching the beginning of a "Previn and the Pittsburg" symphony broadcast. I just remember sitting there and being stunned by the music coming out of this little TV. It was the *Firebird* by Stravinsky, conducted by Andre Previn.

At age 16 Syler realized he wanted to study music seriously, which meant taking piano lessons in preparation for college. His first experience with piano lessons was not what he expected.

> She was a little tiny old lady who gave lessons in her condo on an old organ with whirling Leslie speakers. Here I came with a method book full of oversized notes, a wad of gum, fresh from baseball practice, ready to play my Hannon exercises. There was an unfathomable disparity in the room. I didn't last long. I dropped out.

Syler recounted two meaningful experiences with teachers during his high school and collegiate days:

> There were two important teachers that helped me early on. One was Jim Osterman in Boca Raton, Florida who was my private percussion teacher in high school and was responsible for getting me ready for college. He introduced to me the value of a variety of musical styles from working on Bach at the marimba to [various] jazz drumming styles...he was a true musical egalitarian.
>
> Another was Al Castronovo who was the director of bands at Chesterton High School in Chesterton, Indiana. I was a music education major as an undergraduate and completed my student teaching assignment in 1983 at his school. I can remember at the very end [of that time]...going into his office and saying that I felt the teaching was fine, but I couldn't wait for the end of the day to come home so I could find a piano and work on some writing. He suggested that I not take a teaching job...he advised me to go home, compose and apply to graduate school. So, I went back to Florida, took a job cleaning pools, wrote music by night to build a portfolio and a year and a half later applied to graduate programs. It was at that time, at the late age 23, that I completed my first original composition. Prior to that I was doing mostly arranging of all sorts. I'm grateful to Al for being straight with me and giving his opinion. I think I knew I was heading in the writing direction all along; I just needed to hear it from someone else.

Syler has taken an interesting path towards a career as a composer and has vivid memories of a significant time in undergraduate school where he felt that writing music for a living was a passion that he wanted to pursue:

For me everything has been gradual. I didn't decide when I was young to be a "composer", but it seemed to grow on me over time. I was a drummer as a kid, played around with writing music in high school, then became a percussionist in college, continued arranging things through college...but then I took an orchestration course at Northern Illinois University as a junior and my final project was an orchestration of the art song *"Ich Grolle Nicht"* from the *Dichterliebe* by Robert Schumann. After turning in the assignment, the instructor, who was also the orchestra conductor, told the class that if we wanted to hear our work we should copy the parts. So I copied and copied...I remember to this day what it was like to sit there in the hall and hear it. I was awestruck at how it sounded. The music glowed to me and I've never forgotten that moment, not because it was "my arrangement"...but because at that moment I seemed to realize that what I thought it was going to sound like, based on the way it was orchestrated on paper, was actually the way it came out. This confirmed to me that I was able to translate what I wanted to hear in my head onto paper. Looking back, I think that is when I decided to become a composer, except I had no idea what that really meant, especially in terms of trying to translate composing into money!

His academic pursuit of composition study was not what he hoped for as he felt that he was in training to become a theory teacher, not a composer. After leaving his doctoral studies Syler began an individual pursuit of private composition instruction, a course of study more suited to his learning style and the development of his skills:

As a graduate student at the University of Miami I had one semester of private lessons with Alfred Reed, then as a doctoral student at the University of Texas - Austin I had a semester of lessons with Karl Korte. I was halfway through the DMA when I decided to drop out; [that course of study] wasn't what I needed or wanted. I felt the music I was writing was going in a direction that was against my ear. I've never been a very academic person and I learn best on my own or in private study with someone, so I looked for a private teacher outside of the academic environment. I was familiar with some of Michael Colgass's percussion music and his orchestral piece *Deja Vu*, which I felt an affinity with, so I contacted him knowing that he wasn't associated with a university and asked if he would consider me as a private student. After sending him some scores he consented and on two different occasions I spent a week or two with him; that was what I needed at the time and he was very helpful.

So most of my influences have not been from composition teachers, but through score study, personal experiences and simply opening my ears and listening to a variety of music.

He credits his family for his sense of independence and individuality, referring to them as "independent, supportive, practical, and full of that old 'go figure it out for yourself' Yankee horse sense." Largely a self-taught composer, Syler didn't begin private formal composition study until he was 26 years old, a situation he views as somewhat of a mixed blessing:

Coming to composition late has meant that I'm primarily self-taught. My undergraduate degree is in music education and my graduate degree is in studio and jazz writing...private composition lessons were not a part of either program, so I learned slowly by trial and error and a lot of reading, score study and

listening. I think I learned most of the Classical repertoire through working as a driver and courier for a couple of years when I was in and out of school. I would listen to the classical station 8 hours a day, 40 hours a week and in the process I heard a lot of music. That was a part of the "not letting school get in the way of your education" kind of learning.

Following his Master's degree program Syler found himself interested in the commercial world of film scoring, but after many attempts to move to Los Angeles the circumstances and contacts never seemed to work out. As the years went by he began to feel more interested in writing music as "art" and less interested in working as a commercial "craftsman". However, he would still like to try his hand at a film score if given the opportunity.

Syler has been composing for the wind band since 1988, and, in a similar fashion to other contemporary composers, was drawn to the idiom when he discovered that original works for the symphony orchestra have little chance of being performed. He feels that wind ensembles provide an experienced to almost-professional quality venue where pieces may be heard and subsequently improved upon.

He has also composed numerous choral and orchestral works but his chamber music compositions are few in number due to the difficulties encountered in the funding of those types of commissioning projects. His interest in the color and texture provided by large-scale forms has led to his current interests and projects.

Since 1998 Syler has also been involved in music publishing as the owner/editor of Ballerbach Music and its growing catalog of band, wind ensemble and choral works.

COMPOSITIONAL APPROACH

Syler's music is driven, in part, by his strong literary interest, an interest that led to past employment as a music critic for the Palm Beach Daily News in Palm Beach, Florida and as an amateur author of short stories and poetry. His taste in literature, and in his own compositional style, is highly dramatic and is reflected by a technique that clearly flows from a strong intuitive sense as opposed to abstract or more formalized, theoretical writing. He describes his compositional approach as being grounded in postmodern eclecticism:

By "postmodern" I mean to imply a creative artistic position that has moved beyond modernism and its attempt to disconnect with the past, into a new phase that attempts to reconcile certain aspects of the past with progressive "modern" ideas. And by "eclectic" I mean to imply the utilization of diverse musical materials in the construction of the work. Combining the two results in an attempt to use a variety of musical materials in a progressive "modern" way, and at the same time using musical materials that are well known from our musical past. This is all rooted in a semiotic approach to constructing (not analyzing) a work. (i.e. the use of musical materials that are instantly recognizable and function in a work as an aural signpost, or indicator. My interest in compositional semiotics comes from my literary interests in authors Walker Percy and Flannery O'Connor)

His jazz and commercial music background has also impacted his compositional approach especially in terms of the harmonic language employed in his music as he tends to construct harmonic schemes in a more practical "non-classical" way through jazz chord terminology. The bebop era is highly influential in at least one of his compositions and his intention in the creation of all of his music is that each piece communicates directly with the audience in the same fashion as an improvisatory jazz solo.

My first interests in music were in jazz. Classical music came later in college. As a kid and a drummer I was very into bop and fusion. I probably still listen to more jazz today than classical music. Later as a college teacher I taught History of Jazz courses (and still do), so [Minton's Playhouse] was a conscious effort to create a third stream type of work that used the bop language I've been listening to since I was a kid. I also devoured the Omni book (transcribed solos of Charlie Parker) while writing Minton's.

Syler has written a great deal of vocal/choral music and views that idiom as being a source of inspiration and craftsmanship for his instrumental works. He believes that his vocal writing has expanded his compositional language particularly in the area of voice leading, interior part writing and dependence on a singing line. In his construct, *all* lines become singularly important, an evolutionary step away from the more typical wind band orchestration model where the clarinet section has traditionally taken the role of the string section.

True espressivo playing is very difficult for a collection of woodwinds and brass [and] the wind band lacks an acoustically balanced homogenous sound unit that can cover soprano, alto, tenor and bass voicing. This isn't necessarily bad, because in a way the wind band is the supreme model of a democratic egalitarian approach— the ensembles instrumentation is a metaphor of Americanism. No one group stands out, all must blend together. [By way of contrast] the orchestra's instrumentation is the ultimate metaphor of the old world elitism. A singular group of instruments (strings) gets most of the attention while the rest "accompany". The clarinet family, which in wind band scoring is typically asked to take the place of the string section, is a wonderful sound but has a limited dynamic range and inability to inflect a melodic line with expression akin to a string instrument or the human voice. Therefore, trying to use this grouping as a substitute for the string section falls flat....if one wants to get to something beyond the generic educational band sound this approach won't take you there...

Clearly, Syler has strong feelings about scoring for the wind band and credits his percussion background as being a significant contributing factor to his particular orchestrational approach. Confirmation of these viewpoints came during his private study with Michael Colgrass (also a percussionist) who suggested that percussionists should be

excellent orchestrators due to their physical vantage point in the ensemble compared to other instrumentalists; they have complete aural access to the sounds of the entire ensemble and that from the beginning a percussionist is concerned with timbre and color. (i.e. soft mallet, hard mallet, brass, wood, plastic, etc.) Syler views writing for the wind band as a specific skill that has many inherent problems especially when contrasted with orchestral scoring:

...the orchestra has risen since the Baroque to become the singular refinement of the large instrumental ensemble...out of this instrumentation we get 3 sub-instrumentations with their own particular strengths and weaknesses: the string orchestra, the contemporary percussion ensemble and the contemporary wind ensemble. These sub groupings have distinct particular sounds and require careful writing. Proof of this is in the fact that you can write a simple chord progression for an orchestra and it will sound like 'gold'. Write the same progression for a wind band and it will sound cumbersome, thick, etc. It takes more attention and skill to write effectively for a wind band, or a string orchestra alone, or a percussion ensemble alone.

Syler's view is that an effective composer's approach to wind band scoring should vary drastically in comparison to standard orchestral scoring. Avoiding direct doublings, he treats the wind ensemble as a collection of colors, frequently writing for one on a part in what he describes as a 'democratic, overgrown chamber setting'. He has strong opinions regarding the issue of contemporary composers' approach to wind ensemble orchestration:

Traditional band orchestration has too many people playing too much of the time. That's understandable for pedagogical reasons, but in a purely artistic sense it's a sound that's fat in the middle and too thin on the bottom. This is one distinction between the educational band repertoire and the advanced or professional wind ensemble repertoire. However, it is wise, obviously to orchestrate in a more tutti way if you're writing for a school group...

He views the current wind band compositional situation as dualistic in nature. On one hand, it is now obvious that a younger generation of composers have realized the opportunities available in creating works for the wind ensemble. Doctoral students are able to produce wind works as final project theses as most academic composition teachers now view the wind band as a valid genre. On the other hand, the fact remains that there is still no American professional outlet for the wind ensemble repertoire; the idiom remains available to a seemingly narrow community. His opinions reflect both a frustration and a future hope for the genre:

The point of this is the fact that we now have two very distinct [wind band] repertoires—educational and professional. Unfortunately there isn't a professional outlet for the advanced repertoire outside of the university world. This is precisely what frustrates contemporary composers about the writing for the wind band. It is a great opportunity to write new music and get it played, but no one knows about it. It doesn't get reviewed or played by professionals over 25. And, rightly or wrongly, a professional reputation as a composer is not built in the academic world; it's made in the professional music-making world, which means orchestral writing and maybe opera or musical theater. (Proof of this is in remembering that the major 20th century composers who became known to the general public were not academic composers—Stravinsky, Copland, Bernstein, Ives.) The orchestra is really not interested in new music, nor is the public, [so] the composer today is stuck. (I'm personally of the opinion that we're beating a dead horse, feeding off the carcass and living in the aftermath if you will, of a glorious, but dead, heritage. Proof of this is in the [historical] fact that a living musical culture has always been rooted in the infusion of new works. We don't have that in today's orchestra. We have a museum.)

Because there has been so much new music written for the wind band in the past 50 years, it seems to be akin to the early days of the classical orchestra when it was building its repertoire. The only real catch is that without the establishment of professional wind music-making much of the wind band repertoire will continue to be limited to the educational context, and thus never make it out to the general public. Putting band music in the public schools was a blessing and a curse. What if after Sousa, wind bands continued to flourish as professional ensembles?

Syler has also continued to develop his own ideas on approaching composition from a semiotic position. Semiotics is the study of signs and is usually thought of as a lingusitic concept. Syler see it as an extension of Debussy and impressionism.

I think we forget that Debussy considered himself a symbolist, not an impressionist. He prefered to hang out with the writers, not the painters, and the writers were symbolists. For me this ties in with my interest in trying to develop the priciples of semiotics from linguistics into music as a post-impressionist (symbolist) compositional device.

His approach is to use well-known or stereotyped musics (ex. a field drum is perceived to be miltaristic) that can function as "aural signposts" in an eclectic non-tonal work and as a replacement for traditional cadential points in tonal music. This approach to replacing traditional cadences with a semiotic "signpost" can be heard clearly in the work *Storyville*.

CONDUCTING APPROACH

In responding to queries regarding his advice to conductors considering rehearsing and performing his works, Syler's input reflects the lyric nature of his compositional approach:

1) ...incorporate a sense of rubato into my works. Wind conductors, as a group, seem chained to their beat patterns and obsessed with metronomic tempi, strict rhythms, etc. Because my own compositional approach is essentially a romantic creative impulse (i.e. visceral, intuitive) rather than a classic impulse (abstracted, form based) my work needs to breathe—to flow, to sing. Fluctuations in the tempo and connecting sections are welcome.

2) I believe all of my instrumental works are inherently lyrical; I write what I sing. A conductor should sit down at the piano with the score and sing the entire piece from beginning to end. Then they should try to extract that singing line out of the instrumentalists. I should note that I've written as much choral/vocal music as I've written instrumental music.

3) Because of the above, the conductor must ensure that there is shape to the melodic line. A line has a beginning, middle, and an end. This is basic, but I'm always dumbfounded during live performances at how undeveloped this concept is. I believe this is due, in part, to the nature of much contemporary music and its angular asymmetry, and the fact that an ensemble of woodwinds and brass are not naturally given to espressivo playing like strings or keyboard instruments.

When asked about 'reference music' that conductors should be familiar with when working with one of his scores Syler commented at length regarding music that has influenced him:

...in general, my aesthetic roots have become increasingly more French than Germanic in that they are more centered on the line rather than on the architectonic. I do admit to being an admirer of Ravel. On the vocal/choral side I enjoy the French tradition of Faure, Ravel, Durufle, Poulenc. On the instrumental side I enjoy the Sibelius symphonies, Ravel, Debussy, Shostakovitch, Delius, Copland. Among contemporaries I honestly don't like much of anything I hear with the exceptions being Henri Dutilleaux, Witold Lutoslawski and Michael Colgrass. In short I feel comfortable thinking of myself in terms of a post-impressionist.

I'm of the opinion that after Debussy, [composers] took the Schoenberg road and never really fully continued down the impressionistic road. I also feel that most composers today are unable to develop their own "voice" compositionally, like Copland or John Adams, because of the intrinsic notion of a self-conscious modernism and its tendency to create unique autonomous works each time out. That phase may well be over, being replaced by a vague postmodernism. I believe what's needed is more of a "transmodern" approach; a descriptor used by New York University psychologist Paul Vitz. The idea that art is rooted in the here and now while, at the same time, is also fully appreciating the *pre-modern*. For me, musically, that means going back to the era just before modernism, which puts one either in impressionism or at the fork in the road of late romanticism. A similar situation exists in art history with Paul Cezanne being enormously influential on modern art, in a way paralleling Debussy's "quiet revolution" with the *Prelude to the Afternoon of a Faun*.

Relative to recommended recordings of his music Syler prefers that conductors spend time with the score before submitting to the influence of a recording:

All five of my original compositions for wind ensemble have been recorded on noncommercial CD's (a university, military band, or convention performance [however] I have no recommendations. Some are very good, but I think of all of them as reference recordings. If a conductor is interested in [my] work they should sit down at the piano with the score, (which are all "score in C" scores except for *The Hound of Heaven*), and dig into the music. This is why reference recordings are useful. They can give you the 'once-over' to see if you're even interested. The danger of course is that a bad recording may do a disservice to an otherwise excellent piece of music. That's the chance you take. Still, once a conductor has committed to performing a piece I think they should avoid recordings of it and get into the score for themselves and make it their own. We're all too dependent on recordings, myself included.

WIND ENSEMBLE MUSIC

Syler has composed six works for the wind band all of which display a remarkable musical eclecticism and a particular command of certain orchestrational manipulations in the achievement of very specific programmatic effects. Several of his works are also dependent on the effects of spatial relationships between the members of the ensemble and, for successful performance, will require particular attention to detail in terms of the stage set-up of the ensemble.

The Hound of Heaven (1988) duration: 19'
picc (dbl fl), 2 fl, 2 ob, eng hrn, Eb cl, 3 cl, a cl, b cl, cb cl, 2 bsn, 2 a sax, t sax, b sax - solo trp, 3 trp, 2 cor, 4 hrn, 3 trn, b trb, bar hrn, 2 tba - cb, pno, timp, 4 perc - optional 2 vc
Premiere: 1993. Wittenberg University Wind Ensemble at Wittenberg University, Springfield, OH. Tom Kennedy, conductor.

Winner of the 1993 Arnald Gabriel Award and the 1993 National Band Association Composition Contest, this six-movement programmatic work was conceived after Francis Thompson's poem of the same name. Like many of Syler's works the writing style is rooted in a postmodern eclecticism; minimalism, 12-tone serialism, traditional tonality, aggressive dissonance and a strong sense of singing lyricism permeate the piece. Syler also displays, in this his first work for wind ensemble, the use of musical fragments that are to be played out-of-time with the surrounding music. This device has been employed in all five of his subsequent works and reaches its zenith in *Storyville* and the *Symphony No. 1* through numerous asynchronous and free musical events. The antiphonal trumpet is key to the programmatic nature of the piece. The composer provides the following program notes for this work:

> *The Hound of Heaven* is a programmatic work, in six sections, for large wind ensemble based on the poem of the same name written in 1893 by the British poet Francis Thompson. The allegorical title describes God as the loving hound who is in pursuit of the lost hare, the individual soul.
>
> Section I depicts the fearful attempt to flee from God knowing all the while that he is being pursued. Section II tells of how the fugitive hare tries to escape in his imagination to the beauty of the heavens. He finds it pointless and in Section III decides to turn to the little children. He believes he can find happiness with them, but just as the children begin to respond they are suddenly taken away by death. He now becomes a desperate soul who, in one last attempt, (Section IV), turns to nature for repose. But nature, as beautiful as it is, is unable to fill the void in his heart and he again hears the footfall of his pursuer. There is nothing left now as he has tried everything, and in Section V he is smitten to his knees. In a dream he views his past life wasted on foolish pursuits, none of which has given him love and happiness. The chase is over. In Section VI the loving Hound of Heaven stands over him and the gloom, which he thought would follow this surrender, is only the shade of God's hand coming down to embrace him. He realizes his foolishness and now knows he has found true love and happiness as his pursuer speaks to him with the words, 'I am He Whom thou seekest!'
>
> This work employs a variety of musical styles to fully underscore the poem's story. The antiphonal trumpet speaks between each section and serves as the musical voice of the Hound of Heaven. This work is my attempt to musically depict the depth of the poem's universal message."

Fields (1994) duration: 12'
2 fl (1 dbl picc, 1 dbl a fl), 2 ob (1 dbl eng hrn), 3 cl (1 dbl Eb cl), b cl, 2 bsn (1 dbl c bsn), s sax, a sax, t sax, b sax - 4 trp (1 dbl picc trp, 1 dbl flug hrn), 4 hrn, 3 trb, b trb, bar hrn, tba - cb, pno, hp, 3 perc - solo flug hrn
Premiere : 1996. Banda Sinfonica do Estado de Sao Paulo (State Symphonic Band of Sao Paulo) in Sao Paulo, Brazil. James Syler, conductor.

Fields, described by Syler as a "mysterious abstract Adagio for wind ensemble" is another piece of juxtapositions and is reflective of Syler's creative use of spatial elements. In this work a new feeling of space is achieved through flexible time notation and a stage configured into three chorales; woodwinds, brass, and a core string group consisting of piano, harp and double bass. Three important, contrasting motifs that never clash and literally seem to exist on different "fields" of thought make up the connecting threads of the work. The quiet, unison, hymn-like chorale near the end brings together the distinct elements and illustrates Syler's clear understanding of vocal part writing. Once again, the work utilizes important off-stage instruments including percussion and flugelhorn. The piece is a dark sound poem, a musical prose of time and space.

Minton's Playhouse (1995) duration: 10'
solo quartet: s sax, a sax, t sax, b sax - 2 fl (1 dbl picc, 1 dbl a fl), 2 ob, eng hrn, Eb cl, 3 cl, b cl, ca cl, 2 bsn (1 dbl c bsn) - 4 trp (1 dbl picc trp, 1 dbl flug hrn), 4 hrn, 3 trb, b trb, 2 bar hrn, 2 tba - cb, pno, hp, 4 perc - tape, optional 2 vc
Premiere: 1995 by the U.S. Air Force Sax Quartet with the U.S. Navy Band at George Mason University, Fairfax, VA. for the 18th International Saxophone Symposium. Lieutenant Colonel Alan Bonner, conductor.

Commissioned by the United States Air Force Band, this one-movement Third Stream fusion-type work scored for saxophone quartet and wind ensemble explores the relationship between jazz and Baroque styles in a concerto grosso setting. The saxophone quartet serves as the concertino and the wind ensemble as the ripieno in a technically demanding work employing bebop lines ala Charlie Parker as well as an original jazz ballad written by Syler. He comments on his inspiration for the work in the forward to the score:

> Minton's Playhouse is a composition written as a tribute to the early 1940's nightclub at 210 W. 118th Street in New York City. The weekly jam sessions and after hours experimenting that went on there, and at other area clubs played an important part in the development of bebop, and subsequently marked the beginning of modern jazz. In honor of the 50-year anniversary of this form of jazz this work looks to the past, and at the same time, to the present.

The music attempts to express what might have gone through the minds of those great musicians as they played a standard ballad in the last set of the evening. Their thoughts must have been filled with the anticipation of experimenting with new ideas in an attempt to forge out a new music.

Storyville (1996) duration: 17'
off-stage solo alto sax; off-stage solo soprano - 2 fl, 2 ob, 8 cl, b cl, 2 bsn, s sax, t sax - 3 trp, flug hrn, 4 hrn, 4 trb, euph, 2 tba - cb, hp - 4 perc
Premiere: Texas A&M - Commerce University Wind Ensemble at the 1997 Texas Music Educator's Association Convention, San Antonio, TX. Bobby Francis, conductor.

Commissioned by a nine-university consortium, *Storyville* is a programmatic piece evoking the jazz element s indigenous to the red light district of New Orleans in juxtaposition with the human despair and tragedy found there. Contemporary techniques mixed with early jazz and a quiet dramatic ending by an off-stage soprano voice highlight this work that is intended as a companion piece to *Minton's Playhouse*.

In the program notes the composer describes *Storyville* as a place of violence and despair beneath a facade of pleasure where 1500 to 2200 prostitutes lived and worked. However, musicians from the area were crucial to the early development of jazz and the stylistic melding of a diversity of styles…ragtime, brass bands, blues and hymns. Syler concentrates on the powerful image of the impact of the closing of the district and the subsequent exodus of the prostitutes burdened with the carrying of all of their worldly possessions on their backs as a massed jazz band played the hymn tune *Nearer My God to Thee*. *Storyville* is united by the hymn tune as well as the recurrent use of a descending half-step motif.

The staging and construction of the piece is reminiscent of works by Colgrass as the physical configuration of the ensemble plays an important programmatic and spatial role. Syler utilizes an isolated mixed choir approach with winds as mixed trios and percussion stage front. The trio pods of winds are in several different combinations of high, medium and low voices in a manner that is meant to reflect jazz combo playing. The off-stage saxophone solo and soprano voice solo are the wordless songs of despair while the per-cussion ensemble, from its front stage placement, interrupts the melancholy tunes with bursts of jazz styles. The clarinet row in the back of the stage provides a vague commentary as would the chorus found in ancient Greek tragedies. The total effect is one of remarkable clarity and is marked by several new sonorities not usually associated with the wind ensemble. In his conductor's notes, Syler instructs conductors to pay particular attention to creating a light and resonant sound with emphasis on individual colors. The work does not follow a strict program and the conductor is free to play the role of a painter of sound and texture as opposed to being merely a keeper of time.

O Magnum Mysterium for Soprano and Wind Ensemble (1996) duration: 12'
solo soprano - 2 fl, ob, 3 cl, b cl, 2 bsn, s sax, a sax, t sax, b sax - 4 trp, 4 hrn, 4 trb, bar hrn, tba - cb, pno, hp - 4 perc - optional organ, chorus

Based on the ancient Christmas day text, this one movement work requires very controlled wind playing and attention to balance with the soprano vocal. Dramatic intensity is achieved through the Latin text, ethnic hand percussion and by holding back the wind sound. Originally a choral work, it can be performed with chorus and/or the organ part.

Symphony No. 1 "Blue" (1999) duration: 35'
I. *Impending Blue*
II. *Dark Blue*
III. *Fading Blue*
IV. *Still Point Blue*
V. *True Blue*
Premiere: 1999 by the California State University Long Beach Wind Ensemble and Chorus, Long Beach, CA. John Carnahan, conductor.
standard instrumentation + harp, celeste, solo soprano, large SATB chorus

Created in an oratorio-like form, *Symphony No. 1, Blue* was commissioned by a consortium of 42 United States university and college wind ensembles in cooperation with their choral departments and was completed in June of 1999. The work is highly eclectic in nature with suggestions of a dramatic choral style similar to Orff's *Carmina Burana* as well as sections of beautifully crafted minimalism reminiscent of the style of John Adams. Clear orchestrations, long beautiful melodic lines and a sense of sweeping lyricism combine to demonstrate Syler's command of both a highly developed compositional sense as well as thorough understanding of literary imagery. Syler describes the work in the forward to the score:

> For many years I've wanted to write a large work that would combine my musical and literary interests. So much of twentieth-century fiction presents despairing characters that find their resolution in some form of self-destruction. In writing the text for this work I wanted to create a narrative that would resolve despair in a different way. This free verse lyrical narra-

tive, titled *Blue*, is in the broadest sense about the loss of love and the process of reconnecting with love.

The text presents a continuation of a Kurtz character, the quintessential modern man, from Joseph Conrad's novel *The Heart of Darkness* (1902). Kurtz is a character who epitomizes outward success and inward emptiness. This notion was further developed in T. S. Eliot's poem *The Hollow Men* (1925) with its reference to the Conrad novel in the epigraph "Mistah Kurtz—he dead." In attempting to continue this 'modern man' I've chosen a T. S. Eliot line for the epigraph of the text, "to make an end is to make a beginning" from *Four Quartets* (1943) as an indication of how this character will reach a resolution.

The character descends to a point of ultimate choice and at that moment the choice is made to give up the 'self'; the metaphorical Mistah Kurtz is indeed 'dead.' At this point regeneration of the character becomes, at the very least, possible. The ascending process of change is put into motion as an inversion, or chiasmus, of the descending process of despair. The literary device of chiasmus presents the material of the first half in reverse order in the second half and is used as the musical and narrative structure of this work. The text ends with the notion that this change is realized, but not understood. The narrative has become in itself a chiasmus. Eliot's idea of 'the still point dance' combined with the biblical idea of 'the still small voice' moves the character through a process of despair, stillness, listening, revealing and ultimately knowing.

The music is in five movements that are held together through a chiastic descending arch form. Using this form further emphasizes the cyclic nature of the text and its epigraph. The music is continually descending, harmonically and melodically, until it reaches its nadir and begins to ascend as a type of musical chiamus. The firm establishment of tonality at the end is symbolic of the conclusion of the narrative. The music ends where it began.

Syler states that there are four basic compositional elements of the piece; 1) harmonic motion by thirds, 2) the continual use of the minor third interval, 3) the melodic function of the augmented fourth, and, 4) the chiastic descending arch form.

One new notational technique employed in the piece is an aleatoric device the composer describes as a 'matrix' initially utilized in the first movement at measure 50. (see figure 1). Syler describes the matrix as "an out-of-time pointillistic descending effect" representing a "reverse transposition". If correctly performed the end result should be "the effect of sound being poured out of a saltshaker." His creation of this effect is to support the symbolism in the work, those moments in life where "free will is exercised."

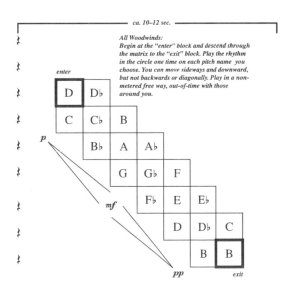

FIGURE 1. *Symphony No. 1 "Blue"* measure 50
© Ballerbach Music
Reprinted by Permission

163

WORKS LISTING

ORCHESTRA MUSIC

Oranges for Soprano and Orchestra (20')
Minton's Playhouse for Saxophone Quartet and Orchestra (10')
Arioso for Clarinet and String Orchestra (9')

CHORAL MUSIC

Siren Song (7')
Dear Sarah (9')
Still Water (3')
O Magnum Mysterium (12')
Tantum ergo (5')
Ubi Caritas (3')
Ave Verum Corpus (4')
The Road Not Taken (7')
Stopping By Woods on a Snowy Evening (4')
Psalm 61 (5')

CHAMBER MUSIC

Oranges for Soprano and Violin, Alto Flute, Harp and Piano (20')
Saxophone Quartet (22')
Bel Canto for Brass Quintet (9')
Arioso for Clarinet and Piano (9')

WORKS IN PROGRESS

New commission for the San Antonio Choral Society, San Antonio, TX
New commission for the Bishop Ireton High School Wind Ensemble, Arlington, VA
Orchestral, solo piano works.

DISCOGRAPHY

Squires, Stephen E., conductor. (1992) **Music for Winds and Percussion—Volume 3.** Northern Illinois University Wind Ensemble. *"Hound of Heaven"* NIU-812.
Lt. Colonel Richard A. Shelton, Commander and Conductor. **Images.** Wright-Patterson AFB, Dayton, OH, Air Force Band of Flight. *"Fields"*
Steele, Stephen, conductor. (2002) **Symphony No.5 by Maslanka.** Illinois State University Wind Ensemble. *"Minton's Playhouse"* TROY500.
The University of Miami Wind Ensemble/The University of Miami Chorale, Gary Green, conductor. **Blue.** *"Symphony No. 1, Blue."* Albany Records. TROY525.

ADDITIONAL INFORMATION

Gausline, Gregg David. *Wind Ensemble Compositions of James Syler.* University of Miami: Doctoral Essay, 2001.
All works are available from the composer's publishing company Ballerbach Music. Additional information on the music of James Syler can be obtained through Ballerbach Music at:
http://www.ballerbach.com